Trust and Hedging in International Relations

Do states trust each other? What are the political and ethical implications of trust? *Trust and Hedging in International Relations* adds to the emerging literature on trust in international relations by offering a systematic measure of state-to-state trust, drawing on literatures from a wide range of disciplines. Looking at how relationships between European microstates and their partners have evolved over the past few centuries, Stiles finds that rather than trusting, most microstates are careful to hedge in their relations by agreeing only to arrangements that provide them with opt-out clauses, heavy involvement in joint decision making, and sunset provisions. In the process, Stiles assesses the role of rationality, social relations, identity politics, and other theories of trust to demonstrate that trust is neither essential for cooperation nor a guarantee of protection and safety. Finally, he explores the ethical implications of a foreign policy founded on trust, in particular whether heads of state have the right to enter into open-ended agreements that put their citizens at risk.

Kendall W. Stiles is Professor of Political Science at Brigham Young University.

TRUST AND HEDGING IN INTERNATIONAL RELATIONS

Kendall W. Stiles

University of Michigan Press
Ann Arbor

Published in the United States of America by the
University of Michigan Press
Manufactured in the United States of America
♾ Printed on acid-free paper

2021 2020 2019 2018 4 3 2 1

A CIP catalog record for this book is available from the British Library.

Library of Congress Cataloging-in-Publication Data

Names: Stiles, Kendall W., author.
Title: Trust and hedging in international relations / Kendall Stiles.
Description: Ann Arbor : University of Michigan Press, 2018. | Includes bibliographical references and index.
Identifiers: LCCN 2017038247| ISBN 9780472130702 (hardback) | ISBN 9780472123575 (e-book)
Subjects: LCSH: International relations—Social aspects—Case studies. | States, Small—Case studies. | Trust—Political aspects—Case studies. | Luxembourg—Foreign relations. | Liechtenstein—Foreign relations. | San Marino—Foreign relations. | Monaco—Foreign relations. | Andorra—Foreign relations. | BISAC: POLITICAL SCIENCE / International Relations / General. | POLITICAL SCIENCE / History & Theory.
Classification: LCC JZ1249 .S75 2018 | DDC 327.101—dc23
LC record available at https://lccn.loc.gov/2017038247

Contents

Acknowledgments

I would like to thank the many individuals and organizations that supported this research. Naturally, the conclusions are my own. I appreciate the research and travel support provided by the Brigham Young University's Center for the Study of Europe and David M. Kennedy Center. I am also grateful to Megan Tyler and Tara Simmons for their able and effective research assistance.

I thank the many scholars who looked over portions of the work in progress, including especially Celeste Beesley, Cornelia Navari, Wade Jacoby, Earl Fry, and Scott Cooper, along with various panelists and audience members at the annual meetings of the International Studies Association and the Academic Council on the UN System. I also express my gratitude to editors at the University of Michigan Press: Meredith Norwich, Mary Francis, and Melody Herr, along with anonymous reviewers. I also thank those involved in producing the final work, particularly Kevin Rennells and Drew Bryan.

Finally, I would like to express my appreciation for the many individuals—scholars, journalists, public officials, and others—who answered my many questions about their countries and gave me advice on how to pursue my research. These include: Jean-Charles Allavena, Jordi Guillamet Anton, Josep Fortó Areny, Marianne Beisheim, Denis Berche, Ester Cañadas, Pavel Černoch, Roberto Ciavetta, Hélène Cristini, Swen Dornig, Patricia Di Luca, Ben Fayol, Gabriel Fernández, Pietro Giacomini, Maria Noguer Gonzalàz, Jordi Guillaumet, Otmer Hasler, Patrick Kinsch, Sonja Kmec, Maria Maten, Meritzell Mateu, Joan Micó, David Oddone, Meritxell Mateu Pi, Panagiotis Potolidis-Beck, Paul Seger, Alvaro Selva, Karen Venturini, Adam Walder, Glenn Weiss, and Dirk Zetzche, and still others who prefer to remain anonymous.

ONE

Trust in International Relations?

During the 2016 US presidential campaign, much was made of whether Americans should trust Russia. Hillary Clinton charged that the Russian government interfered with the election while Donald Trump repeatedly dismissed the issue (Politico 2016). Even after the CIA and FBI went public with their evidence, Trump said America should "move on," arguing that the evidence of hacking was simply too weak to be worth our attention (Wagner and Demirjian 2016).

Likewise, the candidates differed on whether Iran could be trusted to honor the nuclear arms agreement hammered out in 2015, this time with Trump taking on the role of skeptical critic (Morello 2016). He was in good company. Even President Barack Obama expressed skepticism about whether Iran was trustworthy at the time he signed the agreement, hence the strict enforcement provision: "We don't trust Iran. But this deal doesn't rely on trust. It relies on verification" (Radio Free Europe 2015).

These debates relate primarily to the fear of being duped or "suckered," a notion nested in the view of international relation as a prisoners' dilemma in which the worst outcome results from trusting one's partner to be loyal and reliable and then being proven wrong (Axelrod and Dawkins 2006). While most would agree that global cooperation is desirable, fear of being exploited usually take precedence. Current opposition to free trade on both sides of the Atlantic stems largely from the sense that countries are being exploited (Stokes 2016; BBC 2016a).

A growing academic literature argues that despite such fears of exploitation, trust is real and plays a key role in international relations, explaining foreign policy decisions, the formation of institutions, and global solidarity generally (Adler and Barnett 1998a; Lipson 2003; Kydd 2005; Hoffman 2006; Henrich and Henrich 2007; Booth and Wheeler 2008; Rathbun 2012; Brugger, Hasenclever, and Kasten 2013; Keating and Ruzicka 2014; Weller 2015). In reaching these conclusions, however, authors disagree on the meaning of the concept, its sources, and its implications.

This study is an effort to return to fundamental questions about trust. I will discuss a variety of definitions of trust found in both international relations and other literatures, which will inform my working definition of the term. I will develop a method for measuring degrees of trust among states and test theories concerning its origins and effects. In the process I hope to show more clearly the role trust does and does not play in international relations. In particular, I will show that trust is difficult to find, even in the places where one would most expect to find it. Further, I will show that where trust exists, it emerges from a confluence of strategic, social, and ideational factors. Finally, I will show that trust has proven to be as much a boon as a curse in international relations and that states that avoid trusting are not necessarily on a path that undermines international cooperation and solidarity.

In this chapter I will begin with a definition of trust, set against the backdrop of international relations and social science and other literatures generally (Baier 1986; Nooteboom 2002; Putnam 2000; Weber and Carter 2003; Hardin 2002; Becker 1996; Kohn 2008; Fukuyama 1995; Castelfranchi and Falcone 2010). I will settle on a rationalist definition of trust and its ancillary notion of hedging, and then proceed with an elaboration of a method for measuring trust, focusing especially on the structure and content of formal agreements between governments. I will then review some of the findings and conjectures in the literature regarding the sources and implications of trust. I will then provide an overview of my empirical tests and what I expect to learn from them.

Definition and Measurement of Trust and Hedging

To begin, I define *trust* as an expectation on the part of a vulnerable actor [call it the "trustor"] that allowing a more powerful actor [the "trustee"] to take actions in its behalf will produce beneficial results (Booth and Wheeler 2008, 229). I will argue that trust begins and ends with a question: Will another actor look out for my interests when taking actions I cannot control that directly affect me? Trust is the expectation that one's interests will be looked after despite the possibility of exploitation by the trustee.

How does trust work? Examples of trust are abundant where interpersonal relations are concerned, and many have argued that trust is the adhesive that holds social relations together (see Putnam 2000; Fukuyama 1995; Brooks 2011). Each time a patient agrees to a surgical procedure, a consumer buys a used car, an investor hires a financial planner, a couple gets married, a crime victim calls 9-1-1, or a child leaps into a parent's arms, we see evidence of trust in people, institutions, and social systems. Typically, such expectations are born of a combination of cognitive and emotional factors, such as the assessment by the trustor that the trustee is reliable and consistent and has interests that incorporate (or encapsulate) her own, often as a result of kinship ties or affection (Baier 1986; Hardin 2002; Becker 1996).

Trust has been hypothesized to matter in international relations in a wide variety of ways. Some early work on security communities touched on the notion that actors in different states might reach a point where their interests and identities would so fully merge that war between them would become "unthinkable" and trust would become the dominant feature of the relationship (Deutsch, Burrell, and Kann 1957; Adler and Barnett 1998a). More recently, liberal thinkers and international regime theorists have argued that trust is an important component in bargaining, negotiation, and institution building, although they also stress that overcoming distrust is possible with the right mix of procedures and structures (Axelrod and Dawkins 2006; Keohane 1984; Keohane and Nye 2011). Lake has discussed the role of trust in hierarchical interstate relations (Lake 2011), while Kydd has explored the importance of trust in a mediator (Kydd 2006). Trust has emerged as a factor in the democratic peace literature.

On the one hand, some see trust as a result of the democratic peace. Since democracies are generally more reliable at keeping promises, other states trust their commitments (Lipson 2003; Martin 2000). Still others posit that the interplay of democracy, free markets, and international law leads to a process of mutually reinforcing tolerance, learning, and trusting (Cederman 2001; Russett and Oneal 2001). Owen and others argue that trust precedes democratic peace in that those who embrace a liberal ideology take for granted that all liberal states, since they are not interested in conquest or war, will seek nonviolent solutions to conflict (Owen 1997).

Some have argued that trust is important, whether in reference to interpersonal relations between leaders of countries or to the social and economic ties between their respective citizens. They posit that all diplomacy, negotiations, legal commitments, alliances, and even asymmetric economic ties involve a certain degree of trust, a leap of faith in the willingness of others to refrain from taking advantage of another's willingness to become vulnerable (Rathbun 2012). Put another way, international cooperation involves an effort to generate confidence in potentially vulnerable and exploitable actors that potential exploiters will be unable and/or unwilling to take advantage of. Liberals emphasize the role of monitoring and enforcement while constructivists stress changes in interests and identities, but both look at trust as an intervening variable (Hoffman 2002).

Realists, naturally, are skeptical that trust exists or matters (Hoffman 2002). They argue that international cooperation can occur as a result of systemic forces and balance of power, mitigated by institutions to a certain degree, especially when those institutions reinforce the distribution of interstate power. But since the balance of power and international institutions fail as often as not, cooperation will be rare and trust may well be irrelevant (Mearsheimer 1994/95). What is often perceived as trust is in fact something less profound and requires little in the way of new thinking or concepts. It might be a simple calculation regarding the odds that a promise will be kept, taking into account the trustee's interests and her track record (Goldsmith and Posner 2005). It may reflect a harmony of interests that has little to do with the fundamental relationship or any mutual adjustment (Keohane 1984). It may represent mere rhetoric masking fear or confidence that each actor's relative power will determine the outcome.

And even if individuals trust, realists fairly ask what this means for states. Although US president Woodrow Wilson was eager to move forward on the League of Nations Covenant, trusting the world's good will, it mattered little in the end as the Senate rejected it (Rathbun 2012). During the Ronald Reagan–Mikhail Gorbachev era, despite Reagan's interest in negotiating arms reductions, secretary of defense Caspar Weinberger was so opposed to talks that secretary of state George Shultz nearly resigned in disgust (Matlock 2004).

Central to these arguments and debates are problems related to the definition of trust. Scholars often conceptualize trust in ways that make cumulative understanding very difficult if not impossible. Even more serious, they tend to ignore the work being done outside the field of international relations, with the result that the findings do not build on the insights that have been accreting for decades, nor do they engage with that work directly.

The definitions being used are often both too broad and too narrow. Game theorists and economists typically remove noncognitive elements (Axelrod and Dawkins 2006; Adler and Barnett 1998b, 46; Kohn 2008, 12). Kydd, for example, defines trust simply as a willingness to reciprocate cooperative gestures without exploiting the other actor (Kydd 2005, 3). Baier defines this as reliance: counting on people to behave in their self-interest or some form of instinct (Baier 1986). But this is different from trust, which involves delegating something that is important to you to another actor who you hope will look out for your interests. For that matter, not all cooperation entails risk of exploitation, as in the case of coordination games (deciding which side of the road on which to drive), and so trust may often be irrelevant (except for trusting that the other actor will not behave in a reckless, destructive fashion) (Weber and Carter 2003, 144; Hollis 1998). Defining trust as the expectation of cooperation is therefore far too broad.

On the other hand, some have argued that trusting is essentially an innate personality characteristic, divorced from circumstances. Rathbun argues that cooperation begins with a leap of faith by actors who trust generally rather than specifically (Rathbun 2012, 3; Uslaner 2000). Such "generalized trustors" don't require evidence that the trustee in question is even trustworthy with respect to a particular issue, since all actors are assumed to be worthy of trust across all topics (assuming they have the capacity to act). Rather than trust, Becker calls this "credulity" and emphasizes that it is "noncognitive," meaning that it primarily involves "having trustful attitudes, affects, emotions, or motivational structures that are not focused on specific people, institutions, or groups" (Becker 1996, 44). While credulity may help explain why some actors trust, it does not define it. Perhaps more importantly, credulity is a surrender of agency, which is generally considered antithetical to trust (Baier 1986; Hoffman 2006, 15).

Other problems associated with international relations scholars' approach to trust include levels of analysis issues and the role of time. Definitions of trust are sometimes borrowed from psychology, which naturally focuses research on individuals, while in international relations it is primarily institutions that matter. Work on organizational behavior tends to be neglected (note, for example, Wheeler 2013). Likewise, work on international law and credible commitments is sometimes misapplied. In most cases what interests international relations scholars is whether states are willing to enter into long-term relationships, relationships that will outlive those who established them. We've learned that institutions such as corporations and professional bodies must be able to interact with society constructively. They endeavor to create an identity (viz. "brand") that others implicitly trust (Farrell 2009, 134; Potter 2002, 24). This usually means persuading stakeholders that your fellow members have both the capacity and interests to look out for them (Nooteboom 2002, 76).

Knowing this, associations routinely adopt public standards of conduct and peer review. They hope to communicate that members of the profession will behave as though they had their clients' interests at heart (Hardin 2002, 50). Violation of these norms undermines the trustworthiness not just of the individual professional in question, but of the whole profession. The more explicit these are, the less case-by-case trust is required (Farrell 2009, 136). This is particularly true, for both moral and economic reasons, where the recipient of the service takes considerable risk. Thus physicians, police officers, accountants, lawyers, and others who take someone's life or freedom in their hands must meet a very high threshold of trustworthiness, especially since many people hire members of these professions sight unseen (Farrell 2004, 88; Hall 2005, 163). The professional credential must take the place of a personal history (Vitek 1993, 65; Narveson 1971; Kohn 2008, 69, 72). Enforcement therefore helps the group to fulfill broader societal purposes, even though the result may be the unhinging of a particular individual's career and life.

In other words, when institutions trust or seek to be trustworthy they are making commitments to change how they govern themselves and how they interact with other institutions. This is not always captured in individual-level theorizing. In fact, individual-level theories may actually underestimate how much trust can exist and how resilient it can be. In particular, they tend to focus too much on particular moments in time and the agreements that can be reached without considering carefully the long time horizon of promising and contracting. Some even argue that making long-term commitments is inconsistent with trust (Hoffman 2006, 15).

This, however, leaves open the question of whether states have stable interests in the first place, setting aside whether these interests might encapsulate others' interests. This is central to whether states can trust each other. States' interests and preferences can be ranked with respect to their scope and durability, but no state has permanent aims (Thompson 1994, 251–52). Realists assume that all states seek their own preservation, and while this is generally true there are even exceptions to this most fundamental rule. Likewise, states shift their alliance patterns, change their constitutions, alter their economic systems in fundamental ways, and even relocate geographically. At the micro level, states are constantly swapping out political elites and changing policies, practices, and procedures, usually as a result of changes in priorities and preferences. Even the most autocratic regime in the most stable polity adopts new interests from time to time.

Does this mean that states are never deserving of trust? And since international organizations generally derive their preferences from their obviously fickle member states, are they also lacking? The answer is a firm maybe. The fact is that while all states change their interests, there are typically mechanisms that minimize this tendency and bring about considerable stability. States institutionalize decision-making procedures in difficult-to-amend constitutions, ratify treaties that "lock in" both domestic and foreign policies, and make day-to-day policy difficult to enact through systems of shared power and "checks and balances" (Moravcsik 2000). Autocrats are often better able to make binding commitments since they are more impervious to shifts in public opinion (Stiles 2015). But even if an actor's interests are fluid, it can still be trusted, especially since the interests of trustors are also variable. In the case of international organizations, the changes in preferences of trustor and trustee alike might be symbiotic as new norms are promoted, adopted, and disseminated by consensus (Sandholtz and Stiles 2009).

But what about the notion that states can be trusting? Rathbun in particular has attempted to transfer insights about individual intent and behavior to the policies of states (Rathbun 2012). Others who study trust have explicitly anthropomorphized states in order to explain their behavior, often without any reference to levels of analysis or decision-making procedures (Hardin 2004a, 9; Kramer 2004, 154; Horne 2004, 252; for warnings against this practice, see Brugger 2015; Godin 2010; and Peppers and Rogers 2012, 37). But this author questions the validity of these logical leaps.

To begin, where a state is governed by a single individual with full executive powers, it may be possible to say that the state can "trust" since its policies are largely a reflection of the leader's preferences. I say "may" because it is unlikely that the leader's personal vulnerability and particular assessments of others' interests and capacity are likely to match up perfectly with those of the state as a whole. Personally strong leaders—such as Spain's Phillip II in 1588 or Iraq's Saddam Hussein in 1990—have sometimes overestimated their states' strength, with disastrous consequences. Likewise, autocratic leaders have misjudged the interests of other important actors, assuming they overlapped with the interests of the state when they clearly did not (see Josef Stalin's misplaced faith in the Molotov-Ribbentrop Pact of 1939). And some dictators have wrongly guessed that other states had the capacity to fulfill their promises to them (note the failure of Britain and France to prevent the collapse of the tsarist regime during World War I despite the prewar alliance). In such situations, it is best to simply speak of the levels of trust of the sovereign rather than assume this represents the trust of the state.

Finally, theory and concept are not consistently kept separate. There is a tendency to conflate the two with definitions of trust that imply a causal story. This is most pronounced in the case mentioned earlier about trust as a personality trait. But it is also implicit in some rational approaches to trust, in that trust is assumed to be the product of calculations of interest and discount rates on others' behavior. Likewise, the notion of "blind trust" goes too far in merging the outcome and the cause (Volkan 2004).

Returning to the definition of trust provided at the beginning of this section, trust is a conscious decision to allow some other actor control over key aspects of one's life. Trusting always involves some risk on the part of the one trusting (trustor). One can never be absolutely sure that one's interests are important to the trustee's or that her past performance can allow one to predict her future behavior (Potter 2002, 3; Weller 2015, 68). The trustee retains her agency and even has an incentive to betray you in the future, by definition (Weber and Carter 2003, 2; Castelfranchi and Falcone 2010, 38). The trustor is vulnerable—either by choice or by circumstance. At some point, he has put himself in a position that requires another person's intervention (Booth and Wheeler 2008, 229; Nooteboom 2002, 48; Colquitt, Scott, and Lefine 2007, 909). As put by Rathbun:

> Trust is the belief that one will not be harmed when his or her fate is placed in the hands of others. It entails a combination of uncertainty and vulnerability. . . . Trustors put themselves in a vulnerable position because they do not expect harm to come of it. Yet if trust is involved, they do not know for sure. (Rathbun 2012, 10)

To clarify the point, trust involves at least three questions: Is the trustor vulnerable to exploitation by the one being trusted? Is the one being trusted willing to embrace the trustor's aims and interests? Can the one being trusted freely act on this willingness to trust? (Peppers and Rogers 2012) Where one of these components does not apply, one can challenge whether trust is really in play.

Hoffman, drawing on Hardin, explicitly states that trust involves putting your fate in someone else's hands through delegation (Hoffman 2006, 3). Castelfranchi and Falcone agree, putting it succinctly: "In sum, in genuine trust X just counts upon the fact that Y will understand and care for her (delegated) goal. Y will adopt her goal and possibly prefer it against a conflicting goal" (Castelfranchi and Falcone 2010, 87). While this is done out of self-interest, it nonetheless comes at considerable risk. A trusting relationship, according to Hoffman, is the sum total of arrangements that are undertaken to instantiate this trust. At no point, however, is the trustor entirely protected from being exploited by the trustee.

But there is a big difference between giving an international organization authority over, say, hunting for migratory birds as opposed to national defense or border control. Trusting on trivial issues is almost meaningless, which makes laboratory simulations where a few dollars are at stake only vaguely suggestive of real-world decision making, where one's very survival is in play (Hoffman 2006, 291). Liechtenstein evinces more trust when it allows Switzerland to manage the totality of its economic and political security than the United States does the when it allows the World Trade Organization's dispute settlement bodies to rule on Chinese dumping practices, even though the dollar amounts may be much larger where the United States is concerned. Nooteboom has pointed out that in experimental settings, people weigh the degree of trustworthiness of a hypothetical trustee differently depending on the stakes (Nooteboom 2002, 157).

Trust requires that the trustee has enough agency and information to be able to choose whether to take the trustor's interests into account. It is therefore not reasonable to call it trust if the trustee is not aware of the trustee's needs (although, as in the case of a bus driver or a development NGO, an actor can be attentive to the needs of a group to which another belongs, which winds up being the same thing in particular cases). This fact came as a rude shock to those who watched trusted financial institutions push the world economy to the brink of collapse in 2007 (Peppers and Rogers 2012, 63–65). Even more risky might be the tendency of some to trust "the market" and other inchoate forces, since it is clear that intentionality is absent (Hardin 2002, 188).

This issue is addressed more clearly by Hoffman, who relies heavily on Hardin's extensive work on rational trusting. Hoffman defines trust in terms of a willingness to delegate something of value to a trustee with the expectation that one's interests will be protected and not exploited (Hoffman 2006, 1; see also Castelfranchi and Falcone 2010, 87). While Hardin argues that this can be based on the belief that one's interests are "encapsulated" by the interests of the trustee (meaning that what the trustor wants is subsumed by the trustee also wants), Hoffman argues that is can also be based on a belief that the trustee has a sense of honor and will keep promises not to exploit a vulnerable trustor (Hardin 2002, 1; Hoffman 2006, 15). Consider, for example, that an attorney may represent a client as though she were representing herself (Cook, Hardin, and Levi 2005, 96). Likewise, a physician may take as much care with a stranger as with his own child (perhaps better, since his emotions might not impair his judgment). As a result, individuals in dire need of legal representation or medical care—where their very lives may hang in the balance—can count on complete strangers to look out for them. Kydd has observed that the loss of faith in American global leadership stems from a perception that American interests no longer encapsulate global interests (Kydd 2005/06).

Constructivists have argued that interests may come to overlap or even coincide as certain norms are adopted and identities merged. Work on norm contagion and diffusion shows how a combination of interests, dialogue, and modeling can lead to the adoption of new priorities, roles, and identities (Risse, Ropp, and Sikkink 1999; Sandholtz and Stiles 2009; Wimmer 2008). But these arguments are still on the fringes of the debate about trust.

The last question is whether trustees have the authority and capacity to act. There is generally little question that a trustee has power or else the trustor would not approach her in the first place. What is perhaps more interesting is whether a trustee's power is limitless. Hoffman and Hardin agree that all trustees have limited authority to act in behalf of the trustor, although Hoffman believes the scope is necessarily expansive since one cannot always know what choices a trustee will face in the future, including the possibility that the trustor's interests may even change over time. In fact, it is even possible, according to Baier, that a trustee will need to act against the trustor's interests if some higher moral principle conflicts with honoring the trusting relationship (Baier 1986). For example, a trustee may have been trusted by more than one trustor and in order to prevent one from being destroyed she must neglect some minor obligation to the other. Trustees must have some discretion to make such choices. Hoffman argues that the scope of that discretion is one measure of the degree of trust that exists. Baier agrees, pointing out that if a partner in a trusting relationship (such as a marriage) engages in controlling behavior or routinely sets out to deceive the other, the relationship is "morally rotten" (Baier 1986, 255; see also Castelfranchi and Falcone 2010, 90; Colquitt, Scott, and Lefine 2007, 911; Becker 1996, 45; and Grant 1949, 360).

The degree of discretion—the extent to which the trustee can act on the trust invested in her—is controversial in the literature. Hoffman argues that while the trustee should have considerable discretion (if the relationship is founded on trust), she must provide mechanisms for the trustor to have an "effective voice" in the trustee's decision making to ensure that its interests are heard in an ongoing way (note that this need not involve a veto over the trustee's actions) (Hoffman 2006, 15). Likewise, enforcement of the trustee's actions should come after the fact rather than ex ante. But this is more a matter of degree, it would seem, since he recognizes limits to the trustee's discretion and favors putting the arrangement in writing for the sake of future leaders and discussions between negotiators and domestic actors that must approve the arrangement (Hoffman 2002, 377). Baier, on the other hand, rejects not only contracting but even promising as indicative of a lack of trust and instead favors using unwritten and open-ended arrangements as a measure of trust between parties, as found in a healthy marriage (Baier 1986; Kohn 2008, 63).

As its title implies, this study also addresses hedging. Hedging is defined in quotidian terms here as both an attempt to limit one's commitment to something (i.e., the degree of trust) as well as to protect against risk by diversifying one's commitments. The concept is rarely used in international relations, although it sometimes appears in the literature on alliances (Weitsman 2004; Lake 1996; Jackson 2016; Tessman and Wojtek 2010) and discussions of escape clauses and withdrawal provisions in treaties (Koremenos 2016; Van Aaken 2014). In the work on alliances, hedging refers primarily to efforts by states—particularly small ones—to seek friendly relations with the rival of an ally in the hope of preserving some autonomy and security (see Willy Brandt's Ostpolitik of the 1970s. See also the policies of weak Asian states vis-à-vis China in Jackson 2016, 2). Major powers may also have to weigh how much to discount weaker allies' commitments and whether to increase governance measures or simply take steps to hedge against shirking (Lake 1996, 21). Hedging by weak states is most likely, according to Weitsman, where external threats are relatively low, and it will likely increase tensions within an alliance (Weitsman 2004, 28).

But since I'm interested in relationships that address far more than military security (or in some cases don't address it explicitly), it is better to think of hedging as a policy of increasing flexibility in commitments with respect to the degree of commitment, the issues addressed, and the possible partners involved. The vast majority of agreements allow states to opt out under certain circumstances. Koremenos, for example, finds that 45 of the 234 treaties in her dataset provide escape clauses that allow states to opt out of certain commitments (albeit temporarily and only under extraordinary circumstances) without diminishing their overall commitment to the agreement (Koremenos 2016, 127). Even more impressive, 164 treaties in the dataset allow for states to entirely withdraw from the agreement, with twelve months being the most popular period of notification of such a withdrawal (Koremenos 2016, 141).

States also hedge by limiting the scope and salience of their commitments, often carving out certain issue areas as "off limits" while entering in numerous agreements on less vital issues. It is not surprising that full-fledged mutual security agreements are relatively rare in comparison to deals governing economic or immigration issues. And finally, states hedge by keeping their options open to entering into deals with new partners when such a move might be propitious. Kaplan's description of a "loose bipolar" system during the 1970s epitomizes this sort of practice whereby weak states switched sides (Kaplan 1957).

Hedging is thus a strategy common to states and other actors that may be willing to commit to substantial agreements involving such fundamental issues as security and human rights but also want to protect themselves from too open-ended or permanent a commitment. This may stem from uncertainty about the future conditions of the world or the fact that the agreement itself is resistant to enforcement, but a key element is almost certainly a fear that your partners will betray you. I therefore place a desire to hedge as a midpoint between trust and distrust. As mentioned earlier, while distrust can often prevent cooperation from even being considered, trust itself is not a prerequisite so long as actors can include in the agreements some degree of flexibility in addition to a range of monitoring and enforcement measures. As we will see, the measurement of such hedging strategies will allow us to calibrate the degree of trust in a relationship.

I now turn to the question of measuring degrees of trust. I identify eight distinct dimensions, grouped under three different topics. These are: actor vulnerability and exploitability, actor volition, the scope of topics and the salience of issues covered under agreements, the agreements' degree of precision, and whether the actor is marginalized by the treaty's institutional arrangements and is entrapped by the agreement. The first three dimensions fall under the nature of the trustor-trustee relationship. The next two refer to the types of issues in play. The last three refer to the structure of agreements. I will discuss each dimension in turn.

Vulnerability refers to the capacity of an actor to insulate itself from foreign intrusions (see Keohane and Nye 2011). More generally, great powers typically have a greater capacity to insulate themselves from international forces than do weak states—essentially by definition. Where international agreements are concerned, great powers can often unilaterally punish violations (Goldsmith 2003). Weak actors antagonize powerful ones at tremendous risk of recrimination or backlash (Lake 2011).

Trust is thus most likely to be observed in weak actors in asymmetrical relationships, since vulnerability is a prerequisite. In this respect I follow Booth and Wheeler (2008, 241) and Beattie and Schick (2012, 93). Weaker actors routinely face decisions regarding whether to trust their more powerful neighbors. On the other hand, where an actor is invulnerable to betrayal, trust is typically dormant (although some powerful actors still trust: Rathbun 2012; Larson 1997). Great powers can usually insulate themselves from betrayal.

Exploitability refers to a state's attractiveness as a target by more powerful international actors. Not all vulnerable states are particularly interesting to more powerful actors in the same way that not all prey are of equal interest to predators. A wolf would show far more interest in an injured deer than a healthy mouse even though both are equally vulnerable. Likewise, a small, unarmed island state in the middle of the Pacific may be vulnerable, but not exploitable if it lacks resources or appeal as a strategic location or a tourist destination.

Voluntarism refers to the degree to which an actor can control the decision to enter into a relationship. Where asymmetrical relations are concerned, there will likely be considerable variation on this dimension. On one extreme would be colonies that are entirely controlled by the larger power and where the local government or people of the weaker power have no voice in their governance. At the other extreme would be a fully autonomous state that enjoys control over its foreign policy, expressing both elite and mass preferences. We are particularly interested in conditions ex ante since it is understood that many actors choose to surrender some of their sovereignty in the process of negotiating agreements. Measuring this dimension will therefore require taking into account domestic and international political contexts to determine the degree to which elites and masses have shaped the timing and content of agreements.

Trust is in greater evidence where agreements cover a wide array of topics, including issues relating to national survival and sovereignty. We define scope in terms of the range of issues covered by formal agreements. This includes not just a consideration of topics but also the types of policy instruments that are affected by agreements. Thus a treaty has broader scope if in the process of covering a wide array of topics it also addresses policy making at the local, intermediate, and national levels.

Salience refers to the degree to which an issue touches on questions of basic national survival and identity. Because it is unlikely that treaties covering migratory birds or shipping container dimensions will threaten a state's survival or somehow alter its essential character, we would consider these not salient. On the other hand, agreements on the size and deployment of military forces or treaties on providing recognition to ethnic minorities would be considered salient since they might affect state survival and identity.

I anticipate considerable variation along these two dimensions. It is not unusual for even weak states to be selective about which topics will be covered. It is even possible that states that enter into many agreements covering a vast array of relatively trivial issues feel less trust than states that commit to one commitment on national defense or full economic integration. To provide an analogy, it is one thing to accept the fact that your neighbor is a bully. You may adjust your lifestyle to accommodate his explicit and implicit demands, all the while looking for opportunities to go back to normal (perhaps even joining others to confront him). It is another thing altogether for you to give him the keys to your house, grant him power of attorney, and invite him to babysit your children while you go overseas. Any weak actor can make itself more dependent by entrusting another actor with the power to make decisions in its behalf. As we will see, Andorra has striven for centuries to keep France and the Bishop of Urgell at arm's length in order to maximize its policy autonomy, signing as few agreements as possible. Liechtenstein surrendered control over almost all its key foreign and domestic policies to Switzerland in 1923 (until it hedged by signing a deal with the European Union in 1995), but it has never signed a formal security agreement with Switzerland. Luxembourg, on the other hand, was willing to grant France and Germany the power to decide whether it would continue to exist (in the period from 1867 to 1949). Even weak actors can calibrate their degree of dependency.

Trust can also be discerned by looking into the structure and operation of international agreements. Hoffman has written eloquently on this topic (I also borrow from Abbott et al. 2000 and their concepts of "precision," "obligation," and "delegation"). Imprecision and informality refers to the clarity of treaty provisions, the details provided to define key terms and their operation, and so forth. Thus a treaty that looks more like a legal business contract than a broad statement of principles will be classified as precise and formal. To measure this, it will be important to remember that many treaties are quite brief and general but are supplemented by detailed protocols and memoranda of understanding. The entire family of agreements must be seen together to judge.

Assuming that sovereign states were not coerced or duped into signing, I argue that where agreements are vague and informal, it is likely that greater levels of trust were present at the negotiations. Much like with most marriage contracts, agreements that are relatively more open-ended and subject to future interpretation evince a high degree of trust on the part of the actors (Baier 1986). By contrast, contracts that spell out obligations in great detail and provide for specific rules of interpretation and enforcement are indicative of a relative lack of trust in the intentions of the trustee. "Get it in writing" is a policy most often applied by suspicious negotiators. This is not to say that detailed agreements do not serve a purpose even where trust is high—especially where the future is highly uncertain. One can always hope to "lock in" an international commitment in order to increase the odds that a future leader will feel bound to comply (Moravcsik 2004).

Much of the literature on trust states that there is an inverse relationship between trusting and "contracting" (Henrich and Henrich 2007, 123; Kohn 2008, 56; Baier 1986). Where a contract is enforceable by a third party—such as in a fully functioning state with a strong legal system—there is no need for trust. Knowing that your doctor could lose her license or be sued allows a patient to walk into a clinic without trusting a particular doctor but rather the professional and legal frameworks within which she operates (Hardin 2002, 46; Hall 2005, 160).

Marginalization refers to the degree to which a signatory to a treaty has the power to assist in its interpretation and enforcement. Treaties usually disburse such authority widely out of respect for the principle of sovereignty and the voluntary nature of international law. There are many cases, however, where treaty interpretation is delegated to a third party that may or may not be sympathetic to all signatories' concerns. Alternatively, interpretation and enforcement may be left to an executive committee or parliamentary body where decisions are made on the basis of something other than the unanimity principle. In such situations, it is not unusual that weaker actors are given fewer levers to pull.

Where the trustor has voluntarily accepted a marginal role in the implementation, interpretation, and enforcement of the agreement, we can assume a higher degree of trust. Where the trustor insists on the right of unilateral interpretation, a veto over enforcement actions, and so forth, it probably indicates less trust in the trustee. An extreme example of delegation would be the formation of a standing adjudicating body with power to indict or otherwise force actors to appear. Such bodies illustrate the concept of an international "trustee" as employed by Alter (2008).

Entrapment refers to the degree to which it is possible or easy for a signatory to withdraw from an agreement, both formally and informally. Agreements based on trust are more likely to involve a long-term commitment that is difficult to terminate. Opt-out provisions, sunset clauses, and other devices that allow parties to easily withdraw from a commitment are consistent with a lack of trust in the other actor, although other factors may explain the outcome (for instance, concern over the changing nature of the subject matter, such as telecommunications or weapons technology). The Nuclear Non-Proliferation Treaty for many years had a five-year sunset provision that was taken as a sign of distrust, and its removal in 1995 was seen as indicative of greater confidence in the willingness of states to refrain from developing nuclear weapons (Non-Proliferation of Nuclear Weapons 1995; Ruzicka and Wheeler 2010). At one extreme, treaties may provide for a six-month warning of unilateral withdrawal without explanation. At the other, treaties may be termed "permanent." This is especially true of "constitutive" treaties that define actors and basic international processes such as the Vienna Convention on the Law of Treaties or certain human rights agreements (Wood, Slaughter, and Tulumello 1998). There are myriad alternatives in between.

The dimensions I've discussed are summarized in table 1.1. I argue that trust is most in evidence where relatively vulnerable and exploitable countries voluntarily enter into agreements that cover many highly salient issues. Further, trust is most evident where these agreements are relatively imprecise, are of a permanent nature, and provide few avenues for the weaker power to influence its subsequent interpretation and application, and develop this character to a greater degree over time. Conversely, where these conditions do not apply we should infer that actors are operating on some other basis.

Origins and Implications of Trust

What explains trust in states and governments? Explanations generally fall into one of three schools of thought: strategic, social, and psychological. As already discussed, some argue that trust is a strategic decision based on circumstances and aims and flows from a simple calculation of costs and benefits and risk (Kydd 2005). Most of the work on trust in politics relates to citizen-state relations, which in turns adds to our understanding of foreign policy making, especially in democracies. Of course, state-to-state trust is not typically analogous to state-to-citizen relations, so caution should be taken when transferring insights from one area to the other.

Generally speaking, rational theories of citizen trust in their respective states show that it is inversely correlated with perceptions of corruption among government officials; in other words, the use of public institutions

TABLE 1.1. Dimensions of Dependent-Dominant State Relations

Trustor-Trustee Relationship			Issues in Play		Structure of Agreements		
Vulnerability	Exploitability	Voluntarism	Scope of Issues	Salience of Issues	Imprecision and Informality	Marginalization	Entrapment

for private gain in most cases represents a violation of citizen trust, even though it may be technically legal. For example, until 2012 members of the US House of Representatives permitted themselves to vote on bills that directly affected the value of their personal investment portfolios despite the obvious conflict of interest and potential for abuse (Keating et al. 2012). Corruption naturally undermines faith and trust in government in a direct and often personal way, especially where there are inadequate institutional checks (Rothstein 2011). A single corrupt official can undermine trust in the institutions of government since it sends the message that oversight is merely after-the-fact (Montinola 2004, 304; Levi, Moe, and Buckley 2004, 108). In Latin America, for instance, trust in government is inversely related to perceptions of corruption (Clear and Stokes 2009, 324). In the Philippines, surveys have found that citizen trust in one government institution (especially one with which an individual has had direct dealings) carries over to attitudes about other governmental institutions (e.g., trust in Congress is correlated to trust in the small claims court) (Montinola 2004, 303; Lubell 2007, 248). One can analogize that when states violate the terms of their agreements with other states—whether explicit or tacit—trust will naturally atrophy.

Sociological theories of trust emphasize the importance of deep and varied relationships between societies at both the elite and mass level, as well as the role of sociological similarities. This undergirds much of the work on security communities. Security communities are clusters of states that have come to accept the notion that they will never use force to resolve disputes among themselves. This in turn stems from changes in their interests and their perceptions of each other's interests. Ultimately, in a mature pluralistic security community all the members' defense planning is oriented outward, not toward other members (Deutsch, Burrell, and Kann 1957; Adler and Barnett 1998a, 55). This does not mean there is not a kernel of doubt about the other members' long-term intentions. In fact, that doubt explains why ultimately these associations are rooted in trust (Adler and Barnett 1998a, 414). The ultimate bond between states, however, involves not just a sense of confidence and trust between policy elites, but a binding together of ordinary citizens with their foreign counterparts (Booth and Wheeler 2008,

230). This, as with the other, can be achieved through "mutual learning." This is most likely where states that are already economically and military secure are concerned (Adler and Barnett 1998a, 424).

Further, it is worth emphasizing the considerable work on the role of international institutions in developing and promoting international norms. Jolly, Emmerij, and Weiss (2005) have documented the importance of advocacy by United Nations agencies and debates in UN fora in the emergence of such pivotal notions as the responsibility to protect, sustainable development, peacekeeping, and human development. With respect to questions of trust, the UN and the International Court of Justice in particular have reinforced such notions as *pacta sunt servanda*, transparency, and accountability to the international community (Sandholtz and Stiles 2009; Adler and Barnett 1998a; Booth and Wheeler 2008, 244).

Still others argue that cultural convergence is reinforced by practical experience such that trust has both a social and rational dimension. As put by Adler and Barnett in their discussion of security communities:

> In sum, we envision a dynamic and positive relationship between core powers and cognitive structures on the one hand, and transactions, institutions and organizations, and social learning on the other. The positive and dynamic interaction between these variables undergirds the development of trust and the process of collective identity formation, which, in turn, drives dependable expectation of peaceful change. (1998a, 48)

At the psychological level, some argue, as we have seen, that trust is an inherent character trait for some people; they are naturally trusting. This, however, is less than useful in predicting how states will behave over time since elites come and go while institutions endure. In the political realm, some have explored how psychological states might be altered over time and correlate with increased trust, especially in government. It is clear that ordinary citizens are vulnerable to what their governments decide to do, no matter the political system in place. We know that states can destroy wealth, freedoms, lives, and whole cultures and peoples by abuse, error, and neglect. Citizens, unlike many other types of trusting actors, typically have few options other than to accept what is handed to them by the state. Emigration is often not an option, nor are there effective mechanisms of control over state elites available to most average citizens, especially in the developing world. At some point in every citizen's life there comes a moment when you resign yourself to the idea that "you can't fight city hall." Rather than succumb to despair and hopelessness, citizens choose to actively trust governmental institutions. "My country, right or wrong" is how this is expressed. Or, perhaps more negatively, citizens decide that whatever the state provides must be what they deserve and they should therefore be satisfied. Both attitudes make for easily governed masses, although not necessarily for healthy polities (Putnam 2000).

On the other hand, there is evidence that people are expecting more and more from their governments. This is a trend that goes back to the origins of the welfare state in most developed countries as well as the spectacular promises of national liberators and populist politicians in the developing world. As expectations rise, disappointment and even disillusionment are far more likely, even where governments are generally competent, civic-minded, and responsive (Cheema and Popovski 2010; Kohn 2008, 111; Putnam 2000; Uslaner 2000). In fact, the better functioning the government, the greater the likelihood that citizens will hold it to an ever-rising standard of performance. The result, ironically, is that good governments sometimes please no one while citizens come to tolerate poorly performing state institutions.

In any case, these psychological theories suffer from levels of analysis problems. Concepts and theories that were designed primarily to explain individual-level dynamics are simply transferred by international relations scholars to the next level to explain collective action by states and state institutions without sufficient reflection.

There is a debate over whether states have intentions and can therefore keep their promises in a meaningful way. Cook, Hardin, and Levi argue that they cannot since they are collective entities (2005, 4–5). Nooteboom (2002, 53) and Becker (1996, 51) argue that they can. Peppers and Rogers (2012, 37) argue that whatever the reality, we treat them as though they can be trusted.

Before moving on, it is worth asking about the effects of trust. Since trust involves a willingness to make yourself vulnerable on the faith that the one being trusted is looking out for your interests and has the capacity to act on that intent, then any time actors refuse, they are not trusting. We could call this distrust, suspicion, guardedness, or any number of things. As Rathbun points out, the preferred strategy for such an actor would be going it alone (Rathbun 2012, 2). While nontrustors may complain that others lack the will or capacity to act in their interest (perhaps due to pessimism about human nature generally or the doubts about certain actors specifically), this attitude is most likely to be expressed by efforts to make oneself less vulnerable to opportunism. We will see below that this is reflected in the design of international agreements and institutions. I will only say at this point that it is possible to cooperate without trusting, assuming one has taken steps to prevent exploitation.

It is also worth noting that trust is the only thing that makes one open to betrayal. They are two sides of the same coin. But "betrayal" is not commonly used in international relations. At the United Nations over the past decade it has only been used a few dozen times. In most of these cases, it appears to serve only as a rhetorical flourish in which the listeners are enjoined not to violate the trust of those who will be injured by certain policies due to a failure to live up to the institution's highest ideals or lofty promises (failing to reach the Millennium Development Goals, failing to reduce food prices, failing to protect the earth, failing to intervene to protect victims of genocide, for example). Particularly poignant is the statement in a recent UN film on peacekeeping that when peacekeepers have raped the very people they were sent to protect, they engaged in a "double betrayal" of trust invested in them by those victims and by the world community (United Nations 2006). Reference was also made to the "betrayal" of Rwanda by France and the United States during the genocide for their failure to intervene, a theme that was repeated with reference to failures to protect brutalized people in Syria, Eritrea, Liberia, and elsewhere (Africa Recovery 2000; Abrehe 2005; Captan 2002). Note that in none of these cases did the international community have a strict legal obligation to intervene but rather had a moral "responsibility to protect," consistent with the sphere of trusting (rather than contractual obligation).

The Cases and Tests

I explore several most-likely cases of trust in the hope of learning how it emerges and how it affects international relations. I focus on the relationships between very small democratic European states and their more powerful protectors (See figure 1.1). Specifically, I focus on Luxembourg, Liechtenstein, Monaco, San Marino, and Andorra over the past two hundred years. These cases have the advantage of not only fitting the basic criteria of fairly high levels of vulnerability and exploitability (although there is some variance), but their longevity as sovereign states allows comparison across time. Each state has entered into many successive agreements—sometimes with a succession of partners—so each state provides multiple cases of voluntary dependence. The other microstates of Europe are quite

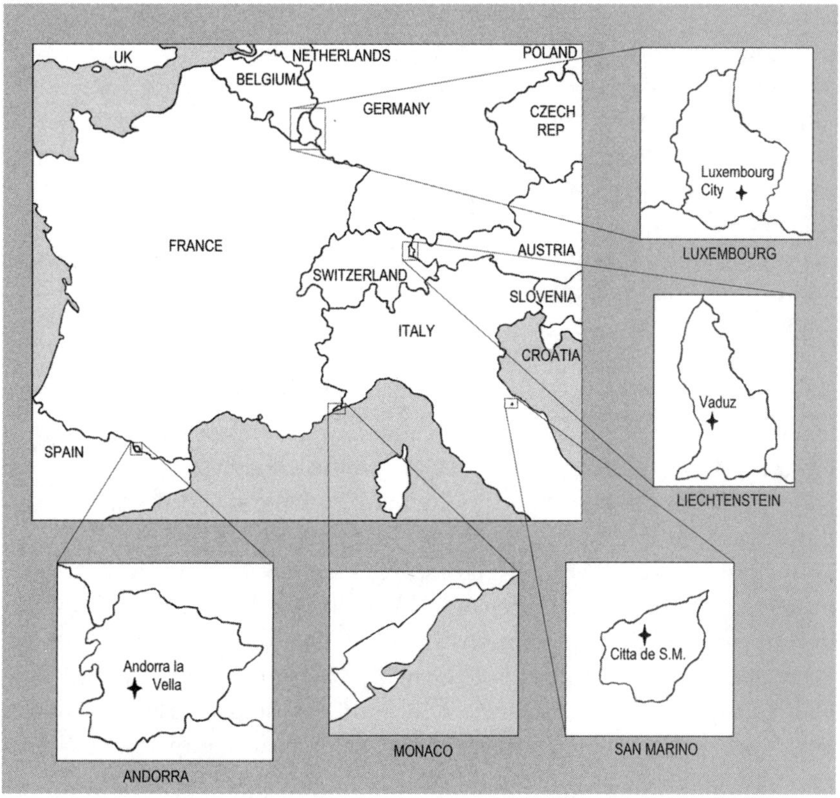

Fig. 1.1. European microstates

different in that they are either not really microstates (Vatican City and the Holy See are better understood as the seat of a billion-member NGO), have not been independent long enough to allow comparative analysis across time (Malta), or are not independent enough to be considered sovereigns (Scotland, Faroes).

Some may object to this choice since these actors are not especially significant on the world stage. But that is the point; vulnerability pushes an actor to make conscious decisions regarding whether to trust. Trust is a daily preoccupation. Nothing can be taken for granted and much is at stake. This is not to say that small states—even those in Europe—will always trust. As we will see, the small states in this study have shown dramatically different levels of trust over the years and across cases. Andorra, for example, has tended to remain autonomous and aloof from France and Spain as much as possible, while Luxembourg embraced dependency on Germany, Belgium, and France in turn. Liechtenstein welcomed dependency on Switzerland for much of the twentieth century until the two countries parted ways with respect to relations with the European Union. For that matter, most small European states have adopted foreign policy orientations that differ markedly from each other. A quick comparison of the policies of Iceland, Ireland, Malta, Cyprus, and Finland should be enough to demonstrate that even weak states view dependency and the trust that evinces as entirely optional (Hower 2008; Hey 2003; Wivel 2016).

These states are also interesting because for many decades they have allowed public participation in policy making, thus allowing the expression of cultural and ethnic ties in foreign policy. They have also been nominally independent for many decades, implying that they could shape their own foreign policies without direct outside control. Further, being endowed with important resources and located adjacent to powerful states means these actors fulfill the criteria of being exploitable.

I will proceed with a series of carefully structured case studies of European microstates. In each case study, I will provide the necessary information to assess each of the various dimensions discussed. For each of the eight parameters I will assign a "high," "moderate," or "low" value along with an explanation. These are not meant to be rigid interval data points but rather an approximate ordinal ranking. Of central importance is how these values change across the different situations for the same country as the historical context evolves, but it is also useful to compare across cases. To determine the relative capability and possible vulnerability, I will compare economic, demographic, political, and geographical characteristics of the microstates in question and their larger neighbors and/or regional bodies to which they have become associated. Some of the variables will include relative gross national product and gross national product per capita; trade and investment patterns; technology levels; relative size and capacity of the governments, foreign services, and militaries; transportation networks; employment patterns, and so forth. These will be reassessed with each new phase of the relationships.

Considerable attention will be paid to the details of the agreements that link the states, as outlined above. I will look at the respective aims of the leaders of the various states, the preferences of the broader public (to the extent that this can be determined), and the negotiation process and context. For each agreement I will consider the scope and salience of the topics as well as details of how the treaty is to be interpreted and implemented as discussed above. I will also consider the actual application of these provisions and the degree of satisfaction with the treaties on the part of elites and masses. These characteristics will then be compared across time and treaty to determine whether any patterns emerge.

Throughout the chapters I will consider the social and ideational links between the microstates and their neighbors such as immigration and emigration, multinational marriages, cross-border labor flows, and so forth. I will also discuss other identity issues such as religious affiliations, ideological beliefs, language usage patterns, mutual perceptions, expressions of affection and trust, and so forth. These will be useful in testing various theories of trust.

I show that while there are some indications that states see each other as having shared if not encapsulated interests, they generally do not trust each other as trust is understood in the broader literature and according to my definition. Rather, the relationships are based on careful and prudent risk assessment and are heavily contingent. Weak states are including a wide range of opt-out provisions, insisting on securing maximum voting powers, and looking for alternative partners. But the relationships I study are generally very healthy and mutually beneficial, serving as models for the world.

The penultimate chapter is a collection of brief case studies that focus on asymmetrical relations involving the major powers. They allow me to explore more fully questions of hierarchy and leadership as presented in Lake (2011), among others, and to increase the variance with respect to a number of independent variables thought to predict trust (such as cultural convergence and ethnic similarity). In particular, it addresses questions of trust in the context of delegation as well as subordination (Castelfranchi and Falcone 2010, 87; Hoffman 2006, 3; Hawkins et al. 2006). The asymmetrical relations in question involve the three major political powers—the United States, the Russian Federation, and the People's Republic of China—and two different subordinate states each, one mostly harmonious and one mostly contentious: US-Canada, US-South Vietnam, Russia-Belarus, Russia-Georgia, PRC-North Korea, and PRC-Vietnam. The differences in levels of trust are more striking in these cases, which in turns allows us to see that cultural convergence and ethnic similarity—along with ideological harmony—are central to the development of trust. The cases also show that trust, where it happens, can be extremely risky for both the weak state and the powerful ally.

In the concluding chapter, I will return to the various theories of trust, as both a dependent and an independent variable in international relations.

I will show that while rationality approaches are the most useful, sociological and psychological theories offer important supplemental explanations. Following this analysis, I will turn to the moral and ethical issues surrounding trust in international relations. In particular, I will return to the question of whether states should trust or whether states should be trustworthy from the perspective of democratic theory and prudent statesmanship. I will look back at the insights that can be gleaned from the case studies and the broader theoretical literature to determine which are most promising with respect to the origins of trust in international relations.

At the end of the day, I find that trust is not a common occurrence in international relations, even in places where one might most expect to find it. While some sociological and ideational factors will contribute to an experiment with trust, structural and situational forces will pull regimes away from the types of open-ended commitments characteristic of trusting relationships. We should not be surprised to see more trust between actors that share identities, particularly those with common cultures, ethnic identities, ideological outlooks, and socioeconomic structures and status. As we will see, in our European cases many elites—as well as ordinary citizens—often commented that they were essentially the same as those in their partner states.

Trust is more pronounced in states where the leader has almost sole control of the country's foreign policy. It correlates with a paternalistic approach to governance that denigrates the role of lower-ranking national actors and citizens as a whole. Only when an entire community has reached a consensus regarding whom to trust can it be said to be ethical. But ultimately even the most vulnerable and least distinctive peoples should be expected to look out for their interests. In particular, I see a great deal of hedging and even some outright distrust, particularly in the wake of betrayal. Both elected and unelected elites will identify primarily with their states and develop a set of priorities and aims that exist separate and apart from those of their larger partners. Consistent with both realist and liberal theory, I find that most agreements would be driven by necessity and be the product of years of careful negotiations. Driven by both structural forces of anarchy and self-help as well as domestic pressures to preserve national identity and security, states will press for treaties—where they occur at all—that are of limited scope and are replete with escape clauses, unanimity requirements, and precise language. Rather than some brief, open-ended statement that commits the weaker party to indefinite and demanding obligations, I see numerous narrow-gauge treaties and protocols designed to limit the larger partner's prerogatives and maximize the weaker party's options.

Even vulnerable small states are willing to keep their options open, casting about for alternatives to the existing arrangement. This might sometimes be forced upon them if their protector implodes, for example, or somehow becomes unable or unwilling to play its part. Even where the relationship is basically healthy, smaller states will continue looking for alternatives where they might achieve the same outcomes but with greater control and flexibility. In particular, small states see advantages to increasing their role in multilateral institutions such as the European Union, where they might possess voting—and even veto—rights.

Regarding the implications of trust, given its infrequency, sweeping conclusions will be difficult. But some preliminary conclusions will be possible. While trust is widely seen as a prerequisite to cooperation, I will show, by returning to the cases, that at best it introduces an element of risk that national leaders are wise not to entertain. As a primarily nonrational psychological phenomenon it runs the risk of turning foreign policy into an extension of a leader's wishful thinking (Becker 1996). We see that national leaders indulging in trusting can lead to disaster, one that is largely inflicted on the public, albeit for the noblest of reasons.

Where trust is high—and formal cooperation also high—many of these arrangements will in the end be detrimental to the interests and security of the weaker parties. The larger parties will either exploit or neglect the weaker parties as they work toward achieving their own priorities. Betrayal will be common, and even where it does not happen to the weaker state directly—as was famously the case for Luxembourg at the outset of each World War—other small states will learn from the cautionary tales around them. The implication is that trusting relationships will likely be short-lived as elites learn their dangers. Empirically, then, trust will be more evident in earlier relationships rather than more recent ones, with hedging and distrust as the more popular approaches over time. The implication is that eventually trust might completely disappear, contrary to the prediction that cooperation engenders trust.

This pessimistic view should not lead to the conclusion that cooperation will inevitably decline over time or that trust is inherently bad. But it should be noted that trust can be counterproductive and trust-based cooperation can be ephemeral. Conversely, we might also see that cooperation does not require trust and that healthy, long-term partnerships should perhaps be laced with a certain degree of skepticism and hedging. These insights might help explain patterns now in evidence between European Union member states, as countries that feel exploited by their larger partners (and even citizens in some of the larger states) seek to extricate themselves from the relationship. Likewise, it might even explain American voters' support for a presidential candidate who openly disdains NAFTA, NATO, the United Nations, and multilateralism generally (Pace 2016). Perhaps an increase in hedging arrangements—including perhaps a return to consensus decision making—and less expectation of trust could reverse these trends.

TWO

Luxembourg

The Dangers of Trust

For centuries Luxembourg's existence depended on the kindness of its neighbors. The local leaders of Luxembourg adjusted to what was handed to them and made the best of a bad situation, sometimes turning necessity into a virtue. The end result was occupation by the kaiser's armies and devastation by Hitler's. These elites learned that the great powers cannot be trusted and that the best solution to vulnerability is integration. Along with its relatively small neighbors—Belgium and the Netherlands—Luxembourg played a key role in the creation and evolution of Europe in the twentieth century. It has moved from pawn to pivot.

This experience of Luxembourg can be divided into four broad periods: occupation and domination by outside actors until the withdrawal of Prussian troops in 1867 and its mandatory neutrality, the country's emergence as a fully recognized autonomous state from 1867 to its admission to the League of Nations, the interwar period of integration with Belgium and continued neutrality, and finally its emergence as a founder of virtually every major European institution until now. Luxembourg experienced a wide range of different levels and types of dependence on a variety of outside actors, making it an ideal case study of trust in international relations. To study Luxembourg is to study several different states at once. In particular, we will see that Luxembourg learned better than most the risks involved in trust and the importance of hedging.

Luxembourg until 1867: Dependence in the Context of Emerging Sovereignty

The founding of Luxembourg is shrouded in myth, as one might expect for a country that still struggles with its essential identity (Péporté et al. 2010). The city of Luxembourg traces its roots to the tenth century CE (Newcomer 1984) while the county of Luxembourg—which encompassed the modern state along with parts of France and nearly half of Belgium—was formally elevated to a duchy by Emperor Charles IV in 1353 (Bartmann 2012, 540). Although the surrounding area is relatively flat, the city itself is perched on a cliff that falls into a deep river valley that makes it almost impregnable from that direction. Once walls were erected around the rest of the city it became a fortress not to be trifled with. The region was prosperous thanks to the many traders who passed through, but the agricultural system was and would remain traditional and the Industrial Revolution would have to wait until the late 1800s. The Reformation had little effect on it as well. The small population had little sense of identity; even the local language was a mix of German and French with unclear origins. Historians and politicians are still trying to reinvent Luxembourg to this day (Péporté et al. 2010). Luxembourg was thus just another locus of peripheral activity, located "somewhere between Vienna and London" (Kayser 1990).

Over the next centuries, the city and its fortress were held both alternatively and sometimes simultaneously by Burgundy, the Netherlands, Belgium, and Austria-Hungary. Following the French Revolution, the territory was annexed by France in 1795. Perhaps needless to say, these invasions and annexations gave the people of Luxembourg a certain fatalism about their status; it was not until the late 1940s that one could begin to think of Luxembourg as something secure and permanent. The result was a quiet cosmopolitanism, a sense that their "country" was intimately tied to the fate of Europe itself, and that there could be much to gain by understanding and welcoming a wide range of foreign cultures and influences.

During the period of French occupation, the duchy knew its only period of republican government as the monarchy was dismantled and the area was merged into the department of Forêts (Newcomer 1984, 11). The political revolution did not take, and in a rare show of defiance against a foreign occupier, in 1798 Luxembourg peasants rose up against the French, to no avail. They are still regarded as nationalist heroes (Péporté et al. 2010, 59).

After Napoleon's defeat in 1814, the status of Luxembourg was a topic of negotiation at the Congress of Vienna, although no representatives of the duchy were invited (nor were the locals consulted [Calmes 1971/1932, 11]). King William I of the Netherlands was granted the duchy (and the title of grand duke) in "personal union" (Final Act 1814, art. 25), meaning that although he could rule (or rather appoint a ruler in his stead) over the territory, the land would not be annexed to the kingdom (Lorenz 2013, 230). Specifically, the treaty provides for a shared governance system involving the Netherlands as the titular head of state and chief administrator and Prussia as the de facto government of the territory. Luxembourg was joined to the German Confederation—represented by William I in his capacity as grand duke—with one vote in the Diet and three votes in the General Assembly (compared with four for Prussia and Austria) (Final Act 1814, arts. 56–58).

The fact that their country was treated as a mere bargaining chip by the great powers came as no surprise to the local population, who had become accustomed to such things (Kayser 1990, 31). But their patience would be tested in the years to come. In 1815, pursuant to the Congress of Vienna Final Act, four thousand Prussian troops (in a city of roughly ten thousand [Calmes 1971/1932, 73]) were dispatched to guard the fortress. Although the great powers had decided that Luxembourg would have its own civil and police administration, the troops ignored the instructions (if they ever received them; the Final Act itself was not published in Luxembourg until 1828) and imposed an informal system of martial law, much to the dismay of local populations (to this day Luxembourgers resort to the epithet "Prussian" when describing Germans who are overly domineering). Despite repeated entreaties, William I did not address their concerns either directly with the Prussian government or through the German Confederation (Calmes 1971/1932, 85). For his part, William I was resented for discriminatory taxes, forcing failed Dutch administrators on the country, and ruling by decree. Tax evasion and peaceful protests spread during the 1820s (Kayser 1990, 40). In spite of the hardships, all of Luxembourg's nobility supported a new basic law offered by William I since it offered freedom of religion and seemed to offer a way out of Prussian domination (Kayser 1990, 31).

Belgians were far less interested in what they considered a mere sop to their desire for autonomy and voted against it, although William I ignored the result and instituted the law anyway. While none of these impositions led to open rebellion, most Luxembourgers supported the Belgian uprising against Dutch rule in 1830 and many traveled to Brussels to join the fight (Péporté 2010, 53). When the Dutch failed to recapture Brussels and the new state's independence was declared, Luxembourgers were not disappointed to hear the rebels announce the annexation of their territory to Belgium's. They sent delegates to Brussels to helped draft the new constitution and vote alongside Belgians for the new king, Leopold (Kayser 1990, 64).

This might have been the end of Luxembourg's story had it not been for the intervention of the great powers, intervening to force a cease-fire in 1831 and pressing for a negotiated settlement between the Dutch and Belgians. Since William I refused to accept the annexation of Luxembourg to Belgium, a final settlement resulted in a compromise in which most of the French-speaking region's duchy was transferred to Belgium via the Treaty of London of 1839. Once again local representation of the duchy was missing and, perhaps unsurprisingly, some German-speaking areas were erroneously granted to the new country. The new rump state was more ethnically homogeneous, to be sure, and while locals lamented the bisection of their country they accepted it as inevitable (Péporté 2010, 5; Newcomer 1984, 195). There was no talk of regaining stolen territory at the time or in subsequent decades; if anything they seemed pleased that if any country were to take half of its territory, best that it be the Belgians, with whom they had forged common cause. Even today most Luxembourgers remain fatalistic and ambivalent about their national identity, and when asked whether they would be willing to see their state merged with another, they seem to accept the possibility without regret, especially if it would result in Belgian citizenship (Kmec 2013). Roughly three-quarters define themselves first as European and only second as Luxembourgers (European Commission 2012).

The year 1839 is generally seen today as Luxembourg's founding year, although an argument could be made for 1815, 1841, 1867, or even 1890, as we will see (Péporté et al. 2010, 31). The confusion about the country's inauguration stems largely from the fact that its sovereignty was accorded to it piecemeal and never asserted energetically. From 1815 until 1890, a foreign monarch ruled. Until 1867, Prussians occupied the capital. Until 1841, Dutch law prevailed. It was not until the 1850s that one could secure Luxembourg citizenship (Kmec 2013). But in 1839 the territory of Luxembourg was established and the international community seemed to acknowledge that the country was to be a permanent fixture (Treaty of London of 1839, art. 6). This even though Prussia sought to annex the territory in 1841–42 and France tried to purchase it in 1866 (Newcomer 1984, 101).

With the abdication of William I in 1840, William II acceded to the

Dutch throne and immediately proved himself more sympathetic to Luxembourg's emerging nationalism and liberalism. A new constitution was promulgated—with the approval of Luxembourg's elite—that instituted a Council of Government made up of local nobles and elected by landowners (who made up just 3 percent of the population [Newcomer 1984, 198]). Luxembourgers replaced Dutch administrators. The duchy was joined to the Zollverein by agreement between William II and Prussia (at Prussia's insistence), giving it access to German markets and protecting its fledgling industry and weak agricultural sector from foreign competition (Gengler 1991, 21). It would remain a member until the dissolution of the treaty in 1919—even after most countries in the system became part of the German Empire in 1871—largely because Germany came to dominate the country's economy (there are indications that Luxembourgers would have preferred being tied to France's economy [Kayser 1990, 91]). The country was caught up in the uprisings of 1848 and a citizens' committee drafted a liberal constitution that was accepted by William II. Parties were legalized, the press was liberated, and a new elected assembly shared legislative powers with the king (Newcomer 1984, 200). This system was reversed by William III upon his accession in 1856, but with the departure of the Prussians in 1867 a new more liberal constitution was instituted.

With respect to our trust-related typology, it is worth asking to what degree Luxembourg was vulnerable and to what degree it represented an attractive target for exploitation (see table 2.1). Clearly the state was subject to the whims of the great powers and even its much smaller immediate neighbors. After all, it lost half its territory in 1839 without even putting up a fight. Throughout this period, except for a relatively brief respite between 1848 and 1856, its constitution was more in keeping with an eighteenth-century model of absolutism. It had no military force although it contributed three thousand men to the Dutch constabulary between 1815 and 1841 (its militia was halved but autonomous thereafter [Lorenz 2013, 230]). The Prussian presence had all the trappings of an occupation force for much of the period. Even its sovereignty was in dispute for much of the period. With respect to its exploitability, the great powers seemed intent on seizing it at the first opportunity, and it was only the balancing between Prussia, France, and the United Kingdom that allowed it to retain a semblance of identity. The Dutch seemed of all Luxembourg's neighbors the least interested in annexing the territory outright, although they for many years were content to squeeze tax revenues from its citizenry.

More interesting from the point of view of trust is whether the people and elites of Luxembourg had much voice in their dependency on their neighbors. As pointed out, there was no overt Luxembourg representation at the critical meetings in Vienna and London that largely decided the country's existence and boundaries. Likewise, its membership in the German Confederation and Zollverein was largely the product of arrangements between Prussian and Dutch rulers. It is clear, however, that over the period in question the country's relationship with the Netherlands became increasingly voluntary. It would be incorrect to say that in 1850 Luxembourg was the mere personal domain of William II. The country's constitutional arrangements with The Hague were endorsed by at least a part of Luxembourg society, and its continued membership in the Zollverein long after the country had its own head of state indicates that there was no fundamental objection to the arrangement. But clearly Luxembourg was not an entirely free agent during this period.

With respect to the scope and salience of issues covered under agreements between the Netherlands and Prussia during this period, it is clear that both were quite significant. It goes without saying that the Netherlands could control much of what occurred within Luxembourg and could also control its foreign relations to a high degree. As mentioned, Luxembourg's small constabulary force was merged with that of the Netherlands for much of the period and it did not have the capacity to enter into agreements with third parties. Where Prussia is concerned, some elements of the country's foreign affairs were off-limits, but many domestic and foreign economic policies fell under its domination. Security in Luxembourg was largely attended to by Prussia, and Luxembourg's membership in the Germanic Confederation and the Zollverein meant that its political and economic relations with other German states and its trade relations with third states were largely controlled by Prussia; at least the kingdom had a veto. Luxembourg was bound to defend all the members against outside threats and from each other (Final Act 1814, art. 63). It was only during the 1848–1856 period that Luxembourg enjoyed something approaching domestic sovereignty.

With respect to the details of the agreements, the Final Act of the Congress of Vienna, the Dutch constitutional arrangements, the German Confederation treaties, and the various treaties associated with the Zollverein were fairly precise with respect to obligations, rights, and decision-making arrangements. The Congress of Vienna went to great pains to establish the boundaries and powers of each dynastic realm, but said relatively little about withdrawal, interpretation, and enforcement of the agreement. Ultimately it was left to an informal arrangement of six great powers operating as a Concert of Europe to carry out these functions on an ad hoc basis.

Because the treaty created William I's status over Luxembourg, these are fairly clear, although largely open-ended with respect to the details of Luxembourgers' rights and duties. William I could have engaged in a very wide range of actions under the terms of the Final Act. Likewise, the provisions regarding the Germanic Confederation are fairly clear where administration and policy making are concerned, but quite vague with respect to the scope of issues that can be addressed, states' obligations to bring items to the Diet's agenda, and which actions are required or permitted. The Zollverein, for its part, is extremely specific where bilateral trade agreements are concerned, providing for specific toll and tariff schedules between particular states. Some organizational structures were set in place to allow for collaborative problem solving, but these were only loosely structured and did not prevent trade crises, something that troubled Prussia and prompted it to strengthen its control of these collective bodies in 1866 with the formation of the North German Confederation (Henderson 1934/2013, 318).

The commitments made—largely in Luxembourg's name—in these various agreements were intended to be permanent. The phrase "in perpetuity" appears numerous times in the Final Act, and the constitutional arrangements with the Netherlands were intended to be perpetual. There are no explicit provisions for withdrawal in the constitution of the Germanic Confederation. Withdrawal is permitted from the Zollverein and was frequently threatened, especially during trading crises. With respect to marginalization, in all cases Luxembourg was a largely passive observer of its fate, with the exception of its evolving relationship with the Netherlands after 1841. Although William I and William II held seats and exercised votes in behalf of Luxembourg in the Diet of the Germanic Confederation, they could do so largely unilaterally since they were under no formal obligation to obtain Luxembourg's approval except perhaps during the brief period of 1848–1856. That said, should Luxembourg ever accede to that seat, it would enjoy considerable voting power, almost as great as Prussia's. Likewise, Luxembourg was represented by the Netherlands at the Congress of Vienna and in the Zollverein's bodies.

These facts, when placed in the historical context, indicate that while the people of Luxembourg were not obligated to trust their neighbors, they often did. There was little in the way of protest or rebellion against the established order, not that these would have likely been effective. Likewise, there was little effort to appeal directly to Paris or London or Berlin to have their concerns heard and addressed by the great powers, an option that was always available. When given the opportunity—in the 1820s and 1840s in particular—they endeavored to use established, peaceful channels to communicate their concerns, and they accepted—however grudgingly—the decisions made in their behalf. That they carried on most of these arrangements even after they gained more control over their fate from 1867 onward indicates that this was not a people chafing under the yoke at any rate. Since they were rarely given the opportunity to select the dependent arrangements in question, and these arrangements were significant and binding, it is perhaps better to say that they hoped that those on whom they were dependent would take their interests into account, even though they had their doubts. One could say this is a precursor to trust.

From 1867 to 1918: Embracing Dependence

The period 1866–1867 was a tumultuous one in and around Luxembourg. Otto von Bismarck was well on his way to establishing a German Empire, diminishing Austria-Hungary along the way (see chapter 4). The Germanic Confederation was dissolved, leaving the status of Luxembourg unclear. France and Prussia both saw the benefit of acquiring a buffer state to gain an advantage in a coming war (which occurred in 1870). France, as mentioned, offered William III five million francs to buy the country from the Netherlands, feeling entitled to compensation for having aided Prussia's efforts against Austria (Kayser 1990, 101; Trausch 2003, 233). But Prussia did not see things that way and vociferously opposed the move, preferring instead to incorporate the duchy into the North German federation (Newcomer 1984, 208–11). The idea of annexing the country to Belgium was also floated (Kayser 1990, 103). Most citizens of Luxembourg and the press were nervous about these machinations. As put in a local editorial, Luxembourg is merely a "state to be fiddled with (état de tripotage), with a dagger pointed at its heart" (Kayser 1990, 103). This stalemate, combined with Britain's preference that neither great power acquire Luxembourg, led to a decision to disarm and neutralize her. As put by Newcomer, "The perpetual irony of Luxembourg again prevailed; the very threats against her integrity sprung the mechanism that made her free" (Newcomer 1984, 208). For the first time, Luxembourg was representing itself at a meeting of great powers designed to decide her fate. The head of government, Victor de Tornaco, and the vice president of the Council of State, Emmanuel Servais, made the trip to London to meet with representatives of the great powers, Belgium and the Netherlands (Kayser 1990, 105). The result was the Treaty of London of 1867. Article 2 declares:

> The Grand Duchy of Luxembourg, within the boundaries established in the 1839 Treaty annexes, and guaranteed by the courts of Austria, France, Great Britain, Prussia, and Russia, will henceforth be a perpetually neutral state. It will maintain this neutrality with respect to all states. The High Contracting Parties commit to respect this neutrality as stipulated in this article. This neutrality is and shall be collectively guaranteed by the treaty signatory Powers, with the exception of Belgium which is itself neutral. (author's translation)

In connection with this declaration of neutrality, Prussian troops were to withdraw from the fortress of the city of Luxembourg (Article 4), the fortress itself was to be dismantled (Article 3), and Luxembourg committed to not raise an army (Article 5). The Netherlands was to supply a force "consistent with public order" and carry out the terms of the treaty. While William III was assured of his continued dominion over the territory, it is clear that his capacity to control it would be limited. The ambiguity of the arrangement was captured by his decree to the people of Luxembourg, dated July 1, 1867, in which he simultaneously praises the people for their expressions of loyalty to him while at the same time pledging his continued efforts to ensure the country's independence (Treaty of London 1867).

Under a new (albeit traditional) constitution (1868) and a new foreign policy status, Luxembourg enjoyed a golden age in the last few decades of the nineteenth century. Its independence was affirmed in writing and guaranteed by the most powerful states of its age. In 1890 William III died, leaving the throne to his daughter Wilhelmina. An arcane rule governing members of the house of Nassau with domains in Luxembourg's territory (enshrined in the constitution's Article 3) prohibited succession to a female heir if a male heir existed in the line, and so the ruling houses of Luxembourg and the Netherlands split, and for the first time since the Middle Ages, the country had its own monarch in the person of Grand Duke Adolph. Ironically, in just over twenty years the successor to Adolph (William IV) also lacked a male heir, but rather than search for a distant relation, he spearheaded a change in the country's constitution (in 1907) to allow his daughter Marie Adelaide to assume the throne, thus assuring a continuing succession of home-grown monarchs. Grand dukes and duchesses enjoyed wide-ranging powers to veto legislation, direct the country's foreign affairs, and appoint judges, but the legislative initiative rested with a sixty-member Chamber of Deputies that controlled domestic policy.

During this period the nation's economy flourished as its iron ore deposits (discovered in 1850) and its ties to the German economy and German-controlled railways allowed it to industrialize at a rapid pace. In 1911 three steel companies merged into ARBED (Aciéries Réunies de Burbach-Eich-Dudelange or Unified Steelworks of Burbach, Eich, and Dudelange) to become one of the dominant concerns in Europe and seen by some as a precursor to the European Coal and Steel Community (Newcomer 1984, 251). The country enjoyed its neutrality, trusting implicitly the assurances made by the great powers in 1867. As put by Trausch, "the country's real foreign policy consisted precisely in not having one" (Trausch 1982, 349, cited by Lorenz 2013, 231).

Grand Duchess Marie Adelaide was well-known to Kaiser Wilhelm II of Germany, to the point that the empire's invasion of the grand duchy in August 1914 was welcomed by some in her entourage and was not seen as the violation of the country's territory or the ruler's trust (or of Germany's legal obligations [ASIL 1915]). During the occupation, she ignored complaints by workers of oppressive German conditions and even visited the kaiser in Berlin (Newcomer 1984, 235). Suspicions of her complicity in German occupation eventually led to her forced abdication after the war and resistance on the part of officials in France and Great Britain to treat the country as an ally. Despite a referendum in Luxembourg overwhelmingly supportive of an economic union with France after the war, Paris declined the offer (Newcomer 1984, 236; Trausch 2003, 240). Liberals and radicals even forced a referendum on keeping the monarchy itself (it passed with 78 percent approval). Amidst the turmoil, France secretly endorsed a Belgian plan to annex the country (Kmec 2013). Once again, the grand duchy's survival was on the line.

We will address how Luxembourg dealt with the postwar crisis in the next section (see table 2.1). For now, let us turn to an assessment of the degree to which trust featured in the country's external relations during this period. On the first two dimensions, the situation was even more worrisome for Luxembourg in that it had been stripped of its military—such as it was—and in discovering and exploiting iron ore had made itself an even more appealing target. The country was moving to the center of Europe—both politically and economically—and the risk of a continental war over its fate was quite high. While this may have also been true in the earlier period, the key difference is that Luxembourg finally had a direct voice in its future. It elected to retain its increasingly loose ties to the Netherlands until a succession crisis created a final rupture, albeit a peaceful and happy one. Even more important, it signed off on and embraced its new status as a disarmed, neutral state, relying on the good intentions of the great powers to ensure its survival and tranquility. At least initially, these factors were strong indicators that the leaders of Luxembourg, while extricating themselves from the need to trust the Dutch, had invested a great deal of trust in the guarantors of the 1867 Treaty of London, a trust that proved to have been misplaced.

As the Netherlands gradually withdrew from Luxembourg, the scope and salience of issues covered under the two countries' agreements and constitutions receded and more and more matters were placed in the hands of the Luxembourger leadership, culminating in the Dutch becoming peripheral players in Luxembourg's destiny (at least until the Benelux agreements are reached; see below). Likewise, the great powers had narrowed the scope of issues covered under the two major agreements: the Treaty of London and the Zollverein. Gone was the obligation to come to the defense of Germany as provided for under the Germanic Confederation. In fact, gone was the obligation to come to any country's defense. The salience of these issues, however, was still extremely high since they involved the country's industrial expansion and its political survival in the event of attack. Luxembourg's economy was inextricably intertwined with Germany's, which was not only its principal customer but also directed its railways and negotiated trade agreements with third parties in its behalf. Were the German economy to collapse, Luxembourg's would follow.

The three sets of agreements—the new constitutional arrangements that initially included and later excluded the Netherlands, the London treaty, and the Zollverein—each had very different characteristics with respect to these last three dimensions. To begin, while the constitutional arrangements were increasingly specific, they also empowered Luxembourg to an increasing degree until by 1890 the country was utterly free of Dutch control. Turning to our definition of trust, we can say that Luxembourg had removed almost all elements of trust from its relations with the Netherlands, choosing instead to go it alone. It no longer leaned on its administrative or police force, was removed from any explicit or implicit defense pact, and was no longer enmeshed in its economy. While the country could conceivably have imposed itself again, the fact that it signed the 1867 treaty offered some assurance that it would not.

The Treaty of London of 1867 was brief and open-ended. As we saw, it simply asserted the neutrality of the grand duchy and committed the great powers (along with Belgium and the Netherlands) to guaranteeing the country's safety from themselves and each other. There is no discussion of how this was to be done, including what penalties would be assessed against those who might violate the agreement. In fact, after the German Empire was consolidated there were claims made in Berlin that this and the nearly identical 1839 London agreement that guaranteed Belgium's neutrality were not binding since they were signed by the Prussian state that had ceased to exist (ASIL 1915). German chancellor Theobald von Bethmann Hollweg is famously said to have wondered why Britain would go to war over a mere "scrap of paper" (which might be better understood as "waste paper" since it was old and obsolete and deserved to be discarded). Obviously there were important differences of opinion regarding the operation of the London agreements.

As mentioned, Luxembourg was far less marginalized at the 1867 London conference, and, although it likely had no alternative, it offered its willing consent through democratically elected representatives. Of course, the commitment was meant to be definitive. Taken together, this is perhaps the most impressive display of trust we will find in this entire study. The fact that it proved disastrous for Luxembourg's people (and to some degree its leaders) will inform much of our discussion in chapter 8.

Regarding the Zollverein, it is important to note that the treaty was reinvented in 1866 in anticipation of complete German unification under Prussian dominance. The Prussian state was able to persuade and pressure the other signatories that its votes on the Customs Council should be increased, that it should have a veto, and that it would represent all the signatories in any trade negotiations with third parties (Henderson 1934/2013, 318). While opinion in Luxembourg was divided over whether these close ties to Prussia and then Germany were healthy in the long run (many favored an economic union with France, especially once the war started), it was difficult to deny that the arrangement provided considerable benefits. At the end of the day, even though the treaty was open-ended (it wasn't entirely clear, for example, what actions could trigger a Prussian/German veto or what were the parameters of trade agreements with third parties) and Luxembourg was both a minor player and able to withdraw only at great cost, it considered the arrangement acceptable. This again indicates a considerable degree of trust, this time in Prussia/Germany in particular.

1919–1945: Bitter Lessons and the Beginning of the Unification of Europe

Coming out of World War I, Luxembourg might be best described as dazed. Running the risk of once again being annexed out of existence, it moved quickly to establish itself as a member in good standing of the international community. As mentioned, the first order of business was to secure the abdication of Grand Duchess Marie Adelaide, which occurred in 1919. She abdicated in favor of her far less controversial sister Charlotte, who would reign until 1964. The monarchy and the Luxembourg elite were eager to recast the country as solidly anti-German by rewriting its history (Péporté et al. 2010, 91), revitalizing the Luxembourgish language, reaching out first to France and then Belgium to form a customs union, even erecting monuments to the country's citizens who joined the French and British armies to fight Germany (Kmec 2013). Next came participation in the founding of the League of Nations and securing membership in the new body. There was resistance to admitting small countries since the great powers doubted they would be able to cope with the body's diplomatic and military obligations. Luxembourg had the added pall of ambiguous World War I loyalties. In response, Luxembourg resuscitated its army with a few hundred troops and assured the great powers that its diplomatic corps was up to the demands (Bartmann 2012, 540; Hardin 1985, 15). It had hoped to be able to retain the neutrality established in the 1867 treaty, but since membership in the League required a willingness to fight against aggressors, the request was withdrawn. The country retained de facto neutrality, however, and by the 1930s was granted formal recognition of its status by the great powers (a vain hope, to be sure [Van Roon 1989, 181]). At the end of the day, Luxembourg was admitted, becoming the smallest state with a proverbial seat at the table, a position it has never relinquished (Bartmann 2012, 537).

The next key step was to quickly gain access to the world's markets, a feat necessitated by the collapse of the Zollverein but complicated by Luxembourg's links to the German economy and its decades of economic protection. Luxembourg's population supported an economic union with France in 1919, but this was blocked by the Allied powers (Magone 2017, 46). Belgium was the most obvious alternative. Belgium was obliging, but demanding. The negotiations were a brief affair since Belgium offered a take-it-or-leave-it plan to incorporate Luxembourg's economy into its own, treating it essentially like a province for economic purposes (Kinsch 2013). Belgium's laws relating to customs, excise taxes, and other forms of trade regulation were to be adopted verbatim by Luxembourg. Given the lack of alternatives and the general sense that Belgium's policies would ultimately be good for the duchy (albeit painful in the short term [Calmes 1971/1932, 243]), Luxembourg negotiators agreed. The Belgium-Luxembourg Economic Union (BLEU or U.E.B.L. in French) was signed on July 25, 1921, creating a customs union and free trade area between the two states (Articles 1–3) with a number of exceptions for coal, steel, and agriculture among other things (Article 3). Article 4 states that "All legal provisions and regulations at present in force in the Grand-Duchy of Luxembourg as regards customs and common excise duties shall be abolished on the date appointed in Article 21 and replaced by the provisions relating to customs and excise in force in Belgium at the date of the ratification of the present Convention." Belgium would negotiate and sign trade agreements with third countries in Luxembourg's behalf (Article 5) and—on a side deal—Belgium would see to the consular needs of Luxembourg's citizens in areas where the grand duchy lacked a consulate (Article 26). Lest there be any confusion, Article 21 reminds the signatories that: "On the ratification of the Treaty, the Grand Ducal Government shall promulgate the laws, regulations and other provisions which it is bound to adopt under the present Convention, and shall give them the full force of law in the Grand Duchy." The treaty was to last for fifty years, renewable in ten-year increments unless one of the parties announced its withdrawal at least one year before the end of each term (Article 29). The treaty also provided for arbitration to settle disagreements of interpretation, with arbitral panels consisting of one person appointed by Belgium, one appointed by Luxembourg, and a citizen of a third country to be approved by both signatories (Article 28).

The treaty was in fact—and in practice—not as rigid as Articles 4 and 21 imply. Luxembourg would be given a period of time to adjust its excise taxes on such things as alcohol and tobacco to conform to Belgian law (Article 6), and both countries could block imports for the sake of health, sanitation, and security (Article 9). And although Luxembourg customs officials would be required to conform to Belgian dress and conduct, no one would be fired or have his pay cut (Articles 15–17). Most important, Luxembourg would have a seat on the various administrative and advisory bodies created to implement the treaty, although until 1935 Belgium would have two seats to Luxembourg's one (Articles 26–28) (Calmes 1971/1932, 245). Although the Superior Council of the Union was designed primarily to monitor and encourage Luxembourg's implementation of the treaty (Annex), in practice the two governments consulted regularly. Luxembourg adopted the Belgian franc as its currency, and to help with payment issues Brussels granted a loan for 175 million francs (Article 22).

As the BLEU arrangements were finalized and implemented, Belgium, with Luxembourg's support, began to work with other small and mid-sized states to widen the free trade system it had helped design. As early as 1932 Belgium and the Netherlands began work on a customs union and worked with the Oslo Group of mostly neutral European states to promote economic cooperation at a time of economic upheaval and uncertainty (Van Roon 1989, 39, 63). While pan-European efforts came to naught, it is important to note that in 1938 the future Benelux countries signed a free trade agreement and established the short-lived Dutch-Belgian-Luxembourg Economic Committee to pursue future trade liberalization efforts. More will be said about this below.

As the drums of war beat more and more loudly, Luxembourg went to great lengths to remind the great powers of its de facto neutrality. While not invited to the Locarno conferences in 1935 that produced a collective security arrangement in Western Europe (Calmes 1971/1932, 246), Luxembourg reiterated its commitment to peace in Europe, which led it to adopt appeasement in the face of German expansion during the late 1930s (Van Roon 1989, 152). It also reasserted its neutrality and sought formal recognition and guarantees from the great powers. As expressed by former prime minister Joseph Bech, "Our peace-loving small country lies at a crossroads within Europe. The Grand Duchy is obligated by virtue of its geographical position and the absence of military resources to pursue a resolute policy of neutrality" (Van Roon 1989, 152). Verbal and written assurances were given in 1936 and again in 1938 (van Roon 1989, 181, 257). At the same time, France and Great Britain made it clear that an invasion of Luxembourg would not prompt military intervention on the duchy's behalf (Calmes 1971/1932, 247). After the invasion of Poland by Germany in September 1939, Luxembourg was pressured by Britain and France to embargo steel exports to Germany despite warnings from Berlin, which mobilized shortly thereafter. On May 10, 1940, Germany invaded, at which point the Luxembourg government appealed to France for aid to no avail (Van Roon 1989, 351). The country was subjected to five years of brutal occupation. The liberation was almost more painful than the invasion as the Battle of the Bulge was fought largely on Luxembourg soil. The country lost one-third of its capital wealth as a result of the war (Meade 1957, 11), making it an enthusiastic candidate for postreconstruction plans, although a more tentative advocate for trade liberalization.

Having benefited from the BLEU arrangements, Luxembourg supported wartime efforts to establish regional and global free trade pacts. It participated in the Bretton Woods conferences in July 1944 and was a founding member of the World Bank and International Monetary Fund. Closer to home, the Grand Duchess met with her royal counterparts-in-exile at a conference in London in the summer of 1944 and on September 5 signed the Dutch-Belgian-Luxembourg Customs Convention, the first step to what would become the Benelux economic union. Although its lofty aims would be derailed by postwar economic turmoil, the convention would in many ways lay the foundation for economic integration in Europe. To a large degree, the agreement was the BLEU writ large. It establishes many of the same economic goals of a customs union and free trade area (Articles 1 and 2). The countries are to reduce trade barriers, harmonize trade policies toward each other and toward third parties, and generally aim at facilitating free trade wherever possible. It sets in place a number of institutional arrangements that mimic and expand on those found in the BLEU, including an Administrative Council on Customs Duties (Article 3), a Commission on Customs Disputes (Article 4), and an Administrative Council for the Control of Foreign Trade (Article 5), the job of which was "to see that a common regime of trade control for the whole Benelux area was built out of these national trade controls and to provide a machinery for the administration of any restrictions on trade with third countries which were common to the whole Benelux area" (Meade 1957, 11). In each of these bodies, membership was split evenly between the Netherlands and the BLEU signatories collectively, implying that Luxembourg would have one seat on a six-seat body such as the Commercial Agreements Council (Article 6). Although clearly a second-tier member of Benelux on paper, Luxembourg was firmly committed to what the institution stood for and was ultimately treated as an equal partner (Meade 1957, 5). Each country had the right to withdraw from the agreement with one year's notice (Article 8). The heads of the three agencies imagined in 1944 were later joined into a Board of Presidents, "set up to act as a steering committee for the consideration of the main issues arising in the formation of the union and for the presentation of these issues to the meetings of the ministers of the three countries for their decision." The board played an "extremely important role" in forging Benelux's future (Meade 1957, 18).

As already mentioned, the last months of the war were devastating to Luxembourg but also to the Netherlands, and it left both countries unable to carry out these lofty commitments for many years. The 1944 charter was not ready for ratification until 1947 after numerous rounds of renegotiation, and the provisions for agricultural liberalization and excise tax harmonization were put off even longer (Meade 1957). We will return to some of this in the next section.

We turn again to asking how this experience relates to our search for trust in international relations (see table 2.1). To begin, little has changed with respect to the country's vulnerability or exploitability. While Germany was in no position to impose its will on Luxembourg in the immediate aftermath of the war, Belgium—with France's blessing—had designs on her. By this point Luxembourg's steel industry was at the heart of Europe's industrialization and would naturally been seen as essential to any great power's rise to military prominence. Its geographic location was perhaps even more precarious since it was now clear that it stood in the path between the two great antagonistic powers, antagonism that World War I did nothing to abate. Luxembourg's thinking at this point was that only neutrality could prevent it from becoming a prize to be won.

Luxembourg's political independence continued to emerge during this period, and for the first time it elected to subordinate itself to a number of institutions, including BLEU, Benelux, and the League of Nations. With respect to its participation in great power politics and its status as a neutral state, however, it had to accept what was given. In fact, its status as a protected neutral state was more ambiguous during the interwar period than before World War I, both on paper and in fact (despite repeated attempts to remedy this). It nonetheless did what it could to remain aloof from major power disputes, joining the efforts of the Oslo Group to urge reconciliation and peaceful dispute settlement (Van Roon 1989). It even tried to paint Germany's expansionism in the most favorable light possible while at the same time endorsing the Locarno Pact guaranteeing continental nonaggression, the Kellogg-Briand Pact of 1928 renouncing war as an instrument of foreign policy, and the League of Nations Covenant. At the end of the day it is best to classify its degree of voluntarism with respect to the great power arrangements as moderate at best.

The BLEU and Benelux agreements covered a great many issues ranging from currency to customs to tax policy. Left aside were social policies and foreign policies, although even these were indirectly affected since Belgium assumed consular and trade negotiation duties for the duchy and excise taxes bore directly on the consumption of alcohol and tobacco, the most socially significant of products. Because security matters were left out of the arrangements it is reasonable to say they were not highly salient, although some would no doubt argue that the production and sale of steel, affected as it was by BLEU, meant that matters of national security were at least indirectly involved.

On the other hand, while the scope of agreements with the great powers were more limited (mostly because the full potential of the League's varied mandate was never fully realized), their salience is clear. All these structures bore directly on the duchy's survival, as became poignantly apparent in May 1940.

Finally, the texts of these various agreements were of roughly equal precision, on balance, in that while they were clear with respect to aims and administration, most provisions were left to future decision makers and were therefore unpredictable. The fact that BLEU consists of a mere thirty articles and the 1944 Benelux deal is even more brief at a mere nine articles (although both agreements were later expanded with numerous appendixes and protocols covering everything from rules of procedure to tariff and excise tax schedules) shows that specificity was not a priority for the negotiators. The League of Nations Covenant was similarly succinct (four thousand words in twenty-six articles including later amendments) and vague enough to be open to a wide range of interpretations (which might have contributed to its failure).

Luxembourg was an active participant in all these arrangements, although it lacked a strong voice. In the case of BLEU, it can be inferred that it held a veto over most policies, except for trade agreements negotiated in its behalf. It also had no control over the value of the franc, and in the 1930s Brussels decided to devalue it, causing considerable distress to Luxembourg (Doerner 1983,143). As was mentioned, Luxembourg was ultimately treated as an equal in Benelux where consensus decision making eventually became the norm, so it was able to protect its interests while not necessarily steering the institution. As a result, it seems reasonable to say that its degree of marginalization was moderate, which was clearly an improvement over past arrangements. Likewise, Luxembourg had a seat at the table of the League of Nations and remained active in the organization—along with France and Great Britain—to the bitter end. As more and more states left the League, Luxembourg's influence naturally grew (although the value of that influence waned). With respect to its neutrality, its voice was also marginal, no doubt less than in the League but probably not enough to categorize it as low.

Finally, these arrangements, with the exception of the 1944 Benelux agreement, did not allow for easy or quick withdrawal, least of which the BLEU treaty, which provided for a fifty-year span. Withdrawal from the League, while possible, would have been catastrophic for Luxembourg, as would have been a withdrawal from Benelux. For all intents and purposes, then, Luxembourg was in no position to take advantage of even the lenient withdrawal provisions of Benelux (for that matter, it is debatable whether Luxembourg could have withdrawn over Belgium's objections since they joined as an economic union).

Taken together, it seems that Luxembourg again trusted its neighbors and partners, although it began during this period to establish a pattern of being more actively involved in the choice of dominant state and in engaging with and helping form international bodies that allowed it to hedge against unilateral betrayal. Although the League of Nations proved inadequate to the task, Luxembourg clearly saw collective security as an improvement over other possibilities (although it still trusted—however nervously—that its neutrality would be protected). And regional integration that was tied to a lesser power and linked to the world economy at large showed considerable promise as a way out of economic isolation or dependence on a fickle great power. Naturally, participation in the League and reliance on the promises of Germany and France did nothing to protect Luxembourg in 1940, and so it would turn after World War II to joining military alliances (while at the same time becoming a founding member of the United Nations and eventually participating in peacekeeping operations). On the other hand, BLEU and Benelux were just the beginning of Luxembourg's integration strategy, a strategy that spilled over far beyond the duchy's borders. It is perhaps not surprising that one of the European Union's founding fathers, Robert Schuman, was born in Luxembourg. One could easily make the argument that without Luxembourg, European institutions and practices as we know them would not exist.

1945 To the Present: Luxembourg at the Center

"Emancipation" is a word used to describe Luxembourg's postwar aims (Newcomer 1984, 273–74; Trausch 2003, 256). Dependence on selfish and powerful neighbors had proved disastrous. Even the Museum of the City of Luxembourg plainly declares that the principal lesson of the previous century was that trust is not a sound basis for foreign policy. The country embarked on a remarkable journey of participation from 1944 onward and has never looked back. While no one imagines that Luxembourg is powerful, there is consensus across parties and from top to bottom in the country that it was to be fully engaged in Europe and the world if it were to have any hope of survival, let alone prosperity.

As put by Frentz:

> Luxembourg has . . . been a driving force behind European integration which is, together with the transatlantic alliance, seen as the best guarantee of sovereignty and security. More generally, the need to reduce vulnerability also explains Luxembourg's strong commitment to multilateralism and international law as a form of shelter.

> Rather than trying to construct a meaningful military force (like, for instance, Switzerland) that would draw on limited resources, Luxembourg embraced collective security by placing itself under the NATO security umbrella at the outset of the Cold War and actively promoted the EU as a peace project. At the same time, Luxembourg has consistently considered that European unity makes sense only in the context of a dynamic transatlantic relationship, and thus has traditionally pursued a pro-NATO, pro-US foreign policy. (2010, 132)

As mentioned earlier, Luxembourg has struggled with having any sense of indigenous national identity, but in the postwar environment what was once a liability was seen as an asset. Luxembourg could fully integrate itself into Europe without fearing the loss of itself. "Luxembourg, the smallest member state [of the EU], has been keen to sustain its own sense of 'national' identity and to resist being 'submerged' within the EU" (Newman 1996, 152, summarizing an argument in Meehan 1993). Nonetheless, the country—in a united policy—has plunged head first into integration. This stems in part from a sense of inevitability, given the country's geography, economy, and culture. In the 1950s, roughly two-thirds of Luxembourgers could count at least one foreign-born grandparent. Most of those working in industry or the service sector had foreign clients or supervisors. Steel production was nearing its peak and the banking sector, secured by laws passed in the 1920s providing secrecy for foreign depositors, was poised to expand dramatically. Increasingly, foreigners living near the border ("*frontaliers*") found work in the grand duchy (Berche 2013). Sixty years later integration had exaggerated these trends. Most of the people working in the country on any given day are nonresidents. In 2012, 96 percent of Luxembourgers said they had socialized with at least one foreigner in the previous year, while 89 percent had traveled outside the country. Eighty-four percent are described as having cosmopolitan attitudes, almost double the next highest country in the EU (Malta at 47 percent) (European Commission 2012, 37, 38). Survey after survey shows that people in Luxembourg define themselves first and foremost as "European" (85 percent in 2012 [European Commission 2012, 21]). Even during the dark days of the Great Recession of 2008, three-fourths of adults approved of the European Union and Luxembourg's place in it.

Because of the breathtaking pace and scope of accessions to international organizations, it is impossible to describe in any detail Luxembourg's postwar multilateralism. Its role as a founding member of the United Nations and most of its specialized agencies and special programs, the

Bretton Woods institutions, the Organization for Economic Cooperation and Development, and the Organization for Security and Cooperation in Europe did not involve dependence or any significant penetration of Luxembourg society or politics at any rate. I will therefore limit my discussion to three sets of institutions that Luxembourg helped found that have in their own way had dramatic effects on almost every aspect of its foreign and domestic policies: NATO, BLEU/Benelux, and the ECSC/EEC and their successor institutions. Even limiting the survey to these bodies leaves us with too much information to provide a full account, and so the focus will be on the questions related to trust, specifically the scope and salience of the agreements, their precision and functioning, Luxembourg's influence and the degree to which the country might excuse itself from the arrangements.

Beginning with the North Atlantic Treaty Organization, historians have generally credited the English foreign secretary Ernest Bevin with hatching the idea of a European-wide anti-Soviet military alliance backstopped by American nuclear power (Henderson 1982, 4–5; Croft 1988, 622). In order to accomplish this, the French would have to be brought on board, and since their greatest fear was of a resurgent Germany he proposed that the Dunkirk Treaty explicitly protect against it (Croft 1988, 621). Once the deal was done in March 1947, they communicated with the Benelux countries to join them as equal partners. This they did a year later. The Brussels Treaty of 1948 stated in Article 4 that if a country were to be a victim of "armed aggression in Europe . . . all the military aid and assistant in their power" were to be provided by the signatories. The treaty was intended to last fifty years. It created a consultative council consisting of the five foreign ministers and a Western defense committee of five defense ministers to meet on a regular basis. The United States and Canada attended as observers beginning in July 1948. In September the signatories created the Western Union Defense Organization (WUDO), a precursor to SACEUR (Supreme Allied Commander Europe), with the illustrious Field Marshal Bernard Montgomery at its head (NATO 1989, 10–15). The alliance also included joint military exercises and projects to curtail subversion (Henderson 1982, 4–5). All of this suited Luxembourg since a key aim coming out of the war was (and still is) to integrate its small military into a European army of some sort (Lorenz 2013, 232).

A military committee was created at the urging of the United States as a way of persuading the Senate that Europeans were serious. This prompted back-channel talks between the British, Canadian, and American foreign ministries (to the exclusion of the continental Europeans) that proceeded in parallel with a stillborn French initiative to create a continental alliance (Henderson 1982, 14; NATO 1989, 16). These machinations exacerbated considerable tension between Great Britain and France, with Luxembourg caught in the middle, and they jeopardized the formation of NATO. But ultimately the United States openly embraced the British proposal and formally invited the other members of the Brussels Treaty to join in talks in mid-1949. Luxembourg was represented in its own right, albeit by a diplomat who found staying awake during the English-only proceedings a challenge.[1]

Although the Benelux countries played a relatively marginal role in the proceedings (they had strong reservations about including a rearmed West Germany and Italy but were overridden), they were satisfied with a key provision: the principle of unanimity in decision making. This naturally meant that even Luxembourg had a veto over whether, why, and where NATO would go to war, as well as whether and which countries to admit to the alliance (Sandler and Hartley 1999, 25).

Luxembourg was included on the full range of NATO institutional bodies, including the Regional Planning Groups (it was included in the all-important Western Europe unit [NATO 1989, 36]). Its military commanders participated in the military committee, which advised the NATO Council (made up of permanent representatives from each alliance member, much like the UN Security Council). The staff is directed by a secretary-general, and although two Belgians and three Dutch have held the post, no one from Luxembourg has been appointed. As provided for in Article 13, Luxembourg has the right to withdraw with one year's notice, but only after the treaty had been in force for at least twenty years (i.e., August 1969).

While never a key player (Pouliot 2016, 104), Luxembourg has remained active in NATO's decision making, serving on the committee that works to standardize equipment and materiel and on the committee that established the standard caliber for small arms (NATO 1989, 19, 274). It was included in the Mutual and Balanced Force Reduction talks with Warsaw Pact members from 1973 until the end of the Cold War (NATO 1989, 234). In 1968 it joined Eurogroup, an informal association of defense ministers that proposed ways to increase European contributions to NATO (Sandler and Hartley 1999, 215).

Two other facets of participation in NATO should be mentioned. One is "burden sharing," meaning the degree to which Luxembourg contributes to the defense of Europe, principally with respect to defense expenditures. Historically, the small states in NATO have been accused of exploiting the larger ones by spending less (often far less) than their share on defense (currently set at 2 percent of GDP) (Olson and Zeckhauser 1966; Oneal 1990; Sandler and Hartley 1999; Sandler and Shimizu 2014). Luxembourg is a natural target of this criticism since until the mid-2000s its defense expenditures rarely approach 1 percent of GDP, placing it next to the bottom of the list (NATO 1989, 457; Lorenz 2013, 239; Sandler and Shimizu 2014, 49). Its military forces make up less than 1 percent of the country's adult workforce, also near the bottom. It also spends no funds on defense research and development, although it is not alone in this respect (Sandler and Shimizu 2014, 48). On the other hand, Luxembourg has benefited considerably from its NATO membership, sheltered as it was initially by the presence of Germany as a buffer against the Warsaw Pact and eventually walled behind a long ring of new NATO members after the end of the Cold War. It is the headquarters for periodic NATO summits and since 1958 the NATO Maintenance and Supply Agency (NATO 1989, 256). Using a complex formula to calculate overall benefits relative to costs, Sandler and Hartley show that Luxembourg consistently derived roughly twice as much benefit as costs during the period from 1975 to 1996 (Sandler & Hartley 1999, 45–46).[2]

Since the end of the Cold War, however, Luxembourg has shifted its focus from a more insular, continental view of defense—which probably involved some exploitation of its larger neighbors and the United States—to one involving global engagement within its limited capabilities. In 1992 the legislature approved the deployment of Luxembourg forces on peacekeeping missions overseas, and almost immediately troops from the grand duchy began participating in UN, NATO, and even European Union missions (Lorenz 2013, 232). Forces have been sent to such hot spots as Bosnia, Kosovo, Chad, Somalia, the Democratic Republic of Congo, and Afghanistan, among others (Lorenz 2013, 232; Frentz 2010, 135). Its spending on UN peacekeeping missions alone rose from roughly $50,000 in 1995 to over $2,000,000 in subsequent years, far more than its share based on its GDP (Sandler and Hartley 1999, 105).

Taking all these factors together, it is clear that Luxembourg has enjoyed a wide range of benefits from its membership in NATO. After reviewing Luxembourg's involvement with BLEU/Benelux and the EU we will return to address the question of whether this flows from Luxembourg's trust in its alliance partners.

The economic union between Belgium and Luxembourg continues to thrive, although as it is increasingly nested in and constrained by both Benelux and the EU it is less essential to the grand duchy. Their agreements regarding industrial trade were reshaped by the creation of the European Coal and Steel Community (see below). With the adoption of the euro by both countries in 2002, their monetary union has been superseded. Nonetheless the two nations continue to apply the agreement, meeting twice a year as legal equals to coordinate policies, renewing it and expanding its scope considerably in 2002 (Article 16 calls for coordination across the full spectrum of issues) (Frentz 2010, 141). They have agreed, for example, to allow the police forces of each country to pursue and even apprehend suspects across the border, although not without controversy: Luxembourg police once shot and killed a Luxembourg citizen in Belgium, prompting objections (Walder 2013).

Although willing to remain active in the association, Luxembourg has insisted on enhancing its status over the years. In the 1940s, Luxembourg rejected Belgian proposals to join Bretton Woods and European multilateral bodies as a unit. It feared that by doing so it risked being relegated to the status of a Belgian province (Trausch 2003, 255). Its voting rights have also been expanded. The introduction of the euro was welcomed by Luxembourg in part because it did not trust Belgian monetary authorities to look out for its interests. In 1985 Brussels devalued the franc—mostly to remedy problems its own mismanagement had produced—without consulting and at the expense of the better-managed Luxembourg (Fayol 2013, Kinsch 2013). Likewise, Luxembourg resents the fact that multinationals with regional headquarters in Brussels often adopt strategies when investing in Luxembourg that primarily serve Belgian interests (Fayol 2013). In general Luxembourg's economy has shifted east, especially toward Germany (Walder 2013). Although in 2013 Belgium was still its primary source of imports (edging out Germany by 18 percent), Germany was the top export market, followed by France (Bridgat 2015). From 2008 to 2013, exports to Germany grew by 40 percent while those to Belgium grew only by 27 percent. Luxembourg's exports to Germany are higher than those to Belgium and the Netherlands combined. Exports to Poland and Russia grew by more than 90 percent. While the vast majority of its trade still involves its immediate neighbors and the Netherlands, it is clear that this will not always be so. BLEU's importance will therefore likely wane over time.

Benelux, for its part, remains central to Luxembourg's foreign policy. While initially designed primarily as a Belgian-Dutch agreement to which Luxembourgers were invited as secondary partners, it is now a fully multilateral arrangement with Luxembourg sharing equal status, both legally and procedurally. As mentioned, it was conceived and initiated in the waning years of the war, but it was not until March 1947 that the treaty could be submitted for ratification. It formally came into effect in 1948 but was continually revised and delayed—because of the postwar turmoil in the Netherlands and then Belgium (Meade 1957)—until in 1958 a treaty establishing a Benelux "economic union" was finally signed. Intended to last fifty years, it provided for a free trade area and a customs union (Articles 1, 2) and a promise to coordinate economic relations with third countries. It set up a committee of ministers (Article 15) to meet every other month to push integration deeper and wider, applying the unanimity principle (Article 18). It also created a consultative interparliamentary council (Article 23) made up of legislators from each country, and a Council of the Economic Union (Article 25) analogous to the Board of Presidents mentioned earlier. It also created committees on a wide range of topics: foreign economic relations; monetary and finance; customs, tariffs, and taxes; social questions; and so forth. Arbitration provisions (Articles 41–53) involved a complex process, beginning with the designation of a number of arbitrators (and alternates) from each country for each topic covered under the various committees (Article 28), with four serving on each arbitration panel at a minimum, but up to ten altogether (Article 43). Rulings were mandatory, although resort to the International Court of Justice was provided for. Where the topic of the dispute fell under the purview of the newly created European institutions and treaties, officials from these bodies would have primary jurisdiction (which in practice implied that the Benelux system would wane in significance). In fact, the last panelists were appointed in 1962 and since then all disputes have been handled in the Council of Ministers or some other political body.

The 1958 treaty protected Luxembourg's interests not only by giving it a veto and a prominent place on arbitration panels but also by urging parties to "take into account the special situation of Luxembourg agriculture" before adopting new policies in that area (Article 67). The treaty also explicitly recognized and authorized the BLEU agreement to continue to operate (Article 94). Every ten years the treaty could be denounced with one year's notice (Article 99). A 1972 agreement on the troublesome topic of excise taxes on alcohol and other goods resulted in exemptions for Luxembourg and generally called for flexibility and local adaptation on other issues.

In 1965 the Benelux committee of ministers adopted a treaty establishing a judicial court (which came into effect in 1975). It consists of nine judges seconded from each country's highest courts (Article 1), with three judges from each country (Article 2). Its jurisdiction encompassed not just trade and business law but also social and criminal questions, any areas where the three countries shared a legal regime ("des règles juridiques qui sont communes aux pays du Benelux" [1969 Additional Protocol Article 1]). Its judgments overrode those of national courts (1969 Additional Protocol Article 28). The court heard 216 different cases between 1975 and 2014, with peak activity coming during the 1990s (just over seven cases a year on average). The vast majority of cases involved private firms taking governments to task over interpretation and enforcement of Benelux regulations. As expected given its size, Luxembourg is not an especially frequent participant (Benelux Court of Justice 2015).

Benelux functions as a policy-coordinating body not only with respect to policies within the three member states but also with respect to external relations, especially with respect to the European Union. The three states meet prior to each meeting of the European Council, for example (Frentz 2010, 141). They work to harmonize policies on a wide range of issues and then coordinate their responses to various shared problems. Even more so than the EU, Benelux affects the day-to-day lives of virtually all their citizens (Fayol 2013). The effort has been largely successful and has strengthened the confidence the states have in each other (Walder 2013). In the 2000s, they moved to expand the scope of the Benelux agreement to encompass social and criminal matters, matching the jurisdiction of the court (Frentz 2010, 141). This led to the 2008 Benelux Union treaty. Its purpose is described in Article 2:

> The Benelux Union seeks in particular: a) the maintenance and development of an economic union including the free movement of persons, goods, capital and services, and bearing on a concerted policy in economic, financial and social policy, including the pursuit of a common policy in economic relations with non-Member countries; b) sustainable development reconciling balanced economic growth, social protection and protection of the environment; c) cooperation in the areas of justice and internal affairs.

The agreement also provides for multiyear planning on topics including immigration, police cooperation, crisis management, and terrorism (Article 3). It provides for no time limit (Article 39) although each party can denounce it three years after submitting the paperwork, starting ten years after it comes into force (i.e., 2022).

Although, as we will see, Luxembourg has long been an enthusiastic exponent of the European Community concept, it was reticent about what the European Coal and Steel Community (ECSC) offered, in part because its steel sector was its economic cornerstone and it feared much could be lost to integration. Nonetheless, the prospect of subordinating German industry—and by implication its military-industrial complex—to its Western neighbors was too important to jeopardize. It didn't hurt that one of its native sons—Robert Schuman (born in Luxembourg but then French foreign minister)—was at the helm of the initiative. He resembled Luxembourg's Joseph Bech and the other leaders of the ECSC founder states: white, middle-aged, idealistic, Roman Catholic, and ardently anti-communist. These men understood each other implicitly and spoke the same political and cultural language (Kmec 2013). As is well-known, the ECSC was designed to integrate coal, iron ore, and steel production in and around the Ruhr Valley, and was to do so with the creation of a benign cartel—the High Authority—that would subordinate profits to regional security and planned growth. The initial proposal called for a small body that would exercise complete control over the sector at the expense of national planning and markets. All the Benelux countries—Luxembourg in particular—resisted such a radical move, fearing loss of sovereignty and in particular the inability to intervene during market downturns. They proposed instead a High Authority with many members, implicitly representing all the member states (the final number of nine—with no more than two from any one country—tilted toward the Benelux proposal). They also sought—successfully—the establishment of a Council of Ministers where each state could wield a vote (Haas 1958, 249; Nugent 1989, 33). Luxembourg secured four seats in the seventy-eight-member Assembly, more than double what its population at the time would have warranted (Article 21). And by ensuring that the ECSC court would have seven members, it assured itself a presence there as well (Article 32).

Pleading poverty and smallness, Luxembourg was also able to secure special protections, including a slower implementation schedule (Article 37), council consideration of national protections in the event of future market downturns (Articles 33 and 35), and preservation of BLEU's special status (Article 31) (Haas 1958, 250). This was enough to reassure the steel conglomerate ARBED and the legislature. This is not to say the grand duchy prevailed across all issues. At more than three hundred pages and with no explicit provisions for withdrawal or denunciation, the ECSC agreement was complex and utterly binding, although it was gradually folded into and adjusted to the broader European institutions. The High Authority wielded considerable power despite checks by the other three bodies. Luxembourg only reluctantly agreed to the placement of the agency's headquarters in Luxembourg (Pryce 1973, 6) and during the 1950s it ultimately succumbed to the High Authority's demand that it dismantle its system of steel subsidies. It was also thwarted in its attempt to join with Belgium in forming a private steel cartel (Haas 1958, 76, 106–7).

The history of the European Union is better-known and more illustrious, and Luxembourg's role in its creation and expansion has been active and enthusiastic. One could even make the case that the idea was Luxembourg's. After all, it was modeled on Benelux, which itself was modeled on BLEU, which was formed at Luxembourg's initiative. Robert Schuman—the native son mentioned previously—was an active instigator. Part of the reason France became interested in integration was out of concern that Benelux would impinge on its national interests (Middlemas 1995, 17). And it was the Benelux countries that originally proposed a plan for a regional trade agreement at the Messina meetings in 1955 that led directly to the 1957 Treaty of Rome (Dosenrode 2012, 9). As put by Pryce, "The trio of Benelux countries, for their part, were . . . committed to a customs union and looking beyond this to a closer economic union. Once their larger neighbors moved in the same direction, they could not afford to stay outside; in any case, there were many among their leaders who were determined supporters of closer European unity" (1973, 5).

As in the case of the ECSC, Luxembourg secured a seat on the Council of Ministers, wielding one vote out of the seventeen total (6 percent, even though its relative population was 0.2 percent). In the European Parliament, Luxembourg received 6 out of 142 seats initially (a bit over 4 percent) (Bunse, Magnette, and Nicolaïdes 2007, 136–40). It has a representative on the European Commission and has three times placed one of its own in the president's chair (Gaston Thorn, 1981–1985; Jacques Santer, 1995–1998; and Jean-Claude Juncker, 2015–2019). Luxembourg has served as the rotating chair on the Council of Ministers/Council of the EU twelve times since its founding (sharing the record with three other cofounders), and during one ten-year period prime minister Gaston Thorn served as council leader four times.

To say that Luxembourg is overrepresented in the EU is an understatement. Each of Luxembourg's citizens has forty times as much influence than each German on the council and ten times as much influence in the European Parliament, even after its 6 votes were diluted with the enlargement of the EP from 142 to 766 and then to 751 members (Jones 1996, 77; Bunse 2009, 21; European Commission 2015). Even the 145 Luxembourgers who work for the EU overrepresent the country six-fold (European Commission 2015).

This historical overrepresentation of Luxembourg has served the country well. Thorn, for example, understood the workings of the EU like no one else and could negotiate the most complex issues without becoming confused by the minutiae (Majerus 2011, 153). Juncker was courted to become the president of the commission as early as 2004 and had the job locked up in 2009 except for the reservations of one member state's delegate (Anderson and Kaeding 2006, 115; Majerus 2011, 145). Today's Luxembourgish diplomats and functionaries have dealt with EU matters from the beginnings of their careers and have developed numerous relationships with other diplomats and staff members. This is helped by the fact that the country is host to several EU bodies: the European Investment Bank, the Statistical Services and the Publications Office, and the Secretariat of the European Parliament, hosting roughly ten thousand "eurocrats" (more than a third of the total) who, along with their families, make up a large and integral part of the capital city's population of only ninety-three thousand (Majerus 2011, 147). Luxembourg has been strategic about its status as an EU capital. The placement of these offices was as compensation for the relocation of the ECSC staff to Brussels in the 1960s. Luxembourg has vigorously defended its status—and the jobs this generates—arguing successfully against the relocation of the 1,500 EP staff during the Nice Treaty negotiations (Hey 2003, 77–78; Europa World 2015a).

In addition to securing this overrepresentation, Luxembourg was able to secure other concessions during the formation of the EU. The ECSC, BLEU, and Benelux arrangements were protected (Articles 232 and 233). National and internal security measures were partly exempted from free trade considerations (Articles 223–225). And although the "Big Three" EEC members could override blocking votes from the Benelux countries, the commission and court were able to check the council's power to a large degree. Although it opposed it, the so-called Luxembourg Compromise negotiated during its turn as council president in 1966 (when future commission president Pierre Werner was prime minister) enhanced the country's power by giving it a virtual veto over matters deemed central to the national interest (Majerus 2011, 146; Pryce 1973, 19; Nugent 1989, 103). Luxembourg has consistently worked to enhance the powers of the commission and European Parliament over the years, sometimes to the annoyance of France and other member states, as in the case of Thorn's proposal for direct election of Members of the European Parliament in 1975 (Majerus 2011, 158). This is also true of expanding the EU's institutional structures. Pierre Werner spearheaded early talks on monetary integration in 1970 (Pryce 1973, 22; Jones 1996, 184), and Luxembourg diplomats, including especially Juncker, played a key role in the formation of the European Monetary Unit and an autonomous European Central Bank (Moravcsik 1998, 440–41; Hey 2003, 91; Phinnemore 2013, 60). Juncker also created and chaired the "Eurogroup" of Eurozone finance ministers after the euro was adopted in 2002, thus placing Luxembourg at the center of bailout talks following the 2008 financial crisis (Europa World 2015a). In 1990, Luxembourg used its turn as president of the council to put forward an ambitious draft treaty to create a European union based on the now-familiar "temple" structure with three pillars (Beach and Mazzucelli 2007, 46; Jones 1996, 46). Perhaps needless to say, Luxembourg was an enthusiastic supporter of the European Constitution and fought to retain as much as possible of the stillborn agreement in the Lisbon Treaty (Phinnemore 2013, 40; Bunse, Magnette, and Nicolaïdes 2007, 153).

This is not to say that Luxembourg has been able to control events at the EU. The Treaty of Rome itself is an intimidating document, logging in at 248 articles with no expiration or withdrawal provisions (the Treaty of Lisbon provides for withdrawal over a two-year transitional period [Article 49A]). Over the years the *acquis* of the community has accumulated around seven thousand directives and regulations that have penetrated deeply into each of its members' activities and policies. With each revision the powers of the European Union have expanded and the degree of integration has deepened. This is not to say that European institutions have consistently grown stronger. As a "guardian of the Community method" of decision making, Luxembourg resisted in vain the efforts to expand the powers of the larger EU members (Germany, France, and the UK in particular). Only on such questions as retaining its six EP seats and retaining the rotation of the council presidency could one say Luxembourg and the smaller states "won," while they had to concede the system of double majority qualified majority voting (which requires approval of measures based in part on the size of members' populations), the eventual shrinking of the size of the commission (the plan calls for an eventual cap at two-thirds the number of member states, making it likely that Luxembourg would not be represented much of the time [Bunse 2009, 26]). They also failed to increase the status of the commission president by providing for her direct election by the European Parliament (Bunse, Magnette, and Nicolaïdes 2007, 144, 149, 153).

To navigate this diplomatic maze, Luxembourg representatives have found it useful not to draw attention to themselves. As put by Hey, "a well-known adage among Luxembourgish diplomats is 'if you have a good idea, whisper it to your Dutch neighbor.'" (2003, 85) The Luxembourg approach is described as "subtle," favoring persuasion and the use of third parties over overt advocacy and pressure (Middlemas 1995, 146). For example, Gaston Thorn's gregariousness was criticized by Werner for being too visible and overt (Hirsch 1983, 132). During the debate over regional policy in the 1990s, for example, Luxembourg was happy to allow Britain and Germany to take the floor to argue against Spain's proposals (Thorhallsson 2000, 175). Luxembourg officials are most comfortable acting as the "honest broker" (Panke 2010, 185), even using their language skills to help, literally, translate their fellow heads of state's positions to each other (Juncker translated for French president Jacques Chirac during the Dublin meetings on the EMU in 1996 [Hey 2003, 91]). Even when serving as council president, Luxembourg is less active than other states in advancing initiatives and adopting decisions (Bunse 2009, 220). As president of the council in 1985, Luxembourg acted as a conduit for commission proposals (Beach and Mazzucelli 2007, 15; Kassim and Dimitrakopoulos 2007, 104).

Although thinking itself a "model European state" (Kmec 2013), Luxembourg has been frequently taken to task by EU institutions. As of 2005, at only 96 percent compliance with EU directives and regulations, Luxembourg's backlog has been far above the EU average (Anderson and Kaeding 2006, 119). It only rarely challenges commission directives in the European Court of Justice (the first time was in 1983 and the most recent was in 2009) and has been on the receiving end of more than two hundred commission challenges in the ECJ (well over half of those coming since 2000), with which it has largely complied (ECJ/Curia 2015). These have led it to open its public service sector jobs to EU citizens and to extend funding for college tuition to temporary residents (Europa World 2015a). It was forced to accept new investment regulations in 1998, releasing crime data and raising the minimum reserves for banks in 2005, and deregulating postal services in 2006 (Thomson 2011, 141, 199, 218, 265). It has been required to raise pension rates, alter its asylum procedures, and create the office of the ombudsman in response to specific directives and pressures from EU institutions (Europa World 2015a). While they may drag their feet, all Luxembourgish officials know that they will ultimately give in to European demands since the country could not endure sanctions (Hirsch 1983, 131).

It has carved out a small number of issues that it considers essential, in particular its bank secrecy and financial services laws on the one hand and its tax policies on the other. Were it not for the Common Agricultural Program's generous protections of all European farming, this would probably be a third area of concern. With respect to bank secrecy, Luxembourg put forward a cautious community-wide policy in 1997 in the hope of forestalling a stricter approach that was in the offing (Bunse 2009, 50). Its hands were forced not by the EU but by the OECD, which listed it as noncompliant with its money-laundering regulations in 2000 (Europa World 2015a). Since then, the EU has pressed for uniform information-sharing rules with which Luxembourg has reluctantly complied (Kanter and Higgins 2014, A10).

On the question of taxation, Luxembourg has been more stubborn, arguing that until the EU develops a program of fiscal harmonization this area of law should remain within the national orbit. As put by Thorhallsson: "Luxembourg's main interest in the EU is to preserve its tax privileges. Luxembourg has, over the years, been able to maintain its policy of offering no income tax on capital interests. As a result, Luxembourg has received a capital flow from other member states" (2000, 39). It began in the 1970s to propose protections of national rights on fiscal policy, knowing this was a rear-guard action (Hirsch 1983, 131). It has relied on Belgium and Ireland, among others, to take the lead on protecting these measures, preferring not to use its veto to get its way (Interview 2013a; Europa World 2015a). That said, Luxembourg has complied with an EU directive calling for a gradual increase in its taxes on deposits from around 10 percent in 2005 to 35 percent in 2011. Meanwhile, it eliminated a tax on foreign residents' asset to offset the increase. Throughout the debate, Luxembourg politicians have bristled at what they consider hypocrisy since several prominent EU members have arrangements with protectorates and colonies that allow their citizens to shelter income (Fayol 2013). This is not to say they do not acknowledge arguments that Luxembourg became wealthy thanks to the corruption of other Europeans, but they reject the notion that Luxembourg should become Europe's tax collector (Kanter and Higgins 2014, A4; Fayol 2013; Doerner 1983, 142).

Citizens of the grand duchy remain among the most supportive of the EU. In 2012, 72 percent of Luxembourgers felt "attached" to the EU—the highest proportion among EU states—and in 2005, 67 percent and 61 percent expressed trust for European Parliament and the European Commission, respectively (European Commission 2012, 8; European Commission 2005, 24). But the recent downturn in Europe's economic fortunes and the slowdown of Luxembourg's financial sector have tainted the appeal of the EU in the eyes of those under forty. With unemployment rising to an unprecedented 4 percent and the cost of living rising so high that many young Luxembourgers have opted to move out of the grand duchy and commute to work from next door, doubts have been raised about the wisdom of integration. The referendum on the Constitution in 2005—despite coming prior to the financial crisis—passed by a mere 54.9 percent, far less than expected (Phinnemore 2013, 20). In a follow-up survey, the Eurobarometer found that a majority of respondents under forty opposed the Constitution, and of those who were opposed, 37 percent feared it would increase unemployment and 23 percent said adoption was not wise given the country's economic situation (European Commission 2005, 9, 14). There is a general sense among Luxembourg elites and those over forty that the EU had failed to "sell" itself to the rising generation (Berche 2013). An MEP at the 2013 Europe Day events in Luxembourg (observed by the author) almost begged the youth in audience to be patient with Europe and to maintain their faith in the institution, promising better times ahead. Those over forty continue to value the EU as a defender of Luxembourg sovereignty and a promoter of peace (European Commission 2005, 12). But without continued prosperity there are concerns that the social contract could quickly unravel. Recent polling indicates that when respondents are separated by nationality, Luxembourg's citizens are divided on the question of whether the country should be more integrated in Europe. Only 41 percent called for "more Europe" while 26 percent called for less (Wort.lu 2014). Sixty-two percent of foreign nationals, on the other hand, wished for "more Europe" while only 17 percent wanted less.

It is clear that all the major political parties in Luxembourg have almost since the EEC's inception staked out a pro-Europe position. While this was implied prior to Santer, candidates have increasingly spoken out in favor of integration and multilateralism (Dumont 2014, 39). There is a sense that open debate on the issue could undermine Luxembourg's diplomatic leverage (Hey 2003, 85). But regardless, each party values the peace and prosperity they attribute to integration, despite the episodic setbacks and inconveniences.

This review of Luxembourg's post–World War II multilateralism reveals certain common patterns across institutions (see table 2.1). To begin, it is clear that Luxembourg is vulnerable throughout this period. The grand duchy never acquired a unilateral capacity to defend its territory but instead relied on others to assume this task. Likewise, its diplomacy is still largely delegated to Belgium and the EU; Belgium even manages its compliance with the Common Agricultural Program of the EU (Thorhallsson 2000, 57). It lacks capacity for many things common to most states, maintaining a small foreign ministry and approaching most foreign policy decisions in an improvisational, informal way as one might expect in a society where journalists, politicians, eurocrats, and ordinary citizens interact socially on a daily basis with few barriers or formalities (Berche 2013). What is differ-

TABLE 2.1. Features of Luxembourg's Relationships with Neighboring States and Institutions

		Trustor-Trustee Relationship			Issues in Play		Structure of Agreements		
		Vulnerability	Exploitability	Voluntarism	Scope of Issues	Salience of Issues	Imprecision and Informality	Marginalization	Entrapment
1815–1866: Submission to the Netherlands & Prussia	Netherlands	**HIGH**	MODERATE	MODERATE	**HIGH**	**HIGH**	MODERATE	**HIGH**	**HIGH**
	Prussia	**HIGH**	**HIGH**	Low	MODERATE	**HIGH**	MODERATE	**HIGH**	**HIGH**
1867–1918: Submission to the Netherlands & the Great Powers	Netherlands	**HIGH**	**HIGH**	**HIGH**	MODERATE	MODERATE	Low	Low	Low
	Great Powers	**HIGH**	**HIGH**	MODERATE	MODERATE	**HIGH**	MODERATE	MODERATE	**HIGH**
1919–1945: Submission to Belgium & the Great Powers	Belgium	**HIGH**	**HIGH**	**HIGH**	**HIGH**	MODERATE	MODERATE	MODERATE	**HIGH**
	Great Powers	**HIGH**	**HIGH**	MODERATE	MODERATE	**HIGH**	MODERATE	MODERATE	**HIGH**
1946–2016: Submission to European Regional Agencies	NATO	**HIGH**	MODERATE	HIGH	MODERATE	**HIGH**	MODERATE	MODERATE	MODERATE
	BLEU/ Benelux	**HIGH**	**HIGH**	**HIGH**	**HIGH**	MODERATE	Low	Low	**HIGH**
	EU	**HIGH**	**HIGH**	**HIGH**	**HIGH**	**HIGH**	Low	MODERATE	**HIGH**

ent from earlier periods is its attractiveness as a target. In the past twenty years Europeans have noticed the accumulation of wealth and assets in the country and have begun looking for ways to remove them. While questions of justice and rights are at issue, the bottom line is that Luxembourg now has resources that make it an attractive target for the very states to which it is increasingly dependent. It is only in the area of security where Luxembourg is not especially salient and exploitable, since it adds little to regional security and as an enclave its protection is already implied (even if it left NATO).

This makes it all the more remarkable that Luxembourg's leadership and the bulk of its citizenry have long considered these arrangements worthwhile and even preferable to a more autonomous existence, leading them to not only endorse membership in these organizations but to also instigate them and to expand and deepen them. Except for a minority of the rising generation, there appears to be no looking back when it comes to both NATO and the EU. National identity, while still manifested in symbolic areas such as language, is virtually irrelevant in Luxembourg, where the vast majority identify as "European." A future outside of European institutions is unthinkable.

With respect to the scope and salience of the agreements, it is clear that while it is extremely salient, NATO does not address the range of issues one sees covered by both BLEU/Benelux and the EU. On the other hand, BLEU/Benelux leaves out certain matters of national security, although that may ultimately change as the organization becomes more of a political union. Since the EU has a security arm, albeit mostly latent, in addition to covering the full array of economic, social, and cultural topics, one would have to say that the salience of its issues are high.

The agreements in BLEU/Benelux and the EU are extremely precise, especially when one considers the range of decisions, regulations, court rulings, and budget allocations that are carried out from Brussels, Strasbourg, and Luxembourg. Thousands of rules have been handed down over the years, to the point that there is very little in each member's foreign or domestic policy that is not constrained to at least some degree. Institutional arrangements have been made increasingly specific, not that they were vague or informal at the outset. Little is left to chance. NATO, on the other hand, has left states with a higher degree of discretion, which helps to explain its adaptability at the end of the Cold War (when some prominent realists predicted it would dissolve as did the Warsaw Pact [Hallans 2010, 18]).

Finally, as we have seen, Luxembourg took steps to protect its interests by ensuring a seat at the table, usually more seats than its tiny population would have justified. This was particularly the case where BLEU/Benelux is concerned. Not only was its presence felt here from the outset, but its status and prerogatives actually increased over time. It had successfully resisted becoming a mere appendage to Belgium and instead established an equal legal weight with Belgium and the Netherlands. This has not been the case—at least not entirely—where NATO and the EU are concerned, although it is clear that Luxembourg is punching above its weight class. Based on its contribution to NATO's defensive capacity, Luxembourg would be expected to bring the other members their tea. Instead it has a veto on new members and new military operations. And recently it has begun to contribute significantly to a wide range of actions outside Europe, complementing its increased activity in UN and OSCE (Organization for Security and Cooperation in Europe) operations. In the EU, despite enlargement and successive constitutional reforms, Luxembourg retains more than its share of seats and votes across EU institutions, and Luxembourgish diplomats are a significant presence in Brussels. Although it may be tiny, it is anything but marginal.

Finally, while escaping NATO may be possible (as France so clearly demonstrated in the 1960s), the agreement is, for all intents and purposes, a permanent one where Luxembourg is concerned. This is even more the case for BLEU/Benelux and the EU, although it should be noted that the ECSC was eventually dissolved, not for lack of interest in its purposes but because these were largely subsumed under the ever-expanding scope of EU activities and regulations. At any rate, departure from these agencies has never been seriously contemplated (Seigel 2016). One would expect that Luxembourg would be the last one to leave the EU should it ever disband, staying around to turn off the proverbial lights.

What does this tell us about trust? It seems clear that Luxembourg has learned one key lesson from its history beginning in 1815, namely to so fully enmesh yourself in the lives of those on whom you depend that the only way they could abandon you is through the equivalent of suicide. Luxembourg's core interests are largely subsumed under the national and collective interests of each of its neighbors, such that they can serve Luxembourg best by simply going about their ordinary, selfish, day-to-day business. Just as the remora can be expected to be a big fan of the shark, it is no surprise that Luxembourg has embraced and championed a pro–United States, pro-Europe policy. There is no need—as required in a trusting relationship—to hope that the other European actors will take its interests into account (it has learned that even Belgium was more than willing to manipulate its currency at Luxembourg's expense). By securing certain rights to participate and to selectively block the most harmful actions, Luxembourg has hedged against worst-case scenarios, indicating that trust is not at the core of the relationship (although the country has accepted that it remains vulnerable to a great deal of mischief). For its part, Luxembourg could be accused of exploiting its protectors by contributing minimally to regional defense, dragging its feet on a number of policy changes, receiving far more than it contributes to EU bodies, and providing safe haven for much of the region's liquid assets. This parasitic behavior appears to be nearing an end, with the result that Luxembourg will be even more vulnerable to exploitation by its neighbors. It is difficult to know what would be the tipping point that would turn Luxembourg into Denmark or Greece (i.e., a reticent participant or rebellious child), but based on the degree of hedging we have seen, it seems clear that such a possibility exists. Luxembourg's commitment to Europe is not without an asterisk.

Conclusions

Luxembourg has experienced a wide range of attitudes regarding its neighbors. In the earlier years it was compelled to rely on greater powers for its survival, something it eventually embraced as its national identity. Two world wars drained it of enthusiasm for this strategy, and beginning in the 1920s it began to strategically alter its relationship with its neighbors, opting for a union with Belgium after being spurned by France. Despite repeated reminders of their responsibilities regarding Luxembourg's safety and integrity, the great powers in 1939 failed to protect it from wanton aggression, with the result that its leaders were determined never again to expose themselves to such a degree to the fickle preferences of larger neighbors. The experience with BLEU, preceded by many decades in the Zollverein, gave Luxembourg's politicians and civil servants the experience and confidence to press forward in the direction of integration, counting on the protection of institutional arrangements and the rational preferences of postwar European politicians to favor peace over war. As mentioned earlier, the entire continent owes a debt to the foresight and strategizing of this small and weak player, and the result has been a stronger but wiser Luxembourg.

Ultimately Luxembourg's experience is a cautionary tale for those who would argue that trust should be the foundation of peaceful international relations. As we will discuss further in chapter 8, while distrust can poison any relationship, the alternative should not be trust, but rather a clear-eyed but hopeful view of others' intentions. Lasting cooperation may be the result—perhaps even trust in the long run—even though it is based primarily on rational calculations of shared interests.

THREE

Liechtenstein

The Virtue of Hedging

At first glance, Liechtenstein's relationships with Austria (Austria-Hungary after 1867) in the nineteenth century and with Switzerland since the 1920s evince considerable levels of trust. In both cases, the leadership and many citizens made a conscious decision to make themselves dependent on these states for essential functions of government, including diplomacy, trade, law, and currency. It appears that Liechtensteiners not only felt these states were dependable and able to fulfill these important roles but they would do so while taking into account Liechtenstein's needs, consistent with our definition of trust. While these expectations were not fulfilled where Austria was concerned, Switzerland has been a trustworthy partner for the most part. The case, as we will see in chapter 8, provides useful material to test theories of trust both as a dependent and independent variable. In particular, Liechtenstein's "voluntary subordination" to Austria first and to Switzerland second has much to do with cultural and social affinity. As we will see, however, despite Switzerland's reliability, Liechtenstein has sought to expand its options and hedge its commitments across the ninety-year relationship, indicating that more is at work than mere trust.

In recent years, Vaduz has reached out to European bodies, signing an agreement with the European Union to enter the European Economic Area even though Swiss voters blocked a similar move by Bern. This has meant that for all practical purposes many Liechtensteiner economic and social policies are being decided in Brussels (Pelkmans and Böhler 2013,

63). Vaduz remains tied to Bern, however, and in some cases is able to take advantage of differential levels of integration between Switzerland and the EU. Overall, Liechtenstein is willing to integrate with its neighbors, often surrendering control over key aspects of its sovereignty while at the same time retaining the power to contribute to, reinterpret, selectively implement, and even withdraw from numerous carefully crafted agreements.

Liechtenstein Heritage

Liechtenstein is perhaps the most unlikely sovereign state in Europe. It was nearly absorbed by the Holy Roman Empire, the Spanish Empire, the German Empire, and the Austro-Hungarian Empire. It has been repeatedly invaded and pillaged. In some respects, its very poverty may have been its salvation since it was never such an appealing target that states were willing to risk conquering it. It also benefited from being at the fulcrum of the European balance of power for much of its history, meaning that there was always another major power interested in preventing its annexation by another.

In the Middle Ages, the territory now encompassed by Liechtenstein was essentially the personal property of a succession of nobles, the last of which went bankrupt. The Holy Roman emperor divested him of his property and went in search of a more solvent ruler, selling the territory to Austrian prince Johan von Liechtenstein—a member of the ruling Hapsburg dynasty—in 1699 and 1712 in two separate transactions (Malin 2007, 228). The new prince, following the lead of the Viennese, abolished the traditions of self-government that had emerged over time and replaced them with a system of absolutism. He tied his domain to Austria, placing an Austrian as governor and personal representative and even allowing Austrian troops to garrison there during the 1790s (Beattie 2012, 21). The territory was granted a seat in the Council of Electors and the lowest rank for a "free" territory in the feudal, hierarchical system that was the Holy Roman Empire. During the Napoleonic era the territory fell under French domination although with the abdication of the Austro-Hungarian emperor Francis II it gained formal sovereignty for the first time in 1806. It was admitted to Napoleon's Rhine Confederation as a sovereign state (Duursma 1996, 149). As evidence of Liechtenstein's sovereignty, Prince Johann I acted as intermediary between France and Austria to negotiate the peace following the Battle of Austerlitz (Malin 2007, 231). Napoleon interceded to prevent Bavaria from annexing it. The principality withdrew from the confederation in 1813.

1812–1919: Subordination to Austria/Austria-Hungary

Liechtenstein was later accepted into the German Federation following the Congress of Vienna (which it attended). Ties to Austria deepened during this period while relations with Prussia—never warm—cooled significantly. Liechtenstein was already part of the empire's postal system, albeit without any formal treaty to govern the arrangement (this would not come about until 1912 [Liechtenstein 2012]), and in 1812 it was incorporated in its legal system, with Liechtensteiner cases being appealed to Vienna and Innsbruck, initially by imperial decree in Vienna and later by virtue of a treaty between the two countries (Quaderer 2000, 64; Raton 1970, 40). In 1852 it forged a customs union with Austria (see below) which it extended and renegotiated several times.

In 1866, in response to Prussian designs against Austria, the German Federation took a vote on whether to mobilize. By the narrowest of margins and with Liechtenstein—perhaps—casting the deciding vote (there was some confusion because of the convoluted voting system and possible recording errors), the Federation rejected Prussia's request. Otto von Bismarck was furious and repudiated the confederation as an example of dysfunctional democracy. Prussia promptly defeated Austria and then, thankfully for Liechtenstein, let bygones be bygones. During the war, again asserting its independence, Liechtenstein opted not to join either great power but instead deployed its army of eighty men to guard against a possible attack by Italy in Tyrol (Liechtenstein US Embassy 2014). With the end of the war the German Federation was dissolved, as was Liechtenstein's small army. It is worth noting that Beattie found that the disbanding of the army was controversial in that the newly formed Liechtenstein Parliament was eager to do so while the prince would have preferred to maintain it as a defense force (Beattie 2012, 33; Seger 1978, 17).

The relationship with Austria was a relatively natural one since most of the principality's inhabitants and rulers were tied to Austria's territory and royal family. They owed their presence in Liechtenstein to the emperor: they traded good management of the territory in exchange for formal sovereignty (including diplomatic immunity and other privileges). Members of the princely family routinely served in Austria's military and diplomatic services and held property in the Empire, and until the twentieth century they resided in Vienna (Beattie 2004, 36). Austrians filled senior positions in the government by princely appointment, often operating from Vienna. The people of Liechtenstein did considerable business with Austrians in neighboring Feldkirch (Vorarlberg state) and herded their cattle to the Austrian Alps each year. Marriages between Liechtensteiners and Austrians—facilitated by their shared Catholic faith—were common. Despite the suffering precipitated by being closely tied to Austria during World War I, the people were generally pro-Austrian (Beattie 2012, 44). As put by Deiner, "All of these integrating measures combined to give the impression that the border with Austria-Hungary was somewhat less than real. There was not much on the surface that differentiated life in Liechtenstein from that of Austrian Vorarlberg on the other side of the border" (Diener 2010, 142).

This is not to say that there was no distinct national identity or political vision among Liechtensteiners. During the eighteenth and early nineteenth centuries, the prince was sometimes unflatteringly equated with the emperor in Vienna, particularly his tendency to behave autocratically. His denial of civil liberties and mismanagement of the economy were resented as far back as 1719 (Quaderer 2000, 62). Rebellion came into the open in 1809 when Liechtensteiners joined an uprising in Vorarlberg state against land registration policies being imposed by princely representative Josef Schuppler, who was forced to compromise. It was not until the French army marched into Feldkirch that the uprising came to an end. In the 1830s the prince's refusal to revise the absolutist constitution was appealed to Vienna to no avail (Quaderer 2000, 71). In 1848 Liechtensteiners joined with their ideological counterparts in Vorarlberg to present united demands for political liberalization in Austria and Liechtenstein, reforms that were reluctantly granted to both (Tiefenthaler 2000, 59). There was some concern that if some action were not taken Liechtenstein would become as radical as Germany or decide to join with Switzerland, the latter option being preferred by a sizeable minority (Tiefenthaler 2000, 54; Beattie 2012, 29). Many Liechtensteiners served as mercenaries for Switzerland over the years, and in 1854 a Swiss recruitment stationed was opened in Vaduz (Austria demanded its closure, which was granted [Beattie 2012, 35]). The constitutional reform of 1862 resulted in the removal of senior Austrian officials and their replacement by native Liechtensteiners in response to popular demand. Anti-Austrian sentiment eventually solidified with the creation of the Christian People's Party in 1919 around the rallying cry "Liechtenstein for Liechtensteiners."

The customs treaty of 1852 emerged in part from the same factors that contributed to the political awakening in 1848, namely concerns about economic survival. Liechtenstein saw itself as economically isolated, and ordinary citizens saw in a trade union with Austria a way to join with a much larger economy (Tiefenthaler 2000, 58). A new prince of Liechtenstein, Alois II, was more progressive than his predecessor and favored actions that would help bring the territory out of preindustrial poverty. On June 5, 1852, a customs treaty was concluded in Vienna that provided for the principality to be subsumed under Austria's tariff system. For trade purposes, the border of Austria was moved to the eastern border of Liechtenstein, complete with customs agents, tariff schedules, monopolies on calendars, newspapers, and playing cards, and other related laws and regulations. Liechtenstein trade was administered from Feldkirch and one new Austrian customs house was erected in the principality (it flew both the empire's and the princely flags [Article 4]). Austrian agents in Liechtenstein were expected to swear loyalty to the prince (who would cover their salaries) and be answerable to local criminal law. Tax revenues were shared between Liechtenstein and the state of Vorarlberg on the basis of population ratios (Article 7). In a codicil to Article 2, the prince of Liechtenstein accepts the possibility that Austrian law may need to be applied in Liechtenstein regarding private and public commercial transactions (Individual Article 1).

Although the treaty was clearly designed to give Austria predominant control over the relationship, it provided certain protections, guarantees, and escape clauses for Liechtenstein. Austria guaranteed minimum payments on taxes related to state monopolies to protect against trade volatility (Article 8). Austria promised that if it entered into trade negotiations with Switzerland, it would "take into account the special needs of the royal government" and allow the prince a veto over any treaty (Article 13). The treaty was designed to expire after ten years with the possibility of twelve-year extensions unless either party chose to withdraw (Article 14). As it happened, when Austria lost World War I, Liechtenstein was permitted to withdraw from the treaty almost immediately (Duursma 1996, 170).

The trade relationship with Austria proved quite beneficial to Liechtenstein, and it was during this period that the country began to experience industrialization and steady economic growth. The experience of being linked to Austria's economy proved disastrous, however, during World War I as the principality became the indirect target of sanctions against the empire. The currency plummeted, trade came to a standstill, and unemployment skyrocketed. It was with considerable relief and little debate that the prince and his people opted to quit Austria and seek a new protector in 1919.

Looking back at the overall relationship between Liechtenstein and Austria, one can see two parallel trends. On the one hand, Austria's role in Liechtenstein's internal and external affairs was consolidated in many respects. On the other hand, that relationship was increasingly codified and regulated. By the beginning of World War I, arrangements that had been informal were all the subject of relatively detailed treaties (criminal law, postal service, business, consular representation) and agreements on new topics were entered into (currency, visas, customs, diplomatic representation). Throughout, however, the prince worked to clarify and even increase his autonomy and the distinctiveness of Liechtenstein foreign policy. He entered into separate agreements with Switzerland on migration, worker status, and land ownership while cautiously and sometimes belatedly approving treaties between Austria and Switzerland that affected Liechtenstein. He never signed a formal military alliance with Austria, preferring to maintain diplomatic flexibility. For its part, Austria did not consistently respond to Liechtenstein's petitions. A formal legation was sent to Vienna to request an extension of the railway from Feldkirch to Vaduz, but the railway was instead extended only partway (requests made in 1905 and 1927 were also rebuffed [Raton 1970, 43]). Efforts to formalize the postal services took several years and met only some of the countries' demands. At the same time, Austria showed considerable respect for Liechtenstein rights, allowing and even encouraging neutrality during World War I. A senior Foreign Ministry official urged the principality to denounce the customs treaty to send a clear signal to the United Kingdom that ties were cut and thereby avoid sanctions (Beattie 2012, 42).

Returning to our rubric from chapter 1, we can see that Liechtenstein's ties with Austria during the nineteenth century displays many of the features of a trusting relationship (see Table 3.1). Clearly, Liechtenstein was vulnerable to the preferences of Austria and was three times swept up in the riptide of its great power politics, first with France, then with Germany, then with the World War I allies. In each case, Liechtenstein adopted a policy of neutrality, which proved to be extremely foresighted since Austria demonstrated time after time an inability to defend itself, much less its neighbors. In the 1840s, it was largely due to the state's economic distress and isolation that a customs union was pursued. With respect to the attractiveness of Liechtenstein as a target of exploitation, it was not until the 1870s, when the country's industry began to expand, that one could say it offered anything of importance. In fact, it was in part the country's lack of economic or strategic importance that protected it from predation by the various central European powers.

On the question of voluntarism, we need to separate the opinions of the prince from those of his subjects. The people were of mixed opinions about ties to Austria. As we saw, there was a sense during the eighteenth century that the prince was an alien intruder, inspired and supported by

Austria. This sentiment seems to have given way to a more positive assessment of the relationship in the mid-nineteenth century. Some even saw the Austrian emperor as a tool to rein in the prince in the 1830s and may have recognized that Austria's relative liberalization in the 1850s was a stimulus for their own subsequent political reforms. In the 1840s the people were generally agreed that participation in Austria's customs system would bring substantial benefit, or at least reduce their deprivation to some degree. But the political reforms of the 1860s included a dose of nationalism expressed by a decision to evict a number of senior Austrian officials from the principality. By the twentieth century the population was deeply divided on the merits of close ties to Austria. The experience of profound deprivation during World War I solidified anti-Austrian sentiment, and it is reasonable to think that the country may have pivoted to Switzerland even if Austria had somehow managed to win the war. Throughout the century, while loyal to all things Austrian and more than willing to maintain a strong Austrian presence in the country, the prince kept his options open where essential sovereignty was concerned. But more often than not it was the prince—often in tandem with representatives of the public—who took the initiative to reshape ties with the empire. Only rarely did Austria intervene without explicit consent, and during World War I Vienna even suggested that Liechtenstein might want to abandon the customs agreement for its own sake. Taken together, it seems clear that the people and government of Liechtenstein were able to make a conscious decision to increase or reduce their ties with Austria and that the country displayed a fairly high level of voluntarism.

By the 1850s, Liechtenstein and Austria were agreed with respect to a wide range of topics, from trade and taxes to weights and measures, from law and punishment to postal service and currency. Short of an outright military pact, few of Liechtenstein's activities and powers were not directly affected by an agreement with Austria. Naturally, almost everything of significance was covered under the arrangement as well. The exception of a military alliance proved essential to the country's survival as a semi-sovereign state.

The customs agreement of 1852 is the keystone of the relationship and so it is worth our time to look at it more closely with reference to questions of precision, participation, and withdrawal. At a mere 3,700 words and fifteen brief articles and seven amendments, the treaty lacks precision and detail. Many of the provisions are quite open-ended, such as the provision that allows the possible imposition of Austrian law regarding transactions (no trigger mechanisms are mentioned other than the emperor's wishes).

Likewise, the termination provisions are vague and a bit confusing. On the other hand, key details are spelled out, such as the terms of reference of the Austrian customs agents deployed in the principality and the distribution of customs and tax revenues. Compared to treaties of its day, the agreement is typical, but since we will be comparing it to the conventions of the twenty-first century, it is fair to say this agreement is quite imprecise.

With respect to the involvement of Liechtenstein in the implementation, interpretation, and enforcement of the agreement, there is little that would lead us to expect anything but that Austria's interpretation would apply. As mentioned, the prince could veto a future trade agreement between Austria and Switzerland and could demand reassignment of Austrian customs workers. He was also invited to share his opinions about tax rates and other matters, but by and large this agreement was to be administered by Austria. As it happened, there was little need for Austria to impose its will as the period from 1852 to 1914 was one of relative quiescence and shared prosperity.

Finally, while the treaty provided for renunciation, it appears that—on paper at least—such an option would be difficult to exercise. Liechtenstein could give its notice of withdrawal, so long it came at least one year before the expiration of the twelve-year period. Otherwise the treaty would automatically renew for another twelve years (Article 14). At any rate, the arrangement was mooted by the events of World War I and the dissolution of the empire, but it is worth noting that the commitment being made was a relatively serious one.

Looking at the arc of agreements between the two entities, it seems that a paradox exists. On the one hand Austria was allowed to take an ever-increasing role in Liechtenstein's domestic and foreign affairs. On the other hand, this involvement was more and more constrained by treaty language rather than by informal arrangements. The codification of the postal agreement—following nearly a century of informal Austrian control—and the formalization of Austria's role in Liechtenstein's legal system—following roughly seventy years of loosely structured arrangements—are important examples of this process. By the end of the period it was put in writing.

Taken together, it seems reasonable to say that at least the prince of Liechtenstein displayed quite high levels of trust in his Austrian elders, although there were some things—namely his status as a monarch and his country's fundamental sovereignty, particularly with respect to matters of war and peace—that were non-negotiable. Whether the Liechtensteiner people were trusting of Austria is debatable. Northerners were more trusting than southerners, conservatives more trusting than liberals, and all were willing to base their trust on Austrian performance. Taken together, one could say that Liechtenstein displayed a sort of contingent trust, a trust that did not abandon fundamental identity and freedom.

As we will see in chapter 8, much of this can be explained by the conflicting impulses of affinity and cultural similarity with the impulse to autonomy and self-government. Trust provided Liechtenstein with a mixed bag of results. As it turned out, Austria-Hungary was not the best horse to which a small country should hitch its metaphorical wagon and it was only because it could declare neutrality—a neutrality that was respected largely because of the country's lack of strategic and economic importance—that it could survive intact. Neutrality and the early intervention by Napoleon, the one "protector" that Liechtenstein never asked for.

The Turn to Switzerland

Switzerland and Liechtenstein had both experienced dramatic changes in the decades leading up to their new relationship. Switzerland had evolved from an unstable, relatively poor, loose coalition of cantons into a viable, self-sufficient state. At the time Liechtenstein signed its customs union with Austria, Switzerland would not have been a viable option. It had experienced a month-long civil war in 1848 and had built its first railway only a year earlier. It was experimenting with a new federal constitution aimed at allowing cantons considerable autonomy and influence but not sovereignty, which would be concentrated in new institutions in Bern. It was during this period that the banking and industrial sectors were established, both of which led to an era of unprecedented economic growth. It emerged from World War I with its neutrality tested but intact.

Liechtenstein, for its part, was on the ropes. As we saw, Liechtenstein's sovereignty and neutrality were questioned by the great powers of Europe, with disastrous consequences. It could only afford to staff three foreign embassies, and it struggled to manage the most basic functions of international diplomacy or protect its citizens' interests abroad. Its economy was in shambles after several years of wartime sanctions and the collapse of Austria-Hungary's government, economy, and currency. Fortunes were lost and prospects were bleak. The government in Vaduz experienced what Beattie calls a "quiet coup" by nationalists, who put pressure behind the scenes on the Austrian governor to resign and leave the country in late 1918 (Beattie 2012, 50). The provisional leadership of Parliament asked the prince to accept a new arrangement wherein the governor would be a native Liechtensteiner and policies (including foreign) would require mutual consent between the prince and Parliament. Prince Johann II agreed, reluctantly, and thus began negotiations for a new constitution that was finally adopted in 1921.

The relationship between the two entities was generally warm. Both understood the value of neutrality in international relations. Both had embarked on banking and industrial paths that mirrored each others. Both societies considered themselves industrious, conservative, and prudent, although this probably best describes common traits shared by German-speaking Swiss and Liechtensteiners especially. Intermarriage was roughly as common with the Swiss as with the Austrians, and movement across the border occurred on a large scale. Most Liechtensteiners today have a relative who was not born in the principality, although non-European immigrants find the country less than welcoming (Liechtenstein 2001). On the other hand, the Swiss have always been a bit puzzled by Liechtensteiners' attachment to the monarchy, which they themselves rejected many years ago, and they are less reliably Catholic (Seger 2013).

The prince and the leaders of Parliament were in agreement that an overture should be made to Bern at the earliest opportunity. There appears to have been little consideration of communicating with any other European state. The willingness of the Swiss authorities to consider the initiative—it took only three days for the legislature to approve the beginning of negotiations (Raton 1970, 73)—was seen by many as an act of charity flowing from the country's "long tradition of helping those in need" (Seger 1978, 19). Swiss legislators characterized the situation as a chance "to grant our help to a small neighboring country which can regain its balance only with our aid" (Bundesrat message #1748, 21, cited in Raton 1970, 91). Naturally, Switzerland was not especially keen to have instability on its borders, especially in light of upheaval in Austria. Some have argued that the federal, multilingual nature of Swiss governance structures prepared it to deal with yet another foundling (Malin 2007, 238).

Over the course of the next four years the two negotiated a string of agreements that resulted in Switzerland essentially inheriting the role previously played by Austria, even though it took a century for the latter relationship to develop and become codified. In almost every area the arrangements gave Switzerland far more control than had been exercised by Austria, a reflection of Bern's uncertainty about Liechtenstein's willingness and capacity to put its house in order. As we will see, the terms—both formally and informally—have relaxed over time.

In 1919 Liechtenstein formally asked Switzerland to "take over the representation of the interests of Liechtenstein in countries where the Principality has no representation but where Switzerland does" (translated from Duursma 1996, 161). Connected to this, Switzerland was asked to represent Liechtenstein in international diplomacy generally, specifically with respect to its request for admission to the League of Nations. It failed in this respect and did not do an especially good job of making the case (Duursma 1996, 173). It also failed to protect Liechtenstein landholdings in Czechoslovakia, an inauspicious beginning to what would prove an otherwise happy relationship (Beattie 2004, 66). At any rate, the arrangement was consummated with only an exchange of notes rather than a formal treaty and has continued largely unchanged (Beattie 2012, 56). Delegations and missions were mutually recognized and the hard work of negotiating began.

Without consulting the Swiss government, the Liechtenstein Parliament adopted the Swiss franc as its national currency in 1924, a situation that continued without formal agreement until a treaty was signed in 1980. Given the country's tiny economy and its integration into the Swiss customs union, this did not trouble Switzerland. The only demand from Bern at the time was that the principality refrain from printing bank notes or mint coins (Duursma 1996, 166).

The first treaty, negotiated in 1920, addressed postal services. In this and in future instances, Liechtenstein took the initiative. It presented Bern a proposal for a deal that would improve on the one reached with Austria in 1911, particularly with respect to allowing Liechtenstein to print and circulate only its own stamps in the territory while submitting to Swiss administration of the mail service (but local control of its post offices). This was rejected by the Swiss government, which proposed instead an arrangement that would have been even less flexible than the old 1911 treaty. In particular Switzerland originally proposed that only its stamps would be used, but after several months of negotiation conceded the point to Vaduz (Raton 1970, 76). Although Vaduz had hoped to cement the agreement within three months, the entire process, from beginning to final ratification, took nearly a year to produce the twenty-article-long treaty.

The treaty provides that Switzerland's laws and administration would govern the principality's postal system. The postal workers, while recommended by Vaduz, had to be hired by Bern, and the same worker regulations and pay scales would apply (Article 7). Liechtenstein could print its own stamps and keep the profits (and bear the losses), but Swiss stamps were to be used when there were not enough of the local variety (which never happened). Note that profits and losses were settled in Bern, although the equipment and buildings belonged to Liechtenstein (Articles 12 and 13).

Withdrawal from the treaty could take place with six months' notice (Article 19) and disputes could be taken up with an arbitration panel (one each chosen by the two parties and a third chosen by the arbiters if they could not reach an agreement) (Article 20).

Before moving to the customs treaty, it is worth mentioning that the two states concluded an agreement on the control of aliens and border police in 1923 on the same day the customs agreement was ratified. It followed from the fact that Swiss customs officials would be deployed along the Liechtenstein-Austrian border and would be joined by police to handle immigration issues. Simply put, Switzerland was permitted to regulate immigration into Liechtenstein as though it were Swiss territory (consistent with Article 33 of the customs treaty). Swiss police were answerable only to Bern and Liechtenstein gave advance permission for Swiss police authorities to enter the territory to deal with any disciplinary actions over the border guards (only notification was required in each instance). Liechtenstein was forbidden to harbor individuals who had been expelled from Switzerland (Article 7). As a concession to the principle of reciprocity, Switzerland also agreed not to harbor those expelled from Liechtenstein, but only in the neighboring cantons. According to Article 11, the treaty ceases to have effect in the event the customs treaty comes to an end (although terminating the policing agreement does not affect the customs treaty) (Raton 1970, 86). There are no specific provisions for withdrawal, denunciation, or dealing with disputes.

The keystone agreement was the customs treaty of 1923, which required just over three years to negotiate. Liechtensteiners were in desperate need of the agreement, not just to gain access to international markets but also for the revenue it could generate (Liechtenstein's share of the tariffs equaled roughly one-quarter of its total tax revenue in 1925). The Swiss, for their part, were interested in making sure the principality would be committed to paying any debts to Swiss banks or the Swiss government (a well-founded concern as the principality would borrow three and half million Swiss francs from Switzerland over the next five years to deal with a banking crisis and various natural disasters). Some were opposed to what they thought would be substantially increased enforcement costs, but most Swiss were unconcerned about the negotiations (Raton 1970, 79, 80).

The arrangement has been described as "rough," "invasive," and "more restrictive" than those made with Austria (Beattie 2012, 60; Malin 2007, 238). This stems from a combination of vulnerability and hope on the part of negotiators. As put by Raton:

> The Liechtenstein delegates raised certain objections regarding the country's sovereign rights, the lump sum the Swiss were prepared to pay annually, and finally the fact that Liechtenstein would have only a consultative voice in the conclusion of commercial treaties between Switzerland and other countries, especially Austria. But the Liechtensteiners knew very well that for them to maintain customs autonomy was sheer illusion, and they therefore made numerous concessions. (Raton 1970, 80)

Although lip service was paid to Liechtenstein's sovereignty in the preamble, Article 1 declared, "The territory of the Principality of Liechtenstein is connected to the Swiss custom territory and forms a part of the Swiss customs territory." Lest there be any confusion about what this implied, Article 4 stated that all Swiss laws related to customs or other relevant topics—current or future—applied in Liechtenstein (Duursma 1996, 164). Article 5 further specified that the principality must "put into effect, on its territory, Swiss laws affecting commercial, literary and artistic property . . . and acknowledge the authority of the Swiss Federal authorities based on these laws." These were to be enforced in Liechtenstein courts, with appeals moving through Swiss courts (the prince may not grant amnesty with respect to breaches of these laws). Article 25 declares that the Swiss customs officials who would be posted in Liechtenstein were answerable only to Swiss authorities and courts (see the provisions respecting border police).

At the international level, while Liechtenstein was not obligated to adhere to treaties negotiated between Switzerland and third countries, it was barred from undertaking trade talks of its own. The one exception was that the principality would be consulted on any trade deals between Switzerland and Austria (Raton 1970, 81).

The treaty was explicit and detailed, covering forty-five articles and several codicils. It was designed to last five years, but either party could withdraw with one year's notice (Article 41). Disputes could be referred to arbitrators, as in the postal treaty (Article 43). Within six years, however, Switzerland negotiated an amendment to Article 41, insisting that the treaty would remain in effect at least until Liechtenstein paid back the CHF3.5 million Bern had lent to it as an advance on its customs receipts. With respect to receipts, since there was no formula in the treaty, the Swiss government proposed pegging it to an estimate of how much the citizens of Liechtenstein typically paid over a year and settled on CHF150,000 at the outset. This was adjusted upward to CHF450,000 in 1936 but downward again to a low of CHF250,000 during the waning months of World War II (Beattie 2012, 57). As both Switzerland and Liechtenstein entered into more and more free trade agreements over time, tariff receipts gradually shrank to an insignificant part of Liechtenstein's public revenue (roughly 1/30th of 2010 receipts).

Reviewing these initial arrangements with Switzerland, it is useful to return to our rubric (see table 3.1). To begin, Liechtenstein was extremely vulnerable, as we have seen, and was forced to take a leap of faith that Switzerland—or anyone—would be willing to rescue it. Switzerland saw the situation in the same way—as a rescue mission—and saw little in the tiny country that would be worth exploiting. Liechtenstein's royal and parliamentary leaders took the initiative to establish a relationship with Switzerland and seem to have had the full support of the people. Perhaps this degree of trust stemmed from Switzerland's republican heritage, diplomatic neutrality, and lack of territorial ambitions, as well as a sense of its own lack of appeal as a target to be acquired. If anything, it was Switzerland that feared being exploited since it knew well the dangers of extending benevolence—and especially credit—to a potentially irresponsible actor.

The scope of the agreements entered into in the 1920s was extremely wide, as we have seen. The only issues that were not directly addressed were questions of Liechtenstein's constitutional order and its national defense. Otherwise everything was touched upon in one way or another. And perhaps even more significant is that Liechtenstein accepted the application of laws as yet unwritten and unimagined. With respect to salience, virtually every vital issue was covered. Even with respect to security arrangements, the placement of Swiss officials—including members of the military—on the Liechtenstein-Austrian border created a de facto military alliance since any attack on the principality would involve an attack on these Swiss troops. Perhaps the Swiss response would invoke only the need to defend its personnel, but the result would be the defense of Liechtenstein as well. And although the country's lawmaking procedures were left intact, the substance of their outcomes were not.

The structure and mechanics of the agreements were as clear as can be. Little was left to chance or to future interpretation. Although Liechtenstein might have preferred a more informal arrangement, this pattern of precision and specificity was often repeated, to the point that it eventually became part of the principality's modus operandi. As explained by former prime minister Otmar Hasler many years later:

> Codification is in our nature—we want to have it in writing. You have to know how to execute the treaty. We like great detail. Liechtenstein's laws are also very, very detailed—that's what we've done in history and what we'll do in the future. It's a tradition. As a small state we want to have security—we want to be sure that what we've agreed will happen. Our sovereignty wasn't easy to secure—we had to fight for it and we want to have it spelled out in treaties. (Hasler 2013)

The initial Liechtenstein-Switzerland treaties provided some important mechanisms for the principality to challenge Switzerland's interpretation (recall the arbitration provisions), but for the most part it was left to Bern to bring the provisions to life. Finally, the treaties allowed for withdrawal according to ordinary international custom, something Liechtenstein officials used as evidence of the country's sovereignty when it later applied for membership in the Council of Europe (Duursma 1996, 181). But withdrawal from the all-important customs agreement was rendered conditional on repayment of its loans to Switzerland. This incident allows us to note an interesting aspect of the relationship between trust and "entrapment" in treaties: for Liechtenstein to accept Switzerland's new terms required additional trust, while for Switzerland, securing a longer commitment reflected its reduced trust in the principality and a lowering of its creditworthiness. This was consistent with Switzerland's generally tougher approach with Liechtenstein than Austria had taken. As we see in connection with the Belgium-Luxembourg customs union (chapter 2), where the power differential is not great, the dominant state may take more precautions to protect its interests, thereby demanding more trust from the subordinate state.

Taken together, there is every indication that Liechtenstein fundamentally trusted that Switzerland would not abuse its new powers, while at the same time it sought protections for the future (see Table 3.1). In some respects, one could say that Liechtensteiners trusted Switzerland to roughly the same degree that they trusted Austria in that while the powers granted to Switzerland were greater, they were more fully codified.

The relationship with Switzerland has proved to be a happy one, despite an awkward beginning (see earlier points about Switzerland's representations in the League of Nations). The relationship has allowed Liechtenstein to grow dramatically, roughly matching and then far surpassing Switzerland's GNP per capita in the late 1960s (Kushnir 2015). In numerous ways the country has mirrored Switzerland's development and diplomatic strategies. It has embraced neutrality and, over time, internationalism. Its economy has also been remarkably balanced, with strong agricultural and industrial sectors and an international financial sector that allows families to protect their fortunes (Zetzche 2013). Many Liechtensteiner industries have been managed by Swiss engineers, and overall economic and social ties are as strong as if the principality were a canton. As we will see, the terms of the relationship have also loosened markedly, stemming in part from Switzerland's willingness to grant Liechtenstein more independence with respect to foreign economic policy and also because of the principality's desire to expand its influence and hedge its bets.

The experience of German aggression during World War II came close to severing this relationship, however. Members of the German high command were actively pursuing an Anschluss with Liechtenstein immediately after Austria's absorption. There was also the imminent threat of a German-Italian invasion of Switzerland and Liechtenstein (Operation Tannenbaum [Halbrook 1998]). Germany also nurtured the local Nazi sympathizers in Liechtenstein in the hopes that they would seize power (Geiger 2007, 141–42).

A few hundred Liechtensteiner Nazis formed a political party in 1938 and began to plot unification with Germany. On March 24, 1939, their putsch was thwarted by a spontaneous popular campaign. The German government immediately distanced itself from the enterprise and dropped plans to annex the country. Nazis were branded traitors by the population, and in April a referendum was held in which 95 percent of voters reaffirmed their commitment to Liechtenstein's independence and its partnership with Switzerland (Geiger 2007, 168). The experience resulted in a greatly strengthened sense of national identity and unity.

Following the war, Liechtenstein followed Switzerland's example and refrained from joining the United Nations and the new European Economic Community bodies, but sought membership in other regional and universal international organizations over time. While some states objected, the country found the path to membership in these bodies much smoother than before World War II, in part because the principle of self-determination was more firmly accepted in international law (Bartmann 2002, 371). It joined the International Court of Justice, despite not being a member of the United Nations and the USSR's doubts about its independence, and in 1955 filed a case against Guatemala over the dispossession of one Friedrich Nottebohm (the case was a key motivation for seeking ICJ membership in the first place [Malin 2007, 240]). Nottebohm, a German-born person who received Liechtenstein citizenship despite his having made only a few visits to the country, had his property in Guatemala seized during the war on the grounds that he was a German national and therefore subject to wartime sanctions. The court ultimately rejected Liechtenstein's contention on the grounds that the ties between it and Nottebohm fell below a minimum standard justifying naturalization (*Liechtenstein v. Guatemala* 1955). It is worth noting that Liechtenstein's sovereignty was never challenged throughout the proceedings. Liechtenstein also joined the Universal Postal Union in 1962 and the International Atomic Energy Agency in 1968. In 1978 it joined the Council of Europe, where its influence exceeds its size thanks to a system of voting that favors small states in the Parliamentary Assembly. A two-thirds majority is required for proposals that go to the Committee of Ministers (the organization's governing body) (Council of Europe 2015). To allay fears that it would abuse this privilege, Liechtenstein agreed during the membership talks to refrain from casting a deciding vote on budgetary issues (Bartmann 2012, 544). Ironically, it was the Council of Europe that would make life uncomfortable for the principality's leadership—especially Prince Hans-Adams II—when in the early 2000s it lodged objections to the constitutional reforms undertaken at the prince's initiative (and which expanded his day-to-day powers while creating the possibility of a referendum that would eliminate the monarchy) on the grounds that it weakened democratic norms (Beattie 2012, 231). The prince would also lose a case before the European Court of Human Rights for his refusal to approve a judge's appointment in 1999 (Beattie 2012, 219; *Willie v. Liechtenstein* 1999).

In 1960 Switzerland helped found the European Free Trade Association, a loose trade association that offered an alternative to the tight arrangements of the European Economic Community (and the only alternative for many after admission to the EEC was blocked for some states during the 1960s). Liechtenstein joined indirectly by virtue of a special protocol applying Swiss policies to the principality (Raton 1970, 100). When the EFTA established ties to the EEC and the European Coal and Steel Community in 1972, Liechtenstein was also a participant, both during the discussions and later once the deal was struck by the use of protocols related to Switzerland's participation (EFTA 2000, 6). EFTA-EEC ties grew closer during the 1980s, leading to a proposal to establish the European Economic Area. Spurred in part by a desire to be a full party to these negotiations, Liechtenstein—with Swiss support—became a full member of the EFTA in 1991 (Pelkmans and Böhler 2013, 14).

Membership in the EFTA tied Liechtenstein's manufacturing sector more deeply to Europe, although it lodged a wide range of reservations—parallel to Switzerland's—exempting trade in services (Annex M). The EFTA also provided considerable protections for each member. Each member held a vote on the council, which generally acted on the basis of unanimity (Article 43). Financial regulation was largely left to the states. Members could adopt safeguards to limit trade during periods of social or economic distress (although these were expected to be narrowly conceived and lifted once the troubles had passed [Article 40]). The dispute settlement provisions included consultations (Article 47), followed by arbitration and possible withdrawal of trade benefits (Annex T). States could withdraw after giving one year's notice (Article 57). Particularly after becoming a full member, Liechtenstein was able to protect its interests while benefiting from greater access to European markets. Prior to that, while it was dependent on Swiss policy making, it had enjoyed access to an even larger market (Denmark, the United Kingdom, Sweden, Portugal, Austria, and Finland were all members at the outset).

Other developments clarify the evolving relationship between Liechtenstein and Switzerland and between Liechtenstein and the broader world. In 1980, the status of the use of the Swiss franc in Liechtenstein was formalized (recall that the legislature in Vaduz had unilaterally adopted the currency in 1924 without consulting Bern). The agreement—at sixteen articles—is brief, but it provides for some powerful institutional arrangements. Substantively, it lodges control over monetary policy to the Swiss authorities, who had already adjusted interest rates and money supply without consulting Vaduz (Article 1). With regard to enforcement, the Liechtenstein National Bank and the country's police force are to follow Swiss law and regulations, and cases are appealed to Swiss courts (Article 6). With regard to institutional arrangements, the two states established a joint commission to address "interpretation or application" of the treaty. The commission consists of three Swiss and three Liechtensteiner authorities who meet on an ad hoc basis (Article 13). In the event of a dispute that the joint commission cannot resolve, a sophisticated arbitration system is provided for in Article 14 that includes a three-member panel selected by each state (with the third selected by the two arbitrators). If the states cannot appoint arbitrators quickly enough, the president of the European Court of Human Rights will make the selections (it even provides that the vice president of the ECHR will make the decision in case the president cannot). The treaty also provides for a quick six-month withdrawal period (Article 15). The most important decisions regarding money supply, interest rates, and exchange rate policy are the purview of the Swiss National Bank, over which neither the Liechtenstein nor the Swiss governments have any control (Potolidis-Beck 2015).

Liechtenstein joined the Council of Europe as an observer in 1974 and as a full member in 1978, which led to its extension of the suffrage to women in 1984 and the abolition of the death penalty in 1989 (Batliner 2007, 23). It joined the Organization for Security and Cooperation in Europe in 1975. It also joined the United Nations—something the prince and legislative leadership favored more than the general citizenry—in 1990 (twelve years before Switzerland [Hasler 2013]) and has been remarkably active ever since, focusing on relatively narrow issues that are neither banal nor explosive, such as seeking compromise on the Security Council and clarifying the definition of "aggression" under the International Criminal Court (Batliner 2007, 16; Liechtenstein 2015). Finally, it joined the World Trade Organization as a full member (it was previously linked through Switzerland) in 1995, although Switzerland still negotiates on its behalf regarding trade in goods (Potolidis-Beck 2013).

Clearly the relationship had evolved from 1923 to the eve of the European Economic Area decision. The principality was no longer a diplomatic refugee seeking asylum but rather a confident, ambitious microstate with skills and assets. Early debts were repaid and officials on both sides of the Rhine had developed comfortable working procedures and expectations. Why Liechtenstein sought increased autonomy when the dependency arrangement was so profitable and amicable is curious. Some of it no doubt stemmed from the very confidence just mentioned in that the prince and the political elite felt the country had something to offer the region and the world. The high-tech industry and financial sectors were confident they could compete with foreigners on their own terms and sought the opportunity to establish more bilateral and regional ties than were possible by being so closely tied to Switzerland. The prince was attracted to the possibility of increased prestige and influence in global affairs as evidenced by the active role Liechtenstein has played in the organizations it has joined (it is a key member of the "small states" voting bloc at the UN, for example [Seger 2013]). It also appears that the country's leadership sought additional ways to protect Liechtenstein's interests in view of how European integration was impinging upon it anyway. While Switzerland and the Swiss were better able to insulate themselves from the legal and political demands placed upon all European states (whether or not they were members of the European community), Liechtenstein increasingly found it could not. Rather than simply seeking shelter under Bern's protection, the leadership—and eventually the citizenry—moved toward becoming as actively involved as possible, limited by the willingness of the European authorities and states and by the special needs of the country.

With respect to our rubric, it seems appropriate to make some adjustments to reflect the situation in the early 1990s (see table 3.1). The principality, while still vulnerable, was far stronger than ever before during this period, and through a variety of economic and political means it could defend itself better than ever before. Unless it develops a world-class military capability (a remote possibility) it will never be invulnerable, but this was clearly not the destitute waif of 1919. And because of this, there was more in Liechtenstein that might be worth taking. While it still enjoyed the advantage of being "under the radar" to a large degree, the country was increasingly enjoying the fruits of its liberal banking and tax laws, to the point that other Europeans would probably argue that Liechtenstein was exploiting them! As we will see, this phase did not last.

While the prince and the leadership of the political and business communities strongly favored the special relationship with Switzerland and the possibility of expanding ties to other countries and organizations, there were some indications at this stage that the mass public of Liechtenstein was more ambivalent. As we will see, this gap in opinion helped precipitate a constitutional crisis.

The treaties between Liechtenstein and Switzerland and ultimately between Liechtenstein and other European states continue to cover a wide range of topics, most of which address key issues of national prosperity and independence short of a military alliance. The structure of the agreements, however, began to change during this period. Increasingly Liechtenstein authorities have asked for more and more precision and detail in the substance of the agreements (the 2001 version of the amended EFTA agreements—to which Liechtenstein contributed—consist of fifty-nine articles, twenty-one annexes, and several protocols, and Liechtenstein's reservations go on for twelve pages) and increasingly rigorous interpretation and dispute settlement arrangements. Likewise, the agreements coming after 1975 provide for clear withdrawal, sometimes in as few as six months.

What does this say about the degree of trust displayed by Liechtenstein? While almost every Liechtensteiner public official is quick to say they trust Switzerland and believe Bern has the principality's interests at heart, the policies indicate a concern that the country is better off increasing its options so that it does not have to rely entirely on Swiss intentions and practices.

Membership in the European Economic Area

Both Switzerland and Liechtenstein—along with the other EFTA members Iceland and Norway—welcomed European overtures to formalize a new partnership with the European community in the late 1980s. The principality helped negotiate the terms of the European Economic Area as a full member of EFTA with full voting rights (including a veto). The negotiations centered on finding a balance between the EFTA countries' desire to have access to the markets of European Union member states while retaining exemptions and the possibility of veto. For their part, European negotiators wanted to limit access to a degree while retaining control over policy and enforcement. The compromise resulted in a hybrid arrangement whereby EFTA members were permitted access on condition of implementing in a timely fashion the rules and regulations emanating from the European Commission and rulings handed down by the Court of Justice of the European Union (Part I of EEA).

Specifically, the agreement commits the EFTA states to honoring the EU's "four freedoms": free movement of goods, persons, services, and capital (Article 1). They are not included in the Common Agricultural Program, the EU's security and foreign policy arrangements, and other ancillary projects (Pelkmans and Böhler 2013, 23). They are expected to contribute to the regional development program, however, and may undertake bilateral arrangements as desired.

In order to comply with the "four freedoms" provision, EFTA countries are required to internalize the EU *acquis* (the cumulative body of EU law) as it pertains to these elements and to continue updating their domestic law to reflect all new rules, regulations, and rulings in the future. To put this commitment in perspective, it is estimated that the EU and CJEU produce one new rule each day on average (in 2012 they produced nearly a thousand new regulations [Pelkmans & Böhler 2013, 30]). Monitoring this flow of law is an EFTA office in Brussels created by the EFTA parties on their own. Enforcement comes initially by means of an EFTA surveillance body that was created by the three EFTA states as a parallel to the European Commission, and like the commission, it is staffed by subject matter experts who monitor new regulations and state implementation. The more important body is the EEA Joint Committee, which is composed of the EFTA block, the commission and the EU members (Article 93). It is to meet at least monthly to determine which new EU rules are to be implemented by the EFTA states. There are no clear criteria for determining this, so some negotiation and discretion are permitted (Pelkmans and

Böhler 2013, 35). While an EFTA court was created to enforce EEA rules, ultimately the CJEU has the power to deal with disputes between states—including EFTA members—and can hear cases involving private parties in the EFTA states as it does with EU members. It is important to recall that although the EFTA states are policy takers, they do not cast any votes in Brussels at the Council of Ministers or elect members to the European Parliament (Frommelt and Gstöhl 2011, 30).

While the powers of the EU are considerable, it is important to understand that EFTA members were able to secure some relatively generous powers of their own. To begin, since the Joint Committee operates on the basis of consensus, the EFTA states jointly possess a veto. Furthermore, since the EFTA states must reach a consensus of their own when addressing the Joint Committee's agenda, each state has its own veto. The implication is that Liechtenstein's thirty-five thousand citizens can stop EEA policy from moving forward (a power it wielded when it temporarily blocked Slovakia's and the Czech Republic's request for accession to the EEA in 2003 [Europa World Plus 2013]). Through this and other informal mechanisms—including the right to observe proceedings in Brussels—the EFTA states have the ability to nudge EU policy from time to time, something Liechtenstein has also attempted to do (Frommelt and Gstöhl 2011, 31). States can naturally register reservations to the agreement; Liechtenstein has exempted itself from some of the provisions on the free movement of persons on the grounds that real estate is so scarce and the population so small that allowing free movement would almost certainly drive up home prices and could threaten to alter the identity of the country (see below). It has also reserved the right to maintain banking secrecy and retain the state monopoly on alcohol sales (EEA Final Act). They can also—as in the WTO—temporarily suspend implementation of regulations for the sake of social or economic emergencies (the "safeguard clause" [Articles 112–114]). And the withdrawal provision involves the standard twelve months' notification (Article 127).

Perhaps most important, and in response to a key demand of the EFTA countries, Article 102 allows the signatories to opt out of certain EU regulations. This cannot be done without some difficulty and with severe consequences, and so this approach has been termed the "nuclear option" (Lindsell 2015, 58). According to the treaty language, the EEA Joint Committee makes itself available to any signatory that has not (whether by design or neglect) implemented an EU rule that was determined to be applicable. The aim is to negotiate language or rules that will be mutually acceptable, in other words to find a way for the state to implement the law to the greatest extent possible. Such an exercise is to take up to six months (Article 102 (4)). Article 102 (5) describes the consequences of failure to comply: "If, at the end of the time limit set out in paragraph 4, the EEA Joint Committee has not taken a decision on an amendment of an Annex to this Agreement, the affected part thereof . . . is regarded as provisionally suspended. . . . Such a suspension shall take effect six months after the end of the period referred to in paragraph 4." Article 105 reaffirms that the provisional suspension will become permanent barring some effort by the delinquent state to comply.

There is some debate over how this would work in practice. Pelkmans and Böhler (2013, 53) argue that refusal to implement a particular regulation would negate the benefits derived from all the regulations covered by the annex in which it is written, potentially affecting trade in hundreds of goods and services. On the other hand, Lindsell (2015, 59) believes that retaliation would only involve the particular rule in question. The language of the treaty is ambiguous, although all are in agreement that withdrawal of privileges would affect all three EFTA members even if only one is refusing to comply. This naturally puts Liechtenstein in an awkward situation, one that arose when Norway resisted implementing the EU regulations liberalizing trade in postal deliveries for letters weighing less than fifty grams (Pelkmans and Böhler 2013, 53; Lindsell 2015, 59). The crisis proved a bit less "nuclear" than some had feared in that the lengthy deliberation and implementation period (at least one year) was extended for three years, during which period the government in Oslo went from left to right and Norway backed down. But it became clear that EU members and commission representatives were loath to activate the penalties associated with Norway's actions even though it had the right to do so for at least two years. For its part, Liechtenstein was threatened with Article 102 sanctions in 2002 over banking transparency and in 2007 over free movement of persons, and in both cases a negotiated settlement was reached (Lindsell 2015, 54). Perhaps thirty-five thousand Liechtensteiners surmised they might have less ability to resist the EU than five million Norwegians.

Regarding migration, as mentioned, Liechtenstein placed a reservation on the free movement of persons. Rather than making this permanent, the EEA Council (the highest body of the EEA) in 1995 acknowledged the principality's special situation and indicated it would look favorably upon activation of the safeguard clauses regarding the issue for the time being. Liechtenstein naturally had hoped for something more permanent but instead felt compelled to repeatedly resort to the safeguard measure, which "did not find much favour among the contracting parties and provoked long negotiations about the" details of Liechtenstein's policies (EEA Protocol 15; Frommelt and Gstöhl 2011, 36). In 1999—when Liechtenstein occupied the rotating chair of the EEA Joint Committee—the decision was made to allow the country to apply the safeguard provision in renewable—and reviewable—five-year increments. Because the provision is now in place and would require a positive vote to be removed, Liechtenstein has an effective veto over the issue. At any rate, it is difficult to imagine that EEA members would have forced the country to lose its identity (Dózsa 2008, 100).

At the end of the day, while Liechtenstein now answers to a multiplicity of state and EU actors in Brussels, it has more control over its destiny than it did under the Swiss customs union (Frommelt and Gstöhl 2011, 28). And with access to half a billion consumers, the upside is remarkable. For the first time, Liechtenstein's decisions can have a direct effect on European policy (World Trade Organization–Liechtenstein 2000).

The decision to join the EEA was controversial back in Liechtenstein, as manufacturers and financiers feared being unable to compete with EU enterprises (Frommelt 2016, 134). The understanding had always been that this would be an action taken in tandem with Switzerland. This was not to be, however. From the outset, Prince Hans-Adams II, business leaders, and the leadership of the Parliament were eager to accede to the EEA treaty, and in September 1992 a vote was cast favoring moving forward (Frommelt and Gstöhl 2011, 30). The prince, however, insisted that Liechtenstein hold its referendum on the issue prior to Switzerland's plebiscite, on the assumption that a negative vote next door would have a chilling effect at home. The legislature balked and the prince threatened to dissolve Parliament and move the royal family (and its considerable wealth) to Vienna (Europa World Plus 2013). Parliament instead agreed to issue a joint statement in favor of the EEA in exchange for Hans-Adams II agreeing to delay the referendum until after the Swiss vote. The general expectation in Vaduz was that the two referenda would pass comfortably and that the relationship with Switzerland would carry on largely unaffected (Interview 2013c). Swiss authorities were shocked when the vote came in at 49.7 percent in favor and 50.3 percent opposed. For their part, Liechtenstein's leaders were pleased with 55.7 percent approval.

The astonishing outcome immediately presented the two countries with a dilemma: whether or how to allow Liechtenstein to move forward? Swiss authorities magnanimously declared at the outset that they would "emancipate" the principality from its full obligations under the customs treaty (Pelkmans and Böhler 2013, 15) and that it would work out an arrangement that would be beneficial to Liechtenstein (Potolidis-Beck 2013; Hasler 2013). The split on the EEA question prompted the two states to consider various interpretations of the terms of their economic union. Talks were also held between the EU and the European Free Trade Area to allow admission of Liechtenstein without Switzerland in 1993 that came into force in 1995. In essence, the protocols that had originally been drafted to cover both countries together were reworked to exclude Switzerland, a case of the dependent actor achieving considerable new autonomy and powers (Duursma 1996, 187).

The crux of the new arrangement involved a system called "parallel marketability" (Pelkmans and Böhler 2013, 15). The EU parties to the EEA accepted the presence of Swiss officials, laws, and enforcement mechanisms in Liechtenstein while at the same time insisting that in the event of conflict between them and EEA-EU law, the latter would prevail. Switzerland would be allowed to govern imports from EEA states to ensure compliance with Bern's safety and content provisions, while on the other hand Swiss exports moving through Liechtenstein to EEA states would be treated as coming from outside the EEA and would have to comply with EEA regulations before moving on (Pelkmans and Böhler 2013, 32–33). Since Liechtenstein had made arrangements to subcontract this certification to Austria, this meant that Austrian officials would have to approve Swiss pass-through exports to EEA countries. While the prospect may have been a bit galling, the fact is that Switzerland benefited a great deal from its association with Liechtenstein and the latter's access to EEA markets. Switzerland has also benefited from Liechtenstein's easier access to EEA financial centers (Lomas 2012).

Liechtenstein and Switzerland had to revisit many provisions of their customs union (Seger 2013). For example, a special arrangement had to be made to ensure that Liechtenstein corporations were not taxed twice with respect to the EEA and Swiss environmental regulations (Frommelt and Gstöhl 2011, 18). More importantly, a "market surveillance system" was set, following two years of tough negotiations, that allowed Liechtenstein to assess compliance with the parallel marketability provisions (Nell 1996, 18), a difficult burden for the small country (Pelkmans and Böhler 2013, 21). All these arrangements, as well as a series of bilateral agreements between Switzerland and the EEA, had to be finalized before Liechtenstein's accession to the treaty was permitted. At that point—in 1995—another referendum was held, which produced almost the same result, a vote of 55.8 percent in favor.

While the rearrangement of Swiss-Liechtenstein trade relations has been extremely inconvenient—especially for the Swiss who would have preferred harmonization (Hasler 2013)—the result has been generally positive. Over time, the supremacy of EEA has been accepted in Vaduz (Dózsa 2008, 100), which has made policy making more clear and predictable. Its implementation of EU directives has exceeded its EFTA counterparts (Frommelt 2016, 137). Liechtenstein benefits from ongoing talks between Switzerland and the EU and sometimes receives the same concessions made in Brussels to Bern (as in the case of the 2007 treaty [Frommelt and Gstöhl 2011, 57]). Business leaders and other Liechtenstein elites continue to strongly support the EEA accession and 81 percent of Liechtensteiners surveyed in 2015 believe it is the best foreign policy option for the country (European Free Trade Association 2015; Frommelt and Gstöhl 2011, 19). This may stem in part from the consensus between the country's major parties on the issue, itself a result of considerable pressure by the prince, as we saw (Beattie 2004, 213), and the absence of a euro-skeptic, nativist movement (although all agree that some limits on immigration are warranted). Liechtenstein is still entirely dependent on the preferences of the Swiss National Bank (as are the Swiss) with respect to the franc's value on international markets. While they generally favored the move by Switzerland to cap the rise in the franc's value in 2009 (Potolidis-Beck 2013), its decision to let it float in 2015 was more unsettling (*Economist* 2012; CNN Money 2015; Liechtensteiner Vaterland 2015). On the other hand, by joining the EEA without Switzerland, Liechtenstein is shielded to a degree against a possible change of heart by its neighbors to the west. For example, the 2014 referendum on immigration in which 50.3 percent of Swiss voters approved a proposal for new quotas to limit "mass immigration" has prompted EU officials to threaten to revisit the gamut of EU-Swiss bilateral agreements, a move that should not affect Liechtenstein even in a worst-case scenario (*Guardian* 2014).

Before moving to an assessment of the Liechtenstein-EEA arrangement, it is worth mentioning that Liechtenstein also signed the Schengen Agreement, although it could only follow Switzerland's accession (although if Switzerland withdraws, Liechtenstein can remain [Pelkmans and Böhler 2013, 60]). The agreement forced Liechtenstein to take over responsibility for issuing most visas (Potolidis-Beck 2013). The arrangement has strict enforcement mechanisms: noncompliance with new regulations within one month will prompt suspension unless the supervising mixed committee decides otherwise within ninety days. In addition, Liechtenstein may not vote although it may participate in deliberations (Pelkmans and Böhler 2013, 62–63).

Taking all these factors together, Liechtenstein has carved out an unusual form of voluntary subordination, submitting as it has to a state and a multilateral body (which itself includes a subset of states to which it is indirectly subordinate). One would reasonably infer that Liechtenstein is extremely comfortable as a policy taker, but this would miss the key point, namely that multiplying the number of actors on whom one is dependent may actually increase one's flexibility. As we see in table 3.1, Liechtenstein is relying less and less on trusting others to look after its interests and instead establishing itself as a clearly sovereign entity with the capacity to walk its own road.

With respect to its vulnerability and exploitability, it seems that Liechtenstein has become a more attractive target of exploitation by Switzerland, in that its advanced industrialization and sophisticated financial sector offer far more rewards to Swiss industrialists and bankers than ever before. This is not to say, of course, that they are taking advantage, only that the opportunity presents itself. And with respect to Switzerland, Liechtenstein's vulnerability was still serious, albeit less than at the beginning of the relationship. In fact, one could make the argument that since the principality is enmeshed in so many regional agreements, it is more insulated from Swiss economic intervention. But the fact remains that it has an undefended border and a population of only thirty-five thousand. Where the EEA is concerned, Liechtenstein's vulnerability is relatively higher, given the resources at the disposal of the half-billion EEA residents. Conversely, interest in Liechtenstein's resources and assets is likely less pronounced. With respect to both sets of agreements, Liechtenstein's leadership is happy about the association while its citizenry is more ambivalent. The pressure from the prince to join the UN offended some in the principality. The prince had to reassure the citizenry on the eve of the EEA vote that should there be a divergence between Switzerland's and Liechtenstein's referenda and that every effort would be made to preserve the customs union and related agreements (Beattie 2012, 213). Ironically, after the Council of Europe criticized his constitutional reforms, he complained that those who supported Strasbourg were trying to make the country a "protectorate of the Council" (Liechtensteiner Vaterland 2003, cited in Beattie 2012, 231). It is interesting to note that, among other things the people of Liechtenstein have debated over the years, in 1997 the Constitutional Commission openly considered—and rejected—union with another state (Beattie 2012, 222).

The scope and significance of the agreements are still very great; little has changed in that respect. The most dramatic difference is the level of

TABLE 3.1. Features of Liechtenstein's Relationships with Neighboring States and Institutions

		Trustor-Trustee Relationship			Issues in Play		Structure of Agreements		
		Vulnerability	Exploitability	Voluntarism	Scope of Issues	Salience of Issues	Imprecision and Informality	Marginalization	Entrapment
1812–1919: Submission to Austria-Hungary		**HIGH**	Low	**HIGH**	**HIGH**	**HIGH**	**HIGH**	**HIGH**	MODERATE
1919–1975: Submission to Switzerland		**HIGH**	Low	**HIGH**	**HIGH**	**HIGH**	Low	MODERATE	MODERATE
1975–1995: Submission to Switzerland		MODERATE	MODERATE	**HIGH**	**HIGH**	**HIGH**	MODERATE	MODERATE	MODERATE
1995–2016: Submission to Switzerland & the EEA	Switzerland	MODERATE	**HIGH**	**HIGH**	**HIGH**	MODERATE	Low	MODERATE	MODERATE
	EEA	**HIGH**	MODERATE	**HIGH**	**HIGH**	MODERATE	Low	MODERATE	MODERATE

detail and precision we find in these agreements. The EEA alone has 129 articles, 22 annexes, and 49 protocols (Pelkmans and Böhler 2013, 26). It and the Schengen Agreement are open-ended in that, as with the Swiss customs treaty, Liechtenstein has largely agreed in advance to implement laws that will not be of its own making. This is not to say that the country is entirely marginalized; the opportunities for participation in decision making are considerable and its voting powers in the EEA are, at least theoretically, extraordinary. But ultimately its vote is limited to after-the-fact decisions and comes with great risk. And the ultimate enforcement of the EEA falls to the awe-inspiring Court of Justice of the European Union, perhaps the most powerful international court even conceived (Alter 2009).

As far as the question of entrapment, the lessons of this period are mixed. On the one hand Switzerland made it clear that its treaties with Liechtenstein were voluntary and could be amended at any moment, and on the other hand they are still very much in place despite events that could have easily justified their termination. Likewise, although the various regional treaties adopted by Liechtenstein have generous opt-out clauses, the reality is that once a country has internalized several thousand new regulations, it is very unlikely to back out. With respect to the EEA, for example, Frommelt estimates that Liechtenstein was able to persuade the Joint Committee to allow it to opt out of 40 percent of all the EEA *acquis* (Frommelt 2016, 151).

Regarding the central question of whether trust is in evidence, the answer will again be a mixed one. Clearly Liechtenstein believes that neither Switzerland nor the EU are likely to adopt policies that will be seriously detrimental to it, but at the same time it is actively pursuing hedging and participatory strategies that will ensure that it does not have to rely entirely on the good will of its neighbors. As mentioned earlier, by increasing the number of states, Liechtenstein may be increasing rather than decreasing its overall dependency. As explained by former prime minister Otmer Hasler, where Switzerland is concerned,

> we don't think of them as "foreign." We have relatives across the border. We share values and attitudes. They are part of our daily lives. . . . We trust each other. Where the European Union is concerned, it's more about strategic interest. . . . Our interests do not always coincide; they have a huge bureaucracy and many member states. The EEA treaties have been successful nonetheless. They have actually helped reaffirm our sovereignty. On the other hand, ordinary people don't have the same degree of trust in the EEA and the EU members. (2013)

A former Swiss ambassador to Liechtenstein, Paul Seger, believes that Switzerland is a trustworthy partner—reliable and prudent—which in turn inspires trust (or at least, as we saw in chapter 1, "confidence") on the part of Liechtensteiners (Seger 2013). At the same time, the principality runs the risk of being absorbed into the federation; note that some Swiss newspapers report Liechtenstein events under the banner of "local" news!

The enticement of joining a half-billion-strong free trade area while still maintaining close ties with neighboring Switzerland was enough to convince Liechtenstein to go forward while still taking every precaution to protect its interests and identity.

Recent International Entanglements

If Liechtenstein ever hoped to use the strategy of "hiding" its policies and preferences to avoid international scrutiny, that option has disappeared as the principality has grown to become one of the world's financial centers and a magnet for capital and labor (Wivel 2016, 15). Its gross national income grew during the first decade of the twenty-first century at roughly 3 percent annually, declining by just over 1 percent during the depths of the Great Recession in 2008 (Europa World Plus 2013). Its per capita GNI hovers near the top spot most years (roughly US$137,000 in 2015) and outward foreign direct investment includes nearly two hundred establishments on five continents. LGT Group, the country's largest bank and the largest private bank owned by one family (the Princely House of Liechtenstein) had assets of US$120 billion under management in late 2014 (LGT 2015).

The country for many years had embraced a low-tax, banking privacy policy that attracted tremendous wealth. Beginning in 2000, it also attracted tremendous attention from powerful Western states. During that year, the Organization for Economic Cooperation and Development (to which Liechtenstein did not belong) began scrutinizing the banking practices of various countries to determine whether they could prevent money laundering by organized crime or terrorist groups. Liechtenstein fell short and was "blacklisted" under the Financial Action Task Force (Europa World Plus 2013). Alarmed at the prospect of losing business and facing potential sanctions, the principality—with the prince at the vanguard—undertook a variety of reforms to increase transparency. This was met with apprehension by Switzerland, which had hoped the two would remain united in their resistance to externally imposed banking regulations. Liechtenstein banned numbered accounts in 2001 and later created a financial intelligence unit to monitor international transactions. It was removed from the FATF blacklist in 2001, mostly as a reward for its good intentions (Financial Action Task Force on Money Laundering 2001).

At roughly the same time, European governments—led by French president Nicolas Sarkozy—put increasing pressure on so-called "tax havens" to raise revenue taxes (especially those on corporate profits) in order to minimize tax evasion by their citizens and companies. Liechtenstein resisted these pressures, arguing that its tax rates were not out of line with other states and that at any rate, as a country with few resources, it felt justified in leveraging its status as a sovereign nation to adopt a tax structure that would attract capital to it. The situation exploded into public view in 2008 when the German government paid an informant in LGT to transmit internal records on German citizens' accounts (Esterl, Simpson, and Crawford 2008). The information not only implicated hundreds of Germans but hundreds more individuals from the United States, the United Kingdom, and many other countries. The princely family accused the German government of violating the principality's sovereignty but agreed to cooperate with German, American, and European Union officials to reduce tax differentials. On March 12, 2009, it issued the "Liechtenstein Declaration," pledging to "implement global standards of transparency and exchange of information as developed by the OECD and will advance its participation in international efforts to counteract non-compliance with foreign tax laws" (OECD 2009c). It also entered into a series of multilateral and bilateral agreements with the EU (signed in 2004), the United States, and a host of other states to address tax differentials, double taxation, information sharing, and so forth, while still reserving the right to ensure bank secrecy under new regulations (European Union 2004). It even had to deal with Swiss objections to a plan to withhold taxes from Swiss commuters (Lomas 2012). The result was its removal from the OECD blacklist for tax havens and a note of encouragement from the EU (OECD 2009b; European Union 2012a).

Considering everything together, Liechtenstein is becoming increasingly enmeshed in the legal—and to some degree political—structures of the advanced Western economies, usually with little control over its fate. But it maintains a veneer of sovereignty that is growing thicker by the decade. Trust has clearly been present from time to time, but less than most politicians would like the world (and the Swiss) to think. Liechtenstein authorities have generally been prudent and cautious—especially over the past half-century—and have made considerable effort to get their agreements in writing.

FOUR

San Marino

The Virtue of Trust

San Marino is an enclave republic in northeastern Italy near the city of Rimini. It traces its founding to the early fourth century and its government—originally oligarchical, now democratic—to the thirteenth century (Veenendaal 2014, 73; Selva 2014). It adopted a policy of neutrality in modern times, fighting its last war in 1463 when it helped the Papal States in the struggle against a local power and was rewarded with new lands, its last territorial expansion (Duursma 1996, 222). Artifacts going back to this period already show the three feather-capped towers above the word "Libertas" (Museo San Marin 2014). The pope repeatedly defended San Marino's sovereignty and protected it as an "indirect dominion," meaning that its domestic sovereignty was guaranteed in exchange for the pope's exercising control over its foreign affairs (see especially the treaties of 1603 and 1627) (Libertas 2015a). He also claimed the right to interfere from time to time in the country's domestic affairs, most recently in 1739, which resulted in active resistance against the pope's overly intrusive emissary, Cardinal Alberoni, a plebiscite in favor of the status quo (supported by Europe's major powers), and his withdrawal by Clemens XII (Duursma 1996, 209; Selva 2012, 73). The country found itself able to survive in part due to diplomatic manipulation of its proximity to the domains of Umbria, Rimini, and Romagna and its strategic location at the top of a small mountain, and by virtue of the fact that, like other microstates we discuss in this volume, it had nothing of great value to make it a desirable target (Interview 2014a). Even today, with a population of thirty-two thousand people and a GDP of just over one billion US dollars (for a healthy GDP per capita of US$36,000) but few natural resources or manufacturing, there is little in San Marino that would attract international attention or envy (World Bank 2015).

More important than its diplomatic prowess, luck has played an important part in San Marino's international relations (Bravo 2003, 283). Rather than pressing the issue, the pope could have just as easily imposed his rule on the small republic, but he chose to restrain himself. In the 1790s, after conquering the Papal States, Napoleon was in a position to annex San Marino to his new Republic of Italy, but instead demurred. It seems that he found much to admire in this plucky republic and was also concerned about public disapproval of the French Republic obliterating one of the few republics on the continent (Interview 2014a). In fact, he offered additional lands to San Marino, which the consuls general graciously declined. For twelve years, relations between the two states were governed by a treaty of friendship (Duursma 1996, 209). Even when the pope tried to reassert his claims to the territory after 1815, he refrained from imposing himself, restrained by public opposition in San Marino and challenges to his rights by the Sammarinese and other Italian kingdoms and principalities. Victor Emmanuel II considered absorbing San Marino when consolidating the new Italian kingdom. His prime minister, Camillo Benso, Count of Cavour, had decided the country was a haven for deserters and brigands and had decided to annex it, while the king was grateful for the shelter that had been provided by the republic for Guiseppi Garibaldi and several hundred of his nationalist fighters in the 1840s. As it happened, Cavour died before he could act on his intentions, and his successor—Bettino Ricaslo—was willing to allow San Marino to retain its sovereignty on condition of Italy becoming its "protector," something the San Marino government had resisted (Interview 2014a; Libertas 2015a; Libertas 2015b). As we will see, Italy adopted a generous, laissez-faire approach to its relations with San Marino. It was more sensitive to international pressures and refrained from intruding directly into San Marino's domestic affairs except for two episodes during the 1950s and more recently in the 2000s. And today, San Marino is part of the ongoing discussions between the European Union and European microstates, which have been mostly a blessing.

Throughout its history, San Marino has prided itself on its sovereignty, although it has also willingly entered into asymmetrical agreements with its more powerful neighbors. These decisions have been a subject of some discussion—usually limited to the elites—and so are far more voluntary than many of the agreements we will discuss in this work. While it has consistently striven to expand its autonomy, it has nonetheless been willing to accept a submissive role. This has generally been to its benefit despite its vulnerability and has validated the trust involved in making these commitments. San Marino's elective dependency has elements of serendipity that separate it from our other cases and help show that trust can emerge (and decline) outside of strategic calculation.

San Marino's External Relations Prior to the Risorgimento

San Marino was essentially a monastery and parish during the early Middle Ages, but by the end of the thirteenth century it was being treated as a political entity with unique rights. It was exempted from feudal tribute, including to the local bishop of Montefeltro (Selva 2012, 76–77). In 1355, Cardinal Albornoz interceded in San Marino's behalf when, while granting secular authority to the count of Montefeltro, exempted the territory around Mount Titano from his domains. San Marino's special status was reinforced over the years by a number of actions, particularly by the Church, which wanted to limit secular power in the area (Selva 2012, 79). Pope Alexander VI intervened in 1503 to dislodge the prince of Romagna (Cesare Borgia), who had seized the mountain six months earlier (History of San Marino 2015).

By the beginning of the seventeenth century, the leaders of San Marino worked to consolidate and clarify its various constitutional arrangements into a "Leges Statutae" or "Statutes of 1600" that clarified the role of the Great and General Council, the Council of the Twelve (similar to the British Law Lords), the General Aregno (an assembly of the heads of all Sammarinese families twice each year that gradually grew into disuse), and the powers, selection, and terms of the captains regent, the unique dual executives selected by the Great and General Council to serve for six months at a time (Selva 2012, 66). In the process of carrying out this exercise in constitutional codification, the Sammarinese were able to show continuity and foresightedness, and in the process asserted their rights and authority to govern themselves as they saw fit. It was also from this point that the country began referring to itself as a "republic."

This is not to say that San Marino was autonomous or even sovereign. As mentioned, the Papal States still exercised sovereignty over the republic, although from a distance. That this relationship was acceptable is evidenced by the fact that San Marino approached the pope about establishing a more explicit treaty of protection and friendship in anticipation of troubles involving dynastic succession in neighboring domains. This was granted in 1603 and confirmed in 1627 (History of San Marino 2015; Duursma 1996, 208). In granting this protection—which was already implied by earlier agreements—the pope also reiterated his recognition of the republic's sovereignty. San Marino easily survived the turmoil in the region while maintaining its internal sovereignty as a result. As evidence for the light touch of papal authority over the next century, conditions in the republic deteriorated to the point that it became a haven for criminals due to the "abuse of the right of asylum" and a willingness to employ other privileges of sovereignty in ways that harmed its neighbors (Duursma 1996, 208). By 1739, Cardinal Alberoni had convinced Pope Clement XII to give him authority to take action. Under the pretext of searching for two wanted men, the cardinal directed armies to occupy the country outright in an attempt to remove its internal sovereignty and make it a "direct" dominion (History of San Marino 2015). The response was dramatic, as explained by Duursma:

> The majority of the San Marinese population objected to this intervention and gained support of other Cardinals and the Austrian, Spanish and French ambassadors in Rome. An apostolic delegate was therefore appointed by the Pope to organize a plebiscite on the freedom and maintenance of the Republic, which was approved by a more than three-quarters majority. (Duursma 1996, 209)

After an occupation that lasted less than four months, papal troops were removed in 1740.

Following the association with revolutionary and imperial France between 1798 and 1815, the Holy See attempted to reassert itself as the protector of San Marino. The move was controversial because the local government—in particular nationalist captain regent Antonio Onofri—believed that since the country's status was not discussed in Vienna and was not addressed in the Final Act, that its status would remain that of a free and independent republic, while Rome believed that silence implied a return to the status quo. European leaders were ambivalent, although the Kingdom of Sardinia and other Italian leaders interested in unification were happy to make use of the country's ambiguous status. Garibaldi and hundreds of his followers took refuge in the republic in July 1849 on their way to continue the fight from Venice, something that earned the enduring friendship of Italian nationalists (Duursma 1996, 223) and enduring suspicion from Austria and the Papal States (Veenendaal 2014, 73; San Marino Site 2015). Napoleon III ultimately interceded in San Marino's behalf and gave it some reprieve from foreign intervention until the unification of Italy, discussed below.

As can be seen, San Marino's sovereignty was earned incrementally, to the point that one would be hard-pressed to identify its day of "independence" (Selva 2012, 83). It appears that the local secular leadership of the country was always intent on securing more and more autonomy, and the notion that San Marino has always been free is a commonly held belief. But with respect to our question, it appears that it was not until the sixteenth century that the Sammarinese were capable of reaching out to foreign powers for the purpose of securing their protection from foreign threats and self-rule at home. Certainly by the time the Statute of 1600 was adopted the country was self-aware and had the capacity to act in the international sphere. It makes sense, then, to mark out a period beginning in the early 1600s until Italian unification as one epoch in San Marino's foreign policy.

With respect to our measures of trust, it is easy to say that during this period the country was vulnerable. Despite having a capital perched on a mountain and surrounded by formidable battlements, most of the territory was flat and easily accessible, as evidenced by the ease with which successive armies occupied it over the years. More troublesome is the question of San Marino's desirability. While various dukes and bishops were interested in the land across the centuries, it appears that the interest was more speculative than strategic, more a series of real estate transaction than conquests (Selva 2012, 77). It is instructive that it was San Marino's very sovereignty that ultimately drew the attention of the major powers, first as a refuge for criminals then as an asylum for militants. While not unusual for microstates surrounded by more heavily regulated states, it would be odd to say that San Marino was an attractive target simply by virtue of its statehood.

The degree to which San Marino participated in arrangements with the Papal States and France on a voluntary basis is relatively clear, absent a public opinion survey. It seems that during the period from 1603 to 1739 that the leaders of the government were satisfied with—and even sought out—the laissez-faire arrangements with the Papal States, themselves a manifestation of a gradual weakening of papal authority across northern Italy. San Marino could even be accused of abusing what was a relatively benign relationship as it violated the spirit of the accords. It is important to note that when the Holy See acted to protect transnational law and order (a right implied in the agreements), San Marino was able to garner the support of numerous officials—religious and political—in Rome to reverse the decision and restore the status quo. Clearly what was left was far more acceptable to the government of San Marino, although it would be difficult to know how strongly they wished for complete autonomy.

The experience with France appears to answer this question, however, in that there is every indication that France secured San Marino's support without coercion (although one could argue that being suddenly surrounded by French vassal states and armies might have persuaded the republic's leaders to prudently seek an accommodation). But it is clear from what came next that the Sammarinese were not cowed into subservience, but rather embraced the republican ideals advanced by France—to the point that they preferred to work against the Papal States and imperial Austria after 1815—at considerable risk to their own survival (see table 4.1). Their endorsement of Italian republicans and their willingness to join the fight also speaks to a commitment to national self-determination. In the final analysis, while it is reasonable to say that San Marino willingly entered into asymmetrical relationships with the papacy and France during the period from 1603 to 1815, its submission to Rome after 1815 was largely involuntary and deeply resented.

The technical aspects of the agreements between the various states are not always easy to ascertain since some of the key documents come in the form of papal briefs and private legal contracts rather than formal treaties (Selva 2012, 74). In general, though, the agreements were relatively narrow in scope and did not involve matters of national defense (Duursma 1996, 234), something that is more apparent in practice rather that in the text. Perhaps the most detailed of the agreements during this period were the free trade treaties between San Marino and the French-dominated Italian governments in the early 1800s. The lack of precision has been a source of tension, as we have seen, but is also indicative of trust. San Marino apparently lacked the authority to interpret or escape from the agreements, also consistent with trust (at least initially where the Papal States are concerned), a situation that caused considerable grief once that trust was lost.

All these events show a small country emerging much more confidently as a sovereign state than is true for the other cases in this project. As its sense of autonomy increased, its willingness to submit to an asymmetrical relationship seems to have declined, at least so far as this period is concerned. Trust, it seems, was consistent with the country's gestation period but not after its birth.

San Marino's Elective Dependence on Italy from 1861 to 1971

The unification of Italy in the 1860s included the dissolution of the Papal States and along with it San Marino's special relationship with the Holy See. As part of the negotiations, San Marino was treated separately and offered a different status within the new state, namely "protective friendship" (Duursma 1996, 256). In essence, this meant that San Marino would retain its domestic political institutions but commit itself to never forming an alliance with a country other than Italy (Selva 2014). On the other hand, it is reasonable to question whether San Marino enjoyed sovereignty, especially in light of how Italy interpreted its prerogatives in subsequent decades (Libertas 2015a). Italy, for its part, would enter into a trade and monetary union with the small republic, returning a share of the proceeds from duties collected by Italy on goods moving through Italy into San Marino (Articles 22–25).

While the agreement of 1862 was not a military alliance, the fact that San Marino was an enclave meant that any land army would have to pass through Italy first and by implication would encounter Italian resistance before reaching San Marino's borders. Since naval and aerial attacks would have been absurd in 1862, this meant there was a de facto guarantee of San Marino's protection from invasion (Duursma 1996, 256). As put by Duursma:

> Italy's protection was no more than a diplomatic or perhaps military effort to defend San Marino's freedom and independence in a world where a small State like San Marino could not appeal to an international court or exert any pressure on larger States with which it could enter into conflict. (1996, 256)

The agreement was implicitly one-sided in this respect, since it did not secure any assurances of San Marino's support for Italian war aims. On the other hand, San Marino agreed not to enter into an alliance with a third state (Article 29).

Italy in 1862 was naturally unstable and insecure, having barely won its independence. A key concern was ensuring that San Marino did not remain a haven for criminals and deserters, not to mention gun runners and smugglers (a likely scenario given the republic's heritage). Cavour, already suspicious of the government's intentions and capacity, wrote to it in 1861 demanding a return of Italian weapons left over from the war

(Cavour 1962, 340). In the 1862 convention, more than half of the provisions (Articles 4–20) address the capture and extradition of Italian deserters and criminals. Specifically, it not only required San Marino to apprehend and transfer these individuals, but it barred it from offering them citizenship as a means to avoid prosecution (Article 6) or offering them asylum or pardons (Article 10). Criminals were to be prosecuted in the country where the crimes were committed and according to their laws, unless said crimes were extremely grave, in which case they could be prosecuted by the arresting country *in situ*—but with penalties no lighter than the then-minimum under Italian law (Article 8, exchange of letters). There were no exceptions for "political crimes," something that will be added in subsequent iterations. Finally, it was understood that sentences imposed by either Italian or Sammarinese judges (the latter being seconded by Italy [Duursma 1996, 215]) would be recognized reciprocally (Articles 1 and 2).

At thirty articles, the 1862 convention was relatively detailed, although since so much of it addressed a fairly narrow topic it was not particularly broad in its scope. As with almost all subsequent treaties between San Marino and Italy, this agreement was meant to be of limited (albeit renewable) duration of ten years with a provision for denunciation with six months' notice (Article 30). There was no provision for consultation, although as we will see in practice the two states communicated regularly regarding interpretation and implementation of its provisions, Italy's voice usually being the dominant one.

For the next thirty years, relations between the kingdom and the republic were amicable if strained. San Marino was eager to increase its revenues and become an advanced, industrial economy, and therefore it took full advantage of any privileges accorded to it in the 1862 treaty. It also sought opportunities to clarify and expand its sovereign prerogatives through successive renegotiation of the 1862 agreement (Libertas 2015a). To begin, it welcomed the opportunity to produce its own postage stamps and recognized that they might become collectors' items. Rather than merely producing enough to cover local postage needs, it aimed for the European market of collectors as a whole, thereby creating a strong revenue stream for the state (Severini 1995, 128). It also took the clause allowing the minting of coins to the extreme by minting far more currency than could be used, with the result that its value plummeted, harming the regional economy of Italy in the process. Even though paper currency was not discussed in the treaty, local authorities decided that the rules governing coins also applied and began overproducing scrip, also to the detriment of the currency's value at home and within the region (Severini 1995, 127, 130).

Aside from pushing the boundaries of treaty interpretation, San Marino directly violated a number of its provisions, particularly in the area of contraband and smuggling. Since it was given permission to produce a certain number of goods that were covered under Italy's excise tax, it produced more than was called for—including gunpowder—which raised serious concerns for Italy due to the lost revenue and unfair competition this produced (Severini 1995, 137). The country also continued its tradition of granting asylum to fugitives and political outcasts, sometimes even granting them citizenship and sweeping pardons. As we will see in chapter 7 and as we saw in chapter 2, much of this behavior constituted exploitation of the powerful by the weak (Venturini 2014). On the other hand, the government in San Marino was also struggling to keep crime in check, and in 1874 it acknowledged the need for assistance from Italy, which deployed police forces in and around the country to help establish law and order (Severini 2003, 254).

From the beginning of the relationship, Italian authorities felt that San Marino was more like a naughty child than a state, but its fondness for small republics prevented it from being overly harsh in the first few decades (Musi 2003; Severini 2003, 252). This was an advantageous arrangement for San Marino, which strongly endorsed its ties to Italy during the nineteenth century. The period might be considered a golden age, as the country was able to begin to attract foreign capital and increase its economic output for the first time. By the 1890s, however, Italy had had enough and called for new talks on a new fundamental treaty. Each of the behaviors discussed above was addressed and the rules were either clarified or tightened to minimize future problems. In consideration of its willingness to undertake reforms, Italy also increased the amount of San Marino's annual payments. The 1897 treaty illustrates the way agreements become more precise to the degree that trust has degraded. The treaty included forty-seven articles, all of which were brief, including new provisions clarifying and limiting San Marino's privileges regarding currency production (Article 38) and barring copyright and patent infringement (Article 42), tobacco and gunpowder production (Article 44), and so forth. Again, the agreement was designed to last ten years (renewable) with a six-month denunciation provision (Article 47).

World War I was devastating to San Marino's economy, in part because the republic was still overproducing coin, although it was able to survive the war physically unscathed. San Marino approached Italy with requests for increases in the annual payments and other privileges. Explaining the government's approach, Captain Regent Olinto Amati explained to the council in late 1914: "We have no right to censure the Government of the King [of Italy] if it strictly pursues its state's interests; we must, however, put ourselves in a position to defend well our own interests." (Libertas 2015a).[1] When fascism came to Italy it came also to San Marino, albeit it was a fascism of a softer variety (Interview 2014; Selva 2014). Cooperation between the two governments increased, in part driven by a shared desire to rein in lawlessness in the republic (Severini 2003, 263). Italy deployed more police in the country, increased annual payments in 1914 and 1921 (Severini 1995, 130, 158), provided substantial help in building a railway between Rimini and the republic, encouraged San Marino's tourism industry (Severini 1995, 168), concluded a renewal of an 1865 postal agreement that allowed the republic to administer Italian postal law at home (carrying the expenses and reaping the profits) (Duursma 1996, 228), and ultimately adopted a sweeping new treaty of protective friendship in 1939. San Marino, for its part, was generally compliant with its treaty expectations, although it was beginning to see that its small size could be turned into an advantage since it could often escape sanction for violating international norms, especially if it had a friend in Rome willing to turn a blind eye (Severini 1995, 125).

The Treaty of 1939, in fifty-eight articles, repeated many of the provisions of the 1862 and 1897 agreements, including what had become stock language on apprehending and extraditing deserters and fugitives and not abusing the right of asylum in their behalf (Articles 12–35), albeit with provisions regarding the nonextradition of political fugitives (Article 13). The treaty also reiterated restrictions on producing and selling goods subject to Italian excise taxes and the production of currency (Articles 45–53). It added new language barring actions that might undermine Italy's tax system (Article 47, paragraph 3), a clause that would be invoked in the late 1940s as we will see. It was silent with respect to security arrangements, leaving San Marino free to continue its policy of neutrality (Bartmann 2002, 369).

Like its predecessors, this treaty did not provide for joint consultation, although in practice each country knew well what the other was thinking. Also like previous agreements, the treaty was designed to last ten years (renewable) with a six-month denunciation provision (Article 58). The treaty was enthusiastically welcomed in San Marino and continues to be the touchstone of Italian-Sammarinese relations, although considerably modified by numerous amendments (it would be revised a dozen times until the last alteration in 1984 [San Marino 2015]). In addition to the formal arrangements, an exchange of secret diplomatic notes established a deeper customs union between the two states (Severini 2003, 267).

The next twenty years would be difficult ones in the republic, although much stems from having forgotten the lesson of the previous decades, namely that overstepping legal bounds is only effective if San Marino has a tolerant friend in Rome. As a defenseless neutral state, San Marino was unable to prevent the intervention of German and Allied troops and air strikes, including a British air raid on June 26, 1944, that resulted in sixty-three casualties, or one-half of 1 percent of a population of eleven thousand (Geiger 2007, 149; Gori 2014; di Luca 2014). It was host to roughly a hundred thousand refugees, including German and Italian Jews and a number of anti-Mussolini partisans (di Luca 2014). On the positive side, a considerable amount of foreign capital flowed into the country, not because of low taxes but because it provided a safe haven for deposits during the war. This taste of the benefits of being open to international capital movements may have shaped the country's decision to lower its tax rate in 1942 (Severini 1995, 174).

The experience with fascism and war turned most of the people of San Marino to leftist parties, and in 1945 a communist-socialist coalition won forty of the sixty seats in the Great and General Council, the first time communists had come to power through free and fair elections in Europe. Their opposition to fascism brought them in line with Allied priorities in the immediate aftermath of the war (Cruciani 2010, 20). This would not last once the Cold War began in 1947. Since Italy, for its part, had turned to the Christian Democrats and joined NATO, this generated friction until the government in San Marino became conservative again in 1957. From the perspective of San Marino's leftist politicians, all Italy did for the next twelve years was aimed at removing them from power, while from Italy's point of view the pressures it applied were driven by the need to protect Italian interests and promote stability and order (Cruciani 2010, 281).

Italy and San Marino negotiated a new agreement in 1945 that increased annual payments, a routine that was driven by the fact that previous agreements had no automatic formula to adjust the amount. This arrangement naturally gave Italy considerable leverage, which it used to great advantage during the 1940s and 1950s. At about the same time, protests came to Italian authorities from the Vatican and local church leaders regarding San Marino's liberal policy of granting marriage annulments to foreigners (Severini 1995, 176–77). Considering it a violation of moral and ecclesiastical law, the Vatican urged Italian authorities to persuade San Marino to end the practice. The ratification of the 1945 agreement was suspended pending talks over the issue; the agreement was modified with Articles 5 and 6 to prevent Italian citizens from having marriages annulled (Cruciani 2010, 33). Meanwhile, another agreement was reached in 1948, which would also be held up for the sake of leveraging additional concessions.

San Marino had also offended Italian authorities by attempting to create a radio station, something that was seen as both an economic and political (even security) threat to Italy and Western interests generally (Cruciani 2010, 85; Visani 2012, 183). Already under threat from a large communist presence at home, conservative Italian interior minister Mario Scelba—famous for his aggressive measures to contain political threats from both the right and the left—refused to accept a stream of left-wing propaganda from this enclave microstate (Cruciani 2010, 91). Italian legislators—perhaps looking for a way to save scarce money and bring about regime change in San Marino—responded to San Marino's actions by refusing to consider ratifying the 1948 deal, which also came with a suspension of the already overdue payment (Cruciani 2010, 89).

San Marino was placed in a difficult situation. In 1939 these Italian payments made up half of the country's state revenue, and although the expected share would be less it was clear that many of the government's new welfare and development policies would have to be shelved unless a new source of revenue were found. Resentful of Italy's betrayal and of Rome's intrusion in its domestic affairs, the government refused to alter its marriage policy and instead approved the founding of an equally objectionable casino (Cruciani 2010, 86), although ironically the idea for a casino can be traced back to an Italian suggestion in the 1870s (Severini 1995, 133–34). The law provided that half of the casino's proceeds would go to the state. To add insult to injury, the government entered into talks with Massimo Maxim (Cruciani 2010, 90) (probably not his real name), a Romanian Jew who was suspected to be a spy and/or have connections to organized crime, to set up the casino.

Needless to say, this action simply added fuel to the fire in Rome, and Scelba immediately took steps to thwart the plan, including. He set up a roadblock around the republic to check identity cards of visiting Italians and arranged for the establishment of gambling facilities in Rimini, on the grounds that San Marino's actions represented a violation of the 1939 treaty (Cruciani 2010, 85–87; Duursma 1996, 225). The measures were also intended to stop rumored gun running by communists (Cruciani 2010, 69). While both were reversed for a time, the policy of blockading the country—especially in the evening when visitors were most likely intent on gambling—was strengthened (although enterprising young Sammarinese helped Italians avoid the roadblocks, for a fee [Selva 2014]). The policy stayed in place for two years until the government of San Marino acquiesced to Italy's demands. The move could not have come too soon for Scelba, as Italy was beginning to tire of the considerable pressure to lift the siege being applied to it from abroad (Severini 2003, 275). An initial agreement was drafted in 1951 whereby San Marino agreed to close the casino while Italy withdrew its border guards and released some of the funds (only half of what was expected, however). Eventually, in 1953 a new agreement was signed that increased Italy's contribution in exchange for San Marino's abandoning its annulment policy and plans for the casino and the radio station (Articles 5 and 47, paragraphs 4 and 5). For the rest of his term in office, Sammarinese secretary of state for foreign and political affairs Gino Giacomini and most of his people considered the 1953 agreement unfair and unwelcome. The country's endorsement was given under duress and deeply resented (Cruciani 2010, 126, 209). Duursma argues that Italy's claim that San Marino was in violation of the 1939 treaty was most likely baseless—particularly where the casino was concerned since nothing in the treaty mentioned any bar on establishing gambling businesses—and its codification of these provisions in 1953 represented a tacit acknowledgment by Italy that it had overreached (Duursma 1996, 226).

Little did San Marino's leftist leadership know at the time that things would only get worse. In 1956, several moderate socialist members of the council decided to distance themselves from the policies of the Soviet bloc (Cruciani 2010, 60, 114) and left the governing coalition (Cruciani 2010, 213). When the last of them made the move on September 18, the communist-socialist government suddenly found itself in the minority—by one vote. The twenty-nine leftist delegates adopted a questionable maneuver that they claimed allowed them to remain in power by essentially voting for their former colleagues in absentia (Hamblin 1957). Once the term of the legislature expired on October 1, San Marino was left with either one, two, or no governments, depending on one's perspective. Recognizing (and having planned for) the development, the new Christian Democrat majority refused to take their seats (leaving the council without a quorum), declared a provisional government, and set up a headquarters in the town of Rovereta. The leftist legislators holed themselves up in the walled city and organized a militia, supported by some Italian communists who infiltrated the country. The provisional government received the explicit recognition of Italy and a steady stream of official and semiofficial (as well as armed and unarmed) well-wishers (including an encouraging letter from the American consul from Florence and advice from the CIA [Severini 1995, 222; Veenendaal 2014, 74]). Over the next two weeks, with secret encouragement from the United States (Visani 2012, 192), Italy deployed police and troops in and around the republic to seal it off (Cruciani 2010, 269). Many observers feared civil war would break out and possibly drag all of Italy into the fray. Although not a shot was fired, epithets, recriminations, and passionate rhetoric were hurled across the political divide. The fact that almost all the protagonists were blood relatives no doubt tempered things. As explained by a leftist militiaman at the time: "It just wouldn't do for anyone to get hurt" (Hamblin 1957, 87). With defeat inevitable, an increasing number of leftist coalition members argued for surrender, while for their part the rightist coalition leaders were emboldened. Ultimately the leftist leaders, "for the good of the Fatherland," stood down (Cruciani 2010, 279). Italian police and carabinieri were officially deployed inside the republic under the supervision of their Italian commander, who assumed control of the state for a day until the new right-wing coalition was given power. Eventually, several of the leftists were convicted of crimes against the state but later essentially pardoned (Severini 1995, 224). Even today, the opinions of ordinary Sammarinese on the events of 1957 reflect their ideological leanings (Veenendaal 2014, 74).

Clearly as a reward for managing to take power, the Christian Democrat government was showered with Italian largesse. Italy's annual payment was increased and debts were forgiven. The United States provided grants and assistance and the United Kingdom finally offered reparations for its accidental bombardment of 1944. Armed with cash and international support, as well as low tax policies and banking secrecy, San Marino enjoyed a period of considerable economic growth during the next two decades. It returned to its tradition of pushing the envelope of what its treaties with Italy allowed by engaging in what was known as "triangulation" (Interview 2014b). This involved reselling Italian goods purchased duty-free to foreigners abroad at higher prices. The effect naturally was immediately deleterious to Italian manufacturers, but Rome looked away for the time being. In addition, the country became a tax haven and its banking secrecy laws attracted money from suspicious characters from across the globe. Since it readily accepted deposits in cash, Italians and others routinely traveled to the republic with bags of currency to avoid regulations at home. Banks also used passbooks, which could be transferred to just about anyone, with no records kept (Interview 2014b).

The result was a country whose economy grew at a healthy rate while Italy's stagnated. Meanwhile, the country grew increasingly confident of its status and privileges. As we will see, this was reflected in a more assertive foreign policy, including efforts to join a wide range of international organizations after having spent much of its history keeping its head low. To illustrate, San Marino began the application for League of Nations membership, but it failed to provide additional information when requested and quietly allowed the process to end (Geiger 2007, 157; Duursma 1996, 234). It also declined an invitation to join the Permanent Court of International Justice (Duursma 1996, 234–35). In its bilateral relations, this assertive policy led to efforts to negotiate yet another agreement with Italy, one that would more accurately reflect its status as a diplomatic equal (Bravo 2003, 289).

Looking back at the first century of the San Marino–Italy relationship, it appears that what began as a serendipitous partnership for the republic deteriorated into a difficult and abusive marriage. It is clear that the expectations of 1862 were not fulfilled for either party and that blame for the situation can be spread widely. San Marino clearly sought to rewrite the rules of its subordination to Italy by defying the rule of law—both customary and codified—with the result that Italy lost its patience and overreacted. Times were best when the two countries were governed by similar regimes, and they were at their worst when San Marino represented an ideological challenge to the authorities in Rome (secular and religious).

Throughout this period, San Marino continued to be extremely vulnerable—even more so with the advent of aerial warfare—and its growing wealth makes it increasingly attractive as a target (see table 4.1). With respect to the willingness of the country to enter into agreements with Italy, the picture is mixed. Clearly there was enthusiasm for the relationship and the specific provisions of the treaties in 1862 and again in 1939, but almost as soon as the ink was dry the attraction waned and the country sought more and more clever ways to skirt its obligations. Whether its commitment to the subsequent agreements between 1874 and 1939 and again between 1945 and 1960 was genuine and heartfelt is doubtful, but rather the country's leaders appear to have either signed under duress or with guile, or both. The low point clearly came in 1953 when San Marino authorities openly criticized Italy and the oppressive agreement they were compelled to sign; even international opinion seems to have concurred with the unfairness of the agreement. It is worth noting, however, that where the average Sammarinese was concerned, agreements adopted after 1906 had the benefit of greater legitimacy given the much wider political participation in the country as a result of democratic reforms undertaken that year.

The scope and salience of the agreements with Italy, while not creating an explicit military alliance, clearly were high as they covered the bulk of domestic and international affairs in the republic, especially as interpreted by Italy. This is not to say the scope and salience could not have been higher still, and as we will see in the next section there was room for expansion on both dimensions.

Regarding the structure of the agreements, there is a steady increase over time in the degree of precision and formality, driven mostly by a desire on the part of Italy to constrain its wayward child of a neighbor. At the same time, San Marino authorities were eager to see more precision, mostly in the form of money on the table and limits to Italy's powers, both of which were gradually secured. The process illustrates the point that as trust declined, precision increased, although note should be taken regarding the source of the pressure to increase the specificity of agreements.

All the treaties considered here have virtually the same provisions regarding interpretation and escape. Simply put, San Marino is given no explicit powers to influence the interpretation and implementation of the agreements (short of ratification itself). But each country has the right to allow the agreements to lapse after ten years or in six months after denunciation, both of which are fairly liberal provisions. Clearly San Marino—at least in 1862 and again in 1939—was willing to allow events to take their course with respect to interpretation, meaning that it must have known that Italy's wishes would predominate and presumably trusted that this would lead to acceptable outcomes. On the other hand, it reserved the right to protest and oppose Italy's interpretations, which it did repeatedly (usually to no effect). The escape clauses, however, show a certain degree of hedging on the part of the republic, a sign that it wanted to keep its options open.

It seems clear that San Marino's trust in Italy—strongest in 1862 and weakest in 1953—is directly informed by events and subject to adjustment. As explained by Captain Regent Amati in 1914, San Marino is ultimately driven by self-interest rather than some blind devotion to Rome or the expectations that its needs will be met by the Italian government. Instead, by word and deed the San Marino authorities are continually attempting to renegotiate the terms of the relationship to their advantage, resisting mightily when pressured by Italy to comply with its version of the deal.

San Marino's Relations with Italy and the European Community/Union Since 1971

The period since 1971 has been one of rapid maturation in Sammarinese foreign policy, driven mostly by a strong desire on the part of elites to bring the country into Europe and the world as a modern, diplomatically sophisticated state (Gatti 2003, 327). Politicians on both the right and the left were in agreement in this regard and shared a desire to facilitate growth in the service sector and build a tradition of governing under grand coalitions. The move was further aided by changes in the international system that took Cold War ideological struggles off the front burner (Clark 1980, 344).

In the late 1960s, San Marino approached Italy regarding revisions of the 1939 agreement with respect to the status of their respective diplomatic missions (Duursma 1996, 227–28). In 1968 these were raised to full ambassadorial rank, which was the beginning of a rapid expansion of San Marino's diplomatic visibility. It systematically increased the number of its embassies to fifteen by 2012 (but down to twelve in 2017), including a legation in Washington, DC, in 2007 (Bartmann 2012, 547, 550). San Marino also undertook to join regional and global institutions, reversing a policy of relative isolation, joining the Organization for Security and Cooperation in Europe as a founding member, followed by successful applications to the Council of Europe and the United Nations in 1988 and 1992, respectively (Duursma 1996, 243, 254). An important motivation for these actions was validation of sovereignty (Europa World 2015a). Italy had shown something less than enthusiasm for the moves; it tried to block Liechtenstein's membership in the Council of Europe in the 1970s out of fear that San Marino would be next (Bartmann 2012, 543–34). But when these bodies accepted San Marino as an equal, it was easier to work with individual governments. The statement by the Council of Europe's rapporteurs charged with assessing San Marino's legal status was especially gratifying. They concluded that its relations with Italy "cannot be defined as those of protectorate and protector. They are in fact based on equality between sovereign States; they contain nothing of the trusteeship implicit in the concept of a protectorate" (Council of Europe 1988, cited in Duursma 1996, 243). San Marino has been active in these bodies, taking its turn as chair of the Committee of Ministers of the Council of Europe in 2006–2007 and participating actively in the European Court of Human Rights since 1989 after it ratified the convention and incorporated it into its domestic law. Its commitment to the International Covenant on Civil and Political Rights has been questioned, however, since the implementing legislation clearly indicates that the treaty's status is subordinate to the constitution (Duursma 1996, 220).

As part of its push to assert its autonomy, San Marino renegotiated the 1939 treaty with respect to Italy's influence over its foreign policy. The result was the 1971 agreement that removed the "protective friendship" language and replaced it with the following:

> The relations between the Italian Republic and the Republic of San Marino will be inspired by feelings of perpetual friendship and good neighborliness. The Republic of San Marino reaffirms its neutrality and certifies that it will maintain the deepest friendship and widest cooperation with the Italian Republic in order to preserve its ancient freedom and independence. (Article 1, author's translation)

The implication is that Italy's duty to protect San Marino is diminished while the small republic's policy of neutrality obviates the need to bar its establishing alliances with third parties (Duursma 1996, 224).

Perhaps even more important, the 1971 treaty created a joint commission via an exchange of letters coincidental with the treaty negotiations (September 10). Made up of delegates from each country, the commission meets alternately in Rome and San Marino and is tasked with "examining . . . problems of common interest and proposing appropriate solutions" (Article 1, author's translation).

The next decades would show a dramatic shift in the Italy–San Marino relationship away from a tendency for both parties to push their rights to the extreme toward something approximating a partnership. Negotiations in a wide range of topics became an annual—almost monthly—occurrence, with the aim to clarify and codify as many questions as possible. In some cases, San Marino was able to extract additional resources from Italy, repeatedly increasing its share of the customs revenue and increasing its tobacco quota. In 1987 it scored a victory by obtaining Italy's approval for a jointly managed television station, ending its media silence (Interview 2014a; Duursma 1996, 231). In 1991 a currency treaty, while limiting San Marino's prerogatives with respect to minting and printing currency, extended new privileges to its banking sector (Duursma 1996, 232). Even the restrictions on currency issues were welcome as they established clear equivalence in the two countries' monies (Articles 2 and 3; Interview 2014a).

Looking at the San Marino–Italy treaty-making trends overall, while the two entered into sixty-five agreements between 1862 and 1970, another eighty-eight treaties and agreements were concluded between 1971 and 2014, going from an average of two treaties every three years to almost two each year (San Marino 2015). It is worth noting that the trend is accelerating, with two and a half agreements per year during the 2000s and three and a quarter per year in the 2010s. The topics being addressed have also shifted and multiplied. Between 1971 and 1999, twenty-four of the forty-three agreements addressed the long-standing issues of trade, coinage, and neighborliness, while since 2000, this was the case for only six of the forty-two. New topics include joint development cooperation (including a new regional airport and development zone) (fifteen out of forty-two), the environment (seven), and police collaboration (six). The agreements have also tended to be far more precise, although not necessarily longer. One of the most specific is a 2008 agreement regarding international adoptions that runs to nearly four thousand words with twenty-four articles. A 2014 agreement regarding joint policing of the regional development zone provides detailed street maps showing precisely the jurisdictions of each country's authorities. At any rate, because many agreements cover the same topic, they amount to lengthy agreements that leave little room for confusion or misinterpretation. They almost all provide for a ten-year renewable term and a six-month denunciation window; they are also covered by the joint commission.

While more will be said about recent developments regarding San Marino's compliance with tax and banking regulations, some of which severely strained the relationship, there is a sense on the part of many Sammarinese—especially the elite—that the relationship has been a positive one. The San Marino economy grew at roughly 6 percent per year during the 1990s, largely because of Italy's support and investment. Unemployment rates were insignificant, hovering around 2 percent (Europa World 2015c).

There is, as was mentioned, a great deal of overlap between the two countries' cultures (Interview 2014a; Interview 2014b). The small republic is clearly less besieged than during the earlier periods and does not fear that it will one day be absorbed into its larger neighbor (it is clear that it would do not so voluntarily, either [Venturini 2014]).

Historically, Italian authorities have tended to disregard San Marino until a crisis erupts. They sometimes have difficulty imagining life in the small republic. Events in the republic are routinely reported under "national news" in Roman newspapers (Interview 2014a). Relationships between San Marino and Italian authorities have grown cordial and even respectful; officials in Rome are quick to pick up when their San Marino counterpart calls (Interview 2014b). There is increasingly convincing evidence that Italy is taking San Marino's interests into account (Interview 2014b). Overall, at least until 2008, the relationship developed something approximating guarded trust; both sides believed their interests were protected in the detailed, explicit, and numerous agreements, and each began to develop a sense of mutual respect.

We will return to the San Marino–Italy relationship through the lens of events since 2008, but to understand them it is necessary to discuss San Marino's evolving relationship with the European Union and its predecessors. To begin, San Marino's trade and currency agreements with Italy inevitably brought it further into the continent's rule-making structures. As early as 1968, agreements with Italy brought San Marino inside Europe's customs territory, meaning it would have to account for many European standards and regulations in its production methods, content, and trade practices (Duursma 1996, 230). San Marino opened a mission in Brussels and initiated negotiations of a bilateral customs union with the European Economic Community in the mid-1980s, the first microstate to do so (Duursma 1996, 246). The talks became formal in 1986 and intensified during the 1990–91 period (Interview 2014b). European authorities were sympathetic to San Marino's intentions—and those of other microstates as well—and was even open to a formal association agreement early on (Duursma 1996, 253; Interview 2014a).

In 1991 San Marino and the European Economic Community signed a customs union agreement (EEC 1992b). In it, San Marino was formally included in the European customs zone and gained access to the European market, on certain conditions and with certain limitations. Tariffs were to be frozen, then harmonized over time in order to achieve genuine "national treatment" for San Marino's goods in the community and vice versa (Articles 2 and 6). San Marino accepted no fewer than seventy-eight European directives and decisions upon acceding to the agreement (EEC 1992a), meaning that many of its industrial production methods and administrative policies and procedures would have to be adjusted. Naturally, San Marino did not have direct decision-making authority within the EEC, but through the creation of a cooperation committee San Marino officials could participate in the interpretation and application of the agreement (Article 23). The committee not only provided for San Marino representation but also a San Marino veto since the committee may only act by consensus. The agreement also established a fairly sophisticated arbitration mechanism that protected San Marino from arbitrary EEC decisions (Article 24). That said, the EEC reserved the right to take action when violations are exposed (EEC 1992a, Article 5; European Union 2010, Article 5).

San Marino was able to include escape clauses and derogations on a number of issues, including especially exemption from the free movement of labor and free trade in services (Bartmann 2012, 544). Article 10 provided for broad derogations where public safety and morals, public policy, and public health are threatened, as well as the preservation of national treasures, gold and silver, and industrial intellectual property. The list was so long that EEC negotiators insisted on adding a caveat that they could not be used arbitrarily or to give Sammarinese companies an unfair advantage. The agreement was designed to last five years (renewable) and could be denounced with a six-month lag (Articles 26 and 27). San Marino failed to secure mutual recognition of degrees and titles and exemption from the EEC rules on product content (Duursma 1996, 247).

Overall, the deal was a significant step forward for San Marino, although it entailed risks. The country enhanced its diplomatic status considerably and positioned itself for increased economic growth and integration into Europe. Since the EEC also pledged to advocate for San Marino's interests when it negotiated with third countries (although not barring San Marino from communicating directly), its diplomatic capacity was suddenly expanded (Duursma 1996, 253–54). Once the follow-on agreement could be signed in 2010, yet another coordinating body was instituted, giving San Marino yet another opportunity to express its voice and influence future bilateral relations (European Union 2010, Article 2). On the other hand, since for ten years France stalled its approval of the cooperation agreement that was signed at the same time as the customs union, San Marino got a taste of European politics (European Union 2011a; Interview 2014a; the move was apparently in retaliation for San Marino's opposition to France's nuclear testing policies). It also obligated itself to much of the community's future policy changes, particularly with respect to the customs code (European Union 2010, Article 3).

San Marino joined the euro zone by means of an EU-sanctioned bilateral agreement with Italy in 1998 (Europa World 2015a). The agreement not only made the euro San Marino's official currency (Article 1), but it also allowed the country to mint its own euro coins with local emblems (Article 3). But once again, San Marino's move was blocked, this time by the Dutch. It would take a visit to The Hague and promises to support the appointment of a Dutch diplomat to a UN post before the agreement could be finalized (Interview 2014b).

While agreements on fiscal and banking policies will be discussed below, it is worth mentioning that San Marino has signed or incorporated a number of other EU policies and regulations, including the free movement of persons under the Schengen Agreement (European Union 2012a). It did not, however, adopt the EU's value-added tax procedures, with the result that "[c]ompanies from San Marino therefore encounter difficulties with the cost of import VAT. Both San Marino operators and purchasers operating on the EU market have to bear additional costs, which derive from the import VAT payment charged on trade with EU Member States."

(European Union 2012a) The country also encounters obstacles to exporting goods to EU member states because it cannot access or does not have the expertise to comply with the EU's technical requirements and legal documentation (European Union 2012a).

In order to address a wide range of such issues more efficiently than through a piecemeal approach, the two bodies have informally discussed a new status for San Marino. While the European Union favors a joint association agreement with Andorra, Monaco, and San Marino (European Union 2012b), San Marino has preferred to work independently, a strategy that is generally supported at home as a way to bring some stability and predictability to the relationship (Interview 2014b; Ciavatta 2014; Selva 2014). The result has been steady, albeit very slow, progress toward a bilateral association agreement that would elevate San Marino to the status of such prospective EU members as Turkey. As of January 2017, there were doubts they could reach the March 2017 target due to the need for EU negotiators to turn their focus on withdrawal talks with Great Britain (Monaco Life 2016). Delays have come primarily from the San Marino side as governments have become more unstable and staffing of ministries more intermittent since 2000 (Interview 2014b; La Tribuna 2014, 7). At one point, San Marino's delegation resigned in protest over the slow pace of negotiations (Ciavatta 2014). Even the people of San Marino seem to have some reservations; perhaps they are influenced by the ambivalence many Italians show toward the EU as well as the turmoil regarding banking and tax policy that will be discussed below (European Union 2012b). A referendum on the move was originally called for 2010 but then set aside as policy makers initiated formal talks. The referendum was finally held in October 2013, but it provided only ambiguous guidance. A slim majority of those voting favored formalizing deeper ties to the EU (the modality was left unclear in the wording of the question), but since only 43.4 percent of the electorate turned out, the number of those voting fell below the 35 percent threshold (of all eligible voters) to make the vote binding (Europa World 2015c). Opposition stemmed from older voters' concerns that deeper integration would erode Sammarinese identity and sovereignty and lead to an influx of foreign workers (Oddone 2014). The government took the vote as an endorsement of its pro-EU strategy and continued the negotiations. Ambivalent at first, Italy has also backed the move, as expressed in a 2014 historic visit by the country's president, Giorgio Napolitano (ANSA 2014). As he put it, "I hope that San Marino can consider the path toward the great European family a decisive priority." With that endorsement, the Council of the European Union formally initiated talks on an association agreement—with Andorra and Monaco as well as San Marino—to begin in early 2015 (RTT News 2014).

While the association agreement talks were being planned, San Marino was the target of considerable pressure from the EU, the Organization for Economic Cooperation and Development, and the government of Italy for its long-standing tax and banking practices. Italy estimated that it loses €120 billion each year to tax evasion, some of which (perhaps as much as €500 million) involves Italians moving funds into San Marino banks (*Guardian* 2013). In addition, concerns also have been raised about ties between Sammarinese officials and organized crime. Corruption was rampant during the 1990s, aided by domestic policies that were out of sync with international norms (Selva 2014). In 1986, charges of financial impropriety were leveled against senior socialist politicians, leading to the collapse of the government and early elections in 1988 (Europa World 2015). In 2009, Italian authorities investigated a series of tax evasion and money laundering cases that led to the arrest of several senior executives in San Marino's largest bank, the Cassa di Risparmio della Repubblica de San Marino (now run by a former diplomat familiar with international banking standards [Europa World 2015; Interview 2014b]). A probe was initiated in San Marino in 2012 to uncover Mafia ties to national politicians (Ciavatta 2014). In 2013 in Italy, several prominent Italians were caught in a tax evasion scheme that had been facilitated by the recently defunct San Marino Investimenti (SMI) group, leading to the arrest of several former executives (Europa World 2015). And in 2014 a former captain regent was arrested for money laundering (Oddone 2014).

Even before these scandals, the United States and major European powers were sending strong signals that policies that allow this type of conduct would no longer be tolerated. The OECD began the new strategy in 2000 by announcing that several "tax havens" (including Monaco, Liechtenstein, and Andorra as well as San Marino) would be placed on the organization's "blacklist" of noncooperating countries and subjected to pressure and possible sanctions until they took steps to increase tax rates and transparency (Europa World 2015). San Marino immediately indicated its willingness to comply and as a result of reforms passed by the legislature was placed on the "gray list" in 2002 and was instructed to undertake negotiations with the EU and a wide variety of developed countries.

Within a few years, San Marino—along with other "gray list" countries—concluded an agreement with the European Union on tax policy. It required the withholding tax rate on savings to rise to 15 percent, then 20 percent after three years and 35 percent after another three years, at which point there would be little incentive for international depositors to favor San Marino's banks over their own (European Union 2003, Article 7). As an inducement to comply, San Marino was permitted to keep one quarter of the tax income, passing the rest along to the country of residence of the depositor (Article 8). Information on accounts was to be shared upon request from the national's home country (Article 13), and San Marino authorities were expected to meet every three years with EU officials to assess progress (Article 15).

In San Marino's favor, the agreement established a remedy for double taxation (something the Social Democrats had promised during the 2002 campaign) and allowed for a one-year denunciation provision (Articles 10 and 17). Because the agreement was multilateral in nature, it only came into effect after three-fourths of participating non-EU states ratified it, and it could be dissolved if one-quarter of them withdrew (Article 16). The agreement, along with additional reforms and two dozen bilateral agreements, contributed to the OECD's decision to remove San Marino from the gray list in 2009.

Italy, for its part, put pressure on San Marino by holding up ratification of the 2002 double taxation agreement for nearly a decade in order to induce agreement on a tax transparency treaty of its own (Europa World 2015). The reason for the strategy had much to do with the recession of 2007–2008 and the fiscal and economic crisis this precipitated in Italy. As was mentioned, Italy believes that €120 billion—or roughly 12 percent of its annual revenue—is being lost to tax evasion. In 2006 Italian economic and finance minister Giulio Tremonti invited San Marino authorities to adopt stricter standards on information sharing, a move that was blocked by bankers in the small republic (Selva 2014). As conditions worsened, Tremonti announced that San Marino would be on Italy's "blacklist." In 2009, the government announced a once-only amnesty program for Italians with tax-delinquent accounts overseas, at which point some €600 million left San Marino's banks, roughly a third of total deposits (Europa World 2015). Italy carried out audits on Italian firms that did business in San Marino, which had a chilling effect on foreign direct investment (Interview 2014b).

The economy in San Marino began to sputter and unemployment rose to 7 percent, and it is easy to understand the source of the recriminations. Tremonti's name became anathema in the country and charges of hypocrisy and cruelty were leveled against Rome (Oddone 2014). "It's as if Italy wants to paint us as a country that doesn't want to cooperate. . . . The Italian position has become incomprehensible," said San Marino foreign secretary Antonella Mularoni (Bloomberg 2010). Antonio Macina, director of tourism, said, "We are a hard working people and we feel very hurt and offended by all this. It's the Italians coming here who are causing all the problems, not Sammarinesi going to Italy" (*Telegraph* 2009).[2]

Ultimately, the Italian strategy worked and San Marino adopted additional rules on bank transparency in 2008 (Europa World 2015). In addition, the government signed an agreement with the European Union in 2012 on banking regulations that was designed to bring San Marino into compliance with the full EU *acquis* on banking practices (European Union 2012b). While relatively brief at twelve articles, the treaty called for San Marino to implement a total of 104 rules and regulations in phases. Thirty-two rules must be implemented within one year, with the deadline for the others coming at either four or six years (Article 8, paragraph 1 and annex). It also required San Marino to put in place a Financial Action Task Force as mandated by the OECD (San Marino had been dragging its feet on this). Failure to comply would lead to restrictions on the amount of currency it would be permitted to mint (and the loss of seigniorage that goes with it) (Article 8, paragraph 3). Although a joint committee would allow San Marino a voice in the future, it would be only one of four actors to be represented (Italy, the EU Commission and the European Central Bank are the others [Article 11]). The European Court of Justice would receive and rule on any disputes, a provision that clearly did not favor San Marino (Article 12). The treaty could be denounced with one year's notice (Article 12).

After all these actions, Italy finally ratified the double taxation treaty in 2012 and removed San Marino from its blacklist in 2014. Praising Sammarinese authorities on the occasion of his state visit, Italian president Napolitano said, "Italo-San Marinese relations have begun to take on unprecedented intensity and weight also thanks to recent choices—not always easy, but certainly farsighted and courageous—taken by San Marino in the economic-financial sphere" (ANSA 2014).

The words gave some hope that future relations would improve. But the damage was already done. Unemployment topped 8 percent (Oddone 2014) and deposits were at half the pre-amnesty levels (Ciavatta 2014). The more stoic among San Marino's elite admitted culpability and recklessness in the country's past approach given their inherent vulnerability. Foreign secretary Antonella Mularoni said:

> It's been a very bad time for San Marino, but we are responsible for many of the problems we have encountered. Relations with Italy have been very, very tense. But we cannot afford to have a bad relationship. Italy can create problems for us because we are so small

and because we rely on them for so many things—even our water. (*Telegraph* 2009)

The country is working to reduce its public sector (which employs one out of six Sammarinese workers) and raise taxes to cut deficits, which will most likely serve to strengthen the country in the long term. There are limits, however, to what the public will tolerate. In 2014 two austerity measures were reversed by large majorities in two referenda (Europa World 2015) and national strikes have taken place. All this helps to explain the ambivalence noted earlier regarding San Marino attitudes toward the EU. On the one hand, officials in San Marino hold out hope that despite the distance—both physical and political—to Brussels, the country will get a fair hearing there. And it may mean Italy will be overseen and restrained by regional authorities far more effectively than by San Marino itself. On the other hand, where one's economy has been founded at least in part on spurning international norms, the adjustments are sure to be painful. As put by law professor Alvaro Selva, Sammarinese will have to learn to make money honestly (2014). It will likely require a generational shift in leadership, something that began with the 2012 election.

Returning to the measures of trust, San Marino continues to be highly vulnerable, and well aware of it. Its exploitability has increased from the previous period in that its relative wealth and its ability to attract foreign capital make it a target for other states. It was clear, for example, that Italians had moved much of their money into Swiss banks during the 1990s, but Tremonti chose to focus on San Marino instead (Selva 2014). San Marino was also targeted by other large European states after the financial crisis; it would no longer be ignored (see table 4.1).

For the most part there was high willingness to engage with Italy as defined in their treaty arrangements. San Marino clearly welcomed opportunities to collaborate with Italy on a wide range of issues, from economic development to environmental protection to police issues. But on at least two key questions—fiscal policy and banking—San Marino was compelled to agree. Given the centrality of these topics, it would be unreasonable to say that San Marino's free will was untrammeled. Where Europe is concerned, the same can be said, although one would have to say that it enjoyed a bit more free will since San Marino initiated and by and large set the pace for the negotiations. But since Italy, the EU, and the OECD were united in pressuring San Marino to accept regional agreements on fiscal and banking policy, once again it would be inappropriate to score this dimension as "high." Hence the equivocal "moderate" for both cases.

TABLE 4.1. Features of San Marino's Relationships with Neighboring States and Institutions

		Trustor-Trustee Relationship			Issues in Play		Structure of Agreements		
		Vulnerability	Exploitability	Voluntarism	Scope of Issues	Salience of Issues	Imprecision and Informality	Marginalization	Entrapment
1627–1861: Submission to France-Papal States		**HIGH**	Low	**HIGH**	MODERATE	MODERATE	**HIGH**	MODERATE	**HIGH**
1815–1861: Submission to Papal States		**HIGH**	Low	Low	MODERATE	MODERATE	**HIGH**	**HIGH**	**HIGH**
1862–1971: Submission to Italy		**HIGH**	MODERATE	**HIGH**	**HIGH**	**HIGH**	MODERATE	MODERATE	MODERATE
1971–2016: Submission to Italy & Regional Agencies (since 1991)	Italy	**HIGH**	**HIGH**	MODERATE	**HIGH**	HIGH	Low	MODERATE	MODERATE
	Regional Agencies	**HIGH**	**HIGH**	MODERATE	**HIGH**	MODERATE	Low	MODERATE	MODERATE

With respect to the scope and salience of the issues in play, it seems reasonable to say that for both Italy and the EU the range of issues is high. Both actors have addressed the gamut of questions relating to trade, finance, and fiscal policy and have engaged in cooperative arrangements across a wide range of ancillary questions. The scope of Italy's involvement is certainly broader than the EU's, but both cover a wide range of issues. With respect to their salience, what separates San Marino's agreements with Italy from those with the EU is security and police matters. These additions are offset by a distancing of Italy from guaranteeing San Marino's security, however, with the implication that the salience of the topics covered would fall on the low end of the "high" category. Because EU agreements do not address security, their salience falls within the "moderate" range.

Regarding the agreements, taken as a whole San Marino has entered into detailed and specific agreements with both the EU and Italy. Particularly when one adds the protocols, annexes, and multiple treaties dealing with the same topic, the agreements leave little margin for interpretation. This degree of precision seems to have originated primarily from the more powerful actors rather than from San Marino, particularly with respect to the contentious issues of fiscal and banking policy. The stakes were higher for the major powers given their need for tax revenue as well as their well-founded fears of organized criminal and terrorist activity and the opportunities availed by bank secrecy and excessively informal regulation. While San Marino would almost certainly have accepted more informal arrangements that gave it more interpretive latitude, its counterparts insisted on precision. This interpretation is reinforced by the fact that some of the EU language was reproduced in agreements with other states.

On paper, the agreements between San Marino and both Italy and the EU seem to provide it with considerably more rights with respect to interpretation and enforcement. In practice, however, some other considerations warrant labeling San Marino's marginalization as only "moderate" rather than "low." Where Italy is concerned, while the agreements seem to give San Marino considerable opportunities to influence the terms—see the joint commission emerging from the 1971 treaty, for example—in practice Italy engaged in diplomatic blackmail similar to what they had done during the previous period. In particular, its decision to delay ratification of a double taxation treaty for years and to sabotage the San Marino banking system with its tax amnesty program in order to secure concessions demonstrate that the small republic lacked real influence over the meaning of its agreements with Italy. Certainly, consultations have been meaningful where less salient issues are concerned—joint development projects and so forth—but this is cold comfort where the survival of the country's economy is at stake.

The EU has created collective decision-making bodies, to be sure, but ultimately the power to create and enforce are both located in Brussels. Even in the treaty language it is clear that San Marino's conduct will be closely monitored by Brussels, which will not hesitate to impose sanctions if it finds them warranted.

Finally, while all the agreements provide for fairly generous terms of denunciation or sunset provisions, in practical terms the commitments being made by San Marino are understood to be deep and enduring. Particularly where customs unions and free trade associations are concerned, withdraw is not a practical option. And it seems clear that San Marino does not intend to take advantage of the denunciation provisions, although one cannot ignore their availability. Hence the decision to say that in both cases San Marino's entrapment is "moderate."

Taking everything together and in context, one could say that San Marino is showing more evidence of trust in Italy than in the EU, although it trusts Italy less than in the previous period. In fact, it appears that San Marino's turn to the EU reflects its frustration and loss of faith in Italy. On the other hand, its relationship with the EU has yet to bear fruit and has been beset by significant challenges. At this point, San Marino authorities would be justified in thinking that no one is really looking out for the country and that its best strategy is to simply comply with expectations in the hope that it will eventually be granted greater latitude in the future. Perhaps its attitude toward the EU will change if its association agreement gives it genuine access to EU decision-making fora, or if in the future the EU is able to defend San Marino's interests and perhaps rein in an overly aggressive Italy.

Conclusions

Overall, San Marino has trusted its larger neighbors at various points in time and often found the result to be rewarding. The experience of the 1862–1947 period certainly confirmed its general sense that Italy could be a reliable and capable partner. Italy's overall laissez-faire approach suited the plucky (and sometimes renegade) republic well. But since 1947 San Marino, to cope with a less tolerant—even aggressive—Italy, has hedged, first by attempting to resist it, then by distancing itself from it, and finally by embracing multilateralism. The strategy has been only partially successful, and the people of San Marino have been left profoundly ambivalent about their future. The leadership is doubling down on the multilateral strategy, but the result is a growing gap between it and the rest of the people. While it comes nowhere near Luxembourg's experience, one has a sense that San Marino has felt betrayed, even though it is far from innocent. Other than a few very bad days in the summer of 1944, most of San Marino's pain has followed its own exploitation of its more powerful neighbors. So in a way it betrayed what little trust was placed in it, indicating that trust can be a two-way street, even among states.

FIVE

Monaco

The Limits of Hedging

Monaco has been dependent on a wide range of different European powers under a wide variety of arrangements, from annexation to formal and de facto independence. Unlike those in Luxembourg, these arrangements were almost always being renegotiated by the local lord, then the prince of Monaco—not always successfully, of course—culminating in a much clearer sense of national identity, at least for the few thousand Monegasque citizens of the principality. Unlike in Luxembourg, the presence of foreigners was never entirely welcomed by the masses and was a matter of serious concern. As long ago as 1910 the prince was accused of selling out the country to wealthy squatters. The uproar led to a new constitution that limited his powers (*New York Times* 1910). The prince has thenceforth had to play a two-level game to appease the locals while ensuring a steady flow of capital from wealthy foreigners.

Monaco also differs from Luxembourg in that it has never been free to chart its own foreign policy course. While it has enjoyed considerable domestic autonomy, its diplomacy is constrained by a requirement to never act against France's fundamental interests. Its diplomacy has been an appendage to that of France, and it has only been able to participate in international organizations once France's blessing was first secured. It did not join the United Nations until 1993, and the Council of Europe required considerable domestic and foreign policy reforms before admitting it in 2004. Since 1641—except for a period of dependency on the

Kingdom of Sardinia from 1815 to 1861—Monaco's destiny has been tied to that of France. In 2005 a 1918 treaty with France was finally revised to guarantee that the principality's sovereignty was "inviolable," something that had never been clear.

In order to establish the presence or absence of trust, it will be important to differentiate the degree of free will that was involved in Monaco's commitments to its various protectors over the years, both at inception and over the course of the relationships. In general, as we will see, Monaco's princes have generally entered into these arrangements with their eyes wide open, often taking the initiative. The people, on the other hand, had little say in the country's foreign relations until the 1960s and were often dissatisfied with what the prince had done. The convergence of public and princely preferences did not arise until the twenty-first century with the enactment of constitutional reforms and the ratification of a new treaty with France. Nonetheless, the case allows us to observe the interplay of dependence, protection, and autonomy, which in turn allows us to see the place of trust both at home and abroad.

Monaco's Dependencies Through 1918

The future rulers of Monaco—the Grimaldi family—were the losers of a power struggle between families in Genoa in the late twelfth century. One hundred years later, the Grimaldis seized the fortress at Monaco from the family that had earlier prevailed in Genoa and attempted to establish their control over the area (it would take until 1419 before this was resolved) (Duursma 1996, 262; International Business Publications 2009, 28). The family's domain included not just the present-day Monaco but also the much larger communes of Menton and Roquebrune to the east along the coast (roughly twenty times more area than Monaco alone).

From the beginning the Grimaldi princes entered into arrangements with various local sovereigns as well as with Spain and France, thereby ensuring their protection and the recognition of their sovereign rights, at least internal sovereignty (Grinda 2010, 11; International Business Publications 2009, 29). In 1542 a treaty with Spain would have made the principality a fiefdom, but the Grimaldis insisted on language that at least gave lip service to its sovereignty. A Spanish military unit was deployed in the territory and the Grimaldi's self-proclaimed title of "Prince" was formally recognized. However, Spanish domination proved oppressive and Prince Honoré II began as early as 1631 to sever ties in favor of France (Brégeon 1991,

129; Grinda 2010, 32). Sensing disloyalty, Spain reduced the prince's powers and increased its garrison in 1636, which only hastened Monaco's alliance with France. In October 1641, Honoré II conspired with his loyalists to outmaneuver the Spanish troops and compel their withdrawal, at which point French troops arrived to take their place (Delorme 1997, 106–7).

In September 1641 Prince Honoré II and King Louis XIII signed the Treaty of Péronne, establishing a permanent French garrison of five hundred troops in Monaco and assuring French military protection (Articles 1 and 10). The preamble to the treaty portrayed France's previous actions as nothing less than the "deliverance" of the principality and stated that the terms of the treaty were "proposed by the prince himself." There were certainly concessions made to Monaco's sovereignty throughout the treaty: the prince was to be the commander of the garrison, even in times of war (Articles 2 and 4), and the king would cover the costs (Article 6). Any new French officers had to be cleared by the prince (Article 8), and the prince's sovereignty was formally asserted (Articles 7 and 10).

On the surface the agreement appeared ideal for Monaco's interests in that it retained internal sovereignty while outsourcing its military defense to France. The treaty did not explicitly address Monaco's foreign policy although the language implied that Monaco could act unilaterally to use its French troops in defense of the principality. The treaty was "a perfect bilateral and consensual act. . . . It [was] more a treaty of friendly protection rather than a rigid modern protectorate." (Lisimachio 1983, cited in Brégeon 1991, 130, author's translation).

For 150 years this arrangement seemed to suit both parties, except for a brief period in the 1740s when French and Spanish troops (now allied) passed through and lingered in the principality en route to Italy over the prince's protests (Delorme 1997, 189). In the early years of the French Revolution, events moved quickly to alter the domestic and international affairs of the principality. In 1790 Monegasques demanded of the prince (Honoré III) the formation of local councils, to which he consented, only to reverse himself two years later. The revolutionary French regime seized properties of the prince (who, along with his recent predecessors, resided in Paris) in France in violation of the Treaty of Péronne (attempts were made to offer compensation later [see French Republic 1793c]). French troops moved through Monaco in mid-1792 and, with the support of local Jacobins, provoked an uprising that resulted in the overthrow of the monarchy (Brégeon 1991, 203). Local assemblies were created and a referendum (of dubious validity) was held, which supported annexation by France, an act that was confirmed by the National Assembly in Paris

(French Republic 1793a; French Republic 1793b). This would have spelled the end of the Grimaldis and the sovereignty of Monaco had it not been for Napoleon's defeats in 1814 and 1815. The initial peace talks in 1814 brought the Grimaldis back to the throne and the restoration of the status quo of January 1792 (including the provisions of the Treaty of Péronne), to local celebration (Delorme 1997, 255). French troops returned in July. But as punishment for the One Hundred Days campaign of Napoleon in 1815, the signers of the Treaty of Vienna took the Piedmont-Savoy-Nice region controlled by revolutionary France to form the kingdom of Sardinia, based in Turin (Article 85) and severed all ties between the principality and France. None of this was discussed with the prince or the people of Monaco at the time (Duursma 1996, 163). The arrival of Sardinian troops was met with a formal diplomatic protest to Turin (Delorme 1997, 260). In 1817 the king of Sardinia negotiated (read: imposed [Brégeon 1991, 219]) a treaty with Monaco in Turin that essentially duplicated the terms of the 1641 agreement, putting Sardinia in France's place. Half a battalion was deployed in Monaco under the same command structure as had been the case with France, and the same pledges of protection and recognition of sovereignty were offered. In addition, Monaco adopted Sardinia's currency and something approximating a customs union (Articles 5, 7, and 8). The areas of Menton and Roquebrune, however, were placed in a subordinate position and the citizens were required to swear fealty to Sardinia (Brégeon 1991, 218).

Life in Monaco during this period was challenging. The prince relied on oppressive taxes and state monopolies to rebuild the nation, thereby alienating citizens who might otherwise have joined him in opposition to the Sardinians, who were bent on restoring absolutist privileges. Tensions boiled over during the political upheavals of 1848 when Italians in Sardinia secured a new (temporary) constitution granting some civil rights, and the citizens of Menton and Roquebrune demanded the same of Charles III. Dissatisfied with the prince's minor concessions, they declared themselves "free cities" and voted for unification with Italy (Delorme 1997, 285). Charles III and those living in Monaco proper appealed to France while planning ways to suppress the rebellion. But when the crown in Turin recognized the status of the separatist cities and placed them under direct Sardinian administration, Charles III stood down and eventually accepted the new situation, all the while asserting his sovereign rights (Delorme 1997, 285). During the Risorgimento, Count Cavour and King Victor Emmanuel II of Sardinia developed close ties to Emperor Napoleon III of France, fighting mostly in concert with him to bring about Italian reunification. Once Austria had been defeated and the peninsula mostly unified, and as part of their arrangement, France was awarded the Italian regions it had controlled during the Revolution in 1860 through the Treaty of Turin and ties between France and Monaco were restored to their 1814 status (Duursma 1996, 263). Monegasques celebrated the departure of the Italian troops (Delorme 1997, 289). Menton and Roquebrune, for their part, were unified with France and in 1861 Charles III renounced all claims to them in a treaty with France signed on February 2 (Article 1). As a generous palliative, the prince was compensated for lost lands with a four-million-franc indemnity (Article 2). A joint commission was set up to determine the status of various personal properties of the prince in Menton and Roquebrune (Article 3). Even today, Monegasques who wish it are permitted to retain their citizenship even if living outside the principality's new boundaries (Article 7).

Finally, the two states agreed to a customs union (Article 6). The customs union was spelled out in an 1865 treaty (which also addresses a range of issues pertaining to neighborhood relations). It eliminated all duties for overland transactions (Article 1), with some French excise taxes applicable in Monaco (Article 6). Monaco's customs agencies were to be filled entirely by French officials, answerable to France (Articles 11 and 12). Unlike previous agreements, this one was to last five years (renewable without denunciations) and could be denounced by either party (effective one year later) (Article 23). The prince was permitted to enter into treaty relationships with other states so long as said treaties did not undermine the 1865 agreement (Article 2).

This arrangement clearly did more than merely subcontract security, and the new relationship with France starting in 1861 had the ring of a protectorate, albeit mostly a voluntary one. A secret arrangement concluded in 1861 further committed the prince to enter into no parallel dependency with any other state (Council of Europe 2004, para. 14). But with the French approval of a casino in 1866 and the completion of a rail line in 1868, Monaco's new gaming and tourism industry exploded. As early as 1869 the prince could afford to eliminate the income tax thanks to the flood of foreign money. The prince, thanks to a generous contract with his French partners, profited handsomely from the casino's success, and before long the gap between rich and poor had grown stark. By the turn of the century the bulk of the local population was Italian, and they and the Monegasques were barred from gambling or even working in the casinos (*New York Times* 1910). Meanwhile the prince received well over one million dollars a year, and the ultra-rich paraded through the streets, flaunting their wealth and questionable morals (Somerset Maugham described Monaco as a "sunny place for shady people" [Walsh 2013]). In 1910 mobs storm the princely palace, demanding limits on his authority. While deliberating how much to concede, the foreigners who managed the casino pointed out that since they were the de facto rulers of the country, the prince has no authority to alter the government (*New York Times* 1910)! Ultimately, to save his monarchy, the prince agreed to a constitution that creates a National Council, which shares some legislative powers.

The French government allowed these changes to occur. But as World War I was coming to an end, it became clear that the current prince might not be able to pass the throne along to a francophone heir, and that the alternative would be for the crown to pass to a German national, Paris took steps to ensure French interests would be guaranteed, in writing. We will turn to this after making an assessment of what has come so far.

Returning to our central questions regarding the evidence of trust in Monaco's subservient relationships, table 5.1 summarizes the key findings. To begin, although the geographical position of Monaco—particularly the rump principality post-1861—situated as it is in a natural harbor surrounded by cliffs and promontories, give it some tactical advantages over invaders, the fact remains that the country is small and vulnerable to attack by land and sea and is particularly vulnerable to a siege. Until the 1860s the country offered little to a potential invader, which—as has been the case with other countries discussed in this book—worked to its advantage. After the country's economy began to explode with the growth of gaming and tourism along with increasingly sophisticated banking, Monaco became a prize worth taking. It is perhaps not surprising that France's relationship with the principality took a turn toward the imperious.

While it is always difficult to ascertain the degree to which the subjects of a monarch approve of his or her foreign policy, there are strong indications that not only did successive princes of Monaco approve of the relationship with France from 1641 to 1815, but the people did as well. They welcomed the French even as they helped to oust the Spanish in 1640. When given the opportunity (albeit at bayonet point) to vote for inclusion in the newly founded French Republic, the former subjects of the prince supported the move. And at least those living in Monaco proper in 1848 were willing to publicly declare their desire to associate again with France despite being under Sardinian authority (there are even indications that those in Menton and Roquebrune were interested in annexation by France [Duursma 1996, 263]). For his part, the prince seems to have been eager for close ties to France after 1641 and found his subordination to the Italians between 1815 and 1861 both involuntary and generally unwelcome, although he seems to have tried to make the best of it in signing the 1817 treaty. But if there was any doubt that the Italians did not have his interests at heart, it was demonstrated when they endorsed the rebellions of 1848. The use of the term "moderate" to describe the degree of voluntarism in Monaco's dependent relations between 1641 and 1861 refers to these mixed feelings on the part of the prince and the people across time. But to be more precise, the support for the arrangements of 1641 to 1815 was high, while the support for the 1815–1861 situation was somewhere between low and moderate.

As to the degree of support on the part of the prince and his people for the 1861–1918 relationship with France, I describe this as "moderate" because there was a growing split between the two. Even the prince was naturally distressed to find his realm diminished by nine-tenths, but he made the best of it and ultimately established close ties with the French leadership and a wide range of French entrepreneurs and midlevel officials who occupied virtually all the positions of economic and even political power in the principality. The people, for their part, were increasingly alienated and marginalized and came to view relations with France as mostly harmful.

The scope of the agreements with France and Sardinia until 1865 were generally limited to questions of security and ancillary topics. Informal arrangements governed economic and neighborliness for the most part. On the other hand, because the survival of the principality was at stake (as demonstrated in 1848), there were few issues that were more salient. After 1861, France and Monaco began to codify their relationship in areas other than security matters. The 1865 customs union in particular was an effort on France's part to have Monaco internalize much of French law and practice. Meanwhile, since the core of the relationship was still a guarantee of protection against invasion, the agreements remained highly salient throughout the period from 1641 to 1918.

Regarding the structure and form of the various agreements, until the customs agreement they were all brief, vague, and open-ended. The 1641 and 1817 agreements with France and Sardinia, respectively, were essentially identical and took the form of royal edict, consented to explicitly by the prince of Monaco. They each referred to the sovereignty of the prince but did not specify what this means, viz. it was not clear where the boundaries lay. They asserted that the prince may command the foreign troops, but they were unclear on what would happen were both the principality and the respective kingdoms to fight against a common enemy; would the Monaco-based detachment fall under the general command of the larger power? And, obviously, the question of how to treat a rebellion and declaration of independence by subjects of the prince was unaddressed even though this proved to be of central importance. Much was left for future negotiation and interpretation, both of which favored a unilateral approach by the great power.

After 1861 the agreements between France and Monaco were far more lengthy and precise and left less room for interpretation. At twenty-four articles, the customs agreement had a very modern feel to it, and was among the more detailed agreements of its type for its time. It much more resembled the Belgium-Luxembourg and Switzerland-Liechtenstein treaties of the 1920s than the typical nineteenth-century contract. It specified which French duties and excise taxes would be applied in the principality, for example, as well as how the earnings would be shared. But the agreement still left open how it might be adjusted to include new goods or remove items from the list, for example.

With regard to the questions of marginalization and entrapment of Monaco, all the pre-1861 agreements were formulated as unilateral commitments by the French and Sardinian monarchs. We know that Monaco's princes were involved in the talks, but there is little evidence of even-handed give-and-take (especially where the 1817 agreement is concerned, which was framed as an act to implement the Treaty of Vienna). Monaco was clearly cast as the petitioner whose fate was in another's hands. The treaties were designed to be permanent and had no provisions for denunciation. Only the 1865 customs agreement provided for denunciation and an automatic lapsing of the treaty (with the option of extension).

It seems clear that Monaco's leadership and for the most part its people entered into these agreements as an act of faith in their would-be protector. There is little hedging, meaning that should the great power withdraw its commitments, Monaco would have no recourse other than to begin anew the search for another protector. While it would be unreasonable to say that Monaco was a mere protectorate—an extension of a great power's global policy—its external sovereignty was thin indeed. The first sign of Monaco taking steps to protect itself from great power exploitation came in the 1865 customs agreement, but even then the likelihood of Monaco denouncing the treaty and going it alone was extremely low. As we saw, the trust invested by Monaco in France from 1641 to 1815 ultimately left it unprotected and vulnerable to conquest by a rival power. And as we will see, France eventually abused its privileges during the twentieth century, again demonstrating to the Monegasques that trust is a risky policy.

Monaco's Relationship with France from 1918 to 2005

Monaco remained neutral during World War I, as it had done since the 1740s. But members of the royal family served in the French military, and the principality's loyalty to French aims was unquestioned. During this period, the House of Grimaldi encountered a number of serious questions regarding succession to the throne. Simply put, Albert I was a bachelor and his only children were born out of wedlock, which meant that according to existing law he would not be able to pass the throne to them. The next strongest claim was from a German cousin, an officer in Germany's recently defeated military no less. The interests of France and the prince coincided perfectly in that neither wanted the throne to pass into German hands. Laws at home were altered to allow an adopted child to inherit the throne, and France and Monaco negotiated a treaty that would allow for the country to become an independent territory within France in the event that there was no heir to the throne who was either Monegasque or French (Articles 2 and 3 of 1918 treaty). Since the treaty also provides for French approval of each new prince (or regent), it might have even been possible for France to have caused such a vacancy by simply refusing to accept a new sovereign (Duursma 1996, 282).

The 1918 treaty continues the tradition of the 1641 protective agreement in that Monaco was to be protected as though it were part of French territory and its sovereignty and independence guaranteed (Article 1). Future occupation of the territory "in case of emergency" was implicitly granted in advance by the prince (although he must be asked for his assent after the fact [Article 4]). In a departure from the earlier agreements, Monaco's loyalty, while previously implied, was codified. Article 1 states, "For its part the government of His Serene Highness the Prince of Monaco undertakes to exercise its rights of sovereignty in perfect conformity to France's political, military and economic interests" (author's translation). In Article 2, it was made clear that Monaco is to consult France regarding any foreign policy initiatives. Needless to say this duty was not reciprocal. France also promised to help Monaco secure access to international organizations, although it was not clear that France would facilitate Monaco's outright membership or merely allow it to share France's seat at the table (Article 5). In a follow-up letter, the question was clarified, in that Monaco could have participated in conferences and organizations that did not deal with military, political, or economic matters (leaving "scientific, moral or social issues") (Monaco 1918). This probably meant that Monaco would have been barred from participating in organizations of which France was not a member (Duursma 1996, 278).

The treaty included only seven relatively brief articles and provided for no termination or denunciation, although the interpretation of Article 1 as articulated in subsequent diplomatic letters seemed to imply an escape clause: "The purpose of the provisions of the second paragraph of article 1 is to define in a general manner the obligations of reciprocity incumbent upon the Prince *in return for the friendly support of France*, without prejudice to the sovereignty and independence of His Serene Highness" (Monaco 1918, translated by League of Nations staff, emphasis added). As put by Duursma:

> This then implies that Monaco's obligations towards France are only invocable if in turn France lends its friendly support. Moreover, the exercise of Monaco's sovereign rights has to be in perfect conformity with the French political, military, naval and economic interests only in so far as it does not prejudice the Principality's independence. (1996, 275–76)

It was largely left to France, however, to determine what constituted its core interests and at what point Monaco was failing to protect them. Although tolerant of the arrangement with France, in later years princes of Monaco came to resent the intrusions on sovereign questions and welcomed the chance in 2005 to jettison the whole of it.

France continued to press Monaco for additional concessions over the following decades. Frustrated by the ability of French residents to hide assets in Monaco, in 1925 Paris persuaded Monaco to sign an agreement on "fiscal frauds," which opened up the otherwise secretive Monegasque financial sector by requiring accounts and safe deposit boxes to be unsealed in the event of the holder's death (Article 1) as well as requiring Monaco to provide the French government with a list of assets in Monaco owned by nationals of France or by nationals of any other country residing in France (Article 2). The customs agreements of the nineteenth century were clarified and expanded to allow more direct French control of the collection and distribution of customs earnings. More importantly, in 1930,

France and Monaco signed a sort of joint constitution named the Franco-Monegasque Convention of 28 July. In it the two parties agreed that in addition to French troops being deployed in the principality, French officials—seconded from the Ministry of Foreign Affairs for the most part—would occupy senior positions in the Monegasque government. Specifically, the minister of state (the functional equivalent of the prime minister) and the government counsellor for the interior (over justice and home affairs) would be French officials, serving for five years (although their selection required the prince's approval) (Article 4). This meant that a French official would have a veto over legislation since he or she could decide whether to move it forward at the prince's request. It also gave the French official a veto over constitutional amendments and reforms. In an analysis of Monaco's sovereignty undertaken in 1996 while the treaty was still in effect, Jorri Duursma came to the conclusion that these provisions did not negate the country's sovereign status, although much depends on the degree of interference by France in the work of its seconded officials. Since they are removed from the French administrative hierarchy upon assuming the new role (they are usually end-of-career officials) and swear to uphold the interests of Monaco and its prince, she concludes that the provisions are not excessively intrusive, although they violate the International Convention on Civil and Political Rights (Duursma 1996, 271, 310–13). As we will see, the Council of Europe reached the opposite conclusion. While in some ways France was merely helping out a small country that lacked the manpower to fill all its posts (even today some Monegasque officials point out that there are few locals who are able and willing to serve in these lofty positions [Allavena 2013]), the clear intent was to ensure that Monaco would never be able to violate the terms of the 1918 treaty and that France's interests would be guaranteed.

During the Second World War, Monaco remained formally neutral but was nonetheless occupied by Italy, then Germany, and then France in successive waves (Geiger 2007). It was even bombed in the waning months of the war. But it emerged relatively healthy, as did most of southern France, and was able to return to the business of gathering in the wealth of Europe to its casinos and banks. The reign of Prince Rainier III is the stuff of Hollywood; literally, given his marriage to actress Grace Kelly in 1956 and his enthusiastic transformation of the principality into a cacophony of high rises and hotels. Monaco became an engine of growth for neighboring French towns and cities, but it was seen as a drain on the country's resources overall and an easy place for criminals and dictators to hide and launder their money. An agreement in 1950 (Monaco 1953) between

France and Monaco was designed to further increase information sharing about foreign assets in the principality and required Monaco to collect taxes on assets owned by French citizens (Article 1). This did little to prevent either money laundering or tax evasion. Charles de Gaulle decided enough was enough in 1958 and began pressing the prince for a revision of Monegasque fiscal and banking law to prevent capital flight. He claimed that Monaco's part in allowing and even encouraging a drain on French resources constituted a breach of Article 1 of the 1918 treaty (Duursma 1996, 276). The prince disagreed and refused to cooperate. For the next four years he was subjected to a series of aggressive actions and threats from Paris (as put by Allavena, deGaulle "showed his teeth" [2013]). To begin, frontier customs posts were erected to put trade with the principality entirely in French hands. France boycotted Monaco exports of pharmaceutical goods (Duursma 1996, 277). When this failed, de Gaulle threatened to cut off gas, electricity, and even water (Weber 2007, 68). Rainier III finally capitulated and agreed to a new set of fundamental treaties on taxes, duties, and good neighborliness (Monaco 1963a, Monaco 1963b, Monaco 1963c). The most onerous was the tax agreement, which required Monaco to impose French tax rates on companies operating in Monaco with at least 25 percent of their operations outside of the principality (Monaco 1963a, Articles 1 and 2). Specifically, the corporate tax rate began at 15 percent in 1964, then increased in 5 percent increments each year until it reached a 40 percent rate (Article 5). French income taxes would also be assessed in Monaco on French citizens, unless they could show that they lived there continuously since 1957 (Article 7). The agreement also provided for additional information sharing, although it maintained previous arrangements to prevent double taxation. And the agreement could be denounced, taking effect six months later (Article 26), although Monaco could only do so at its peril, as was made clear by France's previous actions. As put by Duursma, "Thus, Monaco was compelled to conclude conventions which led to the introduction of certain taxes in its territory without it in fact wanting this taxation" (1996, 278). The customs agreement (Monaco 1963c) continued earlier commitments to make Monaco part of France's economy, but increased the republic's control by requiring that all customs agents in Monaco be French citizens, appointed by Paris, with the prince's approval (Article 8). These were to administer French custom law, which was to be internalized by Monaco (Article 1 of protocol; Marshall 1993, 57). The treaty created a joint commission to monitor and interpret the treaty and a six-month denunciation provision (Articles 12 and 13). It also provided a formula for sharing the revenues, although France over time ignored economic changes that would have warranted an increase in Monaco's share (Marshall 1993, 59; Monaco 1972).

Finally, the neighborhood agreement (Monaco 1963c) reiterated some provisions of earlier treaties, including the free movement of citizens of each country and a prohibition against Monaco's harboring French deserters or exiles (Articles 1, 12 and 13); these last two provisions were perhaps needlessly reciprocated. This agreement also provided for a six-month denunciation (Article 24).

As the century came to a close, France again applied pressure on Monaco to modernize and harmonize its tax and banking systems, although this time it was joined by the rest of Europe and the Organization for Economic Cooperation and Development (OECD). In the wake of scandals and rumors of large-scale money laundering, Monaco was on the defensive and gradually conceded the need for financial reform. French police were given increased powers, beginning in 1963 with provisions that allowed them to pursue suspects into Monaco without notification (Monaco 1963c, Article 11). France was also empowered to grant and deny visas to foreigners seeking a long-term stay in Monaco (Monaco 2000a, Articles 1–3) and securing information from the principality about the identities, addresses, and activities of foreigners residing in Monaco (so long as they are citizens of a country "tied" to France) (Monaco 2000b, Articles 4 and 10).

In 2000, the OECD announced that Monaco would join several other European microstates as uncooperative with respect to fighting fraud and money laundering (Europa World 2015b). At about the same time, France exercised its prerogatives under the 1930 treaty and refused to extend the term of a Frenchman whom it considered insufficiently aggressive in prosecuting fraud. The combined pressure resulted in legislative reforms and a new agreement with France (Monaco 2001) that allowed Monegasque financial institutions to override the principality's secrecy laws when cooperating with France in investigations of money laundering.

In 1998, following its successful United Nations membership bid, Monaco applied to join the Council of Europe. It immediately encountered obstacles as members raised questions about its level of genuine democracy and its full sovereignty (Grinda 2010, 52). A fact-finding team of jurists from the European Court of Human Rights was dispatched to assess the situation, in much the same way the council had done in eastern Europe during the previous decade. While some in Monaco resented this sort of second-class treatment (Allavena 2013), officials worked closely with the visitors. They returned and issued a report detailing the good and the bad of Monaco's political situation. A few years later, following reform efforts in Monaco and new negotiations between Monaco and France, the group issued its final recommendation to the council, returning frequently to the content of the report (Council of Europe 2004). As was expected, the report raised concerns about Monaco's first-past-the-post electoral system, which had consistently returned supermajorities and even one-party legislatures over the years (Council of Europe 2004, part III). The report also called for a lowering of the voting age and increased efforts to involve women in politics. Finally, it called for strengthening the powers of the legislature (Council of Europe 2004, part III). On the international front, it challenged directly the notion that a state could be fully sovereign when its key political leaders are required to be foreigners assigned and employed by a foreign government. Given the important legislative and executive functions of these officials, it was hard to understand how this could be compatible with full internal sovereignty (Council of Europe 2004, part VII). As put by the report: "the 1930 treaty limited the Prince's power freely to appoint the Minister of State and several other senior officials, whatever their nationality, and that this raised doubts about Monaco's internal sovereignty in the conduct of affairs of state and the administration of justice" (Council of Europe 2004, sec. 2, para. 60). Perhaps most problematic was the provision in the 1918 treaty regarding Monaco's possible annexation, which was entirely unacceptable and would have to be changed prior to admission, or at least be well on the way (Bartmann 2012, 544). As we will see, the response to these questions and concerns opened a new chapter in Monaco's domestic and foreign affairs.

At this juncture, an assessment can be made regarding the place of trust in Franco-Monegasque relations between 1918 and 2002 (See table 5.1). To begin, Monaco was still vulnerable and, as we saw at the end of the previous period, exploitable. In fact, during this period Monaco acquired one of the highest per capita incomes in the world. While the Monegasques themselves were a small minority in the territory (roughly one-fifth during most of the period), they were able to secure important privileges and benefits that dramatically increased their influence and security, except where senior government posts were concerned. Tight naturalization laws helped strengthen and perpetuate these privileges, creating increasing resentment among ordinary French residents (that is to say, not those in power in government) who not only could not practice law, medicine, or any number of professions, but had to pay French taxes as though they were in Nice. Politics within Monaco increasingly shifted to efforts to protect these hard-won benefits—including the wealth stemming from gaming and banking—

while preventing France and the French from undercutting them. The struggle was mostly unsuccessful.

France repeatedly imposed agreements on Monaco that belied its guarantees of sovereignty. Certainly one could not say that the republic has invaded, occupied, or annexed the principality, but it is clear that Monaco was less than free to enter into these new agreements, beginning with the 1918 treaty and culminating in the tax and banking agreements coming at the end of the century. Even the Council of Europe seemed to feel some pity for Monaco.

The agreements with France seem to cover an ever-widening array of topics while still addressing the core issues of security and economics. Monaco adopted more and more French rules and regulations over the twentieth century, to the point that it was almost an extension of the Palais de l'Élysée, like any French department. Its fiscal and financial policies, police and court systems, trade policies, and even its insurance industry were all governed by French law to a large degree. Its foreign policy was still constrained by a myriad of agreements, even more so than during the 1861–1918 period. The one area where France exercised less control was over Monaco's participation in international organizations. Its inclusion in the United Nations was the culmination of a long string of successes and failure in this regard. And ultimately, it would be an international organization—the Council of Europe—that would have the most dramatic effect on the reassertion of Monaco's sovereignty during the twenty-first century.

With respect to the structure and terms of the agreements, we have seen that for the most part these were brief and general, although made more precise over time through the means of exchanges of letters and follow-up agreements. Thus the 1918 treaty was clarified over time, along with the 1865 customs agreement and the 1930 pseudo-constitution. As these new arrangements were drafted, Monaco's rights were sometimes lost but often strengthened with the addition of termination and especially denunciation clauses. In addition, some new consultative bodies were formed that gave Monaco the opportunity to consult on a more equal basis with its much larger neighbor. Of course, there is nothing that even remotely resembles the Luxembourg-Belgium joint committees or even the Liechtenstein-Switzerland institutions of the same period. But it appears that incremental change was happening. Had I opted for an artificially precise measure of these last three dimensions, on a scale of 1 to 10, for instance, the informality, marginalization, and entrapment scores could be said to have shifted from 6 to 4, still within the "moderate" range but tending toward the "low."

The foundation of the Franco-Monegasque relationship seems to have become unmoored during the period under consideration in comparison to the previous period, especially compared to the 1861–1918 era. Increasingly, the prince was pressured—nearly forced—to accept strict agreements on issues over which he had previously had sovereign control. His ability to resist French pressures appeared extremely limited. But he managed—increasingly—to insert clauses in the arrangements that minimally protected his interests (beyond that boilerplate and increasingly insincere pledges to guarantee the prince's sovereignty). As mentioned, more and more agreements came with escape clauses and even some national prerogatives were curtailed. The lower level of voluntarism combined with increasing levels of hedging indicate an overall loss of trust on the part of Monaco vis-à-vis its larger neighbor. It would be wrong to say that trust was absent, but it had clearly diminished.

Monaco-French Relations and Monaco-Europe Relations Since 2002

Returning to the Monaco application to the Council of Europe, what is perhaps most remarkable is that the principality immediately undertook far-reaching reforms in response to the concerns raised. The voting age was lowered to eighteen, a mixed voting system was introduced to increase the ability of minority parties to secure seats (which may have also facilitated the electoral success of the opposition party in 2013 for the first time), and other actions were taken that prompted the council's Parliamentary Assembly committee to report:

> Since they first lodged Monaco's candidature with the Council of Europe, the country's authorities have not ceased to co-operate with the Parliamentary Assembly. They have remained in permanent contact with its rapporteurs and in a relatively short space of time have instituted a vast programme of constitutional and legal reforms to bring the country's laws and institutions into line with Council standards. (Council of Europe 2004, paragraph 69)

The council granted membership with some reservations in that Monaco had not yet signed a number of European human rights and social agreements, among other things. As of early 2015, Monaco had ratified the European Torture Convention and signed (but did not ratify) the European

Social Charter and its Protocols, as requested by the council. It has ratified the Convention for the Protection of Human Rights and Fundamental and Protocols 4, 6, 7, 13, and 15, but had not ratified Protocol 1 and had not signed Protocol 12 on the grounds that it could interfere with rights to discriminate on the basis of nationality with respect to housing (Council of Europe 2004, app. 6). The reservation attached to the Human Rights Convention ratification states the view that the Constitution of Monaco takes precedence over it, flowing as it does from the authority of the sovereign prince, "who is its source" (Council of Europe 2015). Monaco further pointed out that under the Constitution "the person of the Prince is inviolable" and that offenses against the prince are punishable by at least six months' imprisonment. Finally, the principality reserved the right to discriminate in public hiring on the basis of nationality. Clearly Monaco is aware of its indigenous institutions and is eager to put limits on the powers of international institutions. This said, Monaco has been taken to the Strasbourg court several times and has also lost a number of cases—mostly related to due process rights of accused persons—and has paid compensation to individuals (Caselaw 2011). On the other hand, Princess Caroline in 2004 won a case regarding whether publishing photos taken of her in public places violated her privacy (it did [Out-law 2004]). Monaco has dragged its feet with respect to increasing the powers of the legislature, however, in that it still may not initiate legislation despite calls from the council (Freedom House 2014).

More challenging was the council's call for France and Monaco to renegotiate the 1918 and 1930 treaties to increase the principality's internal and external sovereignty. Negotiations on the topic lasted three years and culminated with a new fundamental treaty in 2002 and a treaty on administrative cooperation in 2005. At eight articles and 650 words, the 2002 treaty is brief and direct, framed in the context of the United Nations Charter and fundamental international law. It repeats pledges of French protection and bars Monaco from acting against France's "fundamental interests . . . in the areas of politics, economics, security and defense" (Monaco 2006a, Article 1, author's translation). It also reiterated the right of France to deploy troops in emergencies, although the term "emergency" is limited to cases in which the survival and functioning of the state are in dire jeopardy (Article 4). Most important, the 2002 agreement ended France's right to annex Monaco in the event of a succession crisis. Questions of succession are left entirely to the Monegasques, although France is to be informed of a change of ruler (Article 3). Finally, the two states agreed to interact with each other at the level of ambassadorial representation and to conduct regular consultations, and the treaty created a joint commission to facilitate this (Articles 5 and 7). The treaty is open to revision by mutual consent, although no explicit termination or denunciation provisions are mentioned (Article 8).

The 2005 convention, which superseded the 1930 treaty and also posted a mere eight articles, addresses the issue of French officials being seconded to senior posts in Monaco by declaring that all government officers are to be Monegasques unless the prince chooses otherwise, in which case French officials may be appointed (Articles 5 and 6). Further, Monaco is allowed to discriminate in favor of Monegasques for all government appointments, although France permits them to compete for positions in the French administration (Article 3 and 4). Finally, and important for this study, Article 1 articulated a way for this and all Franco-Monegasques treaties then in effect to be denounced or terminated:

> The Parties conclude agreements, conventions or texts of some other nature in all areas in which they judge it necessary to so do with the aim of guaranteeing their shared community, as recalled in the preamble to the October 24, 2002 Treaty. Conventions currently in force will remain so unless the two governments decide otherwise. (Author's translation)

While reiterating a common provision of customary law, this is a rare codified assertion that implies that Monaco will not be compelled to endure treaties that have grown intolerable. Further, it emphasizes the requirement of consensus in dealing with future difficulties.

Taken together, the agreements demonstrate a maturation of the relationship. As put by Grinda, the negotiation was driven by and satisfied "the necessity of bringing this [1918] agreement up to date and of adapting its content and form to the new principles of public international law, notably to [*sic*] sovereign equality between the States. . . . Henceforth, these contacts [between France and Monaco] can only take place by close dialogue between two partners confident in each other and respectful of their reciprocal fundamental interests" (Grinda 2010, 43).

That the prince welcomed the new agreements is evident, but it is also worth noting that these would not have come about without the instigation of the Council of Europe. The public invitation to France to reconsider the terms of its 1918 and 1930 treaties came close to "naming and shaming" in that the council made it clear that France was impeding Monaco's ability to join the organization. While the conclusion of new agreements was not a prerequisite for Monaco's membership, evidence that the negotiations were well under way was. For perhaps the first time in its history, Monaco benefited from intervention on its behalf by Europe as a whole. This signaled a shift in Monaco's overall approach to European institutions, as we will see.

Before moving on to discuss Monaco's relations with Europe, it is important to note how these new agreements with France affected day-to-day relations. In fact, there were fewer changes than one might have expected. France opened an embassy in Monaco in 2002 (Bartmann 2012, 546). It also altered the 1963 fiscal agreement in 2003 to allow Monaco control over tax collection, still according to French law and schedules. The share of TVA revenue was increased to one-sixth of the total (Monaco 2006b, Articles II (3) and III (2)). On the other hand, French wealth taxes would be collected on French citizens residing in Monaco according to a 2003 amendment to Article 7, and smaller firms that have at least 25 percent of their activities outside of Monaco were subject to French tax levels (Monaco 1963a, Articles 3 and 7). All real estate transactions involving French residents in the principality were to be reported (Article 21). And finally, according to a 2003 amendment to the neighborhood treaty of 1963, names and other identifying information on all long-term residents from any European Union country were to be reported to Paris (Monaco 1963c, Article 3). While these agreements are still open to denunciation according to the original terms of the treaties being amended, it is clear that France is intent on ensuring that Monaco fulfills the increasingly strict terms of the agreements.

Turning to European institutions, Monaco has for many years been making its way into the European Union's orbit (European Commission 2012, 17–18). Because of a customs union with France, many EU directives have been applicable to Monaco for many years. In 2003, Monaco and the European Commission formally agreed as to which EU directives relating to trade in medicinal products, medical devices, and cosmetics would be applicable to Monaco; the number came in at 190 (Council of the European Union 2003). The exercise was repeated ten years later and showed that an additional 128 new and previously existing directives needed to be adopted by the principality (Joint Committee of the EU and Monaco 2013). In 1998 Monaco formally accepted the euro as its currency, a decision necessitated by the elimination of the French franc, and began circulating it on the first of January 2002 (Monaco 1999). In general, as French laws that apply in Monaco are adapted to reflect new EU directives and European Court of Justice rulings, these are applicable to Monaco. In this sense Monaco is a passive EU member in that Paris and Brussels together can tie Monaco's hands (Grinda 2010, 60).

Recognizing this problem, Monaco and the EU entered into an agreement in 2003 that establishes an EU-Monaco joint committee made up of EU and Monegasque representatives to monitor and—to a degree—enforce Monaco's compliance with relevant parts of the EU acquis (Council of the European Union 2003, Article 2). Its primary function is to play the role of arbitrator in the event of a dispute between Monaco and the EU, rendering its decisions on the basis of consensus and equality of status (Article 4). But if the joint committee cannot reach an agreement on how to proceed within ninety days of considering a dispute, "the Agreement shall cease to apply six months after that period expires" (Article 4). In addition, either party may denounce the agreement, to take effect six months later. In other words, the EU and Monaco both acknowledge that Brussels cannot explicitly compel Monaco to comply with EU directives, although both seem to hope (given the persistence of the arrangement) that consensus can be achieved. With respect to our measure of "entrapment" it is clear that it is possible for Monaco to walk away from this agreement, although this does not mean it can ignore what is happening in Brussels (knowing this, Monaco has established a diplomatic presence there). Also note that with respect to marginalization, the agreement does not provide Monaco with a voice in EU policy making.

In addition to creating the joint commission, Monaco and the EU have entered into a variety of formal agreements by which Monaco has agreed to adopt on a case-by-case basis a number of EU rules governing tax, banking, and monetary policy. In 2003 Monaco agreed to raise its tax withholding rate on interest from savings, starting from 15 percent in 2005 to 35 percent after July 2011 (European Community 2003, Article 7). It also agreed to collect and disseminate (when needed for investigations and prosecutions) information on bank accounts and interest earned on the assumption that states have a right to tax overseas accounts of residents (Articles 3, 7, 9, 12, and 13). On the other hand, Monaco will be permitted to retain one-quarter of the revenue (Article 3). The agreement—which was also signed by Andorra, San Marino, and Liechtenstein—may be denounced at any time and will then come to an end one year later (Article 16). It does not provide for any sort of joint governance or interpretation.

With respect to antifraud and money laundering regulations, the EU has essentially delegated the issue to the OECD. Following its placement on the list of uncooperative states in 2002, Monaco enacted a wide range of regulations and laws governing banking transparency and company registration. It negotiated and signed numerous agreements with other developed countries. The agreement with the United States includes thirteen articles, three of which (Articles 5, 6, and 7) are very detailed with respect to the type of information that is to be shared and under what circumstances, as well as conditions that would bar the sharing of information (OECD 2009a). Of particular interest is a fairly broad exception to the duty to share information: "The competent authority of the requested Party may decline to assist . . . where the disclosure of the information requested would be contrary to public policy" (Article 7(1)). Recognizing the domestic measures and international commitments made by Monaco during the 2000s, the OECD removed it from its list of uncooperative states in 2009, although it continued to monitor its compliance with international standards. In 2011, a review board determined that Monaco was dragging its feet—and perhaps even regressing—with respect to "the international standard with regard to the availability of accounting information, in particular for non-trading partnerships, foreign-law trusts established in or transferred to Monaco and foundations" (OECD 2011, 9). In general, though, Monaco has received encouragement and some praise from the OECD, particularly for its recent commitment to the Multilateral Convention on Mutual Administrative Assistance in Tax Matters (OECD 2014b). The Council of Europe has been less positive, citing several gaps in its ability and willingness to monitor transactions and ownership, urging Monaco to strengthen its regulation of not just bankers but accountants, lawyers, and even jewelers (Council of Europe 2014).

Monaco still seems to many to be that sunny place for shady people, however. This is perhaps inevitable when the country's dominant economic strategy seems to be to attract as many of the world's super rich as possible (Christini 2013). Tax evasion is still not policed as aggressively as most governments would like, nor is fraud (Osborne 2012). One of the ECHR cases in which Monaco was involved stemmed from a massive private Ponzi scheme in the 1990s that, while successfully prosecuted, exposed the government to financial liability for failure to monitor the perpetrator's company (*L'Express* 2015). The Monaco branch of PNB Paribas has been accused of laundering money in Africa (Radoman 2013). The prince's close relationship with the casino managers and foreign development companies has led to numerous charges of favoritism, including one from the legislature, which lamented the lack of transparency in the decision to hire Bouygues Construction to work on a maritime reclamation project aimed at extending the territory into the sea (Europa World Plus 2015b). It has been claimed that the reason this project did not go forward sooner was because the best bid originally came from a firm that was not connected to the prince (Interview 2013a).

In 2015, Monaco, along with San Marino and Andorra, entered into talks regarding an association agreement that would bring its status under the EU to roughly the same as Liechtenstein or Turkey. Naturally, the talks addressed not only transparency and open markets but also more difficult issues surrounding migration. Early on, Monaco was assured by European negotiators that it could maintain its integration into the European customs union by virtue of its trade agreements with EU member France (Monaco 2016). While the talks were to reach completion in March 2017, the British "Brexit" referendum likely put UK-EU talks to the fore at the expense of talks with microstates.

Overall, it appears that France, the OECD, the EU, and the Council of Europe have together exerted enough pressure that law and regulation have improved dramatically in the principality during the twenty-first century, but it also seems clear that one way the country is exercising its sovereignty is to drag its feet. An interesting question to ask is whether these various external actors will be able to enforce the new standards in the future without violating Monaco's sovereignty.

While Monaco remains highly vulnerable and exploitable, during this period its relations with France are much more elective than in the previous period, particularly where the 2002 and 2005 treaties are concerned (see table 5.1). This does not appear to be so much the case where regional agencies (EU, Council of Europe, OECD) are concerned given the resistance and resentment connected to Monaco's response to pressure from these bodies. As mentioned, constitutional reforms were undertaken even though the citizens of Monaco overwhelmingly supported the status quo. With respect to banking and fiscal policies, the assent seems grudging at best. Nonetheless, it is clear that these agreements are not being imposed on Monaco and the measures taken to enforce them seem far more tentative and respectful of its sovereignty than in the past.

With respect to the range of issues in play and their salience, it is still the case that the agreements between France and Monaco are comprehensive in their scope and touch on vital matters of national security. Where regional bodies are concerned, however, since Monaco is not a member of NATO, the topics covered under regional arrangements exclude security matters, although one might imagine it becoming involved in a continental war by virtue of the lack of respect states have shown for its neutrality in the past. This is not to say regional bodies are not addressing matters of high importance, only that there are even more important issues that are left untouched.

TABLE 5.1. Features of Monaco's Relationships with Neighboring States and Institutions

		Trustor-Trustee Relationship			Issues in Play		Structure of Agreements		
		Vulnerability	Exploitability	Voluntarism	Scope of Issues	Salience of Issues	Imprecision and Informality	Marginalization	Entrapment
1641–1918: Submission to France & Sardinia/Savoy	France	**HIGH**	**HIGH**	MODERATE	MODERATE	HIGH	MODERATE	**HIGH**	MODERATE
	Sardinia/ Savoy (until 1865)	**HIGH**	MODERATE	MODERATE	Low	**HIGH**	**HIGH**	**HIGH**	**HIGH**
1918–2002: Submission to France		**HIGH**	**HIGH**	MODERATE	**HIGH**	**HIGH**	MODERATE	MODERATE	MODERATE
2002–2016: Submission to France & Regional Agencies	France	**HIGH**	**HIGH**	**HIGH**	**HIGH**	**HIGH**	Low	MODERATE	Low
	Regional Agencies	**HIGH**	**HIGH**	MODERATE	MODERATE	MODERATE	Low	**HIGH**	Low

With respect to the nature and structure of the various agreements, as we have seen, things have changed dramatically where France is concerned. The 2002 and 2005 treaties set aside vestiges of a quasi-protectorate and replaced them with terms that reflect contemporary international legal norms to a far greater extent. They are generally more clear and specific. For example, the 2002 treaty spells out what constitutes an "emergency" that would warrant the deployment of French troops rather than leaving it to the discretion of authorities in Paris. Likewise, the various fiscal agreements spell out more clearly what can and cannot be taxed and how. When combined with various ancillary agreements and exchange of letters, it seems that Monaco can feel more confident that it will be able to anticipate a French response to most scenarios. This is even more the case where regional agencies are concerned since in many cases Monaco has acceded to multilateral agreements, which, as we have seen in other chapters in this volume, tend to be far more exhaustive and precise. In the case of the fiscal agreement with the EU, for example, nearly one thousand words are dedicated to defining a few key terms such as "interest payment" and "beneficial holder" (European Community 2003, Articles 2–6). As mentioned, hundreds of specific EU directives are listed in the annex to the 2003 and 2013 agreements on trade in medical equipment and cosmetics (Council of the European Union 2003; Joint Commission 2013).

With respect to the degree to which Monaco can participate in the development and enforcement of these mutual agreements, France has provided additional avenues of access, including especially the joint committee that emerged from the 2002 treaty and the call for regular consultations. This does not mean that Monaco can contribute equally to formation of policy options and treaty language, but it comes closer to giving Monaco a veto over onerous terms. This is obviously a long way from the type of even-handed dealing one would find between, say, France and Great Britain, but it warrants the description of only "moderate" rather than "high" marginalization. With respect to regional agencies, however, Monaco is mostly a policy taker. As mentioned, France and the EU together have been shaping a wide array of Monegasque policies for years. Likewise, the OECD and the Council of Europe gave Monaco a "take it or leave it" offer with respect to constitutional change and reform of the country's banking and fiscal policy. While the council's recommendations were tied to a promised benefit—namely membership—the OECD's demands were punctuated with threats. Only in a few areas has Monaco been able to influence the content, and this has mostly involved foot dragging with respect to the most objectionable proposals. It remains to be seen whether the joint commission created by agreement with the EU will translate into a genuine give-and-take, although this seems unlikely.

Finally, while the costs in political terms may be high in practice, Monaco has far more legal escape routes than before. The agreements with France are to be upheld only by consensus, meaning that the 1962 boycott scenario is extremely unlikely in the future. Several new treaties explicitly provide relatively quick denunciation terms, which is a big change from the previous periods. Where regional bodies are concerned, while the verdict is mixed, it seems that escape clauses are generally reasonable. Perhaps the most generous of these is the provision that allows Monaco to walk away from the agreements with the EU whenever the joint commission fails to reach a consensus on how to settle a dispute. While some might consider this a "nuclear option," the fact remains that this provides an important protection against entrapment.

It seems clear that Monaco's efforts to protect its interests have paid off. Where relations with France are concerned, this was greatly helped by the intervention of the Council of Europe in its behalf. This is not to say, however, that the country's sovereignty is sacrosanct, and Monaco has been vulnerable to pressures from outside just like other European microstates, not to mention Switzerland and Austria.

Does this mean that trust is no longer an important element in Monaco's external relations? Certainly the country has been engaged in far more hedging in the current century, stemming in part from what it considered an ill-advised level of trust in France. The picture is muddied by the council's intervention since this took the initiative away from the prince. But it is clear that the council's advocacy and pressure were welcome in Monaco, indicating that it had lost faith in existing arrangements and had lost confidence in France's willingness to consider Monaco's interests when making decisions. Since it appears that what took place caught the prince by surprise, it would be too much to say Monaco had planned this outcome. But the denouement spared the country years of resentment under the old system.

Where Monaco's relations with regional agencies are concerned, since these were less voluntary and more easily discontinued, it is unlikely that trust governed the decision making. Only the fact of Monaco's marginalization—again offset by the largely involuntary nature of the agreements—indicates there may have been some degree of trust. After all, if Monaco did not believe these agencies were ultimately interested in its welfare, why would it have tolerated being bound at all when it was marginalized?

Taken together, the level of trust on the part of Monaco relative to France and Europe's regional bodies seems relatively low, and its relations are driven far more by calculations of interest and hedging against exploitation.

Conclusions

Monaco's story since 1641 seems like a gentler version of Luxembourg's. While its territory was a crossroads of great empires and was invaded repeatedly, it benefited from being far from Germany and close to Italy. It was willing to entrust its fate to various neighbors in part because the stakes were not so high. By 1861, its survival (albeit as a much smaller state than Prince Charles III would have preferred) was not especially in doubt, unlike that of Luxembourg, which was forced to disarm itself in 1866 and float like a leaf on the stream of great power politics (see chapter 2). At the same time, its treatment at the hands of Sardinia and France during two centuries left it increasingly skeptical of its neighbors' empathy. It launched a quixotic campaign to assert control over its own fiscal and banking system during the 1950s and early 1960s, after which it grudgingly accepted its fate, but without much faith in its neighboring cousin. With a nudge from the Council of Europe, it was finally able to change its destiny and emerge as something more closely resembling a modern state, complete with the guardedness that goes with it. Even in its relations with the much more powerful regional actors, it is playing the game of reaching agreement on terms, then dragging its feet on implementation; time will tell whether this strategy is sustainable. At any rate, it is what is to be expected from an actor that has lost confidence in its neighbors.

SIX

Andorra

Eking Out Autonomy

Andorra has been in a dependent relationship with two entities simultaneously—France and the Bishopric of Urgell—since the thirteenth century. At least since the late eighteenth century the arrangement has had the explicit approval of the Andorran government and was probably accepted by earlier governments for centuries. While its sovereignty was in doubt until 1993, it is clear that it has at times exercised autonomy, in part by playing the two overlords against each other. It has been able to manipulate its situation—to a degree at least—to achieve its primary ends as a result. Largely ignored as a useless enclave between France and Spain—at least until the 1960s—the country's two principal economic activities were herding and smuggling (Deane 1961, 57). Even the smuggling was ignored, as it was the natural result of free trade agreements between Andorra and its neighbors. Following a path similar to San Marino's, Andorra found its room to maneuver increasingly limited by its larger neighbors, who became increasingly intolerant of the loss of revenue to smugglers and duty-free shopping. At the same time, the quasi-feudal status of the principality was increasingly offensive to European policy makers, who pressed for a written constitution and a relative withdrawal of the overlords from Andorran domestic and even foreign policy (an outcome eagerly sought by the Andorran people). The net result is an independent country with more-or-less figurehead co-princes that behaves and is treated like other European microstates—with both the privileges and the duties this entails. Overall,

Andorra's historic attachment to its co-princes indicates that there exists a certain degree of trust in this dependent relationship, although it is clearly couched in a cool awareness of strategic constraints and opportunities.

Roughly one thousand years ago, the Roman Catholic Bishop of Urgell, in northeastern Spain, came into possession of Andorra by way of a grant from Charlemagne's son to the Count of Urgell, who apparently couldn't be bothered with administering the territory, although the details are sketchy (Llobet 1947, 11). It boundaries were set by 1007, however (Angelo 1970, 95). The mountain valley, with only 5 percent arable land, had little economic appeal and a few thousand inhabitants, although it had some use as a strategic bulwark against the spread of Moorish invaders (Leary 1912, 7, 17). In fact, poverty was an explicit aim until at least the mid-1800s. As put by a contemporary observer: "Two ruling ideas have governed the Andorrans for centuries past, and seem to have existed independent of any special tradition. One is, that they must not become rich; the other, that no feature of their government must be changed" (Taylor 2002/1876, 221). The fear was that by exploiting such resources as lead and silver, they would draw attention to themselves and increase the likelihood of annexation.

Later on, one of the bishop's successors invited another count—this time of Castellbó (also Caboet [Duursma 1996, 317])—to administer the region, but he showed little interest in the job, and the bishop's secular power increased (Llobet 1947, 13). When the French Count of Foix married into the house of Castellbó, he decided that Andorra worth be worth having after all as part of his effort to control northeastern Spain (Catalonia) and defend Protestantism, and an unlikely military struggle erupted between the bishop and the count (the last time war occurred in Andorra [Villaró 2013]). Eventually the king of Aragon and other local lords and clerics urged the parties to undertake a settlement that was common in the thirteenth century: a feudal condominium suzerainty.

The basic outline of the roughly three-thousand-word Concordat of 1278 (also known as the Treaty of the Pareatge or Paréages, approved by the pope in 1282 and then renegotiated in 1288) was a relatively simple one, best understood as an arbitral award (Angelo 1970, 96): Andorrans were permitted to govern local affairs as they saw fit, while the Count of Foix and the Bishop of Urgell would exercise joint control over the territory, with secular and spiritual matters tended to by the count and bishop, respectively (a major concession by the bishop [Llobet 1947, 15]). They would also offer their protection to the territory in exchange for a tribute (*questía*) (Article 1) that would be paid on alternate years to each "co-prince" (Fernsworth 1934). The co-princes would rule from afar but would send one delegate each (*veguers*) to steer or validate whatever Andorra's local governments did.[1] In addition: "the Bishop and the Count, shall always jointly and equally administer high justice over the said men of Andorra" through bailiffs (*bayle* or battles) (Article 2). In practice, they were selected by the *veguers* from a list prepared by the General Council (Angelo 1970, 104). The co-princes were entitled to enlist Andorran men to serve in their armies as needed, provided they were not expected to fight against each other. Needless to say, Andorrans would not have any international status and their relations with the outside world would be carried out by the co-princes. Technically, the bishop's sovereign rights over Andorra were acknowledged and the French count's rights flowed from a fief from the bishop (Leary 1912, 27). The treaty requires papal approval within four years, subject to a fine of "50,000 Malagoran sous" for foot dragging. The treaty was to be perpetual, with no provision for denunciation. Needless to say, the Andorrans were not consulted. In modern terms, the system worked a bit like a homeowners' association in receivership, in that the local government of Andorra did little more than maintain roads and supervise the use of common lands and forests while the co-princes addressed activities that are normally associated with statehood (Angelo 1970, 110).

As it happened, time was on the side of the count as his dominions were absorbed into larger and larger houses, ultimately residing in the House of Navarre, which was lorded over by the Count Henry II, who was then elevated to the throne of France after joining with the Bourbons in 1589 to become Henry IV (Taylor 2002/1876, 204). Thereafter it was confirmed by several royal edicts that the kings of France—and by implication any French head of state regardless of title—would always be co-prince of Andorra (Angelo 1970, 97). On the other hand, the secular powers of the Bishop of Urgell declined along with those of most ecclesiastical rulers (Llobet 1947, 17), while Spain remained on the margins, having no formal authority in Andorra but growing political and military clout. In all of this Andorra was a spectator, but it nonetheless survived intact (Llobet 1947, 19). In 1659, for example, France and Spain concluded a treaty following an Anglo-French victory against Spanish forces in the Netherlands that resulted in a large portion of Catalonia being ceded to France—but leaving Andorra untouched (despite considerable mistrust of Catalan politics on France's part and the latter's claim to the Bishopric of Urgell [Serra 2008, 84, 86]). Until the 1700s, the *veguers* often insinuated themselves into domestic policy making, but this met with increasing local opposition on the grounds that it exceeded their authority as outlined in the Pareatge (Brutails 1904, 261).

The internal government of Andorra—as well as many details regarding the rights and powers of the co-princes—were not codified, although it generally resembled a hereditary oligarchy managed by the heads of various Andorran clans (Taylor 2002/1876, 214). A number of treatises were drafted that offered a sense of what was expected of everyone and gave advice on how to cope. The *Manual Digest* (known as the "Andorran Bible") was drawn up by Andorran notary Antoni Fiter i Rossell (allegedly) in 1748 and provides not only a detailed handbook for Andorran governance but also such Franklinesque advice as "be honest," "be discrete," "be prudent in business," "be tolerant," and so forth (Maxims 5, 7, 8, and 11). It also offers sage advice to Andorran diplomats and politicians on how to survive in the world by, among other things, negotiating carefully, avoiding conflict with neighbors and the co-princes, and ensuring that those put into positions of responsibility are men of integrity, discretion, and experience, and so forth (Maxims 6, 10, 17, and 18). In other words, "keep a low profile" (Maten 2013), a principle that has been a touchstone for Andorran politics from the beginning ("doing the Andorran" is a local expression meaning, variously, don't provoke anyone or don't take a firm position on controversies). This began a long tradition of political neutrality (Duursma 1996, 334). The *Politar Andorrà* was written by legal scholar Antoni Puig in 1763 and provides a more succinct version of the manual. Original prints of these classic works are kept under lock and key in the Andorran archives (opening it requires six keys, one each from representatives of the original six parishes [Leary 1912, 117]). Another more recent text by Brutails provides a comprehensive description of Andorran government, employing contemporary concepts and referents (Brutails 1904; Angelo 1970, 102). In 1740, legal proceedings of the country's Tribunal des Corts were specified.

Even the roles of the co-princes and their representatives have largely been defined by custom. As we will see, with the end of monarchy in France in 1870, the decision was made to allow the president to assume the role of co-prince, even though the French constitution does not permit him to exercise sovereignty in more than one country (Duursma 1996, 343). The question of how sovereignty is to be shared was also never clarified, and both co-princes often took it upon themselves to press their advantage in the hope of expanding their authority. A constitutional crisis erupted in 1793 when the Revolutionary French government refused to accept the annual *questía*, seeing this as a feudal holdover and entirely unbefitting for a republic to receive. The new government declared it would no longer fill its role as co-prince and granted Andorra independence. While this was no doubt intended as a gift, from the Andorran point of view this action threw their very existence into doubt since it would either mean becoming subject to the bishop alone or being entirely thrown to the wolves as a tiny, independent country (Deane 1961, 58–59). It also meant that the tax exemptions and free trade privileges the Andorrans had enjoyed since 1532 could be revoked (Emerson 2007, 30). The bishop, to his credit, concurred that the status quo was more desirable than the alternatives and joined the Andorrans in urging the French to reconsider in 1801 (Llobet 1947, 21). In 1806, Napoleon—himself no enemy of titles and feudal traditions—agreed and accepted the position of co-prince. It is also said that he had some affection for the principality since he had camped there during his Spanish campaign, again recalling San Marino's history (Deane 1961, 59). He reportedly told a delegation from Andorra, "I have heard of this Andorra and have purposely abstained from touching it, because I thought it ought to be preserved as a political curiosity" (Taylor 2002/1876, 199). At any rate, an argument could be made that the French head of state is a co-prince on the basis of Andorran popular sovereignty (Fernsworth 1934).

Nineteenth-Century Dependency: 1806–1933

After 1806, France found itself being challenged by increasingly assertive bishops who for much of the nineteenth century interfered with the domestic politics and economic life of the Andorrans. In 1855 the bishop "took it upon himself to pardon a man who had been condemned to death by the Tribunal des Corts, and the country was at once thrown into commotion by this illegal interference" (Leary 1912, 133–34). The bishop blocked the construction of a casino a few years later and again in the 1870s (Taylor 2002/1876, 225). In 1865, the bishop attempted to bring about some internal administrative reforms by issuing a unilateral decree, which ultimately led Andorran leaders to resign in protest. This led the Bishop to appoint a new *veguer*, whose task was to imprison several of the most recalcitrant Andorran officials. For a time, the bishop abdicated his role and the French *veguer* judged unilaterally (Brutails 1904, 251). In 1880, the bishop ordered the destruction of new telegraph lines in an attempt to keep the country from being morally polluted by the outside world, this despite his support for the tradition of smuggling (Leary 1912, 136). In each case Andorran leaders brought the bishop's overreaching to the attention of France, usually with some success. In the case of the telegraph lines, since France had funded their erection, it had a keen interest in reversing the Bishop's actions, although it took more than a decade (and the deployment of French troops on the border) before the problem was resolved. Even the pope was enlisted to restrain the Bishop in 1894 on the grounds that he was exceeding his authority with an edict that all public works required his approval and that Andorra could have no direct communication with foreign states (Leary 1912, 137).

In the 1880s, France delegated dealings with Andorra to the Prefect of the nearby department of Pyrénées Orientales, while Spain used the military governor in Urgell as its commissioner. Spain largely ignored Andorra, however, despite the close ethnic ties with the principality (Andorra shares Spain's Catalan heritage). In another territorial boundary treaty with France concluded in stages at Bayonne in 1856, 1862, and 1866, Andorra was not mentioned even though there were questions. It did take the time to sign a customs agreement in 1867 that mirrored one signed by France, through an exchange of letters (Faure and Klaousen 2000, 112). This overall neglect naturally gave the bishop greater latitude. The legal system was time-tested by 1900 in that local Andorran *bayles* would handle most criminal and civil cases, which would be appealed to a foreign judge appointed alternately by one or the other co-prince (Leary 1912, 123). Final appeals could be heard in nearby French or Spanish cities and sentences longer than a few weeks would be served in France.

At the turn of the twentieth century, Andorra was still a backwater. The capital of Andorra-la-Vella had only six hundred inhabitants and the country's economy was still dominated by herding and smuggling (Leary 1912, 84–85, 102). Although incomes were low and relatively equal (the richest man in the country was worth the current equivalent of only about one-half million dollars), the people were not living at subsistence levels. The country had no police and no army, there was only one letter carrier to serve the whole territory, and schools were entirely administered by nuns and priests. The political system had modernized a bit with the New Reform of 1866 that increased male suffrage from a small number of clan leaders to all the heads of household (781 out of a population of around 4,000 [Emerson 2007, 30]) and established a new and more powerful General Council (Angelo 1970, 109). France was generally tolerant of livestock smuggling, setting a flexible upper limit on trade so that even when livestock were intercepted they were simply counted as falling under that limit. Andorrans routinely bought tobacco duty-free from France only to resell it to French customers for less than the customers were paying for it at home (Leary 1912, 105). Some effort was made to tighten enforcement in response to complaints from local producers in France (Spain, with the bishop's support, had largely ended the practice in the 1790s [Emerson 2007, 31]), mostly by requiring easily forged certificates. France also allowed itself to be exploited in other ways, paying more than ten times the biannual tribute to build the telegraph mentioned earlier, for example.

As we have seen, the influence of the two co-princes has risen and fallen at various times, a matter of considerable interest to Andorrans. As put by contemporary observer Lewis Leary, "Political difference of opinion within the Valley often hinge large upon the question as to whether Urgell or France shall be relied upon as the more trusted adviser and protector," with France becoming the preferred option after 1880 (Leary 1912, 140). By the turn of the century, however, the French co-prince began to overreach, claiming, for example, the exclusive right to represent Andorra in all foreign relations, which provoked considerable debate in the principality (Llobet 1947, 23). As early as 1863, France refused to recognize a treaty between Spain and Andorra regarding territorial demarcations on the grounds that Andorra lacked the authority to sign it (Duursma 1996, 351). This despite the claim by some in Andorra that the original treaties actually granted that power to the regime (Maten 2013). France repeatedly interfered in Andorran efforts to accede to various multilateral agencies and conventions, including the Opium Convention in 1925, the Permanent Court of International Justice in 1926, and the Universal Postal Union in 1932 (Duursma 1996, 353, 355, 365). The League of Nations refrained from inviting Andorra to join, most likely because France had made it clear that it lacked sovereignty.

It was in this context of finding its powers constrained that the General Council undertook a series of unilateral legislative actions that profoundly challenged the rights of the co-princes. In 1931, the council approved a contract to build a casino in the country. This was soundly vetoed by both co-princes (the bishop for moral reasons, the French for fear such a business would compete with nearby French casinos [Maten 2013]). This precipitated violent protestations by the council against the co-princes (Duursma 1996, 319). To add insult to injury, the council approved a contract with Spain to build a telephone network (Duursma 1996, 319). The Andorrans further moved to "to establish their own postal system . . . to conduct their own schools, name their own notaries and pass upon the qualifications of Andorrans to hold office" (Fernsworth 1934). Finally in 1933, following demonstrations from Andorra's youth, the council adopted a new law extending suffrage to all men twenty-five and older. This proved to be the last straw and, accusing the Andorrans of "disobedience and disrespect" to the co-prince, the French deployed sixty gendarmes (with prior approval from the bishop) to ensure the dissolution of the council and new elections (Duursma 1996, 319; Fernsworth 1934). The Andorrans appealed to the League of Nations on the grounds that France had violated the Kellogg-Briand Pact of 1928 that barred the use of force between states, but the league demurred on the grounds that Andorra was not sovereign (Duursma 1996, 353). Oddly enough, several of the most controversial laws were later adopted by decree by the co-princes or at the initiative of its far more compliant post-1933 legislature (suffrage was extended and a French company was tasked to build a telephone network).

For its part, Spain had moved to the sidelines following its failed attempt in 1931 to pressure the bishop into resigning as co-prince in favor of the new republican regime in Madrid (Duursma 1996, 319). This may have created an opening for the French assertiveness in question. But once the gendarmes were deployed:

> Spain intervened. The Minister of State, Fernando de los Rios, issued a note pointing out that the rights of the co-Princes in Andorra were exactly equal. The incident had the important consequence that Spain once more renewed relations with the Bishop of Urgell, recognizing him for the future as its diplomatic representative for Andorra. . . . The extremer phases of French activity in Andorra would seem to have been checked by the firm position taken by Spain, who has made it clear that she has an equal interest there with France and that the balance of power must be maintained. (Fernsworth 1934)

Put another way, Spain implicitly accused France of violating the 1278/1288 agreements, although one could argue that since both co-princes were in agreement and the powers of the General Council clearly did not cover the things it was trying to do, this is probably not accurate. But the "Andorran Revolution," as it came to be known, is an important watershed in the life of an otherwise placid principality and warrants serving as a bookend to the nineteenth-century period.

As with several other microstates discussed in this work, Andorra was both vulnerable and not especially attractive as a target of exploitation. This, as we have seen, gave it reason to hope to escape the turmoil of European great power politics. It was not only poor but had the advantage of being inaccessible, which made it unlikely that it would become a battlefield, like Luxembourg. Further, since Franco-Spanish relations were largely peaceful after the Napoleonic invasion, Andorra could hope to avoid conflict, something it managed to do for centuries. The Bishop of

Urgell probably found the principality a bit more attractive since his flock there covered much of the cost of running the Church.

Of particular interest, as shown in table 6.1, is the evidence that Andorra not only tolerated but generally welcomed the role played jointly by the French leader and the local bishop, to the point that it worked hard in the early 1800s to prevent a divorce, as it were. During most of the nineteenth century, France proved a capable and reliable "ally" to the Andorran people, serving as a bulwark against the bishop's intrusive tendencies (the co-prince it never chose). It was not until the last few years of the period under consideration that Andorran contentment with the co-princes turned to bitterness. Having tested the limits of the relationship, the General Council was forced to accept a constitutional surrender.

The agreements governing the co-principality were relatively broad and important, addressing as they did the essential features of domestic and foreign policy involving police, justice, public expenditures, treaty making, and so forth. Implicitly, at least, the secular co-prince was tasked with defending the territory while the ecclesiastical co-prince was tasked with saving their souls. Rarely have sovereigns had such sweeping responsibility and authority (but since the bishop did not deal with security issues directly, I have categorized his role as less salient). Only on matters involving the use of public lands and other local matters did the co-princes defer to the Andorrans.

The nature of the agreements binding our actor together are at the extreme end of the precision-imprecision spectrum, since they are for the most part based on a broadly worded thirteenth-century treaty and hundreds of years of custom. It was not until the eighteenth century—a full five hundred years after the Pareatge—that attempts were first made by private individuals to codify Andorran constitutional law and practice. It is clear from our discussion that neither co-prince nor the General Council nor Spain entirely understood the limits of their respective authority.

During the nineteenth century, it appears that Andorran leaders had at least informal access to the French leader, while channels to the bishop were less open, hence the distinction in Table 6.1 regarding "marginalization." At any rate, however—and as demonstrated by the events of 1931–1933—there were clear limits to Andorra's capacity to influence the operation of its agreements with its co-princes. It would not be until the 1980s that Andorrans would have genuine access to key decision making. Finally, since these agreements were binding on all three actors in perpetuity, Andorra was committed. In fact, that the co-Princes were dual made any renegotiation of the arrangements twice as difficult and therefore twice as unlikely. As we saw, even when France tried to extricate itself from its 1278 commitments during its revolutionary period, it was pulled back in.

How does all of this inform our basic question of whether Andorra's policies were driven by trust? Certainly, Andorra was in a weak position throughout this period, a fact made all the more obvious by what occurred in the 1931–33 period. At the same time, it seems clear that while Andorra was not consulted regarding the establishment of the Pareatge, by 1793 it had internalized it, such that when the relationship was threatened, it worked to re-establish it. This might have stemmed from the fact that it derived considerable material benefit and the alternatives were even less appealing, but it seems that to at least some degree it trusted that a system of co-Princes would be worth preserving. In some ways, one could argue that it was the system of balancing that Andorrans trusted more than either the French president or the Bishop of Urgell. Certainly the scope, salience, informality, and other features of the arrangement added to Andorra's vulnerability in many ways, but still it opted to maintain its key feature (with the brief exception of the 1931–33 period, of course). We will see in the next section whether the bloom was off the rose after Andorra was forced to comply.

Second Period: 1933–1993

While Andorra was largely spared the suffering of World War I, the turmoil in Spain during the 1930s spilled over across its borders. In 1936, eighty thousand Spaniards and one hundred thousand Frenchmen crossed into Andorra for asylum (Deane 1961, 57). To help keep the country from becoming a means for the Spanish civil war to threaten France, Paris deployed troops on the southern border of Andorra with the consent of the local leadership from 1936 to 1940 (Duursma 1996, 320). After the fall of France, Andorra resisted demands by Germany to turn over refugees, deserters, and partisans, conceding only that it would limit their stays until they could each recover from their injuries and trauma, which proved a remarkably elastic phrase (Deane 1961, 59). In the waning months of World War II, both France and Spain put troops in Andorra with the consent of the bishop (Duursma 1996, 320).

The period immediately after World War II would reshape almost everything about the principality. It opened its doors to foreign workers who found jobs in the expanding service and energy sectors. Day trippers came to the country to take advantage of its duty-free shopping while during

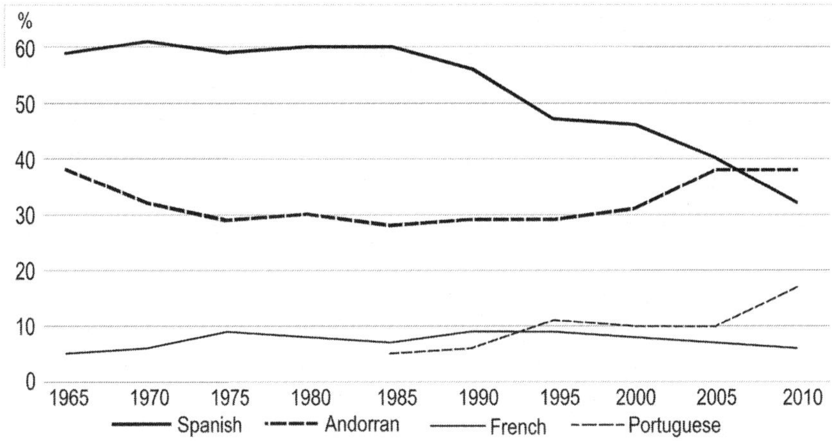

Fig. 6.1. Andorran population by nationality, 1965–2010 (percentages). (*Source:* Data from Andorran Department of Statistics.)

the winter the ski resorts did a thriving business. Many Spaniards remained in the country year-round, with the result that by 1965 they made up the majority of the country's population, far surpassing the French and even the native Andorrans. Figure 6.1 shows the trends for the share of population in Andorra of different nationalities. While the Andorran tradition was to settle disputes as much as possible through informal negotiation (the principal duty of the *bayles* was to help the parties reach a settlement rather than go to court), foreign residents did not share this tradition. Add to this the need to engage with foreign investors and traders and it is clear why as early as the 1950s local Andorran officials began to search for ways to codify their customary laws (Guillamet 2013; Deane 1961, 65). From then until the adoption of a constitution in 1993 the laws and regulations of Andorra became increasingly formalized and congruent with modern European legal traditions. The growth of the country's population from the historic range of five to eight thousand to roughly eighty thousand in 2015 also required a new form of administration and law enforcement.

The reforms regarding domestic politics paralleled—and depended on—changes to the roles of France, Spain, and the bishop. In addition, European integration and norm congruence on a regional level had a direct effect on all aspects of Andorran politics. For example, as France became increasingly integrated in Europe's free trade area during the 1950s and 1960s, Andorra increasingly served as a conduit for duty-free goods from France to the Spanish market. In turn, Spanish depositors increasingly availed themselves of Andorran banks (Emerson 2007, 34). For example, Andorran citizens could purchase French automobiles duty-free, and so Spaniards would pay a local to buy the car in their behalf, at which point it would be taken to Spain and resold and both the Spaniard and the Andorran would pocket the profits (Deane 1961, 65). Andorra's duty-free shops, many of which were perched on the French border, were almost entirely frequented by foreigners. Finally, the country continued its tradition of smuggling and otherwise flouting regional legal norms.

The result was an increasingly significant loss of tax and trade revenue for both France and Spain. In the 1940s, the French president, in his capacity as co-prince, banned and then jammed Radio Andorra to prevent it from piggy-backing on wavelengths that were assigned to other countries (Duursma 1996, 343). In 1959, Spain sealed the border with Andorra in an effort to bring smuggling to an end, with the result that the country was virtually cut off during the winter since its roads to France were snowed in (Deane 1961, 61). In an effort to maintain control over its trade with Andorra, France denied that the principality was part of the European internal market in 1965 despite the long-standing free trade agreement between the two (Duursma 1996, 359).

But tensions were even higher with respect to the question of international representation. As we have seen, as early as 1930 Andorran officials chafed at France's policy of unilaterally carrying out the principality's diplomatic activity. The frustration did not abate after World War II and reached a crisis point as Spain came to support the view that Andorra should be free of French diplomatic domination. In 1952, Spain attempted to sign a copyright convention in behalf of Andorra and in 1954 signed a convention on looting, only to see France intervene to annul the action (Duursma 1996, 355). France attempted to block Andorra's application to participate in the 1957 World's Fair, fearful that it would signal the principality's independence (a threat by Andorra to seal its borders with France prompted Paris to relent [Deane 1961, 61]). For its part, France continued to sign multilateral treaties, claiming that they applied to Andorra, over the local authorities' objections. In 1970 France declared explicitly that Andorra's signature on any international convention should be considered invalid since it lacked sovereign prerogatives (Duursma 1996, 356). In 1978 France blocked an attempt by Andorran officials to join the World Tourism Organization, on the same legal grounds. As recently as 1984, it barred Spain and the Bishop of Urgell from representing Andorra at a regional meeting of the International Telecommunications Union (Duursma 1996, 356).

Much of the French president's approach can be explained by the fact that the French constitution does not explicitly provide for the person holding the office to exercise sovereignty in more than one state. By emphasizing France's control over Andorra, this question could be answered by alleging that Andorra was merely an extension of France and therefore not sovereign. Even French courts generally granted Andorran residents something akin to citizenship, adding to the ambiguity (Duursma 1996, 342–44). Not to be outdone, Spain declared in 1941 that Andorrans were not aliens, implying that they enjoyed a form of Spanish citizenship as well. Even Andorrans themselves contributed to the uncertainty by routinely holding multiple passports despite the principality's prohibition against dual citizenship (Micó 2013).

In addition to Spain's support for Andorra's autonomy in diplomatic matters, international organizations increasingly questioned France's assertions. With decolonization in the developing world, self-determination increasingly approached the status of peremptory norm, implying that whenever a dependent territory—particularly a democratically governed one—claimed that a dominant state lacked legitimacy, the onus was on the dominant state to justify its claims (Bonanate 2003; Cardoso Reis 2013). UNESCO, the ITU, the European Commission, and the Council of Europe each made overtures of their own to Andorra during the 1970s and 1980s, forcing France to adjust the way it presented its authority to the world. In 1973, an agreement was struck that allowed representatives of the General Council to accompany representatives of the two co-princes at certain international meetings (Emerson 2007, 39), although this did not include granting Andorrans any powers over treaty making. In 1975 the General Council drew up a request to the co-princes to begin talks over codifying a constitution, including the granting to Andorra the authority to represent itself overseas. While they agreed in principle to the talks, France reiterated its opposition to the latter point (Duursma 1996, 320).

French president François Mitterrand adopted a more generous approach beginning in the early 1980s (Guillaumet 2013). As he met with the bishop and representatives of the General Council, again the issue of French unilateral representation was raised and rejected by Andorra. All agreed that Andorra should remain a morally conservative country and so the issue of legalizing abortion was taken off the table. The talks languished until a 1986 case before the European Court of Human Rights prompted the Council of Europe to intervene. The case involved two non-Andorrans who had been convicted of crimes in Andorra but were serving their sentences in France. It was clear from the outset that the customary legal system that had survived nearly a millennium was creating legal headaches for the Strasbourg jurists and that the best solution would be large-scale legal reform (the case was ultimately thrown out, but not without Andorra's system receiving considerable negative attention [Emerson 2007, 38]). The days of the Pareatge and France's unilateralism were clearly numbered.

Before discussing the important constitutional reforms and Andorra's Council of Europe membership, we will turn to the negotiations on the Andorra–European Community customs union. All these moves involved a waning of French influence and the assertion of Andorra's sovereignty, and they were mutually reinforcing. But the pressure to move forward on Europe prompted by Spain's accession to the European Community in 1986 did much to force the legal and diplomatic issues. As early as 1979, the European Community became interested in Andorra (Faure and Klaousen 2000, 112). At about the same time, Andorran officials met with European Community officials informally and reached the conclusion that the EC "would not take advantage of [Andorra's] size and would offer Andorra a customs regime containing the advantages of the 1867 agreements" (Faure and Klaousen 2000, 113). In 1984 Andorra requested that the French president and the Bishop of Urgell approach the European Community regarding the possibility of a customs union of some sort. The bishop readily agreed, although he had no status in Brussels, while the French demurred. As Spain's accession talks progressed, however, some sort of action on Andorra became inevitable as it was soon to be an enclave in the European community, much like Monaco and San Marino (Faure and Klaousen 2000, 108). Reference to a future agreement on Andorra was included in the talks with Spain and were begun in earnest almost immediately after the accession.

Success in the talks was unlikely given Andorra's size and inexperience in contrast to that of the European Commission and France. For its part, as a member of the EC and an Andorran co-prince, France was in a position to veto any agreement on either side of the table. On the other hand, Andorra was firmly supported by the bishop and by Spain, and early on in the talks the commission took steps that indicated it wished to deal with the Andorrans as an autonomous state (Duursma 1996, 360).

In the face of an essentially united front, France conceded that the Andorrans could not only join directly in the talks but take the lead role. It transferred its policies to the office of the French *veguer* (from the Foreign Ministry) to signal it was acting in the role of co-prince rather than as the French government (and member of the EC with a veto). It also allowed the Andorrans a right of veto over any deal and, in agreement with the bishop, allowed the Andorrans to head the delegation (Faure and Klaousen 2000, 116–17).

With this new authority, Andorra launched the first phase of the negotiations, which involved obtaining Spain's support for its positions. But Spain decided to make demands regarding the legalization of trade unions, an issue that afflicted the many Spaniards in Andorra and that had been raised by the Council of Europe. But Andorra balked and the EC questioned the move, so Spain relented and endorsed the Andorran position. Once the talks began, however, the European Commission proved far less flexible that had been expected. The delegation returned home with nothing to show for its efforts except some diplomatic bruises (Faure and Klaousen 2000, 118). One cannot help but wonder why the French did not warn the Andorrans that their demands were unrealistic. Perhaps they were hoping to prove to them that they were not ready to represent themselves? At any rate, the delegation returned and accepted, hat in hand, much of what the commission had previously required. The deal was signed in 1990 and came into effect in 1991.

The customs union agreement between Andorra and the European Community consisted of twenty-six brief articles and brought Andorra into the EC's internal market with respect to industrial goods only (Article 2, viz. chapters 25–97). Article 7 required Andorra to accept the EC acquis on trade policies and regulations (a total of fifty-two rules [European Commission 1991a]). It was also expected to freeze new tariffs and quotas (Articles 5 and 9). On the other hand, it largely exempted Andorran agriculture and its service sector (Emerson 2007, 48; European Commission 1992). It was allowed to retain its duty-free market, but foreign customers would be limited in how much they could take out of the country (Article 13). A long list was agreed to, including caps of one kilogram of butter, one kilo of coffee, one and a half liters of hard liquor, three liters of wine, and three hundred cigarettes. The last item was a concession on the EC's part, which had hoped to bring all tobacco sales under its rules (Emerson 2007, 48).

As with other microstates during this same period, the EC established a joint committee to govern implementation of the agreement (Articles 10 and 17). Made up of representatives of the EC and Andorra (nothing was said about the role of the co-princes here), the joint committee was to address disputes and seek a negotiated settlement, including both enforcement measures and derogations. Failing that, it was empowered to constitute arbitration panels. Article 20 states that the agreement is of unlimited duration but Article 21 provides for denunciation with a six-month lag. The agreement superseded the existing free trade agreements with France and

Spain (Article 25). Subsequent agreements and joint committee decisions spelled out the mechanics of customs operations and how duties would be shared (Andorra was to receive 10 percent of duties collected by other states on goods bound for the principality [European Commission 1991b]).

The agreement was not as broad in scope as those with Monaco and San Marino adopted at roughly the same time (Marshall 1993, 58), which was probably in Andorra's interests. But with France's and Spain's approval of the deal, Andorra received something far more important: status. As put by Duursma, Andorra was treated as a state by a major international body, one that could effectively limit France's power and authority (Duursma 1996, 364). For the foreseeable future, Andorrans would have direct access to Brussels despite the best efforts of Paris.

This success made other negotiations easier since key questions were at least implicitly resolved. On the constitutional front, Andorra was again aided by a European body: the Council of Europe. As mentioned, the council became interested in Andorra in the mid-1980s as its peculiar legal system came to its attention. It had also received complaints from foreign workers about its inadequate protection of trade unions. On the other hand, the council was satisfied that the country had generally democratic institutions. The General Council looked more and more like a real legislature, albeit with an oversized role for the co-princes (Angelo 1970, 99). Capital punishment had been abolished in the 1950s (the story is told that a firing squad refused to execute the order because everyone knew and liked the convicted individual too well [Deane 1961, 62]). There were concerns about the degree of discrimination in favor of Andorran nationals—particularly those who could trace their citizenship into the Middle Ages—since they had a de jure monopoly on the professions and elective office and de facto control of all other major economic activities (Micó 2013). There were also concerns about the internalization of many generally accepted norms of human rights such as the ban on torture and the right of personhood (Duursma 1996, 329). Ultimately, a list of desiderata was generated and presented to the Andorrans in 1990 in the form of Council Resolution 946 (Council of Europe 1994). In this resolution, the council called for Andorra to adopt a new, written constitution, one that would circumscribe the powers of the co-princes and establish clearly the country's sovereignty. Naturally, the constitution would spell out clearly the powers of the country's other institutions, although they took pains to reassure the readers that they could retain their traditional organs (as had been the case for San Marino) so long as everything was codified. In addition, the council urged Andorrans to explicitly internalize international human rights norms, preferably in the form of a bill of rights (Council of Europe 1994).

Even before the Council of Europe's resolution, Andorra had begun to take steps in the direction of modernizing its domestic political institutions. In 1981 it created an Executive Council that separated the government from the legislature. In 1987 it liberalized its rules on unionization. In 1989, by decree of the co-princes, the rights of the person were established (Duursma 1996, 321, 329–30). It also announced plans to internalize the provisions of the Universal Declaration of Human Rights, although the details were few.

Following a three-year process, a new constitution was drafted in 1993 that incorporated almost all the council's requests. More will be said about this in the next section. Suffice it to say here that it resulted in an almost immediate accession of Andorra to the Council of Europe and the United Nations and its recognition as a sovereign state by France and the rest of the international community.

What does this period in Andorra's history tell us about trust? A great deal, since it shows how trust can be lost. To begin, Andorra is vulnerable to exploitation and must therefore decide whether to rely on the protection of others. Whom to trust in this respect was clear, but whether to trust was not. It is important to note the growing importance of regional bodies in Andorra's foreign policy and the effect they had in restraining its protectors, especially France. Andorra since the 1960s has become an increasingly appealing target. Andorrans forgot one of their fundamental rules: don't become rich. By the end of this period, tourism, banking, and duty-free shopping had given Andorra a standard of living well above the average in Europe and higher than those of its Spanish and French neighbors. It should not be surprising that this attracted attention. At this stage this mostly resulted in diminished toleration of lawbreaking, but we will see that it ultimately led to an effort to limit all of Andorra's historic privileges.

As we see in table 6.1, Andorra made it clear that it no longer endorsed much of the political arrangement it had inherited, especially where France was concerned. The gesture of threatening to suspend intercourse with its powerful neighbor over the World's Fair issue is prima facie evidence that a new relationship was a priority. That Andorrans stuck with constitutional reform for eighteen years is testament to their commitment to change. The public appears to have solidly backed these efforts; as we will see, the new constitution received the support of roughly three-fourths of the voters.

The scope and salience of Andorra's dependent relationships were roughly the same as during the previous period, but with the loss of legitimacy this became a thorn in the side of Andorra's leaders. It was not that there was any effort to join an alliance with some third country, however, just that the need to alter the terms of the existing arrangements was urgent. The agreements also differed little in substance and form, although it can be said that by the end of this period Andorrans were no longer so marginalized. They clearly seized every opportunity to engage with the co-princes and took the initiative (at European prodding) to renegotiate the terms of their fundamental agreements. The result was the grudging recognition of their legitimate grievances and their elevation to quasi-equals, especially in the eyes of Spain and various European players. We will see that with this newfound status and recognition that Andorra has launched a new identity.

Clearly the key shift in Andorra's level of trust is its conclusion that France did not have its best interests at heart and that it would do better to speak for itself as much as possible, especially in the European theater. Ironically, it does not seem that France's policies were particularly damaging to Andorra, unlike its actions in Monaco or those of Italy vis-à-vis San Marino. Rather it seems Andorra's expectations had risen. Faure and Klaousen argue that both the Andorran leadership and the Bishop of Urgell began in the early 1980s to tout Andorra's uniqueness and "nationhood" (to counter France's views), and although the reality of such rhetoric was dubious, it was sincerely believed (2000, 110). As it happened, in the context of the nearly universal acceptance of self-determination and growing interest in microstates on the part of European institutions, the rhetoric became reality, something France did not understand until it was compelled to.

Although more will be said in the next section about Andorra's relationship with European institutions, it is worth noting at this point that its arrangements with the European Community were fairly typical of those we have seen thus far (except for the case of Luxembourg). While it was mostly a recipient of European terms, it was able to secure some protections of its fragile economy while also receiving the recognition that strengthened its hand with Paris. As of 1993, it is reasonable to say that Andorra was willing to trust Europe, but that it was also glad to hedge its bets. As it happened, the standard agreements being drafted by the EC allowed for both.

Third Period: Since 1993

As mentioned earlier, the Council of Europe urged Andorra and its co-princes to codify and modernize the governance structure. Andorran official Giles Menage began the process of drawing up the new constitution with the support of French president Mitterrand (Maten 2013). The public approved the new document with a 74.2 percent vote and it became law in 1993 (Duursma 1996, 321). A monument was erected next to the old parliament building and the moment is emphasized in the country's tourism literature. The key result was a significant weakening of the powers of the co-princes, to the point that they receded significantly from day-to-day Andorran politics (Micó 2013). This is not to say they are mere figureheads. While sovereignty is clearly vested in the Andorran people (Article 3), the co-princes, "in accordance with the institutional tradition of Andorra . . . are jointly and indivisibly, the Head of State, and they assume its highest representation" (Article 43). They are declared equal in power but swear allegiance to the Andorran constitution despite their loyalties to Rome, Madrid, and Paris. In practice this has come to mean that although their assent is still required for laws to be promulgated and treaties ratified, one co-prince cannot block what the other has approved. This happened in 2005 and 2013 concerning laws recognizing common law marriages and civil unions, which were opposed by the bishop but supported by France. On the other hand, engaging in what can best be described as political blackmail, each co-prince has threatened to resign his post and create a constitutional crisis over matters they considered essential: a law legalizing abortion in 2013 in the case of the bishop and Andorra's duty-free shopping and tolerance of tax evasion in the case of France under president Nicolas Sarkozy[2] (Micó 2013; Maten 2013; Fernández 2013). The legislature conceded in each case.

In the area of foreign policy, the place of the co-princes is still ambiguous in that as heads of state they have power to receive foreign ambassadors (including ambassadors from France and Spain) and to ratify all treaties (Articles 44 and 45). Where treaties with Spain and France are concerned, however, the co-princes are to be involved in negotiations dealing with "internal and external security," territorial questions, and "diplomatic representation or consular functions, or concerning judicial or penitentiary cooperation" (Article 66, paragraph 1). After participating in the drafting of these treaties, though, the co-princes were not permitted to veto their ratification (Emerson 2007, 38). This can lead to some curious arrangements. In the case of an agreement involving minor territorial adjustments around the city of Pas de la Casa, the French president was represented in Andorra in his constitutional capacity as well as by the French ambassador to Andorra: the personal representative reporting through his chief of staff and the ambassador through the foreign minister. He had the authority to approve ratification of the treaty for both countries, although he could only have refused ratification for France (Guillaumet 2013). To help establish definitively Andorra's sovereignty, the French government has freed the president to act unilaterally when fulfilling his role as co-prince (Duursma 1996, 369).

Other features of the constitution were designed to secure the approval of the Council of Europe, including a number of human rights provisions, including the recognition of the right to unionize (Article 18), the right to life (Article 8), and universal suffrage (Article 24). The Universal Declaration of Human Rights is said to be Andorran law (Article 5) but since the Constitutional Court (Article 96) cannot apply it to review laws, the significance of this statement is unclear (Duursma 1996, 330). The constitution also disbands the system of foreign courts serving as courts of last resort, resolving a key concern that arose in the European Court of Human Rights, as mentioned earlier. The constitution also provides for the possibility that Andorra may surrender sovereignty to an international body—such as the European Union—although such a move would require a two-thirds vote by the legislature (Article 65).

It is worth noting that not only did the constitution receive more than 70 percent approval in 1993, in a 2013 survey nearly 94 percent of Andorran nationals approved of it (nearly 50 percent gave it their moderate or strong approval while 44 percent found it acceptable [Centre de Recerca Sociològica 2013]). At the same time, 57.2 percent of Andorran nationals indicated they would like see it amended, particularly to allow abortion and to expand the protection of social rights. Regarding their approval of the role of the co-princes themselves, Andorrans trusted them less than any other major political institution aside from political parties, with 64 percent saying they are trustworthy (more than three-fourths of those asked said this of the General Council, the most trusted institution) (Centre de Recerca Sociològica 2013). In general, Andorrans are more progressive than the bishop (most favor legalized abortion and 70 percent favor same-sex marriage), so constitutional conflicts will likely recur in the future. On the other hand, most Andorrans are open to incorporating more political rights, including dual citizenship, shorter residency requirements for naturalization, voting rights for foreign residents, and increased involvement in the European Union (three-fourths of Andorrans approve this last point [Centre de Recerca Sociològica 2013]).

Parallel to the constitutional negotiations were talks on a new overarching treaty to govern relations between Andorra and its two neighboring states, which was concluded in 1993. It clearly asserted France's and

Spain's recognition of Andorra's national sovereignty (Article 1), with the logical implication that each would be represented at the ambassadorial level (Article 2). The treaty also provided for a commitment on Spain's and France's parts to consult with Andorra in the event of a threat to its independence or territorial integrity, although it did not guarantee mutual defense (Article 3; Bartmann 2002, 369).

Articles 4 and 5 are broadly and ambiguously worded, but taken together they committed the three states not to adopt domestic policies that undermine the others' fundamental national interests, including especially internal and external security (since security is mentioned in Article 5 it isn't clear what was covered by "fundamental interests" in Article 4 [Duursma 1996, 336]). France and Spain also offered their diplomatic and consular services to assist Andorra in its efforts to communicate with third states. This led to an awkward moment when representatives of the countries approached the Andorran foreign minister in 1995 proposing to split the world in half and divide representation between the two major powers. She replied that Andorra would do as much as it could on its own and suggested their move was presumptuous (Maten 2013).

The treaty provided for no formal consultations or arbitration, although regular communication was encouraged, and it provided for no denunciation or termination. At eleven articles it is a model of brevity, especially for modern diplomacy. Overall, the three parties have lived by the word and spirit of the agreement, although Andorra has resisted efforts to bring its banking and tax policies in line with world European standards while France and Spain have overreached from time to time. Some follow-up agreements between the three include a brief treaty on migration and travel that commits Andorra to complying with French and Spanish immigration norms and laws and to notify each country of any visitors to Andorra who plan to stay more than ninety days. Article 5 of the treaty provides for a five-year expiration window but with the possibility of renewal, and denunciation with a six-month effect (European Union 2011b). In 2012, the three countries—joined by Portugal—signed an agreement allowing professionals to establish offices in the other countries on a reciprocal basis (European Union 2012a). Since 1993, Andorra has entered into fifteen new agreements with Spain and fourteen with France covering a variety of mostly uncontroversial topics such as student exchanges, regional development, and so forth. In 2007 they also were together awarded a five-year regional development grant from the European Union that provided €257 million to fund cross-border integration efforts, enhance tourism, and stimulate joint natural resource management (European Commission 2008). The adjustment of the border near Pas de la Casa was previously mentioned and represents a practical solution to what had become a sticky situation, namely Andorra's decision to build a tunnel coupled with a request to France to improve access roads, something France was disinclined to do since it would mean funding easier access for French citizens to Andorra's duty-free shops (Timothy, Guia, and Berchet 2012).

This is not to say that relations between the three neighbors have always been smooth. As we will see, the two states mostly went through multilateral channels to deal with the most serious issues of money laundering and tax evasion, although they have also secured bilateral deals on bank account information sharing. In 1997, Spain blocked access to Andorra in order to pressure the government to adopt stricter rules on smuggling cigarettes. The tactic worked (Emerson 2007, 34, 50). For example, in 2013 a cigarette smuggling ring was disrupted by Andorran police (*Bon Dia* 2013c, 13). In 2010 Andorra liberalized foreign direct investment and was rewarded with a relatively generous double taxation treaty with France and another with Spain that came into effect in 2016 (*Andorra Business* 2015; Ministère des affaires étrangères, France 2013; McKenzie 2016). With twenty-nine lengthy and precisely worded articles, it removes any room for multiple interpretations. The tax rate on business is set at 10 percent and capital gains tax is 25 percent (Articles 11 and 13), with the assurance that taxes levied on French residents of Andorra (and vice versa) will go toward their respective liabilities. The final article (29) provides for denunciation with a six-month lag and no termination.

Before moving on to a consideration of Andorra's relationship with regional bodies, we will discuss Andorrans' contemporary views of Spanish and French policies (their views of the Bishop of Urgell were discussed previously). In general, Andorran affection for France is on the wane, a situation that worries Paris (Scalbert 2010). Sarkozy's name is rarely spoken with warmth, and the typical epithet used to describe him is "bully" or the more mild "hypocrite." His heavy-handed approach to Andorra's low taxes was deeply resented, particularly his move to seal off the country after one severe snowstorm by simply refusing to plow the roads on the French side (Maten 2013; Guillaumet 2013). François Hollande, on the other hand, is viewed more favorably by Andorrans mostly because they see him as an improvement on Sarkozy (Centre de Recerca Sociològica 2012). In general, the French are seen as (perhaps predictably) arrogant and with a sense of entitlement, refusing to embrace the local culture by learning Catalan (among other things) (Guillaumet 2013; Fernández 2013). Spain—

especially Catalonia—has won the heart of Andorrans, although they will naturally not go on record favoring the independence movement.

On the diplomatic front, France and Spain mostly leave Andorra to adopt its own foreign policy, although given the remarkable harmony of interests this poses little risk (Interview 2013b). Sometimes Andorra has been used as a political football. Spain pressed Andorra to endorse its favored candidate Morocco as the host of the World Expo, but Andorra voted for South Korea instead. An angry Spanish foreign minister phoned the Andorran head of government demanding he remove his foreign minister in retaliation (he didn't [Maten 2013]). When France and Spain both put forward candidates for posts at international organizations, Andorra tends to lean toward the French candidate but generally votes on the individual's qualifications (Maten 2013; Interview 2013b). As put by one senior Andorran diplomat, the starting point of Andorran foreign policy is getting along well with France and Spain, after all (Interview 2013b).

Perhaps the most significant shift in Andorran behavior was its decision to join many multilateral organizations. It joined the United Nations in 1993 without objection from the French (an important validation of its recognition of Andorra's sovereignty as promised [Duursma 1996, 370]). It was admitted to the Council of Europe virtually without scrutiny since it had already completed most of the elements on the organization's checklist in previous years (Duursma 1996, 358). In the review of Andorra prior to its admission, the Council of Europe urged it to ratify a number of agreements including the Convention on Human Rights and Fundamental Freedoms, the European Convention for the Prevention of Torture and Inhuman or Degrading Treatment or Punishment, the Convention on the Transfer of Sentenced Persons, and the General Agreement on Privileges and Immunities, and to accept the compulsory jurisdiction of the European Court of Human Rights (Council of Europe 1994). It did so by 1998 for all items except for a treaty on transferring sentenced persons, which it ratified in 2000. Other concerns raised in the application were the prominent role of the co-princes in appointing judges to the Constitutional Court and the lengthy residency requirement for naturalization. It would also like to see strengthened collective bargaining rights for workers (Fernández 2013).

In general Andorra has been an active and constructive member of the Council of Europe, taking its turn as council chair in 2012 (*Bon Dia* 2013b, 9). It has been involved in a number of cases before the European Court of Human Rights as well and has almost always seen the cases either thrown out or ruled as nonviolations (Council of Europe 2015). It has also been mostly cooperative with the council's MONEYVAL inspections and recommendations, although more will be said about this.

Within the first ten years after the tripartite agreement, Andorra joined twenty-six international organizations (Emerson 2007, 40). Most of these were relatively uncontroversial decisions, but where the European Union is concerned, issues of great significance are at stake. Andorra has followed the models of San Marino and Monaco, seeking an increased degree of engagement while at the same time protecting its privileges and minimizing its exposure. In many respects, Andorra has been the most tentative of the European microstates (Emerson 2007, ii; European Union 2011a). As mentioned, the customs union covered only industrial goods. The agreement on monetary integration in 2002 did not initially allow Andorra to mint its own euro coins (this was not granted until 2011 and did not come into effect until 2013 [European Union 2011a], *Bon Dia* 2013a, 3). A cooperation agreement signed in 2004 has yielded few tangible results even though it provided for the possibility of joint projects on the environment, communication, education, social and health issues, transportation, and regional policy (European Union 2011a; Emerson 2007, 51). That said, Andorra benefited from participation in a regional development program funded by the EU as mentioned earlier (European Commission 2008). Andorra has generally not been required to implement the EU's four freedoms (Emerson 2007, 13; European Commission 1998).

As has been mentioned, Andorra has profited from a fiscal system based on indirect taxation, leaving its commerce duty-free and its corporations lightly taxed. Likewise, it has attracted Spanish and French deposits by protecting depositor identity and requiring little information about them. The size of Andorra's economy made these policies less of a threat to the rest of Europe, however, than those of Switzerland or Luxembourg, as discussed in earlier chapters. Nonetheless, we have seen that Andorra's system was irksome to its neighbors, and as circumstances changed following the September 11, 2001, terrorist attacks and the 2007–2008 financial crisis they were no longer willing to tolerate it. Andorra's foreign policy in the twenty-first century—like those of other European microstates—has been the story of accommodating these new demands. Overall, Andorra has been remarkably compliant without the same degree of pressure we saw applied to Monaco and San Marino. In fact, Andorra has adopted an ambitious and far-reaching policy program—"Andorra 2020"—that aims to bring the country more fully into Europe and in the process wean itself from duty-free shopping and ski vacationers as the foundation for its economy (Berthélemy, Llimona, and Maresceau 2009, 43).

To begin, Andorra was listed along with most microstates as an uncooperative tax haven by the OECD in 2000 and was urged to increase its tax rates and especially its withholding of taxes on foreign deposits (Department of State 2013). In 2004 it signed its own version of the tax withholding agreement with the EU, as did San Marino and Monaco, meaning that it was required to increase the taxes to 15 percent immediately, then to 20 percent after three years and to 35 percent after another three years (Emerson 2007, ii). It offers some protection against double-taxation, and since the agreement is multilateral in nature, it only came into effect after three-fourths of participating non-EU states ratified it, and it can be dissolved if one-quarter of them withdraw (European Community 2003). Since 2011, Andorra has further increased tax rates and mirrored EU policy by introducing a corporate tax in 2012 and switching from a sales tax to the value-added tax in 2013, along with enacting an income tax and capital gains tax (Europa World Plus 2015d). Andorra was removed from the list of uncooperative tax havens in 2009 and, with the implementation of these new taxes, will no longer be considered a tax haven in 2017.

Tax evasion was addressed primarily through a variety of bilateral and multilateral tax information sharing agreements (nearly thirty were either concluded or under negotiation as of 2015). As with the other microstates, these follow a standard template by which Andorra agrees to share information as requested by a state pursuing a criminal inquiry. Protections are available to protect Andorra's interests, as with agreements signed by San Marino and Monaco. Andorra has gone a step further, however, by being one of the first to sign the OECD Multilateral Convention on Mutual Administrative Assistance in Tax Matters (OECD 2013). It has also endorsed the Common Reporting Standard to bring its banking and accounting practices in line with OECD expectations (OECD 2014a).

Finally, and closely related to the other topics, was the reform of Andorra's banking secrecy rules. There was little concern that international terrorist groups were laundering money through Andorra's relatively small banks, especially since the country has been relatively free of official corruption (Department of State 2013). Nonetheless, since such groups are always in search of the weakest link in the chain, conformity to regional standards was a high priority, despite the threat this posed to the country's financial system. A 2012 report by the Council of Europe's MONEYVAL group on laundering showed that Andorra was partially compliant with almost all its standards (Council of Europe 2012). The most serious deficiency was Andorra's relatively gentle treatment of minor offenses and its overly narrow definition of "terrorism," each of which could provide an opportunity for some types of small-scale laundering (Council of Europe 2012, 5). But otherwise it has committed to the expected OECD, EU, and Council of Europe standards and seemed poised to fully implement most of them.

In 2003 the head of government, Marc Forné Molné, announced, impetuously in retrospect, that Andorra would become a member of the European Union by 2018 (Europa World Plus 2015d). Andorra has renounced this goal (All Andorra 2016) and instead has focused on an association agreement. Talks are underway at the time of writing (January 2016) between the EU and Monaco, San Marino, and Andorra, with a March 2017 target date for completion, although this will likely be affected by the urgency of UK-EU withdrawal talks connected to the June 2016 "Brexit" referendum (Monaco 2016). At any rate, the joint committee has been quite active (issuing more than twenty policies during the 1993–2015 period), putting flesh on the bones of the 1990 customs agreement, specifying in great detail which products will be covered, which rules and regulations will apply, and how all of this is to be managed, as mentioned earlier (European Commission 1999). In 2010 Andorra signed an agreement on customs security measures designed to minimize the spread of unsafe products and contaminated foods, among other things (European Union 2011b). Andorra's investment laws were also liberalized with respect to services (see above) as well as other sectors in response to pressure from the EU and OECD. Foreigners, as a result of laws passed in 2008 and 2012, may own a majority of shares in such key activities as real estate and tourism ventures (Department of State 2013; Europa World Plus 2015d).

For the most part Andorra has been a receiver of policy and has been relatively more compliant than its counterparts, perhaps in part because of France's role in legislating (Reixach 2015). Although one could argue that the EU has shown some restraint in dealing with Andorra, the fact remains that even the joint committee decisions largely reflected EU preferences. The customs security agreement, by which Andorra committed to apply the EU's acquis on the subject (Article 12b), provides only the possibility that Andorra's opinions regarding future policies will be solicited (Article 12i), a natural enough situation for a nonmember state (European Union 2011b). Despite this, the vast majority of Andorrans, as mentioned earlier, would like to see integration with the EU proceed (Centre de Recerca Sociològica 2013). A mere 6 percent favor a reduction of ties (European Commission 2012), even though employment levels have declined since 2009 and everyone is paying higher taxes (Departament d'Estadística, Andorra 2013). Even though there are fewer foreign residents in the country, the country's identity seems to be in flux. The speaking of Catalan is in decline despite efforts by the state to reverse the trend (Servei de Politicá Lingüística 2011, 9). Andorran youths are leaving the country in ever-greater numbers, in part due to the decline of the ski resorts (Fortó Areny 2013). The need for diversification and new investment is clear, although many bureaucratic obstacles exist (Cambra de Comerç et al. 2012).

To what extent is trust evident in Andorra's relations with its neighbors since 1993? Especially where the co-princes are concerned, it would seem there is quite a bit. Using the criteria presented in table 6.1, we can see that Andorra continues to be vulnerable, perhaps in some ways even more so than before since it is increasingly accessible and more frequently visited. Andorra is on Europe's radar. It can no longer bask in the security that comes with obscurity. Likewise, foreigners have learned that Andorra has assets that can be exploited. Of course, two can play at this game, and Andorra came out ahead until the Great Recession. But clearly the potential exists—and is being made more likely by Andorra's efforts to liberalize its economy—for Andorra to become deeply penetrated by foreign capital, regulations, and influence. It is surprising that Andorrans seem less concerned about this possibility than, say, the Sammarinese or Liechtensteiners.

With respect to the co-princes—and Spain by inference—Andorra's relationship since 1993 is more clearly based on the will of both the elite and the masses. The public and elite were actively involved in redefining the fundamental relationships by means of a carefully and publicly considered constitution as well as a tripartite treaty subjected to debate and endorsement in the General Council. Andorra succeeded—with the help of the Council of Europe and the European Union—to establish a far greater degree of sovereignty and recognition than before and to have this status validated repeatedly in the subsequent years. At the same time, there was no interest then and now in expelling the co-princes and proclaiming a republic. In the final analysis a gentler form of dependency has been elected by the people of Andorra, reminiscent of the multiple votes by Puerto Ricans in favor of maintaining its status as a commonwealth of the United States rather than opting for independence or assimilation and statehood.

The scope and salience of Andorra's relationship with its co-princes and Spain are classified as "high" despite the ambiguity of the security relationship. Given the obligation to consult in the event of a threat to Andorra's territory or independence and Andorra's geographic location as an enclave, it is reasonable to infer an implicit and de facto commitment to defend Andorra in the event of attack. At the lower end of the spectrum,

TABLE 6.1. Features of Andorra's Relationships with Neighboring States and Institutions

		Trustor-Trustee Relationship			Issues in Play		Structure of Agreements		
		Vulnerability	Exploitability	Voluntarism	Scope of Issues	Salience of Issues	Imprecision and Informality	Marginalization	Entrapment
1806–1933: Submission to France & Bishop of Urgell	France	**HIGH**	Low	**HIGH**	**HIGH**	**HIGH**	**HIGH**	MODERATE	**HIGH**
	Bishop of Urgell	**HIGH**	MODERATE	MODERATE	HIGH	MODERATE	**HIGH**	**HIGH**	**HIGH**
1933–1993: Submission to France & Bishop of Urgell	France	**HIGH**	**HIGH**	Low	HIGH	**HIGH**	**HIGH**	MODERATE	MODERATE
	Bishop of Urgell	**HIGH**	MODERATE	MODERATE	MODERATE	MODERATE	**HIGH**	MODERATE	MODERATE
1993–2016: Submission to Co-Princes & Regional Agencies	Co-Princes	**HIGH**	**HIGH**	**HIGH**	**HIGH**	**HIGH**	MODERATE	MODERATE	**HIGH**
	Regional Agencies	**HIGH**	**HIGH**	MODERATE	MODERATE	MODERATE	Low	MODERATE	MODERATE

many issues have yet to be addressed systematically (unlike in the France-Monaco and Italy–San Marino relationships), but the trend is for increasingly deep collaboration and integration, if only through the EU.

The fundamental agreements and several of the secondary treaties and commitments are less explicit and precise than one finds elsewhere. The constitution, while apparently detailed and clear, leaves several key issues in limbo or subject to interpretation. Whether both co-princes must ratify all treaties or promulgate all legislation is not entirely clear; experts disagree. It seems likely that this will be resolved only through the accumulation of more practice and custom in the Andorran tradition. Other agreements are both short and long, precise and vague, depending on the topic. The tripartite agreement on travel and immigration is on the imprecise end of the scale, while the recent agreement with France on double taxation is at the other end. Taken together, the agreements are fairly imprecise, especially those that are more significant.

With respect to marginalization and entrapment, the treaties generally offer few opportunities for regular consultation and for Andorrans to influence treaty interpretation and implementation. Naturally, Andorrans have the principal voice where the constitution is concerned, but primarily with respect to domestic affairs. Where foreign relations are concerned, Andorrans must still share responsibility with the co-princes—a rarity in modern times—but at least they have more power than in the past. Where the other treaties are concerned, most do not provide for Andorran input after ratification. Entrapment is high not only because the relationship with the co-princes is enshrined in constitutional law, but also because most other agreements do not provide for an end date or denunciation. Taken together, Andorra clearly shows a willingness to commit to a far-ranging dependence with France and the bishop (as well as Spain in parallel), even though it had the opportunity to walk away. Based on our rubric, this indicates a fairly high degree of trust, but trust in a new type of relationship that gives Andorra more opportunities to shape its future. It also seems that its trust is not entirely invested in either co-prince or neighboring state but in the process of balancing.

With respect to its agreements with the EU and the Council of Europe, it is also clear that Andorrans not only welcomed closer ties but for the most part initiated them. Furthermore, the agreements were validated through legislation, referenda, and opinion surveys, which all point to a general approval of closer ties. Since the agreements don't cover security issues, it is reasonable to say their scope and salience is only moderate, albeit at the high end of the category. The Council of Europe played a key role in the political reforms that took place in 1993, essentially prescribing the basic outline of the constitution and the tripartite agreement recognizing and framing Andorra's sovereign privileges. Likewise, the initial 1990 EU agreement set the stage for Andorra's entry into the regional market, which in turn presaged its conformity with standards on taxation and money laundering. In the end almost every aspect of Andorran life was affected.

As in the case of other microstates, EU agreements are consistently precise and detailed, although the 1990 agreement is less specific than others. Likewise, the expectations of the Council of Europe—particularly regarding membership—leave little room for interpretation. Most of the other arrangements involving these agencies are virtual carbon copies of other treaties we have considered earlier in the book (see especially chapters 4 and 5). Therefore in the case of Andorra, as with the others, these agreements are low on the imprecision spectrum. Likewise, with respect to marginalization and entrapment, Andorra is given opportunities to participate in implementation and interpretation. The joint committee established through the 1990 EU treaty has been quite active, issuing important decisions on a yearly basis that, while clearly reflective of EU preferences, are at least vetted by representatives of Andorra. The Council of Europe provides Andorra a chance to participate directly in council decision making, including a turn in the chair's position. Of course its votes are hardly determinative of council policy. Taken together it seems reasonable to classify Andorra's marginalization as moderate. The same applies to the degree of entrapment in these agreements. In nearly all cases, the treaties provide for a six-month-delayed denunciation or a sunset clause that could bring the agreement to a natural end. In the case of the agreement on taxation of savings, as with other microstates, all depends on other states' willingness to commit and remain committed. But the clear expectation is that Andorra will allow its political system, economic policies, and societal practices to be permanently reshaped by its engagement with regional bodies.

Taken together, as mentioned, Andorra is demonstrating a considerable degree of trust in its protectors. Much of this seems rooted in faith that all these various actors—from the French president to the European Commission—have different interests and aims that offset, with the result that Andorra's interests will have a good chance of being preserved. As we have seen, while the French president may be more concerned about lost tax revenue, the bishop is more concerned about lost souls. And while France and Spain may focus on cross-border migration and trade, the EU and Council of Europe are focused on broader freedoms and rights. It seems that in most situations, there will be at least one actor whose interests will coincide with Andorra's and who can serve to moderate pressures from others.

Conclusions

In the first phase we considered—1806 to 1933—Andorra's conduct evidenced considerable trust in the system established centuries earlier, and again since 1993—after a lengthy period of frustration and disappointment—the basic sense of trust seems to have returned, albeit trust in a very different arrangement involving new actors and new issues. In this sense, Andorra's experience is unique. While other microstates have worked consistently to extricate themselves as much as feasible from their dependent relationships, Andorra—even though it clearly had the opportunity to do the same—has worked to redefine the situation in order to preserve much of its essence. On the other hand, Andorra's trajectory will likely come to resemble that of its counterparts as it becomes more deeply integrated in Europe. Whether its degree of trust in regional institutions will wax or wane is difficult to predict. Andorran officials have already learned that the EU has a mind of its own and that it does not tolerate wide deviation from its expectations. Even during the 1990 negotiations the commission representatives proved quite inflexible. Benefits have been closely tied to compliance and for now Andorra still has far to go. Andorra's willingness to comply depends a great deal on the ability of the economy to redefine itself and rebound.

SEVEN

Trust from Dominance

I have argued that trust is most likely to be in play in the case of weak actors that elect to rely on the protection of more powerful ones, especially where the protector could exploit the weak state. It can be measured in part by looking more closely at the terms of the arrangements, their scope and salience, their precision, and the degree to which the parties can influence their operation or exit. We have seen that while trust is not common where our small European states are concerned, there is enough evidence of its occurrence to warrant a deeper inquiry into its causes and implications, a subject to which I will turn in chapter 8.

In this chapter, I expand the types of cases to include great powers acting as the dominant actors over a variety of weaker states. I look at some asymmetrical relationships between the United States, the Russian Federation, and the Peoples Republic of China and two other states each, one that has been generally satisfactory from the dominant state's perspective and one that has not. Specifically, I will consider United States relations with Canada and South Vietnam, Russian relations with Belarus and Georgia, and Chinese relations with North Korea and North Vietnam/unified Vietnam.

These cases are particularly interesting because they allow us to explore situations in which very powerful actors appear—at least on the surface—to have made themselves vulnerable to exploitation by weaker actors. By looking more closely at conditions surrounding the relationships and the terms of various agreements, we will be able to address whether trust was active. While it is unlikely that major powers or large multilateral agencies would put themselves in such a situation, it is possible, as argued by Rathbun (2011) with respect to the US role in NATO, particularly if a government's leader are personally predisposed to trust. Trust, as pointed out by Lake (2011, 14), might allow for a productive relationship without the investment of time and energy in enforcement. On the other hand, I will also consider the perspective of the subordinate states. It is to all these issues that we now turn.

United States–Canada

Canada indirectly owes its existence to the United States, in that back in 1867 when it formed into a dominion, it did so to more effectively protect itself from Americans' oft-stated plans for annexation (Roussel 2004, 5, 16; Holmes 1989, 20). As recently as 1911, a reciprocal trade agreement collapsed in large part because the deal—already controversial in Canadian circles—was touted as a first step to annexation by US House Speaker Champ Clark, who opined that the treaty would lead to a day when "the American flag will float over every square foot of the British North American possessions" (Taylor 1989, 243; Tansill 1943, 463; Shore 1998, 339). It is therefore surprising that Canada has been willing to submit to US leadership at all, something that stemmed in large part from improved relations between the United States and Great Britain in the early twentieth century (although in 1895 President Grover Cleveland threatened war over Britain's policies toward Venezuela [Shore 1998, 346; Preston 1977, 149]). This did not always serve Canadian interests, however, as when, after securing a US commitment to the creation of a six-member joint commission (three Canadians, three Americans) to settle a dispute over the Alaska panhandle boundary in 1903, the British conceded the US position above Canada's, apparently to induce American support for the UK's South African operations (Preston 1977, 150; Tansill 1943, 230; Wilson 1963, 10).

The United States and the United Kingdom had already settled a variety of questions by means of a joint commission of experts and diplomats and so it was not entirely unexpected that the United States and Canada would follow suit (Roussel 2004, 233, 237; Holmes 1989, 20). In 1909 the United States and the United Kingdom (on behalf of Canada) agreed to a series of arrangements regarding management and use of the Great Lakes and St. Lawrence Seaway, including the creation of the International Joint Commission that included an equal number of representatives from the United States and Canada (Articles 3 and 7) and the power to issue rulings on disputes by simple majority vote (Articles 9 and 10). In practice the body has operated on a consensus basis (Shore 1998, 353).

The United Kingdom refocused its defense away from Canada in 1905, leaving it with fewer than twenty thousand troops to defend thousands of miles of wilderness borderlands (Preston 1977, 160; Shore 1998, 342). The United States for its part had only around ten thousand troops between 1866 and 1900 (Shore 1998, 342). The result was a de facto undefended border, which may have contributed to the tendency to resolve conflicts through nonviolent means (Shore 1998, 335, 342; Taylor 1989, 241). Prime minister Wilfrid Laurier is rumored to have told a colleague in 1902 that Canada need not worry much about its own defenses since the American Monroe Doctrine would lead the United States to thwart foreign aggression anyway (Ropp 1963, 86). Even when Canada began to increase its military strength in the early 1900s, it was with an eye to helping the United Kingdom in the event of a European war, and in fact when war broke out in 1914 Ottawa sent almost all of its forces overseas, leaving it defenseless (Preston 1977, 167, 215; Shore 1998, 347). Although many Americans still nurtured the Manifest Destiny ideology, and Teddy Roosevelt hinted that he could have taken the Alaska panhandle by force had the British not conceded, annexation was no longer official US policy and by the 1930s both countries had ended planning war scenarios involving the other (Shore 1998, 347; Preston 1977, 169).

During the interwar period it became increasingly clear that Canada's defense—especially against such global threats as Nazi Germany and Tojo's Japan—could not be achieved without help from the United States (Stacey 1963, 104). The more cynical in Ottawa presumed that failure to collaborate with the United States would prompt unilateral action from Washington (Preston 1977, 3). Collaboration during World War I had already presaged the United States's assuming Britain's role (Shore 1998, 335). Economically, the two nations were increasingly integrated: by 1891 the United States had passed the United Kingdom as Canada's primary source of imports; in 1923 more direct investment was American and in general the country was becoming increasingly Americanized culturally (Tansill 1943, 429; Martin 1993, 75; Doran 1984, 31). In 1935 they signed a trade reciprocity agreement that exempted Canada from many of the beggar-thy-neighbor policies the United States had adopted previously (Perras 1998, 17; Martin 1993, 76). A key turning point came in 1936 when Franklin Roosevelt, on a visit to Chautauqua and again at Kingston in 1938, declared that the United States would intervene to defend Canada in the event of an attack from a third country (Perras 1998, 35, 43; Preston 1977, 228). Prime minister Mackenzie King reciprocated by assuring Roosevelt that Canada would take measures to ensure that no country would use its territory to attack the United States (Perras 1998, 44).

Between January 1938 and August 1940, the United States and Canada were engaged in behind-the-scenes talks on mutual defense. Canadian leaders resisted several US proposals, including the leasing of Canadian bases to the United States (as the British had done) and allowing American warships to refuel at will in Halifax (Perras 1998, 52; Stacey 1963, 105). These efforts were symptomatic of Canadian fears of being overwhelmed by great powers (Roussel 2004, 233; Gotlieb 2013). Even after the United Kingdom declared war on Germany in September 1939, Canada later made its own declaration of war (Perras 1998, 52). Canada also rejected membership in the Organization of American States for fear of becoming the United States' "second vote" (Martin 1993, 162). Nonetheless, Canada agreed in August 1940 to joint and mutual defense with the United States. The statement issued in Ogdensburg, New York, was brief—a mere six sentences—but it committed the two states to protecting the continent from foreign aggression and to coordinate their defenses (English and Hillmer 1989/1982, 34; King 1989/1940, 100).

A Permanent Joint Board on Defense (PJBD) was to be created that consisted of an equal number of Canadian and American representatives drawn from both military and civilian services, whose task would be to "commence immediate studies relating to sea, land and air problems, including personnel and material" and to "consider in the broad sense the defense of the north half of the Western Hemisphere" (Keenleyside 1960/61, 52). Within ten days of the declaration, the PJBD held its first meeting, meeting eight times in four months to discuss key defense questions and carry out on-site inspections and fact-finding missions to determine the most urgent deficiencies. The committee's decisions were made by consensus, although majority voting was permitted, and were uniformly described as "candid," "business-like," and governed by "mutual confidence" (Stacey 1963, 107; Keenleyside 1960/61, 54). Sensitive information was shared, even during the period when only Canada was a belligerent. When disagreements arose, it was as often as not based on branch loyalties and perspectives rather than nationality. The board issued thirty-three recommendations to the governments of Canada and the United States and all but three were implemented without reservation, a remarkable record (Keenleyside 1960/61, 56).

A further sixty-five bilateral agreements were reached between the two countries during the war years (almost half of all the bilateral treaties signed by Canada [Cohen 1963, 190]). One of these was the agreement in April 1941 at Hyde Park to integrate the production of war-related goods, also a model of brevity at only seven paragraphs (Perras 1998, 96; Preston 1977, 229). This agreement would profoundly affect the Canadian defense industry for years to come (Martin 1993, 76; English and Hillmer 1989/1982, 35). This is not to say that all went smoothly during the war years. Canadians resented being excluded from a variety of wartime joint boards established by Roosevelt and Winston Churchill, although this problem stemmed as much from Churchill's preferences as Roosevelt's (Perras 1998, 106). But it was also clear that after December 7, 1941, the United States had less patience for diplomatic politesse and favored taking command and leaving less to chance. A senior Canadian official concluded in late 1941 that Americans "were ready for Canadian 'cooperation' so long as that meant Canada would follow the American lead and subordinate the policies of Ottawa to Washington" (Keenleyside 1941, in Perras 1998, 103). Despite sometimes seeing their forces sacrificed in dubious missions (see the Dieppe raid of 1942 in which two-thirds of a force of roughly five thousand were killed, wounded, or captured), Canadians were most worried about not appearing to do their part in the war (viz. the heavy involvement of Canadians in the Dieppe raid was at the insistence of Canadian commanders in the United Kingdom [Veterans Affairs Canada 2017]).

Emerging from World War II, Canada's foreign policy mirrored that of the United States in that it did not revert to prewar neutrality as it had in 1918, but instead became fully engaged in the defense of the Western world, joining NATO and the Bretton Woods institutions and ultimately placing some of its forces under US command by way of the North American Aerospace Defense Command (NORAD) (Taylor 1989, 242). The government even came close to signing a free trade agreement with the United States, but withdrew out of concern of appearing to be an American lap dog or disloyal to the United Kingdom (Taylor 1989, 243; English and Hillmer 1982/1989, 35). At any rate, until 1971 US-Canadian relations were at their warmest, primarily because Ottawa accepted Washington's leadership, although it took contrary positions on the Cuban Missile Crisis and the Vietnam War (Muirhead 2004, 448; Stacey 1963, 112). Prime Minster Lester Pearson effused in 1951 that the United States will perform well its new role as leader of the free world and Canada should therefore accept the role of loyal ally without expecting as much attention from

Washington as had been given before (Pearson 1989/1951, 109–111). This observation was never entirely accepted by Canadian elites and proved a source of disappointment and frustration (Anderson 2011, 1036).

Despite some serious reservations about becoming an appendage to US strategic policy, Mackenzie King agreed to a Joint Statement for Defense Collaboration in 1947. This was again a relatively brief document that spelled out a series of collaborative actions, including staff swaps, uniform specifications for war materiel, and shared facilities (Roussel 2004, 233; Ropp 1963, 82). It protected national security and provided for denunciation with no lag period. The agreement has functioned effectively and helped prepare the way for NORAD in 1956, itself a product of joint consultations in the joint Military Study Group (NORAD 2005). The agreement specified that units from the two countries would be integrated under a single command and that the commander and deputy commander would always come from different countries (Article 4) although in practice the top post has gone to an American (the headquarters is in Colorado Springs). The command is accountable to both countries (Article 2) although since the Strategic Air Command—which for the first two decades was the operational arm of NORAD—is entirely under American control, this was a hollow provision. At eleven brief articles with a ten-year sunset provision, the agreement is informal, at least on paper.

NORAD was clearly a priority for American military planners since they were unable to complete an early-warning radar network in the Arctic without it. Canadian authorities were sympathetic to the mission but the public had reservations. In particular, the eventual decision to turn over control of the Distant Early Warning line of radar stations along Canada's northernmost border to the Americans was among the most controversial elements since it raised questions about whether the country had surrendered its sovereignty (Lackenbauer and Kikkert 2010, 7). Even though it cost millions, the John Diefenbacker government welcomed the chance to take full control of the southernmost Pinetree Line that ran mostly along the US-Canada border in the early 1960s, given its symbolic value (as well as its linkage to an arms deal [Stevenson 2013, 299; Stacey 1963, 305]).

Canada's military became more deeply enmeshed with that of the United States with respect to procurement as well with the shuttering of Avro Corporation's production of the Arrow jet fighter (Ropp 1963, 96). In 1957, after struggling with cost overruns and lack of demand, a decision by the US government to halt purchases of Arrows (itself likely encouraged by US defense contractors) led to tens of thousands of Canadians losing their jobs at a time when unemployment was already high (Hobson 2013; Stevenson 2013, 295). The Dwight Eisenhower and John F. Kennedy administrations made a variety of offers to offset the loss of the Arrow, including selling several dozen F-101 jets at cost and offering to sell F-101s and buy other less advanced Canadian planes, all of which were rejected by an indecisive Diefenbacker (Stevenson 2013, 295–97). Ultimately, a deal was struck involving the transfer of F-101s in exchange for Canada assuming control of the Pinetree Line as well as the United States purchasing Canadian planes to help create local jobs (Stevenson 2013, 299). Canadian negotiators also conceded that the American fighters could be equipped with nuclear-capable missiles, a difficult position for the antinuclear Ottawa government (English and Hillmer 1982/1989, 39).

Canada continued to negotiate agreements with the United States at a healthy pace, averaging more than eight new treaties each year between 1946 and 1956 (Cohen 1963, 190). By 1961 the United States and Canada were governed by 187 bilateral and 153 multilateral treaties as well as a number of joint commissions dealing with border issues and economic and security matters (Wilson 1963, 5), making the dyad among the most "legalized" in the world (although until the 1980s joint commissions tended to give the United States the upper hand in practice [Gotlieb 2013]). While Canada participated in the Korean War by way of the UN, Ottawa was not always supportive of larger US foreign policy aims. In particular, Canadian authorities worried about Eisenhower's fierce anticommunist rhetoric and brinkmanship policies and saw its role as a force for moderation (Ropp 1963, 85; Stacey 1963, 120; Martin 1993, 160). Diefenbacker's foreign minister Harold Green famously offered to mediate during the Cuban Missile Crisis, an offer that provoked anger and charges of disloyalty from John F. Kennedy (Martin 1993, 64; English and Hillmer 1982/1989, 38). A few years later a similar reaction came from Lyndon Johnson after Lester Pearson vigorously urged the United States in 1965 to suspend its bombing campaign in North Vietnam to no avail (English and Hillmer 1982/1989, 39). And Canada continued to reject membership in the OAS, despite the organization's keeping an empty seat available to it (Martin 1993, 163). In general, Canadian governments were beginning to develop an international identity that emphasized multilateralism, peacekeeping, moderation, and mediation, which increasingly put it at odds with the United States' hegemonic imperatives (Roussel 2004, 17; Thompson and Randall 2008, 301). As a nation of few people heavily dependent on the sale of raw materials to its superpower neighbor, Canadians were sympathetic to the theory of dependency that was so popular in the developing world beginning in the 1960s, and so Canadian diplomats began to see themselves as a bridge between North and South (Roussel 2004, 22).

A key turning point occurred in August 1971, when the Richard Nixon administration unilaterally took the dollar off the gold standard and imposed a 10 percent surcharge tariff on all imports, including Canada's. The effect was seen as a betrayal in Ottawa, where expectations had developed that the United States would always try to provide Canada with privileged access to its markets (Muirhead 2004, 440). Canada resisted undertaking the policy changes the United States asked of all OECD countries but instead asked for an exemption to the draconian measures. Treasury secretary John Connally rejected the request out of hand, pointing to the large trade surplus Canada enjoyed vis-à-vis the United States, which in his view was prima facie evidence of free riding (Muirhead 2004, 422–23). Ultimately, Canada loosened its currency and allowed it to appreciate, despite fears of job loss across the country as its exports became too expensive for American tastes. But Prime minister Pierre Trudeau—already skeptical of US intentions around the world—saw no need to make further sacrifices and held the line for several months (Holmes 1989, 22; Muirhead 2004, 455). Ultimately, the immediate effects of the Nixon shock on Canada were not as severe as had been expected and so it could to be patient; thanks in part to Henry Kissinger's intervention many of the trade penalties were lifted (Muirhead 2004, 452). Stung by Canada's intransigence, Nixon traveled to Ottawa to explain what he felt was the basis for a new US-Canada relationship, one based on realpolitik:

> Canadians and Americans [must] move beyond the sentimental rhetoric of the past. It is time for us to recognize that we have very separate identities; that we have significant differences, and that nobody's interests are furthered when these realities are obscured. . . . (Canada House of Commons 1972, 1327, cited in Muirhead 2004, 455)

Ironically, Trudeau took Nixon at his word and began to develop what would be known as the "third option," a policy of nurturing relations with countries other than the United States and loosening ties to his neighbor to the south, much to Nixon's annoyance (Muirhead 2004, 456; English and Hillmer 1982/1989, 33). The next ten years would form the nadir of Canada-US relations as Trudeau signed free trade agreements with Europe and Japan while eschewing a similar arrangement with the United States (Biette and Kuschner 2014, 399), visited Havana and declared "Viva Castro!" (Martin 1993, 162), and condemned American nuclear testing on the Alaska panhandle (Preston 1977, 2). His government created the Foreign Investment Review Agency (FIRA) to screen especially obnoxious foreign investment while promoting Canadian energy policy through the New Energy Program (English and Hillmer 1982/1989, 40; Burney and Hampson 2012). He was also direct in criticizing the "Cold War II" escalation of Ronald Reagan and Margaret Thatcher (Martin 1993, 58). In all this he received the backing of the Canadian public, which had largely lost its enthusiasm for the United States (Gravelle 2014, 3). American governments, for their part, waffled between anger and confusion over the new Canadian approach, with the result that statements oscillated between castigation and condescension (Holmes 1989, 19). Congress in particular took aim at FIRA, accusing Canada of turning its back on free markets (English and Hillmer 1982/1989, 40). To be sure, after three decades of relative subservience on Canada's part and what Americans felt was considerable generosity, it is understandable that American officials felt betrayed by this new direction (Anderson 2011, 1039).

Everything changed, however, when Progressive Conservative Brian Mulroney became prime minister in 1984. A true believer in free markets and a fan of all things American, he was unapologetic about reversing the policies of Trudeau's Liberal Party (Martin 1993, 53). He eagerly sought the company of Reagan, a man he much admired, despite the risk of being called a lapdog of the United States (Martin 1993, 57, 82; McDonald 1993). He joined the OAS and immediately supported the US intervention in Panama, the only yea vote besides the United States' (McDonald 1993, 7). He dismantled FIRA, a move that was heartily welcomed in Washington (McDonald 1993, 21). He became a close adviser to George H. W. Bush, coaching him on how to win over French president François Mitterrand and how to interpret developments in Mikhail Gorbachev's USSR (Martin 1993, 158). Put another way, Canadian and American interests were in harmony during the Mulroney years (Holmes 1989, 29; Keohane 1984). As put by Martin, "Remarkably, neither Bush nor Reagan ever felt he had to make strong public criticism of positions taken by the Mulroney government. It was an indication of their degree of satisfaction" (Martin 1993, 155).

This is not to say there were no conflicts. Reagan did little to address Canada's concerns over acid rain, although the Great Lakes Water Quality Agreement and the 1970 Clean Air Act addressed the issue to a degree (Roberts 1989, 80). Mulroney opposed Canadian participation in the Strategic Defense Initiative and feared it would violate the Anti-Ballistic Missile Treaty (Biette and Kuschner 2014, 396; Taylor 1989, 245). In general, Canadian defense spending, while growing under Mulroney, still fell considerably short of US aims (Martin 1993, 167). The United States was also persuaded that the Northwest Passage was an international strait open to peaceful navigation and sent ships through it to bring home the point. Canada persistently objected (Taylor 1989, 250).

The overall good feeling and harmony between the two culminated in the Canada-U.S. Free Trade Agreement of 1988 and subsequently the North American Free Trade Agreement of 1994. Although consistent with Canada's historic push to secure special concessions from the United States, the agreement was a break from the country's historic ambivalence about leveling the playing field (Holmes 1989, 28; McDonald 1993, 16). At 2,106 articles, not including a number of annexes, the FTA was a monument to clarity and specificity. It also provided for a GATT-like dispute settlement system that would guarantee that neither country could skirt the prescribed procedures on trade matters (although it did not necessarily address adverse outcomes [Annex 1901.2, 1903.2, 1904.13; Godsoe 1989/1988, 311]). Canada insisted on this in large measure because of adverse decisions made by US administrative tribunals that demonstrated that Americans could not be counted on to protect Canadian interests (Gotlieb 2013). Article 2101 provided for a full exchange of data and texts on trade law and trends and Article 2106 allowed for denunciation with a six-month lag. The negotiations, while tough, were carefully framed for public audiences to minimize the chances of rejection, especially in Canada. US negotiators were urged not to apply excessive pressure to Canadian diplomats and to avoid using the phrase "free trade" in public comments (Martin 1993, 155; McDonald 1993, 16). The tactics worked in that the FTA became relatively popular among both Liberals and Conservatives (Gravelle 2014, 6). Mulroney's Progressive Conservatives were re-elected in 1988 in what served as a referendum on NAFTA. This is not to say that American negotiators were being overly generous. US trade representative Clayton Yeutter commented that "The Canadians don't know what they've signed. In 20 years they will be sucked into the U.S. economy" (McDonald 1993, 16). Bush and later Bill Clinton consistently viewed free trade in North America as a prelude to hemispheric integration, an agenda that was far broader than most Canadians understood (McDonald 1993, 4). At any rate, as the FTA began to bear fruit, the new Liberal government of Jean Chrétien carried on the negotiations for NAFTA, albeit a bit more quietly than had the Conservatives (Thompson and Randall 2008, 285). Despite efforts to limit US sales of cultural products in Canada, films and books flowed almost without obstacles, another departure from past Canadian policies (Thompson and Randall 2008, 289). But Canadian exports to Mexico and the United States nearly doubled within five years, so many would-be critics were mollified (Gravelle 2014, 4; Anderson 2011, 1034).

Following the terror attacks on September 11, 2001, Canada experienced a wave of sympathy and support for the United States (Gravelle 2014, 6). It immediately came to the aid of its southern neighbor, allowing aircraft that were stranded by the clearing of American skies to land at Canadian airports and tending to the passengers, voting with the United States on anti-terror resolutions at the United Nations, and even deploying two thousand troops to Afghanistan (Thompson and Randall 2008, 306). It adopted tougher antiterror legislation even more quickly than did the United States (Pauly 2003, 101). It also formed a joint crisis management team that could allow troops from both countries to move quickly across the border, and it signed other agreements on border security (Thompson and Randall 2008, 318; Roussel 2004, 239; Pauly 2003, 102). NORAD was once again renewed—this time indefinitely—despite Canada's being indirectly compelled to accept elements of an antimissile system it had previously rejected (NORAD 2012, 10; McDonald 1993, 25).

The enthusiasm was short-lived, however, as Canadians viewed George W. Bush's Manichean approach and disdain for international law as antithetical to everything their country stood for (Thompson and Randall 2008, 304; Pauly 2003, 92–93). Liberal prime minister Jean Chrétien lamented that American and Western arrogance might have contributed to the attack (*National Post* 2001). Canada expressed deep reservations about Bush's war in Iraq, opting not to participate and even persuading Mexico to use its place on the UN Security Council to put forward a compromise resolution before the invasion (Thompson and Randall 2008, 310; Roussel 2004, 241; Pauly 2003, 92). Bush responded with pointed criticism of Canada's failure to support the United States during visits in 2004 and 2005 (Thompson and Randall 2008, 317). Canadians expressed annoyance at the adoption of stricter border controls, although American officials for their part complained of the failure on the part of Canada to secure the border. In 2009, passports were made mandatory for those crossing into the United States (Thompson and Randall 2008, 327; Pauly 2003, 101).

Obama, while in many ways sympathetic to Canada's approach to world affairs, put the relationship even further down his list of priorities (Anderson 2011, 1034). There was little interest in the effects of American stimulus programs on Canadian trade (the "buy America" provisions were resented in Ottawa [Biette and Kuschner 2014, 398]). The United States ignored the spirit of NAFTA as it imposed a ban on beef imports over the mad cow disease scare (Thompson and Randall 2008, 339) and emphasized trade agreements with Asian countries and the rest of the Western hemisphere (Burney and Hampson 2012). And Canadians were disappointed in the failure on the part of the United States to strongly support Canada's bid for a seat on the UN Security Council in 2010 (Biette and Kuschner 2014, 401). And Obama's rejection of the Keystone XL Pipeline project (later approved by Congress over his objection) added salt to the wound (Sands 2012). All of this prompted two prominent Canadians to write in *Foreign Affairs* in 2012 that Obama had "lost Canada" (Burney and Hampson 2012). They charged that the United States had repeatedly "jilted" its neighbor and had failed to "trust and respect its loyal ally." The accusation is naturally debatable, and Americans for their part accuse their neighbors to the north of the same sort of whining Nixon described back in 1972 (Sands 2012). After all, despite these complaints, the two nations continue to sign formal and informal treaties on a clockwork-like schedule, a recent one involving the creation of a working group to harmonize regulations (the Joint Action Plan for Regulatory Cooperation). Joint commissions continue to resolve numerous minor disputes on a daily basis and security cooperation continues to expand. Canada even joined the Trans-Pacific Partnership trade talks in 2012, something Conservative PM Stephen Harper enthusiastically endorsed although incoming Liberal PM Justin Trudeau has demurred on endorsing it (Biette and Kuschner 2014, 399; McGregor 2015; Liberal Party of Canada 2015). The question became moot once Donald Trump, outspoken TPP critic, was elected US president. He pulled the United States out of the talks shortly after taking office.

Trump's election also raises questions about other forms of cooperation that were moving forward under Trudeau, including the status of NAFTA and climate change commitments. The WTO provided a win for Canada when a dispute settlement panel required the United States to suspend country-of-origin labeling for Canadian pork and beef bound for the United States (Global Affairs Canada 2015). Although the talks had taken years, it is interesting that a deal between Canada and the European Union was concluded in late 2016, providing a tariff cut of roughly 99 percent between the parties and providing a bit of a hedge for Canada against possible trade troubles with the United States (BBC 2016b). It is also unclear how committed is the Trudeau administration to security cooperation, especially with respect to fighting terrorism in Iraq and Syria as Canada withdrew some fighter aircraft while deploying new helicopters in 2016 (National Defense 2016; Kennedy 2016).

Returning to our typology of trust, table 7.1 provides some tentative categorization. The first period ends at 1970, although it could just as easily break at the Nixon shock of August 1971 since it is widely agreed that this represented a turning point in the relationship. Prior to this, Canada showed considerable evidence of trust while the United States was less trusting. Looking more closely, Canada was in a vulnerable position, although with a solid resource base and continuing close ties with the United Kingdom it was not as vulnerable as, say, Monaco vis-à-vis France. It still depended heavily on US markets and goods. As a result, and given its small military capability, it was very exploitable, a feature that virtually defines the Canadian psyche. The United States, on the other hand, had little to fear from Canada. Both governments, along with their citizenry, strongly supported the relationship and the numerous agreements entered into, so it is reasonable to rank voluntarism as "high" for both.

Where Canada was concerned, the scope and salience of the many agreements entered into were both high as they directly addressed a wide range of issues, some of which were matters of life or death. Where the United States was concerned, while the issues were certainly important—especially joint defense against Soviet attack—it had far more concerns aside from the relationship with Canada. Its economy was still largely self-sufficient during this period, for example, and Washington had to tend to problems in Europe, Asia, the Middle East, and Latin America on a daily basis. The agreements were numerous and varied, but it is worth noting that some of the most important, as discussed previously, were also among the most informal. In retrospect, it almost seems that the more serious the topic, the more casual the form of the agreement. Naturally, the United States made sure that even though many arrangements involved joint interpretation and implementation, it reserved certain key decisions for itself alone. A key case in point was the security agreements—NORAD in particular—which left considerable unilateral control to the United States (such as its direct control over SAC). The United States likewise—at least informally—seems to have felt it could walk away from some agreements to which Canada was more deeply committed.

After the Nixon shock, the relationship went through a reappraisal (See table 7.1). The nature and form of the agreements shifted as well. In particular, some of the key commitments—the FTA and NAFTA, for example—were far more detailed and specific than had been the case previously. While some agreements were still informal, most were very precise, indicating perhaps a loss of trust by both parties. The basic conditions of the two states did not change appreciably from the previous period.

TABLE 7.1. Features of US-Canada Relationship

		Trustor-Trustee Relationship			Issues in Play		Structure of Agreements		
		Vulnerability	Exploitability	Voluntarism	Scope of Issues	Salience of Issues	Imprecision and Informality	Marginalization	Entrapment
1940–1970	US	Low	Low	**HIGH**	MODERATE	**HIGH**	MODERATE	Low	MODERATE
	Canada	MODERATE	**HIGH**	**HIGH**	**HIGH**	**HIGH**	MODERATE	MODERATE	**HIGH**
1971–2016	US	Low	Low	**HIGH**	**HIGH**	MODERATE	MODERATE	Low	MODERATE
	Canada	MODERATE	**HIGH**	MODERATE	MODERATE	**HIGH**	MODERATE	MODERATE	**HIGH**

While Canada's economy might be more deeply intertwined with the United States' market since the FTA, it has also reached out to other states to diversify its trading network. And while it is also just as dependent on American security guarantees, the urgency of the threat has diminished.

With respect to voluntarism, the key change was an increase in nationalism in Canada during the 1970s. In retrospect, though, it appears that this situation was reversed to a large degree, not only in the 1980s but since then. Public opinion surveys in the 2010s indicate a relatively high degree of satisfaction in Canada (over 50 percent) with the status quo and even some favoring a deepening of ties (Gravelle 2014). That successive governments of different parties continued to endorse the FTA and NAFTA is another indicator of satisfaction with a continental approach. It is ironic that one contemporary Canadian complaint against Washington has been its lack of enthusiasm for NAFTA (Burney and Hampson 2012), a policy that prior leaders had to defend as something other than selling out to the Americans.

Returning to the legal commitments, on balance they should be described in the same terms as during the previous period, with the caveat that there seems to be a reversal of the correlation between salience and imprecision. Overall, it appears that while trust is still in operation where Canada is concerned, this is likely no longer the case for the United States. Canada, it seems, is no longer deserving of the special relationship it once enjoyed in Washington. One cannot resist the metaphor of the older couple—or perhaps long-time roommates—who have lost the intimacy once enjoyed because one of them has grown distracted and bored. Nonetheless, no one is speaking of divorcing or moving out, perhaps because it is simply unthinkable.

United States–South Vietnam

The story of the Vietnam War is one of the best-known in international relations. The United States spent the 2015 equivalent of one trillion dollars and lost 58,000 troops out of nearly three million deployed (National Archives 2015). The war marked a turning point in US foreign policy and contributed to changes in US relations with its European and Asian allies, each of which increasingly went their own way. And domestically, the prosecution of the war and its outcome contributed to the felling of two presidential administrations and a generation of doubt and questioning of those in authority. The cost to North and South Vietnam was far greater as an estimated 750,000 South Vietnamese troops and civilians died while one million North Vietnamese and Vietcong were casualties (recalling that almost all Vietcong were residents of the South, the figures could be reversed [Brigham 2002]). Both countries were devastated economically although the political upheaval in South Vietnam was naturally far more acute, and it ultimately ceased to exist.

Throughout this period, beginning as early as 1945, the US relationship with Vietnam was governed by treaty commitments. The United States offered increasing levels of assistance to France in its struggle to maintain control in Indochina, despite President Franklin Roosevelt's initial preference to see the region under a trusteeship. In December 1950, France, the United States, and the three Indochinese territories signed a pentalateral mutual defense agreement that spelled out how US materiel and aid would be handled and how US personnel would be treated, a combination of a sales contract and a status of forces agreement (Army, United States 2015). Direct aid to France continued until 1954, at which point the United States was covering three-fourths of the costs (Kalb 2013, 41–42).

While the United States and South Vietnam did not sign the 1954 Geneva Accords that called for French withdrawal and a temporary division of Vietnam into North and South, each recognized their importance. The United States warned that it would view any violations of the agreement (read: aggression by North Vietnam) "with grave concern and as seriously threatening international peace and security," a phrase John F. Kennedy reiterated nearly a decade later (Department of State 1961). Vietnam, for its part, repudiated the Geneva Accords as unfair and unwelcome (Miller 2013, 97).

President Dwight Eisenhower provided aid directly to the South Vietnamese regime after the Geneva Accords, granting $300 million to the Ngo Dinh Diem regime (Karnow 1983, 220) despite misgivings about the regime's reliability. In a letter dated October 23, Eisenhower indicated that the aid would aim primarily at assisting in the relocation of nearly 900,000 mostly Roman Catholics in the North to areas in the South, conditioned only on the Diem government's "undertaking needed reforms" (Department of State 1954, 735–36). More importantly, less than two months before making this commitment, the United States orchestrated the creation of the Southeast Asia Treaty Organization (SEATO) that consisted of a mutual defense pact between the United States, United Kingdom, France, Australia, New Zealand, Pakistan, Thailand, and the Philippines. Article 4 reads, "Each Party recognizes that aggression by means of armed attack in the treaty area against any of the Parties or against any State or territory which the Parties by unanimous agreement may hereafter designate, would endanger its own peace and safety, and agrees that it will in that event act to meet the common danger in accordance with its constitutional processes" (Article IV, para. 1). Joint response would also be warranted in the event of nonlethal attacks or threats to any member's territory or sovereignty (Article IV, para. 2). A protocol clarifies that Indochina is included in the "treaty area" mentioned in Article 4, paragraph 1 (France had opposed inclusion of the three Indochinese territories as SEATO members, presumably to prevent their elevation to sovereign status [McNamara et al. 1999, 13]). The United States also clarified in a note that only communist aggression was contemplated in the drafting of Article 4, although other forms of aggression could be discussed. The treaty was intended to be of indefinite duration, although member states could withdrawal one year after notification (Article X). In fact, Pakistan withdrew in 1968, France suspended its financial contributions in 1975, and the organization was disbanded in 1977. Although the defense of South Vietnam was never a full-fledged SEATO operation, some members participated and the United States repeatedly invoked the treaty to explain and justify its involvement in Southeast Asia. They also referred from time to time to the "domino theory" that predicted the loss of Southeast Asia and increased vulnerability to regional US allies should South Vietnam fall to the communists (Williams et al. 1985, 156).

From the outset, Diem and his Washington sponsors worked at cross-purposes. In 1955–1957 Diem's aggressive efforts at consolidating his power and diminishing the power of the communist-inspired Vietcong bore fruit, although his activities increasingly alienated him from the population, especially his "strategic hamlet" tactic and his anti-Buddhist discrimination and eventual repression (Brigham 2002, 100). His regime was filled with officials and officers who had little experience fighting in behalf of the Vietnamese people, although Diem himself was anti-French (Halberstam 1969, 181). He had little interest in the rural development projects the American advisors promoted and sparred with military advisors over the proper role of the Army of the Republic of Vietnam (ARVN) and the Civil Guard (Miller 2013, 113, 196). It became increasingly clear that Diem was far more concerned about a coup than about the Vietcong or North Vietnamese and was using American aid primarily to buttress his political standing and viability (Miller 2013, 192, 213). He wanted US troops and a formal, written alliance treaty primarily to increase the credibility of the American commitment to his regime (Karnow 1983, 251; Miller 2013, 230).

By the time John F. Kennedy came to the White House, opinions about the Diem regime were divided. An agreement was proposed in late January 1961 in which "the US would support 'adequate forces' (i.e., no large increases in ARVN's troop strength) if Diem would institute 'necessary corrective measures' (viz. improve strategy and command)" (Department of Defense 1971, 3). The deal was stillborn and produced no changes. But ambassador Frederick Nolting and vice president Lyndon Johnson were strong advocates of increasing support and were later joined by defense secretary Robert McNamara, Joint Chiefs' chairman General Maxwell Taylor and others, who in late 1961 advised responding favorably to Diem's request for additional aid and the insertion of US troops in the event of a North Vietnamese invasion (Karnow 1983, 251; Miller 2013, 228; *New York Times* 1971, 148–53). The proposal involved a "limited partnership" by which the United States would provide sophisticated weapons and the American crews to maintain and operate them, along with conventional weapons and economic aid in exchange for Diem's undertaking much-needed political reforms and economic development projects. In addition, Americans would expand their role from "consultant" to "co-decision-maker" (Williams et al. 1985, 195). Diem resisted the package as amounting to making South Vietnam an American "protectorate" (Miller 2013, 229). Language involving reforms and shared decision making were dropped from the formal exchange of letters of December 14, 1961, codifying the agreement, and a dollar figure was not provided (Department of State 1961). Informally, political conditions and joint decision making were waived by US officials in Saigon, making the deal fairly one-sided (Halberstam 1969, 224).

The political situation continued to deteriorate in the wake of anti-Buddhist repression, and Diem's sister-in-law took to writing anti-American editorials in the English-language *Times of Vietnam*. Signals in the forms of public warnings were sent to Diem of US impatience about the urgent need for political reforms and a cut in assistance in September (Karnow 1983, 290). In July 1963 the American CIA station chief Lucien Conein was approached by ARVN generals about a coup plot. The American response was tentatively favorable, and in late August Kennedy formally gave support for the plan (Miller 2013, 293; Karnow 1983, 287). On November 1, 1963, a junta seized power and executed Diem and his brother (Karnow 1983, 305). US ambassador Henry Cabot Lodge was quick to congratulate the new leadership.

For the next few years, the regime in Saigon was riven with instability and rivalries. Meanwhile, North Vietnamese commitment to supporting the Vietcong, begun in 1958, was firm and effective. Rural areas were falling quickly to Vietcong–North Vietnamese forces and defections from the ARVN were increasing (Karnow 1983, 342). President Johnson reiterated Kennedy's and Eisenhower's commitments to preserving South Vietnam as a noncommunist bastion, driven not only by a belief in the domino theory but also by a fear of "losing Vietnam" the way Harry Truman "lost China" (Kalb 2013, 89; Karnow 1983, 268). He decided that success would come only if the United States took control of offensive operations, and following passage of the Tonkin Gulf Resolution whereby Congress gave him virtually unlimited power to prosecute the war, he initiated air raids against North Vietnam followed by large-scale bombing runs and ultimately the insertion of large numbers of troops in 1964–1965. This was done with the understanding that the ARVN would shift its mission to defending territory already held while the United States took increasingly unilateral offensive action (Brigham 2002, 112). For its part, the South Vietnamese slipped into a colonial mode, allowing Americans to essentially run the country, pushing back from time to time only to find their authority circumvented and undermined (Karnow 1983, 443–44). Elections in 1967, while open, led the victor—Nguyen Van Thieu—to imprison candidates he had defeated, further alienating the populace (Karnow 1983, 453). The government became increasingly corrupt with large numbers of US aid dollars being diverted (Karnow 1983, 441). The United States generally tolerated these practices, although it despaired at the continuing unrest, repression, and instability (Olson and Roberts 2008, 125; Karnow 1983, 445–50).

During his first year in office (1969), President Richard Nixon negotiated a new framework for US–South Vietnam cooperation that provided for the ARVN taking over the offensive military role played by US troops since 1965. In announcing this policy and reminding his American audience of the previously articulated "Nixon Doctrine," Nixon said, "A nation cannot remain great if it betrays its allies and lets down its friends." He said that from then on the United States "will keep all of its treaty commitments" and "we shall furnish military and economic assistance when requested in accordance with our treaty commitments." (Williams et al. 1985, 281–82). It is worth noting that two of the three principles on which the Nixon Doctrine was founded related to honoring treaty commitments.

At roughly the same time as the relationship was renegotiated, Nixon opened the door to direct talks with the North Vietnamese, which Thieu initially rejected (he had rejected the same offer the previous year from Johnson [Willbanks 2004, 7, Torry 2015]). Eventually Thieu changed his mind and participated in the formal Paris peace talks, although he was never a party to the more important back-channel negotiations between

Henry Kissinger and Le Duc Tho (Kalb 2013, 163; Karnow 1983, 624). Throughout the 1968–1973 period Thieu became increasingly mistrustful of Nixon's intentions and feared that South Vietnam's interests would be sacrificed to the Americans' need to end the war (Kalb 2013, 168). To a large degree his fears were confirmed when in October 1972 he learned about the substance of the tentative agreement that had been struck. Thieu had demanded that any deal not violate his four "no's": no coalition government with the Vietcong, no undermining of South Vietnam's territorial integrity, no North Vietnamese armies left in South Vietnam, and no declaration of neutrality (Olson and Roberts 2008, 205). In fact, the preliminary agreement violated the first three no's in that it allowed for North Vietnamese troops to stay behind and for the Vietcong to govern the territory they controlled in anticipation of joining a coalition government in the future, and it left the demarcation of the border along the 17th parallel unclear (Kalb 2013, 170). He rejected the deal out of hand, then later proposed sixty-nine amendments, something Kissinger himself dismissed as bordering on the insane although he dutifully presented them to his North Vietnamese counterparts (Willbanks 2004, 172). Sensing disarray in the US camp, northern negotiators began withdrawing offers and making new demands, with the result that talks came to a halt in December 1972. Impatient for results, Nixon threatened Thieu with a rupture in relations (even though he had originally said this deal should not be a "shotgun wedding") (Willbanks 2004, 171; Kalb 2013, 172). Thieu's response was defiant as he declared privately that South Vietnam would rather fight alone than sign this unjust treaty (Karnow 1983, 654). Nixon bombed North Vietnam in late December and in January talks resumed, although the original October deal remained the basis, much to Thieu's chagrin. Nixon promised him that he would respond with more bombing if the North Vietnamese violated the terms of the agreement, then gave him an ultimatum (to the effect of "sign with us or we will sign alone"), which Thieu finally accepted in February 1973 (Kalb 2013, 187). Marvin Kalb in *The Road to War* provides this interesting exchange between Thieu and an aide at the time of his decision:

> Thieu: "The Americans really left me with no choice—either sign, or they will cut off aid. On the other hand, we have obtained an absolute guarantee from Nixon to defend the country. I am going to agree to sign and hold him to his word." The aide asked: "Can you really trust Nixon?" Out of options, Thieu replied: "He is a man of honor. I am going to trust him." Here was proof of a presiden-

tial pledge. Nixon had given his word, and Thieu responded on the assumption that the president's word was America's word, and he accepted it. What else could he do? (Kalb 2013, 193)

As the United States withdrew from Indochina, it lavished war materiel on the government, most of which fell into the hands of the North Vietnamese two years later. On the other hand, it cut aid each successive year and refused to intervene to stop the North Vietnamese advance in 1975 (Karnow 1983, 667). The last act by the US government was to evacuate Vietnamese in the face of North Vietnamese attacks. Thieu gave his view that the United States (read: Nixon) had betrayed him in the end (Willbanks 2004, 216).

Table 7.2 provides a summary of the characteristics of the US–South Vietnam relationship. As we can see, the relationship was clearly asymmetrical with respect to the degree of vulnerability each side felt. For South Vietnam, the war was a matter of national survival, while less was at stake for the United States, although there was a tendency to inflate the importance of the situation in US circles (Kalb 2013, 52). While each side was in a position to be exploited, this exploitation would come in very different forms. Clearly, successive South Vietnamese governments sought as much American support as possible, mostly to shore up their own status within the country rather than strike a death blow to the Vietcong. This meant that ultimately the South Vietnamese could pick and choose for the most part which American edicts it would honor. As put by Stanley Karnow, "So despite their reliance on American aid, now more than a half-billion dollars a year, they could safely defy American dictates. In short, their weakness was their strength. As a Saigon government official privately explained it to me at the time, 'Our big advantage over the Americans is that they want to win the war more than we do'" (Karnow 1983, 383). On the other hand, the United States was in a position to take advantage of South Vietnam in that it was far more interested in its place in its geostrategic agenda than in the prosperity and peace of the Vietnamese people (although, ironically, the US government was for the most part more concerned about Vietnamese welfare and freedom than was the Vietnamese government). Each was therefore in a position to be exploited to some degree. As put by David Halberstam, "In all this there is a subtle change; the client state does not really come to life but the illusion does; as such, the proprietor state begins to live slightly at the mercy of the client state." (Halberstam 1969, 184)

Although the Diem government official requested aid from the Eisenhower administration at the outset, thus exercising its sovereign prerogatives, it eventually lost control of the relationship. American leaders, for their part, may have felt they had no alternative to an alliance with South Vietnam, but it is clear from the scope of opinion before 1954 and the ultimate withdrawal in 1973 that this was not accurate. The United States always had more options than South Vietnam.

The agreements entered into covered many key issues for South Vietnam, although from the US perspective the scope was not so broad. For much of the period the agreements dealt with matters of vital national interest to South Vietnam (any doubts about this are dispelled by the sacrifices made by the US government in South Vietnam's behalf; see the beginning of this case study). The various agreements—with the possible exception of the contracts related to the transfer of property and personnel—tended to be vague and unclear. Much was left to the US ambassadors and the South Vietnamese presidents to interpret and enforce provisions of the agreements. In particular, the letters exchanged in December 1961 that created the framework for cooperation until 1965 (or until 1971, depending on one's perspective) were short, opaque, and offered little specific guidance for either party. Even the SEATO treaty provided less assurance than a typical mutual defense treaty since every decision to defend an alliance member would require a unanimous vote (i.e., each party had a veto). Perhaps the most important American commitment came in the form of a short, secret letter from Nixon to Thieu that had no basis in political reality. For the most part the South Vietnamese had hoped for more formal, written commitments from the United States, although they were happy to keep their own promises and obligations vague.

South Vietnam was able to participate in interpreting and enforcing the agreements, although this was not always explicitly provided for and was a matter of subsequent negotiation itself. Successive South Vietnamese governments were relatively adept at dragging their feet and even convincing Americans to waive various demands. In particular South Vietnam was able to constrain and even diminish the role of American advisers during the 1956–1964 period, although this slipped away thereafter. But the South Vietnamese could have significantly diminished the American role prior to 1971 only if the ARVN had been a capable fighting force and the North Vietnamese had disengaged. For its part, the United States could turn the aid spigot on and off at will despite rhetoric implying it lacked control. When it became clear that the ARVN was not a capable fighting force, it could act unilaterally, something South Vietnam could not do. Regarding entrapment, similar considerations apply. There was little in the various agreements that provided explicitly for withdrawal (SEATO being

TABLE 7.2. Features of US-South Vietnam Relationship, 1945–75

	Trustor-Trustee Relationship			Issues in Play		Structure of Agreements		
	Vulnerability	Exploitability	Voluntarism	Scope of Issues	Salience of Issues	Imprecision and Informality	Marginalization	Entrapment
US	MODERATE	MODERATE	**HIGH**	MODERATE	**HIGH**	**HIGH**	Low	Low
South Vietnam	**HIGH**	MODERATE	MODERATE	**HIGH**	**HIGH**	**HIGH**	MODERATE	**HIGH**

an exception), and political realities prevented South Vietnamese leaders from considering alternatives to the US alliance. The United States, on the other hand, could have withdrawn at almost any point, although not without considerable domestic and strategic fallout (both of which came at any rate).

While the rhetoric of a relationship should be taken with a grain of salt, it is worth noting that South Vietnamese leaders from Diem to Thieu were frequently found to accuse the United States of potential, actual, or imagined "betrayal," a term rarely if ever used by American officials, who instead spoke of "disappointment" and "incompetence." Had the South Vietnamese initiated serious talks for a separate peace, one might have heard Americans use the term, but no serious talks occurred. In fact, as we see in table 7.2, it appears that South Vietnam invested some degree of trust in the United States, albeit shrouded in fear and suspicion. South Vietnamese leaders understood that although they could resist and dissemble, in the final analysis the fate of their country, their careers, and even their lives were in the hands of the Americans. American leaders, for their part, decided to defend South Vietnam knowing relatively little about the country and its leadership. For them the problem was more one of slippage in a principal-agent relationship rather than trust. They surmised that they could always take over and at least produce a stalemate as they had in Korea (surely the North Vietnamese would be easier to deal with than the Chinese . . .).

Russian Federation–Belarus

Belarus is largely an accidental country, the product of an unwelcome dismemberment of the Soviet Union, a structure within which it had felt supremely comfortable (Ioffe 2008, 110). While one might be able to trace some form of Belarusian identity across the many foreign occupations and assimilations during the Middle Ages and modern era, it was ultimately incorporated into the USSR as a Soviet Socialist Republic (the highest administrative division) (Balmaceda 2014, 23; Yekelchyk 2008, 13–23; Ioffe 2008, 80). Russification and great wartime sacrifices during the Soviet period seemed a small price to pay for the significant economic growth and political stability the country enjoyed as an essential part of the USSR's energy and military strategies (Rontoyanni 2005, 125; Yekelchyk 2008, 24). Even when Moscow delayed its emergency response following the Chernobyl reactor accident in 1986 (roughly 70 percent of the fallout fell on Belarus), there was no outrage (Savchenko 2009, 149). It was not until

1988, when tens of thousands of skeletons were unearthed in Kurapaty, revealing the extent of Stalin-era massacres of Belarusians thought to be disloyal to Moscow, that an anti-Russian backlash occurred (Savchenko 2009, 150; Rudling 2008, 59), although this proved to be short-lived. Even today, Belarusians, compared to citizens of other former Soviet republics, are the most drawn to all things Soviet (even more so than Russians themselves [Rudling 2008, 58; Rontoyanni 2005, 123]).

Democratic institutions never took root in Belarus and there was never a Baltic-style commitment to Europeanize the country. While the Belarusian Supreme Soviet had declared the SSR's sovereignty in 1990, this was coupled with a call for creating a union of socialist states, essentially ensuring the preservation of the USSR (Savchenko 2009, 155). In March 1991, 82.7 percent of Belarusians expressed in a referendum their preference for preserving the Soviet Union (Rudling 2008, 60). When the country was dissolved in December of that year, the existing leadership simply changed the letterhead and continued functioning, hoping the disruption of ties to Russia would be minimal since it was the source of almost all their energy, export earnings, and inputs for their sizeable industrial sector (Balmaceda 2014, 27). The absence of a clear deal with Russia on energy imports cost the country dearly (it spent one-quarter of its GDP on energy imports in 1992 [Balmaceda 2014, 28]) and so it quickly entered into a barter system to lock in a price for oil at roughly one-third the world price. Although the new constitution called for Belarusian neutrality (Krivosheev 2003, 167; Rozanov 1999, 87), it changed its position under pressure from Moscow (a reduction of its flow of energy with a promise of cheaper oil in the future, what came to be known as "valve diplomacy" [Golani 2011, 27; Krivosheev 2003, 168]) and signed the Collective Security Treaty of the Commonwealth of Independent States in December 1993 (Collective Security Treaty Organization 2015; Rontoyanni 2005, 124; Sannikov 2003, 223; Nikonov 1999, 106). This allowed Russian troops and equipment to remain in Belarus and spared the country's many arms manufacturers from having to compete on world markets (Rozanov 1999, 87; Nikonov 1999, 125). More importantly it provided for mutual defense: "If aggression is committed against one of the States Parties by any state or group of states it will be considered as aggression against all the States Parties to the Treaty" (Article 4 of the Tashkent Treaty). It provided for a five-year duration (renewable every five years) and a six-month lag after denunciation (Article 11). A follow-up agreement allowed Belarus to deploy 1,800 tanks, 2,600 other armored combat vehicles, and 1,614 artillery units to Russia's 6,400, 11,480 and 6,415 (Implementation Agreement).

Alexander Lukashenka, a largely inexperienced midlevel Communist Party official, was able to win 80 percent of the vote in the second round in 1994 on a populist, nostalgic campaign of eliminating corruption and integrating with Russia (Rudling 2008, 63). After his election, he was able to secure public support (by way of referendum) for rewriting the constitution to concentrate power in the hands of the president and to marginalize (and ultimately dissolve) the Parliament, as well as restore the Soviet-era political symbols that had been removed by his predecessors (Rudling 2008, 65; Krivosheev 2003, 165). These actions, combined with increasingly repressive measures against pro-Western opponents and strident anti-NATO rhetoric, sealed his foreign policy direction (Delyagin 2009, 193; Krivosheev 2003, 171). Except for a short-lived and largely tactical flirtation with Western institutions in the mid-2000s, Belarus has remained loyal to Moscow. More than a score of treaties and agreements attest to this (Pirchner 2005, 7).

Belarus and Russia have entered into a staggering number of agreements, some of which are breathtaking in their scope and significance, at least on paper. But a closer look shows that the more dramatic the promises, the less likely they are to be implemented. The most serious of the commitments have been in the area of military cooperation, including a wide range of agreements to collaborate on air defense, military infrastructure, and joint exercises that resulted in Russia's de facto control of Belarusian security (Europa World 2015e; Golani 2011, 23; Sannikov 2003, 223). As we will see, this commitment to defense coordination has not slackened even as the warmth of the relationship has sometimes cooled. Belarus is consistently seen by Russia as its western shield against the encroachment of NATO (Sannikov 2003, 223; Perepelitsa 1999, 82). It has been in the economic and political spheres that agreements have more often than not been adopted for domestic political purposes and ultimately failed to live up to their soaring language.

The first example of this virtual integration (Drakokhrust and Furman 2003) was a stillborn agreement to unify the currencies of the two states in 1994. The agreement did not resolve the key question of where the decisions regarding money supply and lending rates would be decided. Russians assumed this would occur in Moscow and the decisions would be unilateral, as in the case of Switzerland and Liechtenstein regarding the Swiss franc (Nesvetailova 2003, 155). Belarusian authorities had other ideas, preferably involving a new jointly governed central bank (Nikonov 1999, 125). Although commitments have been made on paper to unify the currency on Moscow's terms (most recently in 2010), Belarus has continued to resist (Europa World Plus 2015e; Nesvetailova 2003, 158).

The 1992 Treaty of Friendship, Good-Neighborliness and Cooperation may be the one exception to the long string of vacuous agreements. Short of creating joint institutions, this remains one of the clearest and strongest agreements between the two states. It protects the signatories' sovereignty and territorial integrity (Article 1) and commits them to consult with each other to coordinate their foreign policy positions, especially in security matters (Articles 2, 3, and 5). It also lowers barriers to the movement of persons and anticipates deeper integration (Articles 4, 9, and 17). It provides for a duration of ten years with automatic renewal and a six-month lag after denunciation (Article 26). The treaty has been generally effective, especially with respect to the coordination of foreign policy and the free movement of persons.

In 1995, at the initiative of Lukashenka, discussions took place on some form of economic or political union (Drakokhurst and Furman 2003, 236). The strategy was appealing to both Belarusian and Russian leaders since conservatives and moderates generally supported some kind of restoration. Boris Yeltsin, who had a direct hand in the dismemberment of the USSR, always feared the Communists would be able to carry the nostalgia vote and therefore hoped that talk of integration would help (Golani 2011, 19, 35; Moshes 2003, 211). Likewise, it was widely felt in Belarus that closer ties to Russia would solve the country's economic troubles (Nesvetailova 2003, 153). The trouble was that neither government could determine precisely which elements of their states' sovereignty were negotiable and which were sacred, so the agreements were intentionally vague and provided little clear direction (Drakokhurst and Furman 2003, 240; Nesvetailova 2003, 155). Lukashenka, for example, insisted on retaining Belarus's sovereignty while still angling to one day become the chair of a jointly governed Belarusian-Russian confederation (Moshes 2003, 203; Drakokhurst and Furman 2003, 244).

Russia, for its part, sought to secure more and more control of Belarus's economy, particularly its energy sector (Europa World 2015e; Savchenko 2009, 196). This naturally went against Lukashenka's policy of Soviet-style state ownership of key sectors (Sannikov 2003, 226). For example, in 1993, Belarus's gas payment debt was resolved by the sale of 30 percent of a refinery to Russia (Europa World 2015e). It signed a deal to transfer control of pipelines to Russian oil company Gazprom, but the agreement went unratified (Golani 2011, 28). Some predicted the creation of a "velvet empire" through which Russia would establish de facto control over the country without directly violating its sovereignty (Golani 2011, 26). At other times, Moscow generously rewarded Minsk for its loyalty by forgiving debts. Clearly Russia's view of Belarus was of a useful ally that needed periodic disciplining.

The first of a series of complex and ambiguous agreements was the 1996 Treaty Establishing the Community of Belarus and Russia. While Lukashenka had been urging some sort of general integration treaty, this package was hastily organized by Yeltsin as a last-minute campaign tactic and so was not well-conceived (Golani 2011, 31; Drakokhurst and Furman 2003, 237). It sketched out a series of joint supranational institutions such as a Parliament and a Supreme Council (Articles 10, 13) with an equal number of seats for each state and the power to issue legislation that would override domestic statutes. This structure, however unrealistic, was designed to ensure that Lukashenka would not feel that Belarus's sovereignty was infringed upon (Drakokhurst and Furman 2003, 239). Oddly, he had no objections to the demand that each state establish domestic democratic institutions (Article 2), implying that the agreement was not seen as binding.

The following year, a Charter to the Treaty on the Union of Belarus and Russia was signed that spelled out in more detail the attributes and powers of the joint institutions mentioned earlier. It was negotiated over a two-month period and incorporated some concessions to Lukashenka's need for equal status (Moshes 2003, 207). In fact, an early version of the makeup of the Supreme Council's Executive Committee provided for a rotating chairmanship, something Yeltsin later realized could fulfill Lukashenka's dream: power over both Russia and Belarus (the clause was altered in the final version). At forty articles, it appeared quite impressive and had much of the ringing language about respecting sovereignty, democracy, economic liberalization, and the rest that we have come to expect from Western European agreements (Articles 3, 8, and 9). Likewise, the structure and authority of the principal bodies seemed to jibe with many other supranational institutions. It also provided for the standard twelve-month lag of withdrawal following denunciation. It provided, however, no timetable for implementation (Nikonov 2003, 121) and in fact was never activated since it was replaced in 1998 by a Declaration on the Future Unity of the Republic of Belarus and the Russian Federation—a vague plan of action designed to persuade observers that there was still momentum to the integration program—and eventually by the Agreement on the Establishment of the Union State. The 1997 agreement devoted many of its articles to a list of policy tasks (Articles 8–12), most of which seem directed at two other states ("promotion of democracy," "free economic competition," "freedom of speech," and so forth). It still maintained equal representation of the two states in the decision-making bodies, something that would not survive the final revisions.

Meanwhile, away from the negotiating table and press conferences, relations between Russia and Belarus were souring. Moscow was increasingly insistent that Minsk privatize state-owned firms, a nonstarter for Lukashenka (Drakokhurst and Furman 2003, 238), and did not hesitate to criticize Lukashenka openly. In 1998 a Russian journalist who dared question the regime in Minsk found himself in jail and Yeltsin responded by cutting off the flow of gas until he was released (Golani 2011, 28). At roughly the same time, the Russian economy slipped into crisis and dragged Belarus along with it. The Belarus ruble lost much of its value, something that later led the government to peg it to the dollar (Savchenko 2009, 205). During this time, Lukashenka responded more warmly to EU overtures until he course-corrected and expelled several European diplomats over a trifle (and was punished with EU sanctions).

With something approaching resignation, Belarus and Russia concluded talks on the union treaty in 1999, again mostly for the sake of public opinion at home. The Agreement on the Establishment of the Union State is even longer and more detailed than its 1997 predecessor and reflected an assertion of Moscow's authority and power. It called for the protection and promotion of private property (Articles 8 and 9). It also provided (however unrealistically) for a convergence of macroeconomic indicators, meaning that GNP per capita, inflation, trade balances, and especially shares of privately held firms would be roughly the same in the two states in due time (Article 21 [Nikonov 2003, 122]). It clarified the powers of the principal organs, but inserted some contradictory language (Nesvetailova 2003, 160; Drakokhurst and Furman 2003, 248). For example, while the Supreme Council was to have the power to directly alter domestic statutes, domestic constitutions were to be preserved (Articles 60, 61). In fact, implementation would have to go through four approval processes, each of which could block implementation. Again, no timetable was provided for; Article 2, paragraph 2 seems to hint that it will all take some time ("Achievement of the objectives of the Union State is to be carried out in stages, giving priority to solving economic and social problems"). While membership of the Executive Committee would still be equal and decisions would require unanimity, the Parliament—now bicameral—now provided more seats for Russia (seventy-five seats to twenty-eight seats for Belarus in the lower house [Article 39]).

The reaction in Minsk was skepticism as the union looked increasingly like a shotgun wedding (Shlapentokh 2012, 62). While public opinion polls still favored some sort of union, support for this particular association stood only at 34 percent (Colton 2003, 25–26; but another 22 percent favored outright unification). The agreement was most popular with older, rural Russian speakers, while those living in Minsk or nearer the Polish border leaned against it (Colton 2003, 43–44). The referendum on the question passed by a large margin, which probably means little since by 1999 all votes in Belarus were considered invalid by the EU and OSCE. It is worth noting that it was at roughly this time that Lukashenka began to actively pursue new diplomatic partners, especially China and Iran (Krivosheev 2003, 175). At any rate, the agreements led to few changes in behavior or policy in either Moscow or Minsk (Drakokhrust and Furman 2003; Rozanov 1999, 30). As it happened, this was the last agreement Yeltsin and Lukashenka would negotiate since a few weeks later he surrendered his post to Vladimir Putin.

For the first months of Vladimir Putin's administration, Belarus figured little in his thinking. Rather, he focused his energies on bringing under his control the gangster-oligarchs in the Russian Federation's regions. While he favored a version of free market capitalism, he was most concerned with harmonizing the needs of private firms with those of the state and to restore order within and project power abroad. He was not interested in recreating the USSR (Golani 2011, 20). Where Belarus was concerned, he enthusiastically carried on the policies of velvet empire and valve diplomacy. He held Belarus in contempt as a state that gave Russia little in return for its abuse of Moscow's largesse (Golani 2011, 33; Sadowski 2009, 178). Yeltsin generally agreed with these characterizations, but where he was politically vulnerable and felt the need to glad-hand Lukashenka, his successor was not and felt no need for hypocritical bonhomie (Golani 2011, 29).

Putin had little interest in implementing the Union Treaty and could barely understand why it was agreed to in the first place. At the same time, he completed a customs union agreement with Belarus and Kazakhstan in late 2000 (Agreement on the Foundation of Eurasian Economic Community) in the hope of bringing the former SSRs more completely within Russia's economic sphere on Moscow's terms and ensuring they would not bolt to the EU (Bugajski 2008, 27; Rontoyanni 2005, 136; Nesvetailova 2003, 161). The spare treaty (twenty articles) established decision-making bodies that provided for weighted voting for the first time, giving Russia 40 percent of the votes on the Interstate Council (made up of heads of state meeting annually) and the Integration Committee (made up of deputy heads of state meeting quarterly) (Articles 4–6). The Inter-parliamentary

Assembly was constituted with forty-two of ninety seats set aside for Russia, sixteen each for Belarus and Kazakhstan, and eight each for newcomers Kyrgyzstan and Tajikistan, meaning that so long as Moscow secured the support of at least one other state it could block any action (with two states it could pass a resolution [Article 7]). The Community Court is the most egalitarian institution, with each state appointing two judges (Article 8). The treaty was designed to be of indefinite duration (Article 18) but states could withdraw twelve months after giving notice (Article 9). While on paper the agreement instituted collective management of a customs union, in practice states continued to act unilaterally, particularly Russia itself (Ryzhkov 2014).

Putin continued to consolidate relations with former SSRs, concluding the Charter of the Collective Security Treaty Organization in 2002 that reaffirmed the mutual defense provisions of the original treaty and added provisions allowing joint action against terrorists, drug traffickers, and organized criminal organizations (Article 8). On paper the organization provided for consensus decision making, but the stark imbalance of forces made this implausible, and Russia ensured it would be the strongest member of the joint military staff (Articles 12 and 18).

Also in 2002, Putin articulated his views about integration with Belarus in abrupt and earthy terms. He said that Belarus was to Russia what a fly is to a "chop" (meaning a piece of meat) (Shlapentokh 2012, 59; Savchenko 2009, 211). Belarus, after all, bought only 4 percent of Russia's exports while Russia provided the country with everything essential (energy, credits, defense, food, technology, industrial inputs, markets, and so forth). The country was routinely in arrears on its energy payments (in 2002 it owed $250 million [Nesvetailova 2003, 158]), and its trade deficit with Russia was running at $2.8 billion (Rontoyanni 2005, 130). Russia was providing between $1 and $2 billion a year in subsidies (Rontoyanni 2005, 132) and was tiring of endemic smuggling and alleged siphoning of Russian oil for direct sale to Western Europeans (Golani 2011, 29). He concluded that it was simply unthinkable that Belarus would ever be an equal to Russia and no treaty would change that. He then asked Lukashenka why, if he favored closer integration, he did not just become part of the Russian Federation, either as a whole unit or as six separate administrative divisions (Golani 2011, 21). Lukashenka would become a provincial administrator and his people would benefit from all that Russian citizenship had to offer (including energy prices at a small fraction of world prices).

By this time, government officials in Minsk—none less than Lukashenka himself—had grown accustomed to governing a nominally sovereign state (Ioffe 2008, 159). Incorporation into the federation was therefore entirely unacceptable and frankly insulting, although Lukashenka's public comments were restrained (Savchenko 2009, 212; Ioffe 2008, 79; Rudling 2008, 68). He began in earnest to look for new partners, especially Iran and China (Shlapentokh 2012, 44, 58). Iran was particularly interested in closer ties since such ties would not damage an already strained relationship with Russia. China also increased its lending and investment beginning in 2007 (Shlapentokh 2012, 72, 82).

Under Putin, Russia began systematically using its economic leverage to gain greater control over Belarus's economy, especially its energy and banking sectors. Since these were largely state monopolies in 2002, the first step was to persuade Lukashenka to liberalize the country's ownership rules. While the various customs and economic unions all required privatization of state-owned firms and respect for foreign ownership of assets, it was clear that Lukashenka would disregard these commitments without threats and inducements. The first inducement, offered in 2002, was for energy price reductions of roughly 50 percent (bringing prices in Belarus down to what they were within Russia, or roughly one-tenth of world prices) in exchange for allowing the Russian oil giant Gazprom to buy up parts of the country's pipelines and oil companies (Europa World Plus 2015e). Lukashenka rejected the offer, and shortly thereafter came the threats. Putin declared that since the pipelines in Belarus were built by the USSR they rightly belonged to Russia. He also accused Belarus of profiting from unauthorized direct energy sales and demanded compensation (Golani 2011, 29). Lukashenka dug in his heels and expanded oil sales to the Netherlands and Great Britain, among others (Ioffe 2008, 119). In 2004 he refused to pay the gas bill, resentful of Putin's continuing demand to sell off parts of BelTransGaz, the Belarusian energy company, and was cut off. He then relented, but only after accusing Putin of committing an act of terrorism (Europa World Plus 2015e; Golani 2011, 28). Needless to say, whatever warmth there might have been in the Putin-Lukashenka relationship had cooled (Delyagin 2009, 197).

In 2006 Putin again accused Belarus of profiting from the resale of cheap oil and announced his intention to reduce Russian subsidies to zero—which would have raised the price of energy roughly fourfold—unless the profits were transferred to Russia along with 51 percent ownership in BelTransGaz to Gazprom (Savchenko 2009, 221; Ioffe 2008, 121). He gave Lukashenka until the end of the year to agree to the terms, which he finally did with less than two minutes to spare (Sadowski 2009, 177). Over the next three years Gazprom gained a controlling interest in BelTransGaz and many of Belarus's pipelines (Savchenko 2009, 222–23). It could have been worse; Gazprom accepted the valuation of the company provided by a Dutch firm, which was ten times greater than its own (Europa World Plus 2015e). In addition, energy prices for Belarus were more than doubled (again better than rising to world prices). Belarus had been well and truly "disciplined" (Sadowski 2009, 181).

Having brought Belarus to heel, Putin offered an olive branch in the form of a $3.5 billion loan to offset the loss of illicit profits (Savchenko 2009, 222–23). To test the waters one more time, in 2007 Lukashenka attempted to impose a user fee on his remaining pipelines. Russia responded by interrupting the flow of gas for three days until Lukashenka withdrew the fee (Europa World Plus 2015e). Efforts continued to curry favor with Western European states (including a short-lived loan program with the IMF [Europa World Plus 2015e]) as well as with Iran and China, earning Belarus a listing as one of Russia's foes in 2008 (Golani 2011, 56). There was even talk in Moscow of Russia deploying nuclear weapons in Belarus, which were countered by hints in Minsk that Belarus might try to join NATO (both threats were preposterous [Shlapentokh 2012, 60]).

Over the next two years, it would become increasingly apparent to Lukashenka that he would not survive without close ties to Russia, on Russia's terms. Putin and placeholder president Dmitry Medvedev were sending signals that they were plotting Lukashenka's overthrow (Shlapentokh 2012, 49–51). Given the increasing levels of unrest in Belarus, such a scenario was plausible. Lukashenka even declined to recognize the incorporation of South Ossetia and Abkhazia into the Russian Federation following the 2008 incursion into Georgia in the hope that this would curry favor in the West (Shlapentokh 2012, 49). The policy did not help with EU relations and produced yet another energy embargo by Moscow (which now demanded payments in cash [Shlapentokh 2012, 49]). Lukashenka's efforts to warm up to the EU failed, ultimately because of the demands made on him to release political prisoners and generally promote human rights (Grant 2014, 14).

As Lukashenka gradually surrendered to Moscow's pressure, he accepted a series of customs union agreements, including the creation of a relatively powerful commission (with qualified majorities that favored Russia) as part of the Eurasian Economic Community in 2011 (Europa World 2015e) and the creation of an economic union with Russia and Kazakhstan in 2014. These agreements were far more detailed and clear than those that preceded them, and they gave considerable authority to Moscow while still providing avenues for Belarus to influence decisions (by consensus). As Lukashenka showed more willingness to submit to Moscow, the country was showered with largesse. Russia offered a $14 billion loan in 2011 and offers of building a nuclear power plant in the country. But as soon as it appeared relations were improving, Moscow demanded that Minsk sell the remaining 49 percent of BelTransGaz to Gazprom and withheld disbursement of parts of the loan until the transfer was made (it was [Europa World Plus 2015e]). In general, it became clear that Moscow considered the legal constraints of its various agreements to be ultimately nonbinding and viewed the status of its formed SSRs as something less than sovereign (Bovt 2014; Ryzhkov 2014). To prove the point, during this period the "Putin Doctrine" came into sharper relief and with its declaration that Moscow felt empowered to intervene to protect Russians in the near abroad, all of Belarus felt it was living on borrowed time (Grant 2014, 13; Hille 2014). Lukashenka has taken the initiative to negotiate a treaty with Russia allowing each country to send special forces to the other upon request to fight terrorism, a term some associate with any antigovernment mass demonstrations (*Daily World* 2016). At the same time, Belarus has signed agreements on basic military cooperation and coordination with its NATO member neighbors and has been willing to receive refugees from embattled regions in Ukraine, but leaders are quick to say this does not represent a shift to the West (*Daily World* 2016).

How does Russia's history with an independent Belarus relate to our questions about the existence and functioning of trust in asymmetrical international relations? Clearly Belarus was always vulnerable and exploitable throughout this period, although Lukashenka sometimes pretended it was not (See table 7.3). Likewise, the scope and salience of the agreements have been, from Belarus's perspective, extremely high. In other words, the preconditions for trust have been in place. On the other hand, Russia has been relatively invulnerable, albeit not entirely. Were Belarus to magically transform itself into a Western ally, the effect would likely be intolerable in Moscow. Less serious would be an unpredictable and periodically defiant Belarus that would require continuous special attention and effort, something that approaches reality between 1991 and 2007. But by and large Russia has been in a position to absorb a great deal of disquiet in Minsk.

Comparing the relationship during the first decade since independence to the more recent years, important differences emerge. Perhaps most significant is the almost complete loss of Belarusian agency. While during the 1990s most efforts at integration came at the initiative of authorities in Minsk, the reverse was true after 2001. This naturally challenges the notion that Belarus carried on in faith and trust. As far as Russia was con-

TABLE 7.3. Features of Russia-Belarus Relationship

		Trustor-Trustee Relationship			Issues in Play		Structure of Agreements		
		Vulnerability	Exploitability	Voluntarism	Scope of Issues	Salience of Issues	Imprecision and Informality	Marginalization	Entrapment
1991–2001	Russia	Low	MODERATE	**HIGH**	MODERATE	MODERATE	MODERATE	Low	Low
	Belarus	**HIGH**	**HIGH**	**HIGH**	**HIGH**	**HIGH**	MODERATE	Low	**HIGH**
2002–2016	Russia	Low	MODERATE	MODERATE	**HIGH**	**HIGH**	Low	Low	
	Belarus	**HIGH**	**HIGH**	Low	**HIGH**	**HIGH**	Low	MODERATE	**HIGH**

cerned, it was also less enthusiastic about integration after 2001, but saw it as one of several ways to assert control over its near abroad (along with many other, more aggressive means).

Regarding the types of agreements entered into, during the first period they tended toward the aspirational and ambiguous (intentionally) and suffered from non-implementation and therefore non-interpretation and non-enforcement. But despite this they formed a foundation for future collaboration, especially with the respect to military cooperation. This pattern was largely reversed in the next phase, mostly because Russia no longer trusted its neighbors to behave as they should. Of course it felt itself less constrained by the letter of the law. Belarus was more of an equal in the early years, another thing that was reversed later on. And, finally, Belarus was more captured in the relationship in the second period, if not on paper than clearly in reality (fifteen years of "valve diplomacy" left its impact).

What we see in the Russia-Belarus relationship is the evolution of a neo-imperialist great power that lost patience with a subordinate and adjusted the terms of the relationship to increase its control. Perhaps it was guided by principles of trust in the early years, although from what we have seen Yeltsin was more likely guided by a desire to retain power and simply hoped for the best where Belarus was concerned. Lukashenka, on the other hand, clearly trusted that Moscow had Minsk's interests at heart in the first few years, but gradually came to doubt its intentions, consistent with a pattern we have seen in a number of cases.

Russian Federation–Republic of Georgia

Unlike for Belarus, there is little other than geographic proximity to naturally link Georgians to Russia (Russell 1991). Georgians generally consider themselves European (Nodia and Scholtbach 2006, 34; Gahrton 2010, 21), although several minority groups, such as the Ossetians, have strong ties to groups across the border (Otarashvili 2015). But since at least 1783, with the conclusion of the Treaty of Georgievsk, Georgia has been dependent to one degree or another on Russia (the treaty obligated Georgia to recognize its protectorate status with Russia and to renounce other alliances with great powers). The country achieved independence after a fashion (by coming under German dominance [Katz 2006, 24]) in 1919–1921 but was annexed by the new Soviet Union and declared a Soviet Socialist Republic (Nichol 2008, 1; Lucas 2009, 139) South Ossetia made an attempt at becoming independent as well, only to become an autonomous region within Georgia during the Soviet era, while Abkhazia enjoyed SSR status from 1921 to 1932 only to find itself folded into the Georgian SSR (Katz 2006, 26). Georgia's annexation and Soviet ethnic purges in the Caucasus left the people with a jaded view of the USSR, which dovetailed with their identity as anti-imperialists and increased the likelihood that any Russian policies would be seen with suspicion (Nasmyth 1992, 222; Devdariani 2005, 157), even though Georgians were granted considerable autonomy (Katz 2006, 23).

Georgia was quick to respond to Gorbachev's perestroika, and as early as March 1989 large pro-independence demonstrations occurred (some of which were brutally suppressed by Soviet authorities [Ladaria 2005, 116]). Meanwhile, Ossetians and Abkhaz minorities pressed for inclusion in the Russian Federation (Katz 2006, 26). Nationalist Georgian leader Zviad Gamsakhurdia and his nationalist counterparts in the separatist regions of Abkhazia and South Ossetia began full-scale fighting in July 1989, long before the dismemberment of the Soviet Union (Nasmyth 1992, 221; Allison 2008, 1146). Amid declarations of independence and appeals for national unity, militias, gangs, armies, and foreign "volunteers" (as well as some Russian regulars) from all sides carried out hit-and-run attacks and engaged in protracted battles over the next several years, prompting most to label Georgia a "failed state" from the outset (Babayan 2014, 56; Otarashvili 2015). It was not until the overthrow of Gamsakhurdia, who had become formal leader of Georgia in November 1990, five months before its independence, in January 1992 and the return of former Soviet foreign minister Eduard Shevardnadze to lead the young country that it began to experience the beginnings of stability. He never escaped suspicions that he was elevated by Russia and would always be seen as too deferential to Moscow (Gordadze 2009, 30–31).

Shevardnadze's willingness to accept Russian hegemony over both the Caucasus and especially the separatist regions set the tone for the next decade (Gordadze 2009, 35). The first item of business was the transfer of large amounts of Soviet-era military hardware (Antonenko 2005, 212). Next was a UN and Russia-brokered ceasefire agreement with Georgia's breakaway provinces, which ultimately surrendered control of the areas to a Russia-dominated Commonwealth of Independent States (CIS) peacekeeping operation that was tilted in favor of Moscow; the Joint Control Commission provided double representation of the Ossetians, for example (Aves 1996, 29; Allison 2008, 1146; Gordadze 2009, 31). Where South Ossetia was concerned, the arrangement left 530 Russian forces, joined by 300 North Ossetians (the force was actually composed of South Ossetians under the command of a North Ossetian [Nichol 2008, 2; Senate, U.S.

2008]) and 300 Georgians. In Abkhazia the agreement provided for roughly 2,000 Russia peacekeepers. Within these areas, local Russian commanders had considerable latitude and often provided direct support and cover for separatists (Aves 1996, 28; Devdariani 2005, 163; Antonenko 2005, 211; Popescu 2006, 1). Russian senior officials took up positions in the leadership of separatist governments, particularly in South Ossetia, where they were appointed president, minister of defense, and minister of the interior (Tsygankov and Tarver-Wahlquist 2009, 312; Allison 2008, 1147). Abkhaz rebels with Russian support launched an offensive in 1993 and pushed out Georgian forces and many Georgian civilians, a situation that has changed relatively little since then despite a series of agreements aimed at restoring the status quo (Aves 1996, 28, 30; United Nations Department of Peacekeeping Operations 2009).

As Russian pressures increased and the separatist crises became increasingly frozen, Georgia set aside its aspirations to join European institutions and instead joined the Commonwealth of Independent States in 1993 (Otarashvili 2015). This was clearly a risky move given the number of anti-Russian Georgian politicians who saw this as a capitulation (Antonenko 2005, 217; Nodia and Scholtbach 2006, 41; Goltz 2009, 203) but one that paid immediate dividends since Russia helped suppress the resurgent Gamsakhurdia and his militia (Popescu 2006; Goltz 2009, 195). Within a few years, Georgia had entered into a free trade and nondiscrimination agreement with Moscow, a treaty of friendship and cooperation that resembled an alliance in many respects (it provided for military aid), and a military base pact that allowed a long-term Russian military presence within Georgia while explicitly recognizing Georgia's territorial integrity (Preamble) (Aves 1996, 3; Antonenko 2005, 218; Gahrton 2010, 206). The friendship treaty was ultimately rejected by the Russia Duma on the grounds that it undermined Abkhazia's independence (Antonenko 2005, 220; Filippov 2010, 1831). In total, Georgia entered into ninety-two bilateral treaties with Russia between 1991 and 2005, most of which dealt with security matters, financial assistance, free trade, and regional aid (Slobodchikoff 2014, 55). Some are quite specific and detailed, such as the military bases agreement of 1995 that includes forty-one articles and a variety of detailed provisions regarding the rights and duties of Russian military personnel and commanders, a mixed commission (Article 38), twenty-five-year duration (with automatic renewal for five years [Article 40]), and a withdrawal provision requiring two years' advance notice (Article 40). On the other hand, the free trade agreement of 1994 is short and vague with just twenty-two brief articles, a largely undefined joint commission (Article 17), a commitment to settle disputes through negotiations (Article 16), and no provisions for termination (although it did allow for security-related derogations [Article 12]). In general, the agreements do not provide for joint commissions or formal dispute settlement. Most provide for resort to negotiations in the event of a difference of interpretation, which naturally benefits the Russian Federation (see, for example, the 1995 agreement on the legal status of permanent residents in each other's state [Article 13]).

Even as Russia established its dominance in the region, there were indications that Moscow hoped for a long-term relationship with Georgia based on mutual respect and tolerance. Yeltsin saw himself as an honest broker during much of the 1990s, although in time both he and Putin found it increasingly difficult to deal with Caucasus separatist groups within Russia and Georgia (Antonenko 2005, 223). Both failed to persuade Abkhaz leaders to accept a subordinate role in a federated Georgia, as provided for in a 1995 bilateral agreement between Tbilisi and Moscow (Aves 1996, 33), while all accepted a modest role for the United Nations and the Organization for Security and Cooperation in Europe (OSCE), each of which was allowed to deploy observers and peacekeepers of their own (Aves 1996, 26, United Nations Department of Peacekeeping Operations 2009). Russia even supported an arms embargo against Abkhazia organized by the CIS in 1996 (Antonenko 2005, 247). And in 1999 Russia supported (reluctantly, to be sure) an OSCE-brokered plan for Russian and Georgian troop withdrawals from separatist areas (although CIS peacekeepers were not covered [Devdariani 2005, 172]).

By 1999, however, Moscow policy in the region took an increasingly anti-Georgian turn, spurred initially by Shevardnadze's failure to support Russia during the Second Chechen War and even providing safe harbor to Chechen rebels in the Pankisi Gorge region (Antonenko 2005, 229; Babayan 2014, 66). Moscow launched a series of attacks on the area between 1999 and 2002, all of which were condemned as a violation of Georgian territory in Tbilisi (Nodia and Scholtbach 2006, 34; Filippov 2010, 1832). Moscow authorities also began distributing Russian passports to separatists in Abkhazia and South Ossetia, an ominous turn in light of Putin's 2000 declaration that Russia had the duty to protect all "compatriots" (meaning pro-Moscow Russian speakers in the near abroad) (Lucas 2009, 149).

At roughly the same time, Georgia was leaning further to the West, mostly as a hedge against Russian domination. It worked to bring its national regulations in line with the European Union's acquis in hope of eventually joining the EU and by actively seeking membership in NATO (Gahrton 2010, 22; Nodia and Scholtbach 2006, 34). In 1999 it joined the

Council of Europe and in 2001 joined the US-sponsored Partnership for Peace (Devdariani 2005, 173–78). It helped form the GUUAM association (Georgia, Ukraine, Uzbekistan, Azerbaijan, and Moldova) as a type of nonaligned bloc for former Soviet republics, a move naturally repudiated by Russia (Devdariani 2005, 173).

Russia's pressure prevailed in the short term as Shevardnadze agreed—with US help—to take aggressive action against Chechen militants in 2002 (Gordadze 2009, 43; Devdariani 2005, 167, 178). He also accepted the indefinite extension of the CIS peacekeeping regime (Antonenko 2005, 241). Ultimately, Shevardnadze's ambivalence and his regime's corruption (Katz 2006, 33; Lucas 2009, 140) precipitated his removal by those supporting the putative loser of the 2003 election, Mikael Saakashvili (Chikhladze and Chikhladze 2005, 11; Ladaria 2005, 117). Oddly, despite his openly pro-Western agenda and Putin's previous support of Shevardnadze (Chikhladze and Chikhladze 2005, 11), Russian foreign minister Igor Ivanov stepped into the fray to broker Shevardnadze's peaceful removal from power (Tsygankov and Tarver-Wahlquist 2009, 310) (although the United States also played a key role [Saakashvili 2005, 25]). Moscow even worked with the new Georgian leader to suppress a rebellion in Ajarian (Tsygankov and Tarver-Wahlquist 2009, 310), although it continued and even strengthened its support for separatists in Abkhazia and South Ossetia (Goltz 2009, 232). Antonenko argues that by 2003, Russia was no longer interested in mediation but rather openly supporting the separatists (2005, 242), while Filippov argues that Moscow had set its sights on dominating and humiliating Georgia by late 2004 (2010, 1830).

Saakashvili was quick to turn Georgia decidedly to the West, adopting Estonia as his model (Lucas 2009, 140). In 2004 Georgia was included in the EU's European Neighborhood Policy (Nodia and Scholtbach 2006, 36) and became increasingly eager to see a Membership Action Plan adopted to provide a timetable for NATO membership. He put the question to the public in a referendum in January 2008, where it passed with 77 percent approval (Nichol 2009, 6; Gahrton 2010, 165). With Ukraine, Georgia invited former Soviet republics to organize a Community of Democratic Choice as a way to counter Russian influence (Nodia and Scholtbach 2006, 38). Saakashvili welcomed foreign investment and made a serious effort to eliminate the crony capitalism and corruption left over from the previous regime. The country's GDP doubled between 2003 and 2007 largely as a result (Senate, U.S. 2008). He also adopted a more assertive policy regarding separatist movements, increasing troop strength and increasing peacekeeping forces (Nichol 2008, 3) while putting forward peace proposals that received international support if not separatist interest (Nichol 2008, 3). Russia by this point was no longer particularly interested in pursuing ways to reintegrate separatist regions into Georgia. By 2005 roughly five out of every six Abkhaz and South Ossetians held Russian passports and were therefore deserving of Russian protection (Goltz 2009, 242; Popescu 2006, 5).

In 2006, in a public and dramatic way, Saakashvili arrested four Russian intelligence officers based in Georgia. Moscow responded by rounding up and deporting thousands of Georgian illegals in Russia and imposing economic sanctions—including the suspension of travel and mail service—and might have orchestrated the destruction of parts of the principal pipeline in Georgia (Babayan 2014, 64; Lucas 2009, 142; Tsygankov and Tarver-Wahlquist 2009, 311; Allison 2008, 1166). Georgia responded by filing a case before the European Court of Human Rights (ECHR), to which Moscow responded by criticizing Georgia for taking the most confrontational tactic to deal with the problem (Foreign Affairs Ministry, Russian Federation 2007). In 2014 the ECHR ruled by a 16-1 majority that Russia violated Articles 3, 5(1), 5(4), 13, and 38 of the European Convention for the Protection of Human Rights and Fundamental Freedoms as well as Article 4 of the Fourth Protocol (*Georgia v. Russia* 2014).

Putin sent increasingly clear signals that NATO expansion had reached its limit and that any attempt to include other former Soviet republics would be seen as a threat to Russian national security (Smith 2009, 125). When NATO member heads of state met in Bucharest in April 2008, however, they concluded that although neither Georgia nor Ukraine were yet ready to join, efforts should be made to facilitate the membership process (Nichol 2009, 1). Since German chancellor Angela Merkel and other NATO leaders had already indicated that membership should be limited to stable countries, it is thought that Putin felt that the window for preventing Georgian membership was closing. The best option seemed to be to strike quickly and decisively, perhaps with the result of removing Georgian forces from the separatist regions once and for all and to effectuate violent disarmament and perhaps regime change (Lucas 2009, 145; Felgenhauer 2009, 162; Allison 2008, 1165). Russia had already withdrawn from the Conventional Forces in Europe treaty in 2007 and was building up its forces near the Caucasus (Filippov 2010, 1837). In 2008 it also denounced the CIS-sponsored arms embargo against the separatist regions, after which it deployed an additional 1,500 peacekeepers, just below the maximum allowed in the 1994 ceasefire agreement (Tsygankov and Tarver-Wahlquist 2009, 312; Smith 2009, 129; Finn 2008). Russian troops helped rebuild the railway through Abkhazia and undertook large-scale military exercises in the region (Felgenhauer 2009, 172; Nichol 2008, 4; Allison 2008, 1149–51). By the end of July newly organized units of well-trained and well-commanded troops were primed for whatever might come.

Western governments warned Georgian leaders of the risks of hubris and anger—something Saakashvili apparently possessed in large measure—and of responding to the typical violent incidents with something more than a limited response (Filippov 2010, 1839; Lucas 2009, 148). Ignoring the advice—or perhaps hoping that Russians would not respond—Georgian forces entered South Ossetia in the evening of August 7 at roughly the same time as roughly twenty thousand Russian troops with one hundred tanks moved in the area from the north. (Although a European Union fact-finding team and most analysts have determined that Georgia fired first, the International Criminal Court was not so sure [Gahrton 2010, 188; International Criminal Court—Office of the Prosecutor 2014].) Within days, Georgian forces were retreating to Tbilisi against an overwhelming Russian force that included units moving through Abkhazia and by sea (Felgenhauer 2009, 171; Allison 2008, 1148). Russia justified its action as self-defense to protect Russian peacekeepers and South Ossetian civilians and to reaffirm the integrity of the CIS peacekeeping operation (Allison 2013, 150–55). Moscow further claimed that since Georgian forces were committing genocide that the principle of the responsibility to protect required action (Evans 2009, 27; Nichol 2008, 5). Needless to say, many Western observers and especially the Georgian government rejected all these defenses, arguing that Russian forces had attacked first (Senate, U.S. 2008), that Russian actions were not justified under the CIS mandate, and that no genocide was committed (and that humanitarian intervention would require UN Security Council approval at any rate) (Illarionov 2009, 77; Lucas 2009, 147; Evans 2009, 25). While the events surrounding the outbreak of the war and its justification are still contested, there is widespread agreement that after an August 14 ceasefire both Russian and South Ossetian forces pressed their advantage far beyond what had been agreed by forcing out ethnic Georgians (roughly 140,000) and occupying large swaths of Georgian territory contiguous to the separatist regions (International Criminal Court—Office of the Prosecutor 2014, 34; Mullins 2011; Felgenhauer 2009, 177; Evans 2009, 27; Nichol 2008, 7; BBC 2008).

The war resulted in permanent changes to the Russia-Georgia relationship. On August 26, Russia granted diplomatic recognition to Abkhazia and South Ossetia and shortly thereafter signed treaties of friendship with each (United Nations Department of Peacekeeping Operations

2009; Harvey 2009). It gradually increased its influence in the areas, culminating in treaties of formal alliance and integration in 2015 that virtually annexed the areas to the Russian Federation (Nichol 2008, i; Otarashvili 2015; Soldatkin and Heritage 2015). Russia increased its military presence to 3,800 troops in each region, more than double the prewar level (Nichol 2008, 11). It vetoed the mandate of the UN peacekeeping mission in Abkhazia on the grounds that its recognition of the territory's independence and Georgia's prior aggression made the operation obsolete (United Nations Department of Peacekeeping Operations 2009; Harvey 2009; CNN 2009). Georgia, for its part, severed diplomatic relations with Russia on August 29, 2008, abrogated the 1994 ceasefire agreement in September, and exited the CIS the next year (United Nations Department of Peacekeeping Operations 2009). While many agreements Georgia had entered into with the CIS remain valid, roughly two dozen security-related agreements have been nullified. On the other hand, it entered into an agreement with NATO to form a joint commission, which allowed NATO members to symbolically affirm their support for Georgia's territorial integrity (Nichol 2009, 3; Nichol 2008, 33). That said, full membership in the EU and NATO are no closer to realization. On-again, off-again peace talks with separatist groups were suspended in 2010 (Babayan 2014, 57–58). The less anti-Moscow government of the Georgian Dream Party, elected in 2012 and again in 2016, has not found relations with Russia to be any easier than did its predecessor, and Russian forces appear to be slowly taking Georgian territory by shifting border markers at night (Babayan 2014, 58, 68; Higgins 2016). At the same time, the ICC is moving forward with an investigation into Russia actions during the war to determine whether war crimes or other charges might be filed (International Criminal Court—Office of the Prosecutor 2016).

As advertised, the Russia-Georgia relationship is dysfunctional, although one would have to admit that it is still very much alive despite formal suspension of diplomatic relations. Economic relations continue between the two powers and they are still tied by dozens of bilateral treaties, although there has been little progress on resolving outstanding disputes or deepening the relationship. Considering the last twenty-five years, what do we learn about the role of trust in this relationship?

As we can see in table 7.4, Georgia has always been vulnerable to Russia. This does not take into account the lack of alternative natural allies for Georgia since relations with Turkey and the West have been either strained or immature or both. This contrasts with the situation for Belarus, which can easily pivot to the West if necessary. Particularly since Russia took control of Georgia's pipelines in the early 2000s, the country's economic and political fate are utterly sealed to decisions made in Moscow. Moscow, for its part, has generally been more secure, although Georgia's role as a facilitator of Chechen rebellion was seen as a serious, albeit manageable, threat. Today the fear in Russia that Georgia will develop into a prosperous democracy and thereby present a perverse model of political development appears genuine but of limited significance.

While Georgia's willingness to enter into a relationship of dependency with Russia was mixed during the 1990s, it is clear that since the Rose Revolution successive Georgian governments—and the vast majority of Georgian citizens—view Russia as a threat rather than a protector. Repeated efforts have been made to extricate the country from Moscow's grasp, to no avail. This is key, since it means the relationship has shifted from a disagreeable protectorate to outright vassalage. Russia justified its August 2008 actions as a punishment for Georgia's bad behavior, on the surface for its attack on South Ossetia (a de facto Russian protectorate) but also on a deeper level for its rejection of Russia's role as mediator and sociocultural touchstone (Tsygankov and Tarver-Wahlquist 2009, 308). Russia saw itself as always ready to extend support and encouragement, so long as Georgia didn't lean too far to the West.

Regarding the scope and salience of the treaty relations and informal ties, they were far-reaching in their coverage during the 1990s, although they addressed issues that were more vital to Tbilisi than to Moscow. Over one hundred bilateral agreements cover everything from trade to security to intellectual property to migration. On the other hand, since the 2008 war and withdrawal of Georgia from the CIS and the interruption of diplomatic relations with Moscow, the scope and salience of their mutual agreements have declined. Those agreements, taken as a whole, were in the midrange of precision and formality. As mentioned, some were remarkably detailed and precise while others were brief and vague. Since 2005, however, it has become clear that Russia did not consider itself bound by the letter of the law, leaving both parties considerable latitude to interpret and apply existing treaties as they saw fit. Key among these issues was Russia's formal commitment to Georgia's territorial integrity, which proved to be far more open to interpretation than might have been expected given the ironclad language (not that Tbilisi has consistently honored Russia's territorial integrity, either [Gahrton 2010, 24]).

In general, the treaties provided few opportunities for Georgia to influence their operation, particularly after 2005. There were few joint commissions, and dispute settlement was almost always relegated to simple nego-

TABLE 7.4. Features of Russia-Georgia Relationship

		Trustor-Trustee Relationship			Issues in Play		Structure of Agreements		
		Vulnerability	Exploitability	Voluntarism	Scope of Issues	Salience of Issues	Imprecision and Informality	Marginalization	Entrapment
1991–2001	Russia	Low	MODERATE	**HIGH**	MODERATE	MODERATE	MODERATE	Low	Low
	Belarus	**HIGH**	**HIGH**	**HIGH**	**HIGH**	**HIGH**	MODERATE	Low	**HIGH**
2002–2016	Russia	Low	MODERATE	MODERATE	**HIGH**	**HIGH**	Low	Low	
	Belarus	**HIGH**	**HIGH**	Low	**HIGH**	**HIGH**	Low	MODERATE	**HIGH**

tiation, a mechanism that clearly favored Moscow. Only in the CIS did Georgia have something approximating Russia's voice, although since Russia was able to opt out of CIS-mandated rules (such as the arms embargo against separatist regions) it retained a de facto veto. Many treaties were intended to last for decades, although most provided for the opportunity for denunciation, as evidenced by Georgia's actions after 2008.

Taken together, we can see once again that the great power is in a position to impose its will rather than rely on the good intentions of its subordinate. Georgia, on the other hand, appears to have trusted Russia—however hesitantly—during much of the first thirteen years after independence. The experience and Russia's handling of the trust invested in it left Georgia permanently scarred. But rather than allowing the small republic to chart its own course with a different protector, Moscow imposed its will on an untrusting underling.

People's Republic of China–North Korea

Chinese leaders have long viewed Korea as essential to the country's national security, "a dagger to the throat" through which Japan and other rivals have attacked northern China and Beijing (Chung and Choi 2013, 245; Kim 2002, 105). It was therefore essential that the peninsula be controlled as much as possible, typically by means of vassalage (Senate, U.S. 2012, 22). Korean leaders, for their part, have long considered themselves an extension of successive Chinese states, the "ideal vassal" (Noesselt 2014, 1313). This was particularly true after World War II once the Japanese were forced out of the territory they had occupied since 1910 (Brazinsky 2012, 163; Scobell 2004, 3). Even before the People's Republic was established in Beijing, 100,000 Korean Worker's Party (KWP) cadres volunteered to fight alongside Mao's forces (Chen 1994 107). Once the Chinese Communist Party (CCP) came to power, it quickly moved to replace the Soviet Union as the dominant force in North Korea and assume again its traditional role (Chung 1978, 159).

Kim Il-sung was one who had once fought alongside Chinese communists against the Japanese occupation of Manchuria and gained notoriety as an effective rebel leader, although the details of his life are notoriously imprecise (Cumings 2005). He was the civilian administrator of Korea after the war only because of his selection by the Soviet occupation force. He was therefore intent on establishing his own credentials as a nationalist. In 1949 he began to petition Mao Zedong for the return of Korean fighters in anticipation of an invasion of South Korea (Li 2014, 10; Chen 1994, 110). After consulting with Stalin and Mao and assuring them that he had sufficient forces to win the war, Kim launched the invasion in June 1950 and nearly drove the South Korean and American forces from the peninsula (Li 2014, 9). All three socialist leaders were surprised, however, at the vigor of the American response. The US commitment to defending South Korea and Taiwan forced Mao to redeploy large numbers of troops to the north and delay an invasion of Taiwan indefinitely (Chen 1994, 6; Li 2014, 12). Mao was eager to intervene not only to show loyalty to his socialist neighbor but also to thwart a US invasion of China itself (Scobell 2004, 1). Had his troops been ready, they would likely have intervened at roughly the same time as the famed Inchon amphibious landing of UN/US forces (Chen 1994, 154). Instead, in response to an appeal for aid from Kim—a humiliating moment in the North Korean's career (Chung and Choi 2013, 247; Shen and Xia 2012, 5)—Mao and his leadership (after fierce debate) order the deployment of troops on October 5. The first units crossed into North Korea on October 19, the same day advancing US/UN forces captured Pyongyang (Li 2014, 2). Ultimately the bulk of the fighting was done by Chinese "volunteers," roughly 750,000 of whom would die in the war (Scobell 2004, 2).

The Chinese forces pushed back the UN/US troops beyond Seoul by January 1951, but by April they were forced to retreat beyond the 38th parallel (Li 2014, 56). A spring offensive failed to break the stalemate and nearly 100,000 Chinese troops died in a month of fighting (Li 2014, 103). Ultimately the war ended in 1953 with an armistice rather than a peace agreement. The arrangement provided for both sides to commit to respecting the territorial integrity of the other and to refrain from acts of violence. Further, the agreement established a joint Military Assistance Committee made up of ten representatives of each side and was tasked with monitoring the border (Articles 19–35). Article 62 prohibits unilateral withdrawal from the agreement.

The experience taught Mao that Korea's security trumped the Taiwan issue, and so the People's Republic began funneling massive amounts of aid to Pyongyang (Chung and Choi 2013, 246). Thousands of Chinese forces were left behind to provide free labor and as much money was given during the five years after the war as had been offered during the war itself, bringing Chinese aid to the same level as the Soviet Union's (Shen and Xia 2012, 6). The aid, which came in the form of capital investments, relief supplies, trade agreements, loans, and loan forgiveness, amounted to roughly 10 percent of North Korean GDP (Shen and Xia 2012, 8).

Chinese authorities became concerned about the potential for Korean resentment of its overwhelming aid and military presence and began to consider troop withdrawals a few years after the war. It might have done so except for Kim's decision in 1956 to undertake a purge of foreign-trained and foreign-affiliated KWP members out of fear of foreign domination (Chen 1994, 111). He also announced his policy of self-reliance (*Juche*), which soon morphed into extreme nationalism and economic autarky. Kim demanded the withdrawal of Chinese troops in 1956, but Mao bristled at what appeared to be another ungrateful nonaligned regime in its backyard and refused (Shen and Xia 2012, 15). Kim then turned to the USSR, which increased its support for the regime, forcing Mao's hand. He accepted the demand for troop withdrawals in 1957, expressing regret over any hurt feelings from his earlier refusal and lack of enthusiasm for *Juche* (Shen and Xia 2012, 19). The two countries initiated a new form of communication: summitry. Given the lack of insider contacts following the purge of CCP-affiliated KWP members, the most efficient means of learning about each other was high-level contacts, which themselves became a fairly reliable barometer of the state of Sino-Korean relations for years to come (Chung and Choi 2013, 247).

During the ten years, relations between the two regimes were arguably at their best. Ideologically, they were in almost perfect harmony as both adopted ambitious industrialization strategies (the Great Leap Forward) and rejected Khrushchev's de-Stalinization policies in Moscow (Shen and Xia 2012, 22; Chung 1978, 159). They shared a hatred for the West, which they each blamed for creating a breach in their respective territories (Nanto and Manyin 2011). In 1960 the leaders met secretly and Korea pledged its support for China's side in the Sino-Soviet split (although it recanted after a Soviet official divulged Mao's derogatory comments about Kim as an ersatz Tito four years earlier [Shen and Xia 2012, 28]; it remained undecided on the issue until the collapse of the Soviet Union). Between 1949 and 1960 the two countries entered into no fewer than sixty-eight treaties and contracts on topics ranging from foreign aid projects to harmonized postal traffic (Ginsburgs and Kim 1977).

The crowning moment of this period was the ratification of the Treaty of Friendship, Cooperation and Mutual Assistance in 1961. The agreement remains the foundation of Sino-Korean relations and has been renewed repeatedly (Noesselt 2014, 1313; Byun and Snyder 2014, 155). Korea had always hoped for a tangible commitment from Beijing to the defense of Korea's territorial integrity (although it had hoped for unconditional support of a future invasion of the South, which was not forthcoming; see Article 6). There were rumors of a tacit alliance as early as 1949 and the Korean War experience already demonstrated a de facto commitment (Chen 1994, 109). The rise of a nationalist, autocratic military junta in South Korea and the growing security cooperation between the United States and a rising Japan were enough to tip the balance in favor of a concrete agreement for Mao (Chung and Choi 2013, 249; Sang-sook 2011). The brief treaty (seven articles) was based heavily on the old alliance treaty between the USSR and the PRC and included as its centerpiece a pledge of mutual support in the event of attack (Article 2). Although China insisted that any language regarding unification be qualified (only "peaceful" unification was acceptable, a warning against Korean impetuosity [Article 6]), the North Koreans secured more unequivocal language for Article 2 in that each side agreed to "immediate" intervention (in light of China's delays in 1950) (Sang-sook 2011; Shen and Xia 2012, 34). The treaty could only be abrogated jointly (Article 7; Lee 1996, 60). It is worth noting, as part of its effort at balancing the great powers, North Korea also signed a mutual defense pact with the USSR in the same year, although its language was more tentative and it included a ten-year sunset clause (Shen and Xia 2012, 34; Lee 1996, 60). It was also during this period that China and North Korea came to a tentative agreement (and still largely secret due to opposition from local Chinese) regarding the demarcation of the border, the key element of which was China's concession to allow North Korea to claim the peak of the symbolic and religiously significant Mount Changbai (Hyer 2015, 158). This was followed up with a string of six relatively succinct agreements regarding control over rivers and islands over the next fifteen years (China, People's Republic 2004).

Relations soured during the mid-1960s as North Korea sought heavy weaponry from the USSR, an action that could not help but offend Beijing given the zero-sum nature of the Sino-Soviet relationship (Kim 2014, 147; Chung 1987, 177). As the Cultural Revolution announced its fury against revisionists, even Kim came under attack by the Red Guard (Brazinsky 2012, 163; Lee 1996, 102). To hedge his bets, Kim adopted unilateral tactics, including attacks in 1968 on the South Korean president's mansion and the USS *Pueblo* and strikes against South Korean border villages, as well as the hijacking of KAL YS-11 in 1969 (Kim 2014, 132; Chung and Choi 2013, 250). A few years later, Kim began exploring the possibility of developing a nuclear capability (Moore 2014, 92). As the Cultural Revolution ebbed, good relations were restored as evidenced by increased aid and frequent summit meetings, although it became increasingly clear that Kim's loyalty to Beijing was utterly contingent on his perception of North Korea's and his own regime's needs (Chung 1978, 160). China's hopes of influencing Pyongyang policy—let alone preventing an all-out war on the peninsula—seemed increasingly unrealistic by the 1970s (Brazinsky 2012, 165).

It was of course during this period that Mao opened talks with a number of North Korea's implacable adversaries: the United States and South Korea. To say that Pyongyang was suspicious of China's intentions would be an understatement (Brazinsky 2012, 163). It was only after considerable cajoling and promises of additional aid that Mao secured Kim's consent to the Nixon summit meeting in 1971 and an official renunciation of unification by aggression (Kim 1998, 96). On the other hand, Beijing kept Kim mostly in the dark about its talks with Seoul that began in 1973 (Chung 1987, 194). As aid came pouring into Korea, including discounted oil sales to offset reductions in Soviet oil sales in 1974, the relationship warmed, culminating in a spectacular visit by Kim to Beijing in 1975, an event worthy of a 1930s Hollywood extravaganza (Chung 1987, 181; China, People's Republic 1975). The relationship was praised as a "militant friendship and revolutionary unity" cemented in blood and indestructible (China, People's Republic 1975, 7). But publicly Chinese authorities emphasized peaceful unification of the peninsula and privately blocked a North Korean plan to invade later that year (Lee 1996, 68).

Mao's refusal to back the invasion plan left Kim feeling betrayed (Chung and Choi 2013, 251). Continued increases in Chinese aid did little to mollify his anger, and he began concerted efforts to acquire long-range missiles and continued his probes in the area of nuclear capability (Chung and Choi 2013, 251). He launched an attack on the demilitarized zone (DMZ) in 1976 that resulted in the deaths of two American servicemen (Kim 2014, 133). He tilted further to Moscow and condemned the anti-Mao policies of the Deng Xiaoping (Chung 1987, 192), Beijing rapprochement with Tokyo (Lee 1996, 68), and China's assumption of the role of mediator between Asia and the West (Chung and Choi 2013, 254).

Sensing that it was losing influence, China again increased its support for Kim by offering additional aid in 1982 and granting approval for Kim's plan to be one day replaced his son Kim Jong-il (Chung 1987, 186). Kim, for his part, agreed, at China's urging, to give capitalism a try by opening free trade zones in 1984, but the lack of investors reaffirmed his lack of interest in open markers (Kim 1998, 105). He did enter into state-controlled trade deals with Beijing, each of which was limited to five-year terms and more resembled an aid contract than anything approaching integration (Kim 1998, 106). Trade flows between the two countries nonetheless increased fourfold between 1970 and 1982 (Chung 1987, 188).

China's increasingly public repudiations of unification by force, combined with its awkward mediation efforts with the South, prompted Kim to adopt a more aggressive foreign policy after 1983. Just prior to the beginning of negotiations with South Korea, North Korean agents detonated a powerful explosive at a meeting of South Korea's and Burma's governments in Rangoon that killed most of South Korea's cabinet (Kim 2014, 133; Chung and Choi 2013, 254). In 1987 North Korea shot down the civilian airliner KAL 855. And the country's pursuit of nuclear and long-range missile capability intensified.

The collapse of the Soviet Union provided an opportunity for China to return to its traditional dominance in Korea, as Pyongyang could no longer play the two states against each other (Scobell 2004, 4; Kim 2002, 113). North Korea had no choice but to turn to China for aid as resources from Moscow dwindled to a trickle. Specifically, this liberated Beijing to explore normalization with Western states without fear of losing North Korea, a country that had become an increasingly inconvenient ally at any rate (Nanto and Manyin 2011, 99). In 1992 China normalized relations with South Korea without seeking Kim's formal approval (although he was informed of the planned move [Brazinsky 2012, 180; Kim 2002, 115]), although it could have been seen as a violation of Article 3 of the 1961 alliance (Sang-sook 2011). It even persuaded Kim to drop his opposition to South Korean membership in the United Nations, and in 1991 the two states were admitted as separate entities (Kim 2002, 114; Lee 1996, 121). Despite increased Chinese aid and trade (which reached a peak of nearly $900 million in 1994, up from an average of roughly $500 million during the 1980s [Lee 1996, 140]), North Korea's economy nearly collapsed during the mid-1990s. Its average GDP growth rate during this period was a shocking negative 5 percent and widespread famine is thought to have taken one life in ten (Radio Free Asia 2015a). Its debt-to-GDP ratio reached 50 percent in 1994 (Kim 1998, 107). Doubling down on repression and indoctrination, the new government of Kim Jong-il rejected liberalization and peaceful foreign relations, much to China's dismay (Kim 1998, 99).

While there were periods of relative harmony, the foreign policies of the People's Republic and the Hermit Kingdom increasingly diverged. As the Chinese were signing the nonproliferation treaty, for example, the North Koreans were abrogating it (Lee 1996, 95; Scobell 2004, 10). While North Koreans were preparing to enrich uranium in defiance of international opinion and engaged in repeated provocations, China was endeavoring to recast its overall foreign policy as that of a mature major power (Kim and Lee 2002, 117; Moore 2014, 79). As the Chinese economy was becoming increasingly integrated with the rest of the world, North Korea was determined to maintain as much of its *Juche* policy as possible. Throughout the post–Cold War era, while North Korea could not credibly threaten to tilt to one of China's rivals, it could always rely on its inherent instability as a guarantee that Beijing would never push it to the brink (Moore 2014, 97; Snyder 2009, 132). China has in a sense been a hostage to North Korea's instability, although given North Korea's increasing dependence on Chinese aid and goods it would be more correct to say they are each other's hostage (Plant and Rhode 2013, 62). As put by Kim, "Paradoxically, Pyongyang's growing dependence on Beijing for economic and political survival has led to mutual distrust and resentment" (Kim 2006, 197).

In 1993–94, China bribed and threatened North Korea into talks with the United States over its nuclear weapons program (although North Korea denied the Chinese role [Kim and Lee 2002, 118; Brazinsky 2012, 181; Kim 2006, 189]). China was deeply concerned about North Korea's coming into possession of nuclear weapons primarily because of the risk of provoking a regional arms race, not to mention the increased chances of a devastating (and refugee-creating) peninsular war (Moore 2014, 91; Chang and Choi 2013, 258). At the same time, it feared an overly strict sanctions regime that could topple the Kim government and provoke a flood of refugees or unification of Korea under a pro-US government (Byun and Snyder 2014, 160). In some ways, the 1994 agreed framework was the ideal type of agreement, from China's point of view, in that it aimed to halt North Korea's nuclear program in its tracks in exchange for support for a peaceful nuclear power plant (Scobell 2004, 15; Kim 1998, 110). Even this deal ultimately was too constraining for Pyongyang, which rejected the provision that allowed South Korean firms a role in constructing the power plant and abrogated the agreement (Brazinsky 2012, 183).

China provided considerable support to North Korea during the famine years in the mid-1990s, although trade levels were volatile, generally correlating with diplomatic relations (Snyder 2009, 131; Kim and Lee 2002, 125). It provided one million tons of food relief, for example (Snyder 2009, 120). To avoid the appearance of dependence, Kim made sure that requests to Beijing were private while denials of aid were public (Kim 2002, 120). He was also not above using blackmail to secure even more concessions (in 1996 he threatened to approve direct flights to Taiwan if he did not get 200,000 additional tons of grain! [Moore 2014, 83; Scobell 2004, 5]). Despite China's aid, relations between the two soured in the late 1990s (trade reached a nadir in 1999) and it was not until the NATO bombing of Kosovo that the two decided to cooperate again for fear of becoming the next target (Kim 2006, 186; Kim and Lee 2002, 114). The North Korean economy grew at a healthy pace after bottoming out in 1998. Trade began to expand in earnest after 1999, rising from $400 million to $2.8 billion in 2008 (Haggard, Lee, and Noland 2012, 131). China furthermore turned a blind eye to the routine failure of North Koreans to pay for imports and to smuggling levels that were roughly equal to legitimate trade (Snyder 2009, 113). At a summit meeting in 2000, the two nations formally agreed to consult each other on major foreign policy initiatives, consistent with the 1961 treaty (Byun and Snyder 2014, 165).

The harmony proved short-lived, however, as fundamental differences in interests pushed the two apart in 2002. It was then that North Korean officials candidly admitted (bragged?) to their American counterparts that the country had a full-fledged uranium enrichment program in place and that it would soon be able to generate sufficient material for several nuclear bombs (Scobell 2004, 10). This came as a surprise to China, which tried for the next decade to be more assertive in controlling Pyongyang's behavior (Kim 2006, 190). At several points—2003, 2005, 2006, and 2009 in response to the enrichment revelation and two nuclear tests—China imposed economic sanctions and voted to allow UN-imposed sanctions (Byun and Snyder 2014, 166; Xu and Bajoria 2014; Scobell 2004, 24). Beijing saw the 2006 test as an affront and a betrayal, not only because it destabilized the region but also because it was done secretly in violation of the 1961 treaty and the 2000 agreement (Chung and Choi 2013, 249; Glaser, Snyder, and Park 2008, 3). China suspended aid to pressure Pyongyang to participate in the six-party talks beginning in 2006, although at the end of the day the talks accomplished relatively little given the lack of overlap between the parties' minimum positions and the unwillingness of China to risk destabilizing the Kim regime (Xu and Bajoria 2014; Byun and Snyder 2014, 166; Pritchard 2007, 102).

As the talks collapsed, North Korea went on a binge of provocations, launching a ballistic missile in April 2009, testing a second nuclear weapon the next month, sinking the Korean vessel *Cheonan* in 2010, and shelling Yeonpyeong in South Korea later that year (Moore 2014, 100; Kim 2014, 133; Wong 2011). In 2015, disputes over North Korea's placement of land mines across the DMZ and South Korea's renewed propaganda broadcasts resulted in an escalation that some feared would culminate in war (Sang-hun 2015). China responded to these events in measured tones, accepting UN-proposed sanctions in response to the nuclear test, but equivocating on the other questions, perhaps in part because of some ambiguity regarding the facts (Moore 2014, 89; Byun and Snyder 2014, 168; Noesselt 2014,

1315). In 2015, Beijing relocated troops to the North Korean border but explained it away as "normal deployment" (Reuters 2015). It was becoming apparent to Beijing authorities that the North Korean regime was taking desperate measures to survive in the face of crippling sanctions, moving into illicit trade in drugs, weapons, counterfeit currency, tobacco, and human trafficking (Moore 2014, 82; Eckel 2013; Pearson 2014; Department of State, U.S. 2015). The regime was obviously financially and morally bankrupt and without some minimal guarantees from China would soon cease to exist. Therefore, China became increasingly ambivalent about enforcing the sanctions regime. It supported the 2009 UN sanctions only after ensuring they would be voluntary (Byun and Snyder 2014, 168). It skirted prohibitions against the sale of "dual-use" materials and luxury items (Nanto and Manyin 2011, 95). It has also permitted the shielding of much of Kim Jong-un's considerable wealth in private Chinese banks (Taylor 2013).

The year 2016 may be seen as a tipping point in retrospect. The UN Security Council passed a string of resolutions condemning North Korea's two nuclear tests and several missile launches by unanimous votes, and China agreed to increasingly tough sanctions against the regime, including a measure aimed at cutting North Korean coal exports by 60 percent (Sengupta and Sang-hun 2016, Sengupta and Perez 2016). This latter move was especially significant since coal exports from North Korea to China had actually risen from 11 million metric tons in 2011 to 19.6 million metric tons in 2015 (Hu 2016). On the other hand, China warned against increased US–South Korean military cooperation that included the deployment of Patriot missiles and the THAAD antimissile defense system (Bodeen 2017). At any rate, China's tougher stand did not lead to any diminution of North Korea's belligerency. To the contrary. Except for a brief period in the fall of 2016 when severe floods prompted North Korea to plead for aid, almost all of its actions were aggressive and defiant against the West, South Korea, and even China (Mills 2016; Silva 2016; Moore 2016; Denyer 2016).

Returning to our questions regarding trust. Table 7.5 summarizes the situation between China and North Korea. As we can see, during the period before China's opening to the West, both states were vulnerable to attack and exploitation by outsiders and by each other. China's commitment to protecting North Korea was made not from overconfidence but from insecurity: Korea was to serve as a front line in China's national defense strategy. It feared not only the immediate threat from the US military but also the longer-term threat of Soviet encirclement. As China repositioned itself on the global stage in the 1970s, its vulnerability and exploitability decreased. North Korea's vulnerability was relatively constant across the entire history, although as time went on it became a less interesting target of exploitation. Where China is concerned, in particular, North Korea became a burden rather than a boon.

In the early phase of the relationship, the closeness between the two countries was entirely voluntary, founded as it was on geography, ideology, shared adversaries, and a degree of economic and social interdependence. After 1971 the partnership was more grudging, and especially after 1991 North Korea's commitment to China was almost compulsory by virtue of its lack of alternatives (at least insofar as the self-obsessed Kim family was concerned).

Regarding the nature of the agreements entered into, the fact is that despite having so much in common the two states refrained from anything approaching full integration. While the military alliance was relatively firm, it was limited to mutual defense, not day-to-day collaboration. The two forces are not integrated as one might expect, and clearly North Korea charts its own course with respect to its capabilities, typically in defiance of China's preferences and interests. Even on the economic side, collaboration is constrained. Only recently have the two states considered creating a free trade area, a venture that seems doomed to fail in light of Kim Jong-un's recent decision to rid the country of foreign goods (RFA 2015b; Noesselt 2014, 1314). Agreements have covered such things as cultural and technical cooperation, but are generally limited in scope. There are some arrangements regarding the land and maritime borders, but they are honored mostly in the breach. That said, because the military alliance looms so large in the corpus of these agreements, it is fair to say that as a group they address highly salient issues of national survival (especially where North Korea is concerned).

The structure of the agreements tends to be relatively informal and open to interpretation. The alliance, as had been discussed, is very brief at only seven short articles and allows for conflicting interpretations, something North Korea bristles at while the People's Republic embraces it. Most of the trade agreements are merely contracts spelling out what goods China will sell and on what terms. Likewise, many other deals can be better understood as aid projects rather than typical bilateral treaties. The periodic deployment of troops to the border is an indication of the ad hoc nature of how this issue is regulated, while trade across the border is almost entirely improvised. Bribery, expropriation, nonpayment, embargoes, and boycotts are routine features, leaving especially the larger

TABLE 7.5. Features of China-North Korean Relationship

		Trustor-Trustee Relationship			Issues in Play		Structure of Agreements		
		Vulnerability	Exploitability	Voluntarism	Scope of Issues	Salience of Issues	Imprecision and Informality	Marginalization	Entrapment
1940–1971	China	**HIGH**	**HIGH**	**HIGH**	MODERATE	**HIGH**	**HIGH**	Low	MODERATE
	North Korea	**HIGH**	**HIGH**	**HIGH**	MODERATE	**HIGH**	**HIGH**	MODERATE	MODERATE
1972–2016	China	MODERATE	MODERATE	MODERATE	MODERATE	MODERATE	**HIGH**	Low	MODERATE
	North Korea	**HIGH**	Low	MODERATE	MODERATE	**HIGH**	**HIGH**	MODERATE	**HIGH**

Chinese firms extremely reticent about committing to the North Korean market (Haggard, Lee, and Noland 2012, 138). Likewise, most agreements are of a short-term variety, expiring after five years in some cases. The key exception is again the alliance, which cannot be abrogated except by mutual agreement, something that restricts North Korea more severely than China given Beijing's commitment to the deal. Finally, China naturally has more voice in the nature of the agreements, although it has chosen to restrain itself with respect to punishment and discipline for fear of upending the Kim regime.

There are in this relationship the prerequisites for trust, and China in particular (North Korea to a perhaps lesser degree) seems to have been possessed of it prior to 1971. But today one sees little evidence of the full-throated commitments trust should generate. Rather, both sides are hedging as much as their core interests and fears allow. China downgraded the relationship as it expanded its ties to Western-leaning states. There are even indications that Beijing prefers working with Seoul rather than Pyongyang as it moves toward a genuine free trade agreement and other deeper commitments with South Korea, something the North sees as a betrayal. For its part, and partly in response to China's perceived unreliability, North Korea has moved to nuclear capability as an alternative to playing Moscow against Beijing as it did for so many years. Its focus on unification by any means is a direct threat to China's aims of becoming a serious world power. In the process, the spirit of the alliance has been frayed almost beyond recognition. The only thing Pyongyang can apparently count on is Beijing's commitment to preserving the regime. In sum, the relationship is based less on trust than on necessity.

People's Republic of China–North Vietnam/Unified Vietnam

Across a century from the 1870s to the 1970s, Vietnam and China's relationship devolved from mutual support and brotherhood in times of foreign occupation and war to mutual distrust and ultimately open hostility. It is a classic case of diverging interests leading to a loss of faith in the other's ability and willingness to take both actors' interests into account. After centuries of interaction characterized by Chinese paternalistic domination and the independent spirit of the Vietnamese, France ultimately came to dominate the Indochinese peninsula in the 1880s (Lawrence 2008, 31). The Chinese government provided support for Vietnamese nationalists fighting French occupation, both materially and also in the form of advice and encouragement (Hood 1992, 14; Duiker 1986, 8). Sun Yat-sen was a particularly inspiring figure, although Mao Zedong gradually emerged as a much-needed ally of the Viet Minh under Ho Chi Minh during the 1940s (Ray 1983, 1–3). After Mao came to power in Beijing in 1949, he promptly began providing military and economic aid to the Viet Minh, and on January 18 the People's Republic formally recognized it as the rightful government of Vietnam, two weeks before the USSR did (Ray 1983, 3). In addition to promises to provide thousands of advisors and millions of dollars in equipment and weapons, the PRC mobilized 250,000 combat troops to the border with Vietnam to provide a security backstop, secretly promising to intervene if the French forces advanced too near the border (Chen 1987, 11; Lawrence 2008, 43; Ray 1983, 5). All told, roughly 4,000 Chinese lost their lives out of more than 300,000 support troops and roughly $200 billion was sent to Vietnam between 1950 and 1975 (Chen 1987, 8, 21). Especially between 1950 and 1954, the rhetoric of friendship and trust flowed freely, with each side using terms like "brotherhood" and "unbreakable friendship" and describing the countries' closeness as equal to that of "lips to teeth" (Khoo 2011, 1; Ray 1983, 5). The cooperation verged on harmony as the interests of each country naturally overlapped, namely to advance socialism and expel the Western capitalists. This harmony, however, proved to be short-lived.

As the Vietnamese gained the upper hand over the French in 1954—with Chinese help—a peace conference seemed desirable, especially to the French, Chinese, and Soviets. While supporting the Vietnamese, the Chinese had also been fighting the Americans and South Koreans, losing hundreds of thousands of soldiers in the process, an experience it had no interest in repeating in Southeast Asia (Hood 1992, 19). Considering the possibility of American intervention following the French departure, Chinese officials surmised that a division of the country (with the possibility of peaceful unification) offered the safest way to prevent this (Ross 1988, 20). It hoped that a divided Vietnam, along with a weak Laos and Cambodia, would simply fade from Western minds while giving Beijing the best chance at exercising influence in the region in the future (Hood 1992, 22; Ray 1983, 9). Vietnamese leaders, however, saw the division of the country as a failure and China's support for it as a betrayal, although under pressure they acquiesced to the outcome (Ray 1983, 10).

The question of how unification should be achieved divided the two countries until 1975: Vietnamese officials sought quick military action combined with episodic negotiations, while Chinese officials strongly favored a very long (one-hundred-year) war of attrition that mimicked its own revolution and posed the least danger of foreign intervention (Khoo 2011, 51). Each side felt the other's position was a challenge and possibly a betrayal: the Vietnamese felt China was more interested in geopolitics—especially after the Sino-Soviet split in the early 1960s—than in Vietnam's future, while the Chinese worried that Vietnamese leaders were reckless and unconcerned about China's security (Hood 1992, 22).

After the 1954 division, China continued to provide aid to Vietnam; it was its principal source of economic military aid until 1969, although as early as 1960 Ho Chi Minh began requesting aid from Soviet leaders, first secretly then openly (Ray 1983, 18–19). As the PRC-USSR split widened, each side took note of the other's policies on Vietnam and maneuvered to increase favor with Hanoi (at least for the most part). The USSR was supportive of Vietnam's drive for unification during the 1960s, especially after Leonid Brezhnev came to power in 1964 (Duiker 1986, 48). As the need for heavy weaponry against the arriving American forces increased, China became the second option for support (Ross 1988, 22). Beijing, for its part, castigated Hanoi for its increasingly pro-USSR stand and its increasingly obvious ambitions in Laos and Cambodia, fearing a possible pro-Soviet encirclement of China (the Soviet Union already had troops in Mongolia along the Chinese border and its ties to India were improving) (Ross 1988, 44). Beijing, meanwhile, began nurturing a more mature and even-handed reputation internationally, culminating in a dialogue with the United States, which Vietnam saw as yet another betrayal (Chen 1987, 19). The relationship between China and Vietnam deteriorated further as Beijing began to encourage peace talks in 1969, including yet another move to divide the country (Ross 1988, 24).

By now Vietnamese leaders routinely spoke of the Chinese as "sellouts" and "backstabbers." After the war they began to take action against Chinese migrants in Vietnam and against China's ally Cambodia (which Beijing had been supporting in its military struggle against Vietnam [Duiker 1986, 59]). China, for its part, considered the Vietnamese "ungrateful" and in need of being "taught a lesson" (language consistent with the notion of "discipline" in Lake 2011), which came beginning in 1968, with a significant reduction in aid, and culminated in 1979 in a brief but bloody incursion (Khoo 2011, 57; Duiker 1986, 85). The war was at best a draw, and Vietnam clearly did not learn its lesson as it nearly doubled the size of its military over the next six years, consolidated its control and influence in Cambodia (which it had invaded in 1978) and Laos (with which it had signed a treaty of friendship in 1977), and more deeply entrenched itself in the Soviet camp (Chen 1987, 34). At the end of the day, China's situation in Southeast Asia had become the worst-case scenario it had so hoped to avoid. It would take the end of the Cold War, the withdrawal of Russia from the region, and economic liberalization in Vietnam for the relationship to return to a cooperative one.

Referring to the trust template (See table 7.6), Vietnam was clearly the more vulnerable and exploitable country of the two, and China had already demonstrated a willingness and capacity to take advantage of it. But for its part China felt almost as vulnerable after losing large numbers of troops and fearing Soviet encirclement. From Beijing's point of view, Vietnam was taking advantage of its largesse by siding with Moscow whenever convenient, a sign of betrayal and duplicity. China and Vietnam entered into few formal agreements during the 1949–1979 period although both did so willingly (i.e., Vietnam was not coerced but came to China), and those that were written down tended to be short and vague, although they at least implicitly were broad in scope and covered the most salient issues of national survival. There was no formal alliance or even treaty of friendship, but nonetheless there seemed to be a general understanding of what was expected of each side. Both parties were quick to criticize and condemn the unwelcome actions of the others (which served to clarify the meaning of vague treaty language), although the use of the term "betrayal" was likely designed more to embarrass or provoke than to provide an accurate measure of the speaker's feelings (Khoo 2011, 72). With respect to marginalization and entrapment, while the two parties communicated on a regular basis, it became clear to Vietnam that China called the shots, perhaps the most distressing feature of the agreement from Hanoi's point of view. Likewise, Beijing clearly expected eternal loyalty from Hanoi, something it did not feel obligated to reciprocate. The fact that Ho kept his 1960 visit to Moscow a secret and China surrounded its rapprochement with the United States shrouded in mystery may be good indicators that each side knew it was being disloyal to the other, among other things. Taken together, the relationship's agreements and their context seem to indicate a high degree of trust, but only during the early 1950s. As each state acted in its own interest—China to secure its borders and its place on the world stage, Vietnam to unify its country by any means necessary—the trust quickly deteriorated into mutual suspicion and ultimately distrust and antagonism.

Findings: Evidence of Trust

Looking at our seven cases (eleven if each period is treated as a separate case), we see that trust is a relatively rare commodity. Subordinate states

TABLE 7.6. Features of China-Vietnam Relationship, 1949–79

	Trustor-Trustee Relationship			Issues in Play		Structure of Agreements		
	Vulnerability	Exploitability	Voluntarism	Scope of Issues	Salience of Issues	Imprecision and Informality	Marginalization	Entrapment
China	MODERATE	MODERATE	**HIGH**	**HIGH**	**HIGH**	**HIGH**	Low	Low
Vietnam	**HIGH**	**HIGH**	**HIGH**	**HIGH**	**HIGH**	**HIGH**	**HIGH**	**HIGH**

are more likely to trust: Canada in relation to the United States from 1940 to 1970, Belarus in relation to Russia from 1990 to 2001, North Korea in relation to China from 1949 to 1971, and perhaps Vietnam vis-à-vis China, but only from 1949 to roughly 1964. In each of these cases, however, the relationship deteriorated and trust diminished over time. Only in China's relationship with North Korea between 1949 and 1971 could one argue that the dominant actor trusted its subordinate, although tensions emerged and trust dissipated over time.

More specifically, in only a few cases were the dominant actors genuinely vulnerable to exploitation. In most cases the subordinate state could only cause a serious inconvenience rather than pose a mortal danger. The scope of issues covered in the agreements was often quite broad (it was "high" in six periods and "moderate" in four other cases) and their salience was often relatively high (in four cases and "moderate" in five others), indicating that these were serious commitments. With respect to the structure and formality of the agreements, they showed a considerable range, with five ranked "high," five ranked "moderate," and one ranked "low." Across the board, the more powerful actor ensured it would have the capacity to interpret and enforce the agreements (all eleven cases were ranked "low") while weaker actors were almost all marginalized (three "high" and seven "moderate"). The same pattern generally holds with respect to entrapment, with the dominant actors in a position to withdraw from the agreements more easily.

Of particular importance is the variation on the dimension of voluntarism. In only four of the eleven periods did the subordinate actors clearly elect to participate in the relationship, while in four other cases there was considerable ambivalence. In two cases the weaker party clearly did not wish to be involved in the arrangements as they were structured (Belarus in relation to Russia from 2002 to 2015, Georgia relative to Russia from 2005 to 2015, and Vietnam in relation to China after 1975). On the other hand, the major actors were involved in the relationships of their own free will, although not always cheerfully.

Finally, considering the historical context of the cases, it is worth noting that most of the actors hedged against the possibility of betrayal, for good reason. Dominant actors generally reserved the right to act unilaterally to hedge against failure on the part of the subordinate actor to perform. The United States, for example, relied heavily on its nuclear deterrent and extended radar system rather than the fighting forces of its allies. Likewise, American troops in South Vietnam and Kissinger's secret diplomacy were fallback tactics to make up for the failures of the South Vietnamese government. Russia under Putin was also quite willing to supersede the preferences of Belarus and Georgia. At the same time, several subordinate states hedged their reliance on the dominant states, especially in the case of Minsk and Tbilisi that kept channels open to Western powers and North Korea and Vietnam that likewise maintained strong ties to Moscow to use as leverage against Beijing.

Not only is trust a rather rare—but not unheard of—commodity, but the essence of the relationships under consideration were not even entirely voluntary in many cases. While hierarchical, they were often not legitimate. The fact that trust does not appear to have increased over time is also telling, in that trust, as pointed out in earlier chapters, carries risks that often results in quite negative outcomes for the trusting actor. Trust has often led to disappointment and even resentment, even in the US-Canada case.

EIGHT

Conclusion

This project has been primarily a search for trust in international relations. The conclusion is that trust exists at high levels only rarely, although it exists with some regularity.

It is worth reviewing the findings once more. Despite selecting most likely cases of trust (for the most part), it has been found to be both elusive and ephemeral. Nonetheless it clearly occurs. The following are the clearest cases of trust, although they are not all uncontestable:

- Liechtenstein's relations with Austria from 1812 to 1919.
- Luxembourg's relations with the Netherlands from 1815 to 1866.
- Luxembourg's relations with Belgium and the Great Powers from 1919 to 1945.
- Monaco's relations with France and other European states from 1641 to 1861.
- Andorra's relations with the two co-princes from 1806 to 1933.
- Canada's relations with the United States from 1940 to 1970.
- South Vietnam's relations with the United States from 1945 to 1975.
- Belarus's relations with Russia from 1991 to 2001.
- China's relations with North Korea and North Korea's relations with China from 1949 to 1971.
- Vietnam's relations with China from 1949 to 1979 (or at least from 1949 to roughly 1964).

As we can see, out of fifty-two dyadic periods, only these thirteen qualified, despite a conscious effort to find relationships where trust would be most likely. Democracies are heavily represented, although several autocratic states displayed high levels of trust. States from each of the different regions included in the study qualified. Both weak and powerful states were found to have high levels of trust. And in every case in which a state displayed high levels of trust, this eventually came to an end over time. Only the case of Belarusian trust in Russia through 2001 comes from this century while four come from before 1900.

Trust is thus a phenomenon that has both rational and social elements, both with respect to its sources and effects. This limits its relevance in international affairs since many of the key prerequisites are difficult to find in relations between states. Likewise, given the ephemeral nature of trust, its effects are often mitigated by more powerful influences.

I will now turn to a consideration of several important theories of the sources of trust and its effects, after which I will discuss some ethical and policy questions related to trust: specifically, whether states should trust at all.

Sources of Trust

Trust is generally portrayed as a state of mind that emerges from one's pursuit of interest as shaped by social history. Other factors, including the type of state under which one lives and its performance or one's personal predispositions, have also been put forward as key factors. I will begin with rationalist approaches.

As we discussed in chapter 1, trust is best understood as a particularistic phenomenon through which we assess whether to put our fate in another's hands (Colquitt, Scott, and Lefine 2007, 911). Once we believe that a particular actor merits our trust—mostly because of the actor's good intentions toward us and her capacity to act on those intentions—we are willing to take a risk (Castelfranchi and Falcone 2010, 90; Booth and Wheeler 2008, 241). It is worth asking why someone might hope that a trustee will be considerate. Many economists and psychologists emphasize the cognitive side of the question, focusing on how one gathers information about another's future conduct and intent. The simplest approach is to merely make a guess and then wait to see what happens. This is the basis for the "graduated reciprocation in tension reduction" concept (GRIT) introduced by psychologist Charles Osgood in 1962 and generally held up as a path to bringing hostile, mistrusting rivals to the bargaining table and eventually to reconciliation (Osgood 1962). In more recent versions, the process is described as "Bayesian updating" and involves the refreshing of appraisals based on new information subsequent to each round of interaction (Kydd 2005; Lubell 2007; Teacy et al. 2012; Rathbun 2009, 355; Kramer 2004, 150–53; Macy 2007, 852). The implication is that it is not possible to trust strangers or mere acquaintances (Cook, Hardin, and Levy 2005, 4–5). On the other hand, trust can become self-sustaining so long as betrayal never occurs (Axelrod and Dawkins 2006, 173).

Others dispute this dynamic, arguing that as the risks grow higher, previous levels of trust become increasingly irrelevant (Hoffman 2006, 291). This is based on the premise that where the stakes increase, the trustee will be increasingly tempted to act selfishly at the expense of the trustor. This may stem from the trustee's fundamental unreliability with respect to important questions, or a sense that the relationship was never meant to be altruistic or long-lasting (this may apply to entrapment or con games [Zak 2008]). High-risk trusting may also be rare simply because everyone knows that not all promises are to be kept all the time (Orbell, van der Krugt, and Dawes 1991, 117). Where keeping a promise might actually cause more harm than good, walking away could be the more ethical move (see below). At any rate, it is generally understood that even well-intentioned, capable trustees may renege on any commitment at any time, so past experience may not be a useful predictor of future behavior.

To what degree is this model of trust borne out from our cases? To begin, it is clear that trusting is more often than not the result of pragmatism and prudence. It rarely flows from devotion to a particular protector. Luxembourg's experience illustrates how even weak and vulnerable actors experiment with alternative trustees, in its case moving from Germany to France to Belgium to the United States to the European Union. Liechtenstein switched loyalties from Austria-Hungary to Switzerland without hesitation, although the negotiations required to cement the new arrangement took several years. When the opportunity arose, the principality shifted its attention to the EU. Andorra repeatedly tilted away from the less cooperative co-prince, ultimately seeking closer ties to the EU as well. Monaco and San Marino were not so fortunate to have a ready alternative, but, as with all the microstates, they were eager and able to alter the terms of the relationship to give themselves more flexibility and autonomy.

Where the major powers and their subordinates are concerned, rational calculations and ongoing updating seem to be the norm. Both the United States and Canada shifted loyalties toward each other in response to changing global strategic conditions. The United States embraced and later repudiated South Vietnam, even moving to supplant it from 1965 to 1969. South Vietnam, while committed to the US alliance, also sought alternative terms, mostly to little avail. Russia has behaved strategically where both Belarus and Georgia were concerned, particularly since the accession of Vladimir Putin. On the other hand, both smaller republics, particularly Georgia, have attempted to expand their menu of options. Finally, China has been willing to either embrace or reject both Vietnam and North Korea, although its room for maneuver with the latter has been more limited for strategic reasons. And both Vietnam and North Korea have consciously attempted to play China and the Soviet Union/Russia off each other in order to secure the most profitable deal.

Geography, proximity, and strategic necessity are all key elements in explaining the nature of dominant-subordinate relations and whether they will evince trust, according to our cases. But at the same time the success of these relationships and the degree of trust involved seems to draw on more than strategy. An alternative (or perhaps supplemental) theory of trust points to the role of empathy, identity, and socialization. In some respect these ideas complement rationalist approaches by addressing the question: why would an actor seek to initiate a trusting relationship in the first place? In many cases it seems to be driven by more than cold-headed cost-benefit analysis. The simplest explanation is that trust stems first from interpersonal affection and loyalty (Kohn 2008, 2; Peppers and Rogers 2012, 175; Colquitt, Scott, and Lefine 2007, 912; Castelfranchi and Falcone 2010, 142). This reverses the rationalist view that interaction leads to affinity, but instead proposes that the ability to trust and ultimately the decision to trust flows from being raised in stable families and secure communities (Zheng et al. 2002, 2; Potter 2002, xiii). While it may appear that some people are "born trustors," the reality is that they are simply taught from a very early age that trusting is effective and safe (Uslaner 2000). Alternatively, while everyone may be born to trust, some learn early on that the risks are great (Kohn 2008, 44). As Granovetter concludes, trust is rooted in social relations, but that is not enough (1985, 491). Trust sometimes extends only to members of kinship groups, and this loyalty may even correlate with very low levels of trust in outgroups (Silva, Bradley, and Sousa 2012, 295; Hardin 2004b, 281; Nooteboom 2002, 86; Potter 2002, 24). Low levels of social inequality can help, as can participatory institutions and honest government officials (Kohn 2008, 86; Rothstein 2011; Schoon & Cheng 2011; Rathbun 2009, 359; Cheema 2010, 8; Rowen & and Finin 2010, 138). Ironically, perhaps, it has been found that social structures that provide sanctions for antisocial conduct may actually increase loyalty and trust, although excessively hierarchical or patriarchal systems may lead to generational cleavage (Portes 1998, 9; Traunmüller 2011; Bowles and Gintis 2002, 424; Huang 2007, 553; Brown 2004, 168; Cheema 2010, 6).

Ultimately, though, social relations and mutual identification may become so internalized as to form a sort of prerational phenomenon, one that screens out information prior to rational calculations of whether to trust (Lanho 2001, 177). Similarity, shared values, and common traditions help provide a social and linguistic vocabulary that makes promising and contracting meaningful in the first place (Nooteboom 2002, 23). One might even find oneself trusting someone without fully understanding why. This may be the basis for the "guesses" people make when first considering whether to trust. It is said, for example, that people are naturally attracted to potential partners who most remind them of their parents or siblings, sometimes with unfortunate results (Perrett 2010; Perron 2009). Similar dynamics may apply to choices of business partners, physicians, auto mechanics, and so forth.

With respect to our cases, it is clear that where social ties and similarities are high, the prospects for trusting relations are also high. The relations that show evidence of high levels of trust on the part of the subordinate state are precisely those where the social, cultural, religious, and other key traits are virtually indistinguishable. Liechtensteiners, although connected dynastically to Austria, consider German-speaking Swiss to be kindred souls; communication requires no translation. The Sammerinese generally acknowledge that they are Italian in every respect except for their passports. Part of what has recently drawn Andorrans toward Spain is the close connection they feel to all things Catalan (although they are careful not to tip their hat with respect to possible union with a future independent Catalonia). The Luxembourgers consider themselves the quintessential Europeans and are as comfortable in the EU as one can imagine. Likewise, US-Canada relations are strong in part due to the similarity between the English-speaking parts of the two societies (although Canadians are quick to emphasize the few distinctions that exist).

On the other hand, key cultural distinctions may help explain the relative tension between the United States and South Vietnam, Russia and Georgia, and the PRC with Vietnam and perhaps North Korea. Two exceptions to the pattern are the ambivalent relations between Belarus and Russia on the one hand and France and Monaco on the other. In these cases it seems the heavy-handedness of the dominant partner has undermined what is a natural affinity.

Because these two approaches complement each other, it is perhaps not necessary to decide which is the stronger theory. Clearly social and cultural similarity can facilitate the initiation of a trusting relationship, but lapses in reliability or disdain for the weaker partner—not to mention attempts by the weaker actor to exploit the more powerful one—can to a large degree nullify this powerful unifying force.

Effects of Trust

The most common claim is that trust facilitates cooperation and enhances social capital. To some degree this may be true by definition since some argue that the trustor and trustee both cooperate in that they make conscious adjustments to their behavior for the sake of each other, which itself is a key element of social capital, understood as a network of mutually supportive social relations (Duhigg 2012, 217; Blind 2010, 23; Nooteboom 2002, 102; Raedar 2004, 242; Rathbun 2009, 349, 357, 373; Brooks 2011, 318; Fukuyama 1995, 7, 25). But it is possible to separate trust and cooperation and social capital and treat them as part of a causal chain (Castelfranchi and Falcone 2010, 23). Some of the factors that explain the link are that trust reduces transaction costs, simplifying them and accelerating the consummation of the agreement. Lengthy contract negotiations and complex arbitration mechanisms are generally seen as evidence of distrust and an impediment to fruitful and efficient cooperation (Kohn 2008, 66; Fukuyama 1995, 336). Trust in the state and public law can reduce the need for enforcement and save money (Rowen and Finin 2010, 135).

Conversely, there are many who argue that cooperation and even social capital do not require trust and that trust may even interfere with these outcomes. Rationalists generally argue that cooperation emerges from an awareness of overlapping interests rather than feelings of trust (Axelrod and Dawkins 2006, 174; Cook, Hardin, and Levy 2005; Hane 2004). For them, strong contracts and strong states facilitate cooperation in the absence of trust and are simply part of doing business (Huang 2007, 572; Cook, Hardin, and Levy 2005; Levi, Moe, and Buckley 2004, 108). That said, while trust may not be a prerequisite, distrust can become an impediment to cooperation (Hane 2004; Booth and Wheeler 2008, 230). There is a wide range of ambivalent tolerance between the two within which cooperation can occur and routinely does.

A darker view holds that trust actually impedes cooperation in that it causes people to lower their guard and increases the possibility of victimization. As mentioned earlier, the only way one can be betrayed is by first trusting. Some crimes can only occur after trust has been granted: embezzlement, date rape, conspiracy, fraud, racketeering, insider trading, swindling, and a wide range of abuses by authority figures (Granovetter 1985, 491; Becker 1996, 47). Peppers and Rogers have noted that sometimes efforts by advertisers (and one might add candidates for office) to buttress their reputation for trustworthiness actually backfire as savvy and skeptical consumers (and voters) discount extravagant claims (2012, 19–20).

What can we learn from the cases with respect to the effects of trust? To begin, in almost every case except for the Russia-Georgia and China-Vietnam relationships, there was a high level of cooperation, in that actors adjusted their aims in response to those of their counterparts (Keohane 1984). In all cases agreements were entered into and in most cases standing institutional arrangements were forged. This means out of fifty-two distinct periodized dyadic relations (treating each relationship pair within a given time period as a separate data point), only two could be described as essentially noncooperative. Yet, as we saw, only fourteen of these showed evidence of high levels of trust. This means that high levels of trust were not required in thirty-six cases. In fact, in those thirty-six cases, nine featured low levels of trust according to the measures.[1] This record demonstrates that even where trust could have been expected to play an important part in the relationship, cooperation emerged from other factors. For the others, it is not entirely clear whether trust was the cause of cooperation and enhanced social capital or the effect (see US-Canada relations in particular [Shore 1998]). At the very least the record indicates that cooperation can lead to enhanced social capital (almost by definition) which may or may lead to or require trust.

What of relations that featured high levels of trust? Did they also exhibit high levels of cooperation and/or social capital? In seven of the fourteen cases, trust correlated with an essentially cooperation relationship. In none of those cases, however, did high levels of cooperation continue uninterrupted. In several cases the relationship collapsed entirely (Liechtenstein and Austria-Hungary, and South Vietnam and the United States). Even Canada's relationship with the United States—the most constructive of all the cases—saw a marked deterioration after 1971 for more than a decade. We can also see evidence of the darker view of trust in the cases of Luxembourg prior to 1940 (invaded twice by Germany and unprotected by those sworn to defend it), Georgia after 2005 (invaded by Russia in 2008 and partially annexed in 2015), and Vietnam (invaded by China in 1979) where state leaders accepted arrangements that made them vulnerable to the whims of their respective trustees. All things considered, it appears that trusting is not correlated with cooperation, looking at it from both directions.

The Ethics of Trust

There is broad agreement that trusting is a good thing in general, perhaps even the essential ingredient for a happy community and world peace (Fukuyama 1995; Brooks 2011; Kohn 2008; Baier 1986; Nooteboom 2002; Rathbun 2009; Uslaner 2000). But we have seen that trust also exposes one—by definition—to the possibility of being exploited, with sometimes horrific consequences. In this concluding section I will briefly consider some ethical and policy questions related to trust. Among them:

- What is a "promise"? How does it relate to international relations and trust?
- What are the duties of a trustee? Of a trustor? What does it mean to exploit one or the other?
- Should anyone trust in international relations? Are the stakes simply too high?
- Should leaders of nations adopt a trusting attitude/policy in behalf of their citizens? Should citizens trust their governments to make these decisions?

To begin, what is a promise? Given the anarchical nature of international relations, it is perhaps better to think of treaties as something other than contracts. Contracts, after all, can be enforced by civil courts following tort law and therefore have very different legal and social implications than the vast majority of treaties. An alternative model might be the promise. Although promises can be implied (such as a "social contract" commitment to be a good citizen in exchange for social status and safety) or general (such as a religious initiation through which the individual pledges to serve humanity and/or God with the expectation of salvation in the next life), what interests us most are promises that are specific between two particular actors. They involve a preliminary sacrifice on the part of the promisee, done in the hope that the promisor will fulfill or redeem the promise at a future date (Aileen 1970, 138; Atiyah 1981). In this sense promises are speech acts that exist in reality once they are articulated (Kohn 2008, 53). What distinguishes promises from contracts is that it is generally understood that there is no obvious legal recourse for the promisee in the event the promisor fails to fulfill the promise. Consider the case of the bride and groom whose guests do not come to their extravagant reception despite having promised they would. It is absurd to think they would be billed for the cost of the meal (although it has been tried [Golgowski 2015]), let alone taken to court (Griffith and Goldfarb 1991, 100). This is not to say that promises only address trivial matters. The decision by two people to move in together is best understood as a promise without the force of law, yet it creates substantial obligations and vulnerabilities.

Ethicists are divided on the morality of promising. Promises are meaningful primarily within a particular social setting where promise making is clearly understood according to philosophers as different as David Hume and John Rawls (Rawls 1955, 18; Aileen 1970, 83; Jones 1966, 288; Grant 1949, 362; Pratt 2007, 547). They generate nothing more than social duties as a result. Failure to keep a promise should result in social disapproval or perhaps shunning, but little else. In fact, since it is possible to promise to do something immoral or that would be damaging to society, keeping a promise may be unethical (Jones 1996, 294; Rawls 1955, 18). Others argue that whenever someone relies on a promise, the promisor has created a duty to fulfill it, even if this involves considerable inconvenience (Hall 2005, 157; Grant 1949, 365–66; Raz 1982, 919; Pratt 2007, 571). Aristotle considered promise keeping to be integral to honesty and justice (Aristotle 1984, 1127a–1127b). Scanlon argues that there exists a "right to rely" on the part of the promisee when a promise has been formally entered into (1990, 210). Immanuel Kant asserts that promise keeping is a serious moral obligation (Kohn 2008, 55). It is worth noting in this context that states routinely treat promises as tantamount to contracts that can be enforced in the courts. Our cohabiting couple from the previous paragraph will be considered to be married in a number of jurisdictions after a certain point with the implication that division of assets and tax liability may be covered by statutory law (Pollin 2012). As we saw, the US–South Vietnam agreements in the early 1960s were seen as legally binding by the authorities in Saigon if not by those in Washington.

A middle ground argues that whether a promise must be kept for ethical reasons depends on how the promise is nested in other obligations. As with all commitments, promises can be nullified by the need to fulfill an even more serious obligation. For example, breaking a promise to visit a sick friend can be justified by the need to assist an injured motorist encountered on the way (Grant 1949, 364). This also applies to contracts to some degree (even soldiers are permitted—at times required—to disobey unlawful orders). But the competing norm must be very serious. It is not enough for a promisor to simply decide that a promise has become inconvenient or that her priorities have changed or that she no longer has feelings of respect or compassion for the promise.

It is useful to think of most bilateral treaties as something akin to a very solemn mutual promise. While they create legal obligations in a public setting, they are generally enforced horizontally (i.e., by the parties) if at all. While they are not easily abrogated, there are many conditions that might allow parties to legitimately end a treaty commitment, more so than for a contract. And they are clearly nested in a hierarchy of obligations—both written and customary—that may require that they be ignored when they come into conflict with a more serious commitment (Sandholtz and Stiles 2009). Finally, their significance and meaning are actualized by virtue of constitutive international norms and rules (Hart 1961, 56–57).

Note that promises are not the same as pledges, which are unilateral declarations of intent. In general, pledges do not create rights on the part of the hearers and therefore defaulting on a pledge does not usually harm others. Of course, this depends on the pledge (a spouse's pledge to stop drinking no doubt affects others), but in most cases hearers rely on a pledge at their own peril. Pledges may be accompanied by promises (the drinker may make a pledge while at the same time promising the spouse to change his behavior), but only the latter automatically generate claims. The various pledges on the part of successive Saigon regimes to undertake human rights reforms were seen as nonbinding for just this reason, even though American policy makers might have interpreted them as a promise.

Promising and contracting therefore create expectations and typically involve an increase in the promisee's vulnerability. Acceptance of a promise therefore involves trust. The same is not usually true of pledges. Given the analogy of promising and contracting with treaty making, it makes sense to speak of trusting in international relations—perhaps even more so than in domestic affairs—since there are relatively few contracts of the traditional variety and therefore the obligation to comply has a stronger moral or social component. Trustors in international relations—as Luxembourg has learned—must rely far more heavily on the honor and reliability of the trustee than those in domestic affairs. In answer to the second set of questions listed above, I infer that the moral obligation of the trustee in international affairs—especially where the stakes are often very high, matters of life and death on a grand scale—is extraordinarily high. It is directly proportional to the vulnerability of the trustor in international relations (Yovel 1999/2000, 959). The moral implications of entering into treaties deceitfully in order to manipulate the trustor or with no intent to honor the obligation is very serious, particularly for the more powerful state but also where the weaker state is concerned (Scanlon 1990, 202; Potter 2002, 18).

The validity of this view is confirmed by the response of third-party observers to the breaking of a promise, especially when a powerful actor betrays a weak one. Particularly where the results are catastrophic for the weak actor, a common response is outrage. As we saw, the German violation of Luxembourg's and Belgium's neutrality in 1914 was considered so offensive by British authorities and the British public that the 1839 Treaty of London was displayed under the words "The 'Scrap of Paper'" on army recruitment posters. The invasion of Poland in 1939 was also seen as a "betrayal" and prompted outrage, as we saw in the South Vietnamese response to the Paris Accords in 1973.

Where agreements are multilateral or create powerful monitoring and enforcement bodies, the individual moral duties of forthrightness and compliance are lower for each state since the weaker actors are more likely to see their interests protected (this was clearly Luxembourg's thinking as it joined NATO and the EU). Of course, this is not to say that international institutions cannot abuse weaker members, but in practical terms the interests of members tend to offset each other and reduce the chances of conspiracies.

In situations where trustees are reliable and respectful of weak actors' needs, these weaker actors have a duty not to take advantage (Giddens 1982, 32). In several cases, we have seen that powerful actors have tolerated high levels of noncompliance—even where this resulted in direct injury—for the sake of maintaining the relationship or preserving a reputation of magnanimity (Olson and Zeckhauser 1966). North Korea is clearly abusing China's trust, and South Vietnam abused US trust in the 1960s (although the issue of internal reform is best understood as a breach of a pledge rather than a promise). As Lake has explained, dominant states often resort to "discipline" to bring subordinates to heel (see China's explanation of its invasion of Vietnam as "teaching it a lesson") (Lake 2011). Of course, even mild discipline can cause trust to evaporate, leaving behind raw coercion. And since this typically leads to still more noncompliance and still more disciplining in the future, dominant states are naturally reticent to take this path.

All of this leads us to the third question: Should trust be removed from international relations? Since trust, by definition, is the prerequisite for betrayal, and since the stakes are often quite high, the conservative answer would be yes. We have seen that trust is not a prerequisite for cooperation and instead can lead to pain and suffering, so it seems rational to simply remove it from the equation and be suspicious of everyone. Every realist in the field would certainly endorse this approach (Van Milders 2012).

On the other hand, lack of trust—and especially distrust—has been shown to increase transaction costs, interfere with the creation of successful and mutually beneficial collective goods, and increase the likelihood of conflict escalation (Booth and Wheeler 2008, 230; Kydd 2005/06, 619; Axelrod and Dawkins 2006). Put simply, it makes us all poorer and more insecure. Taken together, policy makers may be facing the horns of a dilemma. This was reflected in the opposing views of the US-Iran nuclear weapons agreement in 2015. While opponents and supporters in both the United States and Iran all agreed that the deal did not guarantee safety or prosperity, the alternative of noncooperation was seen by many as even worse (Fallows 2015). At the same time, the agreement was replete with hedging provisions, including particularly the "snap back" clause that allowed states to reimpose sanctions in the event Iranian progress on disarmament failed to meet certain benchmarks. The implication is that the neoliberal program is most likely best: trust enough to initiate the relationship but always hedge your bets. At any rate, since there is always the possibility that enemies become friends and that friends form security communities, trusting may be a worthwhile alternative (Barnett and Adler 1998, 415, 422).

While some have argued that multilateral institutions generally embody trust (Rathbun 2012), the findings of this study challenge this conclusion. With respect to the European Union and NATO, it appears there are many provisions—both substantive and procedural—that are specifically designed to promote cooperation amid distrust. Not only does the entire EU acquis allow for exit (as was considered by the UK in 2016), membership comes in levels, from the loose association of EFTA members to the closer relations of EEA signatories to the standard members and finally the euro zone members. At each level states agree to particular arrangements but opt out of others while at the same time protecting their interests through weighted voting or veto provisions. Further, most international organizations make it more difficult for states to engage in duplicity or evasion since debates are routinely public and codified. Finally, explicit enforcement arrangements, some of which amount to a "scorecard" on state performance, minimize the need for member states to take a leap of faith in the other members (Stiles 2015).

This leaves the ultimate question of whether heads of state and governments have the right or the duty to trust. The answer to this question involves one's sense of the state's duties to its citizens along with its international obligations. States are in the middle of a trust chain, acting as the trustees of their citizens on the one hand while faced with a choice whether to trust other international actors. Guiding this decision should be a simple principle of delegation: where risks are to be undertaken by the state that will ultimately be borne by the public, the citizenry should be given the opportunity to express its views or even to veto the decision, either directly or through legitimately elected representatives. Particularly where the decision was not foreseeable, the public's voice must be sought. We saw this in Liechtenstein and Canada, for example, when publics and/or legislatures were empowered to speak directly and authoritatively regarding international commitments that involved risk and trust (joining the European Economic Area and approving two free trade agreements, respectively). Legislative ratification of serious treaty commitments is a matter of customary law today. And while plebiscitary democracy has been much maligned since the age of Napoleon, conducting referenda on key questions such as membership in the EU or joining an alliance provides a direct means of obtaining consent and providing some cover for political leaders.

Alternatively, political leaders have an obligation to be as transparent as possible regarding the rationale for a decision to take a risk and submit to constitutional arrangements that make them accountable for it. This naturally leads to the conclusion that only in functioning democracies with a strong system of rule of law and separation of powers can leaders legitimately and morally take serious risks and engage in trusting behavior. Unless the real possibility exists that a leader could be removed from office (preferably before the next scheduled election), taking actions that seriously jeopardize the safety or economic well-being of the citizenry would be a form of collective abuse. North Korea's leadership, for example, has moved past this line in its decisions to rely on Chinese and Soviet support, thereby making its population extremely vulnerable without having to fear any genuine accountability to those who are put in jeopardy. While Canada and Liechtenstein were clearly on the right side of the line, we have seen cases that were more ambiguous. The South Vietnamese government's decision to rely on the United States was done mostly without popular consent given the illegitimate election procedures and corrupt governing structures. Likewise, decisions by various nineteenth-century monarchs in Monaco and Luxembourg were made without public input and were therefore unethical despite being consistent with contemporary notions of sovereign prerogatives. In the process, these rulers exposed their subjects to unwarranted and unwelcome risks.

Combining the answers to these four sets of questions allows one to offer the following recommendations to would-be trustors. To begin, one must avoid distrusting all actors, especially as a baseline response. A willingness to trust can lead to important agreements or at least to productive discussions between states. While the devil may be in the details of these agreements, there is something troubling about states that refuse to even broach the subject of negotiating settlements. States must accept the simple fact that all agreements involve an element of risk since they necessarily involve mostly unenforceable commitments to provide some future benefit in exchange for a short-term sacrifice.

Trust, as we have seen, can come in degrees, however. Trust that is entire and comprehensive is as worrisome as unconditional distrust. Particularly where an entire nation's survival is at stake, every effort must be made to consult with stakeholders before entering into a sweeping, long-term commitment. There is also something to be said for revisiting the basic framework from time to time. As disturbing and upsetting as it might have been, the Brexit vote added legitimacy to Britain's EU membership. Likewise, the periodic referenda undertaken across Europe on the occasion of various revisions to the founding documents have been an important check on executive excess.

Finally, especially where events are fast-moving, relationships are immature, and links are thin, every effort should be made to hedge when making commitments that increase vulnerability and cede sovereignty. These should include relatively lenient opt-out clauses, both comprehensive and issue-specific (the latter is illustrated by the WTO's safeguard provisions). They should also allow for joint decision making with respect to interpretation and enforcement of the agreements, with the implication that all parties should have a veto over both facets, especially in the early years of implementation. These decision-making powers should be revisited on a regular basis, or else some provisions should allow automatic adjustment of voting powers, as in the European Parliament. Special attention should be paid to protecting weaker actors against the more powerful.

Concluding Thoughts and Future Research

This project was an attempt to identify trust in international relations using a definition that is consistent with that used in most of the academic literature, including some international relations research. In the process, I identified a number of particular relationships during different time periods where high levels of trust were in evidence, searching from a pool of most likely cases using a measure that erred on the side of false positives. From this I explored to what degree these cases could be explained by various theories of the origins of trust and whether they helped test the validity of theories on the effects of trust. I determined that trust stems primarily from rational calculations, although affinity and social ties are important factors to explain the initiation of trusting relations. On the other hand, trust did not seem linked in any direct way to increased cooperation or enhanced social capital. From an ethical point of view, while trusting is not an unreasonable frame of mind when engaging in international relations, when states do so their leaders have an obligation to ascertain the consent of the governed—whether before or after the fact—which implies that autocracies are generally unable to trust legitimately. These conclusions are most consistent with the neoliberal approach or the English School and least compatible with either the constructivist or realist theories (Van Milders 2012).

Where do we go from here? With respect to a research agenda, more needs to be done on how trust interacts with other variables to explain international relations outcomes. It would be advisable to focus particularly on interactions between Western democracies where trust seems most likely to manifest itself and serve as a legitimate policy guide. There already exists an emerging tradition of looking at EU affairs from this perspective (Cramér 2009; Anderson and Apap 2002; Weller 2015). In addition, renewed interest in security communities will help clarify the place of trust in regions that share some of Europe's characteristics but offer important contrast (Adler and Barnett 1998a; Pervez 2013; Collins 2013; Acharya 2014).

Additional attempts at measuring trust should also be undertaken on the likely chance that it will reveals different patterns. In particular, efforts could be made to explore in greater depth particular dyads in order to ascertain the state of mind of a wide range of key decision makers. Rathbun's study of US foreign policy vis-à-vis international institutions is a useful guide (2012). Conversely, large-*n* studies using very carefully constructed operationalizations of trust—almost certainly focused on behavior rather than attitudes—could help identify general patterns across time and space, although they would almost certainly need to be supplemented with case study and process-tracing work. It is my opinion that experimental methods would not shed much light on the life-or-death choices of heads of state for reasons stated earlier, although a number of natural experiments can be found (some of which were covered in this book).

Additional philosophical work on the nature of trust and its relation to international law would also be a fruitful area of study, particularly when combined with theories of domestic governance and representation. Work by Kohn (2008), Hoffman (2002), Hardin (2002), Atiyah (1981), Grant (1949), and Baier (1986) could serve as a useful starting point, along with classic works by Hume, Kant, and Rawls. Of particular importance is the question of trusting in behalf of others, a notion that has been relatively overlooked.

It is worth noting that although I have concluded with a skeptical note with respect to the place of trust in international relations, I acknowledge the central role it can play in interpersonal relations and a well-functioning society. Perhaps as borders become increasingly porous, the international society will come to increasingly resemble a cosmopolitan world society in which interpersonal dynamics will be reflected in world affairs (Booth and Wheeler 2008). In that eventuality, the possibilities will test even the more adventuresome imagination.

Notes

CHAPTER 2

1. The delegate, Hughes Le Gallais, missed the first five meetings; this was noted in the press. As put by Henderson, "It would sometimes happen at the Working Party that the Dutch and the Belgians would take up different viewpoints on a particular question. Le Gallais would then be asked for his opinion. With infinite sagacity and solemnity he would reply: 'I agree with the views of my Benelux colleagues'" (Henderson 1982, 57).

2. Using a different formula, Sandler and Shimizu find that the costs and benefits are actually balanced until 2002, at which point benefits outweigh costs (through 2012) (Sandler and Shimizu 2014, 54–55).

CHAPTER 4

1. Original: "Non abbiamo il diritto di censurare il Governo del Re [d'Italia] se adempie anche rigidamente al dovere di fare l'interesse dello Stato cui presiede; dobbiamo, bensì, metterci noi in grado di poter fare accortamente e bene l'interesse nostro" (*Libertas* 2015).

2. It is worth noting that after the amnesty was withdrawn, Italians continued to smuggle cash into San Marino, sometimes stuffing it in their shoes or water bottles to avoid detection from the increasingly vigilant Sammarinese border patrols (*Telegraph* 2012).

CHAPTER 6

1. Although the treaty only explicitly stated that the Count of Foix would appoint a *veguer*, the bishop began doing so in the 1340s without objection (Brutails 1904, 248).

2. Sarkozy was in a political bind, after all, since he had targeted tax havens while technically presiding over one himself!

CHAPTER 8

1. 1867–1918 Luxembourg-Netherlands, 2002–2015 Monaco-France and Monaco-European states, 1971–2015 San Marino-Italy and San Marino-EU, 1933–1993 Andorra-the Bishop of Urgell, 1995–2015 EU/OECD-microstates, 1991–2001 Russia-Belarus, 1972–2015 China-North Korea.

References

Abbott, Kenneth, Robert Keohane, Andrew Moravcsik, Anne-Marie Slaughter, and Duncan Snidal (2000) "The Concept of Legalization." *International Organization* 54, no. 3: 401–19.

Abrehe, Berhane (2005) "Statement by His Excellency Mr. Berhane Abrehe, Minister of Finance of the State of Eritrea at the 60th Session of the General Assembly of the United Nations," New York, September 21.

Acharya, Amitav (2014) *Constructing a Security Community in Southeast Asia: ASEAN and the Problem of Regional Order*. London: Routledge.

Adler, Emmanuel, and Michael Barnett (1998a) "Security Communities in Theoretical Perspective." In *Security Communities*, edited by Emmanuel Adler and Michael Barnett, 3–28. New York: Cambridge University Press.

Adler, Emmanuel, and Michael Barnett (1998b) "A Framework for the Study of Security Communities." In *Security Communities*, edited by Emmanuel Adler and Michael Barnett, 29–65. New York: Cambridge University Press.

Africa Recovery (2000) "OAU Commission: Rwanda Genocide was 'Preventable.'" Vol. 14, no. 2 (July): Briefs page.

Aiken, Henry D., ed., (1970) *Hume's Moral and Political Philosophy*. Darien, CT: Hafner Publishing.

All Andorra (2016) "We Don't Pretend to Be a Full Member of the EU." January 26. Available at http://all-andorra.com/eu-association/. Accessed January 19, 2017.

Allavena, Jean-Charles (2013) Member of the National Council. Interview with the author, May 14, Monaco.

Allison, Roy (2008) "Russia Resurgent: Moscow's Campaign to 'Coerce Georgia to Peace.'" *International Affairs* 84, no. 6, 1145–71.

Allison, Roy (2013) *Russia, the West, and Military Intervention*. London: Oxford University Press.

Alter, Karen (2009) "The European Court's Political Power across Time and

Space." Faculty Working Papers. Northwestern University. Paper 175. Available at http://scholarlycommons.law.northwestern.edu/facultyworkingpapers/175. Accessed March 6, 2015.

Anderson, Greg (2011) "'Forgotten Partnership' at 20-Something," *International Journal* 66, no. 4 (Autumn): 1031–41.

Anderson, Karen, and Michael Kaeding (2006) "Belgium, the Netherlands, and Luxembourg: Increasingly Cautious Europeans." In *The European Union and the Member States*, 2nd ed., edited by Eleanor E. Zeff and Ellen B. Pirro, 107–26. Boulder, CO: Lynne Rienner.

Anderson, Malcolm, and Joana Apap (2002) *Striking a Balance between Freedom, Security and Justice in an Enlarged European Union*. Brussels: Center for European Policy Studies.

Andorra Business (2015) "Double Taxation Treaty Signed with France," April 9. Available at http://www.andorra-business.com/news.asp?ArticleD=18. Accessed May 26, 2015.

Angelo, A. H. (1970) "Andorra: Introduction to a Customary Legal System." *American Journal of Legal History* 14, no. 2 (April): 95–111.

ANSA (2014) Story on visit to San Marino by Italian president Giorgio Napolitano, June 13. Available at https://www.ansa.it/english/news/politics/2014/06/13/napolitano-backs-san-marino-eu-bid_0e5b61f6-de9c-451f-89a6-386cfed43439.html. Accessed June 23, 2014.

Antonenko, Oksana (2005) "Frozen Uncertainty: Russia and the Conflict over Abkhazia." In *Statehood and Security: Georgia after the Rose Revolution*, edited by Bruno Coppieters and Robert Legvold, 205–70. Cambridge, MA: MIT Press.

Aristotle (1984) *Nicomachean Ethics*. Edited by Jonathon Barnes. Princeton: Princeton University Press.

Army, United States (2015) "Mutual Defense Assistance in Indochina: Agreement Signed at Saigon December 22, 1950. Available at: http://www.history.army.mil/books/vietnam/law-war/law-appi.htm. Accessed July 7, 2015.

ASIL (American Society of International Law) (1915) "The Binding Effect Upon the German Empire of the Treaty of London of 1867 Neutralizing Luxembourg." *American Journal of International Law* 9, no. 4 (October): 948–58.

Atiyah, P. S. (1981) *Promises, Morals and Law*. New York: Clarendon Press.

Aves, Jonathan (1996) *Georgia: From Chaos to Stability?* London: The Royal Institute of International Affairs.

Axelrod, Robert, and Richard Dawkins (2006) *The Evolution of Cooperation*. Revised ed. New York: Basic Books.

Babayan, Nelli (2014) *Democratic Transformation and Obstruction: EU, US, and Russia in the South Caucasus*. Florence, NY: Taylor & Francis.

Baier, Annette C. (1986) "Trust and Antitrust." *Ethics* 96, no. 2 (January): 231–60.

Balmaceda, Margarita M. (2014) *Living the High Life in Minsk: Russian Energy Rents, Domestic Populism and Belarus' Impending Crisis*. Budapest: Central European University Press.

Barnett, Michael, and Emmanuel Adler (1998) "Studying Security Communities in Theory, Comparison, and History." In *Security Communities*, edited by Emmanuel Adler and Michael Barnett, 413–44. New York: Cambridge University Press.

Bartmann, Barry (2002) "Meeting the Needs of Microstate Security." *The Round Table: The Commonwealth Journal of International Affairs* 91, no. 365: 361–74.
Bartmann, Barry (2012) "From the Wings to the Footlights: The International Relations of Europe's Smallest States," *Commonwealth & Comparative Politics* 50, no. 4 (November): 535–54.
Batliner, Gerard (2007) "Liechtenstein unter den Bedingungen der europäischen Integration und der Globalisierung." *Liechtenstein Politische Schriften Band* 42: 11–31.
BBC (2008) "Georgia Breaks Ties with Russia" August 29. Available at http://news.bbc.co.uk/2/hi/europe/7588428.stm. Accessed May 26, 2015.
BBC (2016a) "Eight Reasons Leave Won the UK's Referendum on the EU." June 24. Available at http://www.bbc.com/news/uk-politics-eu-referendum-36574526. Accessed December 30, 2016.
BBC (2016b) "CETA: Canada-EU Sign Long-Delayed Free Trade Deal." October 30. Available at: http://www.bbc.com/news/world-europe-37814884. Accessed January 17, 2017.
Beach, Derek, and Colette Mazzucelli (2007) "Introduction." In *Leadership in the Big Bangs of European Integration*, edited by Derek Beach and Colette Mazzucelli, 1–21. Basingstoke: Palgrave Macmillan.
Beattie, Amanda Russell, and Kate Schick (2012) *The Vulnerable Subject: Beyond Rationalism in International Relations*. New York: Palgrave Macmillan.
Beattie, David (2004) *Liechtenstein: A Modern History*. London: I. B. Turner.
Beattie, David (2012) *Liechtenstein: A Modern History*. New and Enlarged Edition. Vaduz: van Eck Publishers.
Becker, Lawrence (1996) "Trust as Noncognitive Security about Motives." *Ethics* 107 (October): 43–61.
Benelux Court of Justice (2015) "Consultation des arrêts et conclusions." Available at: http://www.courbeneluxhof.be/fr/arresten_lst.asp. Accessed May 26.
Berche, Denis (2013) Editor-in-Chief, *L'Essentiel*. Interview with the author, May 2. Differdange, Luxembourg.
Berthélemy, Jen-Claude, Joaquim Llimona, and Marc Maresceau (2009) *Andorre-Union Européenne: Vers le marché intérieur*. Andorra: Ministry of Foreign Affairs.
Biette, David N., and Alexander Kuschner (2014) "Reflections on Foreign Policies, Defense Budgets, Borders, and the Current State of the Partnership." In *Canada and the United States: Differences That Count*, edited by David M. Thomas and David N. Biette, 386–407. Toronto: University of Toronto Press.
Blind, Peride K. (2010) "Building Trust in Government: Linking Theory with Practice." In *Building Trust in Government: Innovations in Governance Reform in Asia*, edited by G. Shabbir Cheema and Vesselin Popovski, 22–53. New York: United Nations University Press.
Bloomberg (2010) "San Marino Says Italian Tax Crackdown Undermines Its Economy." June 15. Available at http://www.bloomberg.com/news/articles/2010–06–15/san-marino-says-italy-s-crackdown-on-tax-evasion-threatens-its-economy. Accessed May 15, 2015.
Bodeen, Christopher (2017) "China, Russia Stay United against South Korea Missile Defense. *Washington Post*, January 13. Available at https://www.wash

ingtonpost.com/world/asia_pacific/china-russia-say-united-against-s-korea-missile-defense/2017/01/13/8cd4dff2-d96e-11e6-a0e6-d502d6751bc8_story.html?utm_term=.322a3174b18c. Accessed January 17, 2017.

Bon Dia (2013a) "Un isard, l'església de Santa Coloma i Casa de la Vall, imtages per als euros." May 17, p. 3.

Bon Dia (2013b) "Traspàs de la presidència del Comitè de Ministres a Armènia." May 17, p. 9.

Bon Dia (2013c) "La guàrdia civil desmantella un grup dedicat al contraban de tabac." May 17, p. 13.

Bonanate, Luigi (2003) "Dalla Pace di Versailles all'ONU." In *Il Piccolo Stato: Politica, storia, diplomazia*, edited by Laura Barletta, Franco Cardini and Guiseppe Galasso, 197–212. Sarravalle, San Marino: AIEP Editore.

Booth, Ken, and Nicholas J. Wheeler (2008) *The Security Dilemma: Fear, Cooperation and Trust in World Politics*. New York: Palgrave Macmillan.

Bovt, Georgy (2014) "Cracks Are Showing in Russia's Customs Union" *Moscow Times*, December 9. Available at: http://www.themoscowtimes.com/opinion/article/cracks-are-showing-in-russia-s-customs-union/513041.html. Accessed July 18, 2015.

Bowles, Samuel, and Herbert Gintis (2002) "Social Capital and Community Governance," *The Economic Journal* 112, no. 483 (November): F419-F436.

Bravo, Luigi Ferrari (2003) "Il Piccolo Stato nei Rapporti Dipplomatici Internazionali." In *Il Piccolo Stato: Politica, storia, diplomazia*, edited by Laura Barletta, Franco Cardini, and Guiseppe Galasso, 283–90. Sarravalle, San Marino: AIEP Editore.

Brazinsky, Gregg Andrew (2012) "Between Ideology and Strategy: China's Security Policy toward the Korean Peninsula since Rapprochement." In *Trilateralism and Beyond: Great power politics and the Korean security dilemma during and after the Cold War*, edited by Robert A. Wampler, 163–88. Kent, OH: Kent State University Press.

Brégeon, Jean-Joël (1991) *Les Grimaldi de Monaco*. Paris: Critérion.

Bridgat (2015) Luxembourg Trade Partners, 2013. Available at http://countries.bridgat.com/Luxembourg_Trade_Partners.html. Accessed April 24, 2015.

Brigham, Robert K. (2002) "Why the South Won the American War in Vietnam." In *Why the North Won the Vietnam War*, edited by Marc Gilbert Jason, 97–116. New York: Palgrave.

Brooks, David (2011) *The Social Animal: The Hidden Sources of Love, Character, and Achievement*. New York: Random House.

Brown, Margaret L. (2004) "Compensating for Distrust among Kin." In *Distrust*, edited by Russell Hardin, 167–91. New York: Russell Sage Foundation.

Brugger, Philipp (2015) "Trust as a discourse: Concept and Measurement Strategy—First Results from a Study on German Trust in the USA." *Journal of Trust Research* 5, no. 1: 78–100.

Brugger, Philipp, Andreas Hasenclever, and Lukas Kasten (2013) "Theorizing the Impact of Trust on Post-Agreement Negotiations: The Case of Franco-German Security Relations." *International Negotiation* 18, no. 3: 441–69.

Brutails, Jean-August (1904) *La Coutume d'Andorre*. Paris: Bibliothèque Nationale de France.

Bugajski, Janusz (2008) *Exporting Eurasia: Russia's European Ambitions*. Washington: Center for Strategic and International Studies Press.

Bunse, Simone (2009) *Small States and EU Governance: Leadership through the Council Presidency*. Basingstoke: Palgrave Macmillan.

Bunse, Simone, Paul Magnette, and Kalypso Nicolaïdes (2007) "Big Versus Small: Shared Leadership in the EU and Power Politics in the Convention." In *Leadership in the Big Bangs of European Integration*, edited by Derek Beach and Colette Mazzucelli, 134–57. Basingstoke: Palgrave Macmillan.

Burney, Derek H., and Fen Osler Hampson (2012) "How Obama Lost Canada: Botching Relations with the United States' Biggest Trade Partner." *Foreign Affairs*, June 21. Available at https://www.foreignaffairs.com/print/1070479. Accessed July 23, 2015.

Byun, See-Won, and Scott Snyder (2014) "China's Approach to North Korea and Northeast Asian Security Cooperation." In *Rethinking Asia and International Relations: North Korea and Security Cooperation in Northeast Asia*, edited by Tae-Hwan Kwak and Seung-Ho Jo, 155–74. Farnham, UK: Ashgate.

Calmes, Albert (1971/1932) *Histoire Contemporaine du Grand-Duché de Luxembourg. Vol 1: Naissance et Débuts du Grand-Duché 1814–1830*. Luxembourg: Saint-Paul.

Cambra de Comerç, Indústria i Serveis d'Andorra (2012) *Andorra té Futur: Anàlisi I propostes per a un accord estratègic*. Andorra: Cambra de Comerç, Indústria i Serveis d'Andorra.

Canada House of Commons (1972) Debates. April 14.

Captan, Monie R. (2002) "Address by His Excellency Prof. Monie R. Captan, Minister of Foreign Affairs of the Republic of Liberia to the 57th Session of the United Nations General Assembly." September 20, New York.

Cardoso Reis, Bruno (2013) "Portugal and the UN: A Rogue State Resisting the Norm of Decolonization (1956–1974)." *Portuguese Studies* 29, no. 2: 251–76.

Caselaw (2011) "Resolution CM/ResDH(2011)135. Execution of the Judgment of the European Court of Human Rights: Prencipe against the Principality of Monaco." Available at: http://caselaw.echr.globe24h.com/0/0/monaco/2011/09/14/case-of-prencipe-against-monaco-106927-43376-06.shtml. Accessed May 6, 2015.

Castelfranchi, Cristiano, and Rino Falcone (2010) *Trust Theory: A Socio-Cognitive and Computational Model*. New York: John Wiley & Sons.

Cavour, Camillo (1962) Letter to "Al Magnifico Consiglio Principe della Repubblica di San Marino." February 4, 1861. In *Camillo Cavour: Epistolario. Vol. 18*, edited by Rosanna Roccia, 340–41. Florence: Leo C. Olschki Editions.

Cederman, Lars-Eric (2001) "'Back to Kant': Reinterpreting the Democratic Peace as a Macrohistorical Learning Process." *American Political Science Review* 95, no. 1 (March): 15–31.

Centre de Recerca Sociològica (2012) *Resultats Enquesta d'Opinió 2012, June*. Andorra: Institute of Andorran Studies.

Centre de Recerca Sociològica (2013) *Resultats Enquesta d'Opinió 2013, July*. Andorra: Institute of Andorran Studies.

Cheema, G. Shabbir (2010) "Building Trust in Government: An Introduction." In *Building Trust in Government: Innovations in Governance Reform in Asia*, edited by

G. Shabbir Cheema and Vesselin Popovski, 1–21. New York: United Nations University Press.

Cheema, G. Shabbir, and Vesselin Popovski, eds. (2010) *Building Trust in Government: Innovations in Governance Reform in Asia*. New York: United Nations University Press.

Chen, Jian (1994) *China's Road to the Korean War: The Making of the Sino-American Confrontation*. New York: Columbia University Press.

Chen, King C. (1987) *China's War with Vietnam, 1979: Issues, Decisions, and Implications*. Stanford, CA: Hoover Institution Press, Stanford University.

Chikhladze, Giga, and Irakli Chikhladze (2005) "The Rose Revolution: A Chronicle." In *"Enough!": The Rose Revolution and the Republic of Georgia 2003*, edited by Zurab Karumidze and James V. Wertsch, 1–18. New York: Nova Science.

China, People's Republic (2004) *Zhonghua Renmin Gongheguo bianjie shiwu tiaoyueji: ZhongChao juan* [The People's Republic of China boundary affairs treaty collection: China-Korea volume]. Beijing: Shijie zhishi chubanshe.

China, People's Republic of (1975) *Chinese-Korean Friendship—Deep-rooted and flourishing. The Party and Government Delegation of the Democratic People's Republic of Korea Visits China*. Peking: Foreign Languages Press.

Christini, Hélène (2013) French national, professor of political science, University of Monaco. Interview with the author, May 14, at the University of Monaco.

Chung, Chin-Wee (1978) *Pyongyang between Peking and Moscow: North Korea's Involvement in the Sino-Soviet Dispute, 1958–1975*. Tuscaloosa: University of Alabama Press.

Chung, Chin-Wee (1987) "North Korea's Relations with China." In *The Foreign Relations of North Korea: New Perspectives*, edited by Jae Kyu Park, Byung Chul Koh, and Tae-Hwan Kwak, 169–99. Boulder, CO: Westview Press and Seoul: Kyungnam University Press.

Chung, Jae Ho, and Myung-hae Choi (2013) "Uncertain Allies or Uncomfortable Neighbors? Making Sense of China-North Korea Relations, 1949–2010." *The Pacific Review* 26, no. 3: 243–64.

Ciavatta, Roberto (2014) Member of the Great and General Council, San Marino (Movimiento Civico R.E.T.E.). Interview with the author, June 25, San Marino.

Clark, Martin (1980) *Modern Italy 1871–1982*. New York: Longman.

Clear, Matthew R., and Susan C. Stokes (2009) "Trust and Democracy in Comparative Perspective." In *Whom Can We Trust? How Groups, Networks, and Institutions Make Trust Possible*, edited by Karen S. Cook, Margaret Levi, and Russell Hardin, 308–38. New York: Russell Sage Foundation.

CNN (2009) "Russia Vetoes U.N. Mission in Georgia." June 15. Available at http://www.cnn.com/2009/WORLD/europe/06/15/un.georgia/index.html?eref=onion. Accessed May 26, 2015.

CNN Money (2015) "Switzerland's Decision to Remove Its Currency Peg on the Franc Is Expected to Wreak Havoc on Certain Industries—and Unlucky Individuals." January 26. Available at http://money.cnn.com/2015/01/16/investing/switzerland-losers-economy-currency/. Accessed March 4, 2015.

Cohen, Maxwell (1963) "Canada-United States Treaty Relations: Trends and Future Problems." In *Canada-United States Treaty Relations*, edited by David R. Deener, 185–95. Durham, NC: Duke University Press.

Collective Security Treaty Organization (2015) Basic Facts. Available at http://www.odkb.gov.ru/start/index_azbengl.htm. Accessed July 15, 2015.

Collins, Alan (2013) *Building a People-Oriented Security Community the ASEAN Way*. London: Routledge.

Colquitt, Jason A., Brent A. Scott, and Jeffrey A. Lefine (2007) "Trust, Trustworthiness, and Trust Propensity: A Meta-Analytic Test of Their Unique Relationships with Risk Taking and Job Performance." *Journal of Applied Psychology* 92, no. 4: 909–27.

Colton, Timothy J. (2003) "Belarusian Public Opinion and the Union with Russia." In *Independent Belarus: Domestic Determinants, Regional Dynamics, and Implications for the West*, edited by Margarita M. Balmaceda, James I. Clem, and Lisbeth L. Tarlow, 21–54. Cambridge, MA: Harvard University Press/Ukrainian Research Institute and Davis Center for Russian Studies.

Cook, Karen S., Russell Hardin, and Margaret Levi (2005) *Cooperation Without Trust*. New York: Russell Sage.

Council of Europe (1988) Parliamentary Assembly, Documents, Working Papers (2–6 May 1988), Doc. 5938, Vol. V, pp. 1–15.

Council of Europe (1994) *Report on the Application by the Principality of Andorra for Membership of the Council of Europe* (Mr. Reddemann, Germany). September 14. Doc. 7152, 1403-13/9/94-7-E.

Council of Europe (2004) "The Principality of Monaco's Application for Membership of the Council of Europe. Report of the Political Affairs Committee to the Parliamentary Assembly." April 8. Doc. 10128. Strasbourg: Council of Europe.

Council of Europe (2012) *Report on Fourth Assessment Visit—Summary: Anti-Money Laundering and Combating the Financing of Terrorism—Andorra*. March 8. Strasbourg: Council of Europe.

Council of Europe (2014) *Fourth Round Mutual Evaluation Report Executive Summary Anti-Money Laundering and Combating the Financing of Terrorism MONACO*. MONEYVAL (2013)12 SUMM. Available at http://www.coe.int/t/dghl/monitoring/moneyval/Evaluations/round4/MON4-SUMMMONEYVAL(2013)12_en.pdf. Accessed May 6, 2015.

Council of Europe (2015) "List of declarations made with respect to treaty No. 005." Status of the Treaties of the Council of Europe. Available at http://conventions.coe.int/Treaty/Commun/ListeDeclarations.asp?NT=005&CM=8&DF=06/05/2015&CL=ENG&VL=1. Accessed May 6, 2015.

Council of the European Union (2003) "Council Decision of 17 November 2003 Concerning the Conclusion of the Agreement on the Application of Certain Community Acts on the Territory of the Principality of Monaco" (2003/885/EC). Brussels.

Cramér, Per (2009) "Reflections on the Roles of Mutual Trust in EU Law." In *Fifty Years of the European Treaties: Looking Back and Thinking Forward*, edited by Michael Dougan and Samantha Currie, 43–62. London: Bloomsbury Publishing.

Croft, Stuart (1988) "British Policy towards Western Europe, 1947–9: The Best Possible Worlds?" *International Affairs* (UK)64, no. 4 (Autumn): 617–29.

Cruciani, di Santi (2010) *Passione Politsche in Tempo di Guerra Fredda: La Repubblica di san Marino e l'Italia tra storia nazionale e relazioni internazionali (1945–1957)*.

Quaderni del Centro Sammarinese di Studi storici #32. Serravalle, San Marino: AIEP Editore.

Cumings, Bruce (2005) *Korea's Place in the Sun: A Modern History* (Updated). New York: W. W. Norton.

Daily World (2016) "Minsk Tacks Between NATO and Russia," December 15. Available at: http://www.dw.com/en/minsk-tacks-between-nato-and-russia/a-367877?maca=en-gk-volltext-newsstand-topstories-en-10709-xml-media. Accessed December 15, 2016.

Deane, Shirley (1961) *The Road to Andorra*. New York: William Morrow.

Delorme, Philippe (1997) *Les Grimaldi: 700 Ans d'Une Dynastie*. Paris: Balland.

Delyagin, Michael (2009) "New Belarus for New Russia: Past, Present, Future." In *Belarus: External Pressure, Internal Change*, edited by Hans-Georg Heinrich and Ludmilla Lobova, 193–202. Frankfurt: Peter Lang.

Denyer, Simon (2016) "A Snub for China, North Korea's Reported Nuclear Test Shows Beijing's Waning Inflence," *Washington Post*, January 6. Available at https://www.washingtonpost.com/world/a-snub-for-china-north-koreas-reported-nuclear-test-shows-beijings-waning-influence/2016/01/06/b0d309e9-a5a4-4cd4-b12a-ab352a53c0cc_story.html?utm_term=.0a02cb61c310. Accessed January 12, 2016.

Departament d'Estadística, Andorra (2013) *Actualitat estadística.ad—April 2013*. Andorra: Government of Andorra.

Department of Defense, United States (1971) *United States-Vietnam Relations, 1945–1967. Study Prepared by the Department of Defense. Volume 2*. Washington: Government Printing Office.

Department of State, United States (1954) "Eisenhower's Letter of Support to Ngo Dinh Diem, October 23, 1954." *Department of State Bulletin*. November 15, 735–36.

Department of State, United States (1961) "President Respond to Request from Viet-Nam for U.S. Aid: Following is an exchange of messages between President Kennedy and President Ngo Dinh Diem of the Republic of Viet-Nam." State Department Archives.

Department of State, United States (2013) "2013 Investment Climate—Andorra. Bureau of Economics and Business Affairs. April. Available at http://www.state.gov/e/eb/rls/othr/ics/2013/204589.htm. Accessed May 26, 2015.

Department of State, United States (2015) *2014 Trafficking in Persons Report: Democratic Republic of Korea*. Washington, DC: Government Printing Office.

Deutsch, Karl W., Sidney A. Burrell, and Robert A. Kann (1957). *Political Community and the North Atlantic Area; International Organization in the Light of Historical Experience*. Princeton: Princeton University Press.

Devdariani, Jaba (2005) "Georgia and Russia: The Troubled Road to Accommodation." In *Statehood and Security: Georgia after the Rose Revolution*, edited by Bruno Coppieters and Robert Legvold, 117–52. Cambridge, MA: MIT Press.

Diener, Alexander C. (2010) *Borderline and Borderlands: Political Oddities at the Edge of the Nation-State*. New York: Rowman & Littlefield.

Di Luca, Patricia (2014) Curator, San Marino Museum of Emigration. Interview with the author, June 24, San Marino.

Doerner, Charles (1983) "Luxembourg: An Example of the Dependent Monetary

System of a Small State." In *Small States in Europe and Dependence*. Luxembourg Papers #6, edited by Otmar Höll, 130–39. December. Vienna: Broumüller.

Doran, Charles F. (1984) *Forgotten Partnership: U.S.-Canada Relations Today*. Baltimore: Johns Hopkins University Press.

Dosenrode, Søren (2012) "The Road to Lisbon." In *The European Union after Lisbon: Polity, Politics, Policy*, edited by Søren Dosenrode, 7–20. Farnham: Ashgate.

Dózsa, Dániel (2008) "EU Relations with European Micro-States: Happily Ever After?" *European Law Journal* 14, no. 1 (January): 93–104.

Drakokhrust, Yuri, and Dmitri Furman (2003) "Belarus and Russia: The Game of Virtual Integration." In *Independent Belarus: Domestic Determinants, Regional Dynamics, and Implications for the West*, edited by Margarita M. Balmaceda, James I. Clem, and Lisbeth L. Tarlow, 232–55. Cambridge, MA: Harvard University Press/Ukrainian Research Institute and Davis Center for Russian Studies.

Duhigg, Charles (2012) *The Power of Habit*. New York: Random House.

Duiker, William J. (1986) *China and Vietnam: The Roots of the Conflict*. Berkeley: Institute of East Asian Studies, University of California.

Dumont, Patrick, Arco Timmermans, and Catherine Moury (2015) "Coping with Domestic and European Complexity: How Consensus Politics Is Maintained in the Low Countries' Governments." In *European Integration and Consensus Politics in the Low Countries*, edited by Hans Vollaard, Jan Beyers, and Patrick Dumont, 24–47. London: Routledge.

Duursma, Jorri C. (1996) *Fragmentation and the International Relations of Micro-States: Self-Determination and Statehood*. New York: Cambridge University Press.

Eckel, Mike (2013) "New $100 Bill: Why North Korea Won't Be Very Happy," *Christian Science Monitor*, October 8. Available at http://www.csmonitor.com/layout/set/print/World/2013/1008/New-100-bill-why-North-Korea-won-t-be-very-happy-video. Accessed August 11, 2015.

Economist (2012) "The Weak Shall Inherit the Earth." October 6. Available at http://.economist.com/node/21564210/print. Accessed March 4, 2015.

Emerson, Michael (2007) *Andorra and the European Union*. Brussels: Center for European Policy Studies.

English, John, and Norman Hillmer (1989/1982) "Canada's American Alliance." In *Partners Nevertheless: Canadian-American Relations in the Twentieth Century*, edited by Norman Hillmer, 32–42. Toronto: Copp Clark Pitman Ltd.

Esterl, Mike, Glenn R. Simpson, and David Crawford (2008) "Stolen Data Spur Tax Probes: Ex-Staffer of Bank in Liechtenstein Offered Information." *Wall Street Journal*, February 19. Available at http://www.wsj.com/articles/SB120333229682874855. Accessed March 10, 2015.

Europa World Plus (2013) "Liechtenstein—Foreign Affairs" Available at http://www.europaworld.com/pub. Accessed March 15, 2013.

Europa World Plus (2015a) Luxembourg. Available at http://www.europaworld.com/entry/lu. Accessed March 25, 2015.

Europa World Plus (2015b) Various items on Monaco. London: Routledge. Available at http://www.europaworld.com.erl.lib.byu.edu. Accessed April 29, 2015.

Europa World Plus (2015c) San Marino—various entries. Europa World online. London: Routledge. Available at http://www.europaworld.com.erlib.byu.edu/. Accessed May 15, 2015.

Europa World Plus (2015d) Andorra—various topics. Europa World online. London: Routledge. Available at http://www.europaworld.com.erlib.byu.edu/. Accessed May 25, 2015.

Europa World Plus (2015e) "Belarus." London: Routledge. Available at http://www.europaworld.com/entry/by. Accessed July 16, 2015.

European Commission (1991a) *Decision No 2/91 of the EEC-Andorra Joint Committee of July 12 on the laws, regulations and administrative provisions applicable to customs matters in the Community to be adopted by the Principality of Andorra*. (91/467/EEC). No L 250/24–29.

European Commission (1991b) *Decision No 4/91 of the EEC-Andorra Joint Committee of 12 July concerning certain methods of administrative cooperation for implementation of the Agreement and the procedures for forwarding goods to the Principality of Andorra*. (91/469/EEC). No L 250/30–31.

European Commission (1992) *Decision No 7/91 of the EEC-Andorra Joint Committee of 31 December 1991 introducing a derogation from the definition of 'originating products' to take into account the specific situation of the Principality of Andorra regarding its output of certain processed agricultural products. (92/116/EEC)*. No L 43/33–34.

European Commission (1998) *Decision No 1/98 of the EC-Andorra Joint Committee of 20 October 1998 amending Decision No 2/96 of the EC-Andorra Joint Committee laying down the arrangements for the implementation of Annex II to the Agreement in the form of an Exchange of Letters between the European Economic Community and the Principality of Andorra*. (98/652/EC). No L 311/21–45.

European Commission (1999) *Decision No 1/99 of the EC-Andorra Joint Committee of 6 May 1999 amending the Appendix to the Agreement in the form of an Exchange of Letters between the European Economic Community and the Principality of Andorra*. (1999/482/EC) No L 191/1–33.

European Commission (2005) "The European Constitution: Post-Referendum Survey in Luxembourg." Flash Eurobarometer #173, July. Brussels: European Commission.

European Commission (2008) "Operational Programme 'France-Spain-Andorra' 2007–2013." MEMO/08/314—Brussels, 20 May.

European Commission (2012) "European Citizenship." Standard Eurobarometer #77, Spring. Brussels: European Commission.

European Commission (2015) Statistical Bulletin—Off & TA. REF: 04:2011:01:20:10.

European Community (2003) *Agreement between the European Community and the Principality of Andorra providing for measures equivalent to those laid down in Council Directive 2003/48/EC on taxation of savings income in the form of interest payments*. No L 359/33–45.

European Court of Justice / Curia (2015) Search engine for ECJ cases. Available at https://curia.europa.eu/jcms/jcms/j_6/en/. Accessed August 23, 2015.

European Economic Community (1992a) *Decision #3/92 of the EEC-San Marino Cooperation Committee of 22 December 1992 on the Arrangements for the Provision of Mutual Assistance Pursuant to Article 13 of the Agreement between the Community and San Marino*. OJEC 93/103/EEC.

European Economic Community (1992b) *Agreement on Cooperation and Customs*

Union between the European Economic Community and the Republic of San Marino. OJEC L 84/43.

European Free Trade Association (2000) In Commemoration of EFTA's 40th Anniversary. Available at http://www.efta.int/sites/default/files/publications/efta-commemorative-publications/40th-anniversary.pdf. Accessed March 3, 2015.

European Free Trade Association (2015) "Liechtenstein Celebrates 20 Years in the European Economic Area." May 11. Available at: file:///C:/Trust/European_Free_Trade_Association_Liechtenstein_celebrates_20_years_in_the_European_Economic_Area_31.01.2017.pdf. Accessed January 31, 2017.

European Union (2003) *Agreement between the European Community and the Republic of San Marino Providing for Measures Equivalent to Those Laid Down in Council Directive 2003/48/EC on Taxation of Savings Income in the Form of Interest Payments*. OJEU L 381/33.

European Union (2004) *Agreement between the European Union and the Principality of Liechtenstein Providing for Measures Equivalent to Those Laid Down in Council Directive 2003/48/EC on Taxation of Savings Income in the Form of Interest Payments. Official Journal of the European Union L 379/84*. December 24. Brussels.

European Union (2010) *Omnibus Decision #1/2010 of the EU-San Marino Cooperation Committee of 29 March 2010 Establishing Various Implementing Measures for the Agreement on Cooperation and Customs Union between the European Economic Community and the Republic of San Marino*. OJEU L 1.

European Union (2011a) *Report to the EU Council: EU Relations with the Principality of Andorra, the Republic of San Marino and the Principality of Monaco*. 11466/11. Brussels.

European Union (2011b) *Council Decision of 18 January 2011 on the signing, on behalf of the European Union, and provisional application of the Protocol extending to customs security measures the Agreement in the form of an Exchange of Letters between the European Economic Community and the Principality of Andorra*. (2011/90/EU) L 36/1–7.

European Union (2012a) Commission Staff Working Paper: Obstacles to Access by Andorra, Monaco and San Marino to the EU's Internal Market and Cooperation in other Areas Accompanying the document "Communication from the Commission to the European Parliament, the Council, the European Economic and Social Committee and the Committee of the Regions—EU Relations with the Principality of Andorra, the Principality of Monaco and the Republic of San Marino: Options for Closer Integration with the EU." SWD/2012/0388 final */ Available at http://eur-lex.europa.eu/LexUriServ/LexUriServ.do?uri=SWD:2012:0388:FIN:EN:HTML. Accessed June 26, 2014.

Evans, Gareth (2009) "Russia, Georgia and the Responsibility to Protect." *Amsterdam Law Forum* 1, no. 2: 25–28.

Fallows, James (2015) "The Real Test of the Iran Deal." *Atlantic Monthly*, July 28. Available at: http://www.theatlantic.com/international/archive/2015/07/the-iran-debate-moves-on/399713/. Accessed October 13, 2015.

Farrell, Henry (2004) "Trust, Distrust, and Power." In *Distrust*, edited by Russell Hardin, 85–105. New York: Russell Sage Foundation.

Farrell, Henry (2009) "Institutions and Midlevel Explanations of Trust." In *Whom Can We Trust? How Groups, Networks, and Institutions Make Trust Possible*, edited by Karen S. Cook, Margaret Levi, and Russell Hardin, 127–48. New York: Russell Sage Foundation.

Faure, Guy Olivier, and Patrick Klaousen (2000) "The Andorran-European Community Trade Agreement Negotiations, 1979–1987." In *Power and Negotiation*, edited by I. William Zartman and Jeffrey Z. Rubin, 107–27. Ann Arbor: University of Michigan Press.

Fayol, Ben (2013) Former Luxembourg Member of Parliament, Member of the European Parliament (1989–99). Interview with the author, April 3, Luxembourg City.

Felgenhauer, Pavel (2009) "After August 7: The Escalation of the Russia-Georgia War." In *The Guns of August 2008: Russia's War in Georgia*, edited by Svante E. Cornell and S. Frederick Starr, 162–80. London: M. E. Sharpe.

Fernández, Gabriel (2013) Web editor at the Diari d'Andorra. Interview with the author, May 17, Andorra-la-Vella.

Fernsworth, Lawrence (1934) "Andorra: The Passing of Europe's Last Feudal State." *Foreign Affairs* (January).

Filippov, Mikhail (2010) "Diversionary Role of the Georgia-Russia Conflict: International Constraints and Domestic Appeal." *Europe-Asia Studies* 61, no. 10: 1825–47.

Final Act, Congress of Vienna (1814) *General Treaty*. Vienna

Financial Action Task Force on Money Laundering (2001) Annual Report—2000–2001. Paris: OECD. Available at http://www.fatf-gafi.org/media/fatf/documents/reports/2000%202001%20ENG.pdf. Accessed March 10, 2015.

Finn, Peter (2008) "Russia's Moves Add to Strains with Georgia" *Washington Post*, May 1. Available at http://www.washingtonpost.com/wp-dyn/content/article/2008/04/03/AR2008043003256_pf.html. Accessed May 26, 3015.

Foreign Affairs Ministry, Russian Federation (2007) "Statement by the Ministry of Foreign Affairs of the Russian Federation Regarding Georgia's Lawsuit Against Russia." Available at http://archive.mid.ru//brp_4.nsf/e78a48070f128a7b43256999005bcbb3/4a297faabfeb0ex3c32572ac002ab55b?OpenDocument. Accessed August 10, 2015.

Fortó Areny, Josep (2013) Professor of statistics, University of Andorra. Interview with the author, May 17, Santa Julià de Lòria, Andorra.

Freedom House (2014) Monaco. Available at https://freedomhouse.org/report/freedom-world/2014/monaco#.VUpK-PlViko. Accessed April 29, 2015.

French Republic (1793a) "Decree of the National Convention Regarding the Reunion to the Republic of the Principality of Monaco and Several Communes." February 14.

French Republic (1793b) "Proclamation to the People of Monaco, Menton and Roquebrune." January 8.

French Republic (1793c) "Observations sur la Réclamation d'Honoré Grimaldi, ci-devant Prince de Monaco." December 16 (26 Frimaire).

Frentz, Jean-Marie (2010) "The Foreign Policy of Luxembourg." In *Small States in Europe: Challenges and Opportunities*, edited by Robert Steinmetz and Anders Wivel, 131–46. Farnham, UK: Ashgate.

Frommelt, Christian (2016) "Liechtenstein's Tailor-Made Arrangements in the EEA: A Small State's Creative Solutions in European Integration." In *State Size*

Matters: Politik und recht im kontext von kleinstaatlichkeit und monarchie, edited by Sebastian Wolf, 313–59. Wiesbaden: Springer VS.

Frommelt, Christian, and Sieglinde Gstöhl (2011) Liechtenstein and the EEA: The Europeanization of a (very) small state. Report #18. Oslo: Europautredningen: utvalget for utredning av Norges avtaler med eu.

Fukuyama, Francis (1995) *Trust: The Social Virtues and the Creation of Prosperity*. New York: The Free Press.

Gahrton, Per (2010) *Georgia: Pawn in the New Great Game*. London: Pluto Press.

Gatti, Gabriela (2003) "Greetings from the Secretary of State for Foreign Business, Republic of San Marino." In *Il Piccolo Stato: Politica, Storia, Diplomazia*, edited by Laura Barletta, Franco Cardini, and Guiseppe Galasso, 327–33. Sarravalle, San Marino: AIEP Editore.

Geiger, Peter (2007) "Der Kleinstaat in der Ära der Weltkriege." *Liechtenstein Politsche Schriften Band* 42: 137–74.

Gengler, Claude (1991) *Le Luxembourg dans Tous ses Etats*. LaGarenne-Colombes: l'Espace Européen.

Georgia v. Russia (2014) European Court of Human Rights, App. 13255/07. July 3. Available at http://www.cnn.com/2009/WORLD/europe/06/15/un.georgia/index.html?eref=onion. Accessed September 8, 2015.

Giddens, Anthony (1982) *Sociology: A Brief but Critical Introduction*. London: Macmillan.

Ginsburgs, George, and Roy U. T. Kim (1977) *Calendar of Diplomatic Affairs: Democratic People's Republic of Korea, 1945–1975*. Moorestown, NJ: Symposia Press.

Glaser, Bonnie, Scott Snyder, and John S. Park (2008) "Keeping an Eye on an Unruly Neighbor: Chinese Views of Economic Reform and Stability in North Korea." US Institute of Peace Working Paper, with the Center for Strategic and International Studies, January 3.

Global Affairs Canada—Government of Canada (2015) "Repeal of U.S. Country of Origin Labelling Reflects Strong Canada-United States Relations." December 18. Available at: http://news.gc.ca/web/article-en.do?nid=1025599. Accessed January 17, 2017.

Godin, Seth (2010) *Lynchpin: Are You Indispensable?* New York: Portfolio.

Godsoe, J. G. (1989/1988) "Only Half a Trade Agreement." In *Partners Nevertheless: Canadian-American Relations in the Twentieth Century*, edited by Norman Hillmer, 311–14. Toronto: Copp Clark Pitman Ltd.

Golani, Helena Yakovlev (2011) "Two Decades of the Russian Federation's Foreign Policy in the Commonwealth of Independent States: The Cases of Belarus and Ukraine." Working Papers: The European Forum at the Hebrew University of Jerusalem.

Goldsmith, Jack (2003) "The Self-Defeating International Criminal Court." *University of Chicago Law Review* 70, no. 1 (Winter): 89–104.

Goldsmith, Jack, and Eric Posner (2005) *The Limits of International Law*. New York: Oxford University Press.

Golgowski, Nina (2015) "Minnesota Bride and Groom Bill No-Show Wedding Guests $80 for Dinner," Available at: http://www.nydailynews.com/news/national/bride-groom-bill-no-show-wedding-guests-80-dinner-article-1.2380660. Accessed October 13, 2015.

Goltz, Thomas (2009) *Georgia Diary: A Chronicle of War and Political Chaos in the Post-Soviet Caucasus*. Expanded edition. Armonk, NY: M. E. Sharpe.

Gordadze, Thornike (2009) "Georgian-Russian Relations in the 1990s." In *The Guns of August 2008: Russia's War in Georgia*, edited by Svante E. Cornell and S. Frederick Starr, 28–48. London: M. E. Sharpe.

Gori, Cesare (2014) *Un Giorno nella Storia: San Marino 26 Giugno 1944*. Republic of San Marino.

Gotlieb, Allan (2013) "The United States in Canadian Foreign Policy." Foreign Ministry of Canada O.D. Skelton Lectures. April 29. Available at http://www.international.gc.ca/odskelton/gotlieb.aspx?lang=eng. Accessed September 18, 2015.

Granovetter, Mark (1985) "Economic Action and the Social Structure: The Problem of Embeddedness." *American Journal of Sociology* 91, no. 3 (November): 481–510.

Grant, C. K. (1949) "Promises." *Mind* 58, no. 231 (July): 359–66.

Grant, Charles (2014) "Smothered by Russia's Bear Hug." *New Statesman*, April 18–May 1, 13–14.

Gravelle, Timothy B. (2014) "Partisanship, Border Proximity, and Canadian Attitudes toward North American Integration." *International Journal of Public Opinion Research*, March 11. http://dx.doi.org/10.1093/ijpor/edu006

Griffith, William B., and Robert S. Goldfarb (1991) "Amending the Economist's 'Rational Egoist' Model to Include Moral Values and Norms." In *Social Norms and Economic Institutions*, edited by Kenneth J. Koford and Jeffrey B. Miller, 39–84. Ann Arbor: University of Michigan Press.

Grinda, George (2010) *The Principality of Monaco: State, International Status, Institutions*. 2nd ed. The Hague: TMC Asser Press.

Guardian (2014) "Switzerland Backs Immigration Quotas by Slim Margin". Available at https://www.theguardian.com/world/2014/feb/09/swiss-referendum-immigration-quotas. Accessed May 31, 2017.

Guardian (2013) "Rome Prosecutor's Office Says E1 bn a Year was Smuggled Into Tiny State on Behalf of High-Profile Clients." By Lizzy Davies and agencies. July 23. Available at http://www.theguardian.com/world/2013/jul/23/italian-investigation-san-marino-tax. Accessed May 15, 2015.

Guillaumet, Jordi (2013) Director of the Andorran Studies Institute. Former chief of staff of the Andorran head of government. Interview with the author, May 17, Santa Julià de Lòria, Andorra.

Haas, Ernst (1958) *The Uniting of Europe: Political, Social, and Economic Forces 1950–1957*. Stanford, CA: Stanford University Press.

Haggard, Stephen, Jennifer Lee, and Marcus Noland (2012) "Integration in the Absence of Institutions: China-North Korea Cross-Border Exchange." *Journal of Asian Economics* 23: 130–45.

Halberstam, David (1969) *The Best and the Brightest*. New York: Fawcett Crest.

Halbrook, Stephen P. (1998) *Target Switzerland: Swiss Armed Neutrality in World War II*. Rockville Centre, NY: Sarpedon.

Hall, Mark A. (2005) "The Importance of Trust for Ethics, Law, and Public Policy." *Cambridge Quarterly of Healthcare Ethics* 14: 156–67.

Hallans, Ellen (2010) *The United States and NATO Since 9/11: The Transatlantic Alliance Renewed*. New York: Routledge.

Hamblin, Dora Jean (1957) "A Civil War in a Nutshell." *Life*, November 4, 79–89.

Hane, Cynthia (2004) "Distrust as a Trade Impediment: European Trade Policy Toward Nonmarket Economies." In *Distrust*, edited by Russell Hardin, 249–77. New York: Russell Sage Foundation.

Hardin, Russell (2002) *Trust and Trustworthiness*. New York: Russell Sage Foundation.

Hardin, Russell (2004a) "Distrust: Manifestations and Management." In *Distrust*, edited by Russell Hardin, 3–33. New York: Russell Sage Foundation.

Hardin, Russell (2004b) "Terrorism and Group-Generalized Distrust." In *Distrust*, edited by Russell Hardin, 278–97. New York: Russell Sage Foundation.

Hardin, Sheila, ed. (1985) *Small Is Dangerous: Micro States in a Macro World*. Report of a Study Group of the David Davies Memorial Institute of International Studies. New York: St. Martin's Press.

Hart, H. L. A. (1961) *The Concept of Law*. Oxford: Oxford University Press.

Harvey, Cole (2009) "Russia Vetoes UN Mission in Georgia." *Arms Control Today*, July 2. Available at http://www.armscontrol.org/act/2009_07–08/Russia_Veto.

Hasler, Otmer (2013) Prime minister of Liechtenstein, 2001–2009. Interview with the author, May 10, Vaduz.

Hawkins, Darren, David Lake, Daniel Nielson, and Michael Tierney (2006) *Delegation and Agency in International Organizations*. New York: Cambridge University Press.

Henderson, Sir Nicholas (1982) *The Birth of NATO*. London: Weidenfeld and Nicolson.

Henderson, W. O. (1934/2013) *The Zollverein*. Cambridge: Cambridge University Press.

Henrich, Joseph, and Natalie Henrich (2007) *Why Humans Cooperate: A Cultural and Evolutionary Explanation*. New York: Oxford University Press.

Hey, Jeanne A. K. (2003) "Luxembourg: Where Small Works (and Wealthy Doesn't Hurt)." in *Small States in World Politics: Explaining Foreign Policy Behavior*, edited by Jeanne A. K. Hey, 75–94. Boulder, CO: Lynne Rienner.

Higgins, Andrew (2016) "In a 'Frozen Zone,' Russia Is Creeping Closer to Georgia." *New York Times*, October 24. P. A4.

Hille, Kathrin (2014) "New Putin Doctrine Emphasises Threat of Political Destabilisation." *Financial Times*, December 26. Available at http://www.ft.com/cms/s/0/ca8a437c-8d1d-11e4–9f52–00144feabdc0.html#axzz3g4oZXJQQ. Accessed July 16, 2015.

Hirsch, Mario (1983) "Who Is In Charge of the Destinies of Small States? The Case of Luxembourg." In *Small States in Europe and Dependence*. Luxembourg Papers #6, December, edited by Otmar Höll, 130–39. Vienna: Broumüller.

History of San Marino (2015) From 1500 to beginning 1800, Napoleon in San Marino. Available at: http://sanmarino.by/en/napoleone.html. Accessed May 18, 2015.

Hobson, Elton (2013) "55 Years Later, Biggest Question Surrounding the Avro Arrow Remains 'What If?'" *Global News*, March 26. Available at http://glo

balnews.ca/news/427985/55-years-later-biggest-question-surrounding-avro-arrow-remains-what-if/. Accessed July 29, 2015.

Hoffman, Aaron M. (2002) "A Conceptualization of Trust in International Relations." *European Journal of International Relations* 8, no. 3: 375–401.

Hoffman, Aaron M. (2006) *Building Trust: Overcoming Suspicion in International Conflict*. Albany: State University of New York Press.

Hollis, Martin (1998) *Trust within Reason*. London: Cambridge University Press.

Holmes, John W. (1989) "Crises in Canadian-American Relations: A Canadian Perspective." In *Friends So Different: Essays on Canada and the United States in the 1980s*, edited by Lansing Lamont and J. Duncan Edmonds, 17–31. Ottawa: University of Ottawa Press.

Hood, Steven J. (1992) *Dragons Entangled: Indochina and the China-Vietnam War*. Armonk, NY: M. E. Sharpe.

Horne, Cynthia (2004) "Distrust as a Trade Impediment: European Trade Policy toward Nonmarket Economies." In *Distrust*, edited by Russell Hardin, 249–77. New York: Russell Sage Foundation.

Hower, Sara Beth (2008) "Do Small States Make Bad Allies?" PhD dissertation, Catholic University of America, Washington, DC.

Hu, Elise (2016) "The 'Livelihood Loophole' and Other Weaknesses of N. Korea Sanctions," National Public Radio, September 15. Available at http://www.npr.org/sections/parallels/2016/09/15/493889932/the-livelihood-loophole-and-other-weaknesses-of-n-korea-sanctions?ft=nprml&f=1001. Accessed October 13, 2016.

Huang, Fali (2007) "Building Social Trust: A Human-Capital Approach." *Journal of Institutional and Theoretical Economics* 163, no. 4 (December): 552–73.

Hyer, Eric (2015) *The Pragmatic Dragon: China's Grand Strategy and Boundary Settlements*. Seattle: University of Washington Press.

Illarionov, Andrei (2009) "The Russian Leadership's Preparation for War, 1999–2008." In *The Guns of August 2008: Russia's War in Georgia*, edited by Svante E. Cornell and S. Frederick Starr, 49–84. London: M. E. Sharpe.

International Business Publications (2009) *Monaco Country Study Guide*. Volume 1—Strategic Information and Developments. Washington, DC: International Business Publications US.

International Criminal Court—Office of the Prosecutor (2014) "Report on Preliminary Examination Activities 2014." December 2. The Hague: International Criminal Court

International Criminal Court—Office of the Prosecutor (2016) "ICC Prosecutor Authorized to Open *Proprio Motu* Investigation." January 27. Available at: https://www.icc-cpi.int/georgia. Accessed January 17, 2017.

Interview with the author (2013a) Long-time Monaco foreign resident and legal expert, May 13.

Interview with the author (2013b) Senior Andorran diplomat.

Interview with the author (2013c) University of Liechtenstein professor, May 8, Vaduz.

Interview with the author (2014a) Senior Italian official, June 25, San Marino.

Interview with the author (2014b) Former senior San Marino official, June 23, San Marino.

Ioffe, Grigory (2008) *Understanding Belarus and How Western Foreign Policy Misses the Mark*. New York: Rowman & Littlefield.

Jackson, Van (2016) "Power, Trust, and Network Complexity: Three Logics of Hedging in Asian Security." *International Relations of the Asia-Pacific* 16, no. 3: 1–26.

Joint Committee of the EU and Monaco (2013) *Decision #1/2013 of the EU-Monaco Joint Committee Established under the Agreement between the European Community and the Principality of Monaco on the Application of Certain Community Acts on the Territory of the Principality of Monaco of July 12 2013 amending the Annex to the Agreement* (2013/513/EU). Brussels.

Jolly, Richard, Louis Emmerij, and Thomas Weiss (2009) *UN Ideas That Changed the World*. Bloomington: Indiana University Press.

Jones, David H. (1966) "Making and Keeping Promises." *Ethics* 76, no. 4 (July): 287–96.

Jones, Robert A. (1996) *The Politics and Economics of the European Union: An Introductory Text*. Cheltenham: Edward Elgar.

Kalb, Marvin (2013) *The Road to War: Presidential Commitments Honored and Betrayed*. Washington: Brookings Institution.

Kanter, James, and Andrew Higgins (2014) "Top Official in EU Faces Rising Furor over Tax." *New York Times*, November 7, A4, A10.

Kaplan, Morton A. (1957) "Balance of Power, Bipolarity and Other Models of International Systems." *American Political Science Review* 51, no. 3 (September): 684–95.

Karnow, Stanley (1983) *Vietnam: A History*. New York: Viking Press.

Kassim, Hussein, and Dionyssis Dimitrakopoulos (2007) "Leader or Bystander: The European Commission and EU Treaty Reform." In *Leadership in the Big Bangs of European Integration*, edited by Derek Beach and Colette Mazzucelli, 94–114. Basingstoke: Palgrave Macmillan.

Katz, Rebecca S. (2006) *The Georgian Regime Crisis of 2003–2004: A Case Study in Post-Soviet Media Representation of Politics, Crime and Corruption*. Stuttgart: Verlag.

Kayser, Edouard (1990) *Quelque Part Entre Vienne et Londres: Le Grand-Duché de Luxembourg de 1815 à 1867*. Luxembourg: St. Paul.

Keating, Dan, David S. Fallin, Kimberly Kindy, and Scott Higham (2012) "Members of Congress Trade in Companies While Making Laws That Affect Those Same Firms." *Washington Post*, June 23, 1.

Keating, Vincent Charles, and Jan Ruzicka (2014) "Trusting Relationships in International Politics: No Need to Hedge." *Review of International Studies* 40, no. 4 (October): 753–70.

Keenleyside, H. L. (1941) "Recent Trends in United States-Canada Relations." December 27, National Archives of Canada, RG25, vol. 5758, file 71 (s).

Keenleyside, H. L. (1960/61) "The Canada-United States Permanent Joint Board on Defence: 1940–1945." *International Journal* 16, no. 1 (Winter): 50–77.

Kennedy, Merrit (2016) "Trudeau Says Canada Will Cease Airstrikes Against ISIS in Syria and Iraq." National Public Radio, February 8. Available at: hppt://www.npr.org/sections/thetwo-way/2016/02/08/4660509/trudeau-says-canada-will-cease-aistrikes-against-isis-in-syria-and-iraq?ft=nprml&f=1001. Accessed February 10, 2016.

Keohane, Robert O. (1984) *After Hegemony: Cooperation and Discord in the World Political Economy*. Princeton: Princeton University Press.
Keohane, Robert, and Joseph Nye (2011) *Power and Interdependence*, 4th ed. New York: Longman.
Khoo, Nicholas (2011) *Collateral Damage: Sino-Soviet Rivalry and the Termination of the Sino-Vietnamese Alliance*. New York: Columbia University Press.
Kim, Ilpyong J. (1998) "China in North Korean Foreign Policy." In *North Korean Foreign Relations in the Post-Cold War Era*, edited by Samuel S. Kim, 94–115. Hong Kong: Oxford University Press.
Kim, Samuel S. (2002) "China and the Future of the Korean Peninsula." In *The Future of North Korea*, edited by Tsuneo Akaha, 104–28. London: Routledge.
Kim, Samuel S. (2006) "Sino-North Korean Relations in the Post-Cold War World." In *North Korea: The Politics of Regime Survival*, edited by Young Whan Kihl and Hong Nack Kim, 183–202. Armonk, NY: M. E. Sharpe.
Kim, Samuel S., and Tai Hwan Lee (2002) "Chinese-North Korean Relations: Managing Asymmetrical Interdependence." In *North Korea and Northeast Asia*, edited by Samuel S. Kim and Tai Hwan Lee, 109–37. Lanham, MD: Rowman & Littlefield.
Kim, Taewan (2014) "Chinese Domestic Politics and Security Cooperation in Northeast Asia." In *Rethinking Asia and International Relations: North Korea and Security Cooperation in Northeast Asia*, edited by Tae-Hwan Kwak and Seung-Ho Jo, 131–53. Farnham, UK: Ashgate.
King, W. L. M. (1989/1940) "The Ogdensburg Agreement, 1940." In *Partners Nevertheless: Canadian-American Relations in the Twentieth Century*, edited by Norman Hillmer, 99–102. Toronto: Copp Clark Pitman Ltd.
Kinsch, Patrick (2013) Professor of law, University of Luxembourg. Interview with the author, May 3, Luxembourg City.
Kmec, Sonja (2013) Associate professor of history, University of Luxembourg. Interview with the author, May 3, Luxembourg City.
Kohn, Marek (2008) *Trust: Self-interest and the Common Good*. London: Oxford University Press.
Koremenos, Barbara (2016) *The Continent of International Law: Explaining Agreement Design*. New York: Cambridge University Press.
Kramer, Roderick (2004) "Collective Paranoia: Distrust Between Social Groups." In *Distrust*, edited by Russell Hardin, 135–66. New York: Russell Sage Foundation.
Krivosheev, Denis (2003) "Belarus's External Relations." In *Contemporary Belarus: Between Democracy and Dictatorship*, edited by Elena A. Korosteleva, Colin W. Lawson, and Rosalind J. Marsh, 164–78. London: Routledge Carzon.
Kushnir, Ivan (2015) Kuchnir's Research Center. Available at http://kushnirs.org/macroeconomics/gdp/gdp_liechtenstein.html#neighbor1. Accessed March 3, 2015.
Kydd, Andrew (2005) *Trust and Mistrust in International Relations*. Princeton: Princeton University Press.
Kydd, Andrew (2005/06) "In America We (Used to) Trust: U.S. Hegemony and Global Cooperation." *Political Science Quarterly* 120, no. 4 (Winter): 619–36.
Kydd, Andrew (2006) "When Can Mediators Build Trust?" *American Political Science Review* 100, no. 3 (August): 449–62.

L'Express (2015) "Monaco condamné dans une incroyable affaire d'escroquerie financière." Available at http://www.lexpress.fr/actualite/monde/europe/monaco-condamne-dans-une-incroyable-affaire-d-escroquerie-financiere_1656380.html. Accessed May 6, 2015.

La Tribuna (2014) "CSU: Governo immobile, inconcludente e chius su confront." June 24, 7.

Lackenbauer, Whitney P., and Peter Kikkert (2010) *The Canadian Forces & Arctic Sovereignty: Debating Roles, Interests and Requirements, 1968–1974*. Waterloo, ON: Wilfrid Laurier University Press.

Ladaria, Nodar (2005) "Contextualizing the Rose Revolution." In *"Enough!": The Rose Revolution and the Republic of Georgia 2003*, edited by Zurab Karumidze and James V. Wertsch, 115–18. New York: Nova Science.

Lake, David (1996) "Anarchy, Hierarchy, and the Variety of International Relations." *International Organization* 50, no. 1 (Winter): 1–33.

Lake, David (2011) *Hierarchy in International Relations*. Ithaca: Cornell University Press.

Lanho, Bernd (2001) "On the Emotional Character of Trust." *Ethical Theory and Moral Practice* 4, no. 2 (June): 171–89.

Larson, Deborah Welch (1997) *Anatomy of Distrust: U.S.-Soviet Relations During the Cold War*. Ithaca: Cornell University Press.

Lawrence, Mark Atwood (2008) *The Vietnam War: A Concise International History*. New York: Oxford University Press.

Leary, Lewis Gaston (1912) *Andorra: The Hidden Republic—Its Origins and Institutions, and the Record of a Journey Thither*. New York: McBride Nast.

Lee, Chae-Jin (1996) *China and Korea: Dynamic Relations*. Palo Alto, CA: Hoover Institution Press.

Levi, Margaret, Matthew Moe, and Theresa Buckley (2004) "The Transaction Costs of Distrust: Labor and Management Relations at the National Labor Relations Board." in *Distrust*, edited by Russell Hardin, 106–35. New York: Russell Sage Foundation.

LGT (2015) Facts and Figures. Available at https://www.lgt.com/en/lgt-group/facts-x-figures/. Accessed March 10, 2015.

Li, Xiaobing (2014) *China's Battle for Korea: The 1951 Spring Offensive*. Bloomington: Indiana University Press.

Liberal Party of Canada (2015) "Liberals Repeat Call on Harper to Release TPP Deal." October 20. Available at https://www.liberal.ca/liberals-repeat-call-on-harper-to-release-tpp-deal/. Accessed October 21, 2015.

Libertas (2015a) "Il cammino di un'idea: Come San Marino si è salvato." Available at http://www.libertas.sm/libri/cammino/cam_11.htm. Accessed May 11, 2015.

Libertas (2015b) "1971: La fine dell'amicizia protettrice." Available at http://www.libertas.sm/libri/Bigi/bi_2htm. Accessed May 11, 2015.

Liechtenstein (2001) *Report on Follow-up to the World Summit for Children*. March 6, Vaduz. Available at: http://www.unicef.org/specialsession/how_country/edr_liechtenstein_en.doc. Accessed March 13, 2013.

Liechtenstein (2014) Embassy of the Principality of Liechtenstein in Washington, DC. "Liechtenstein History." Available at http://www.liechtensteinusa.org/index.php?page=history. Accessed March 3, 2014.

Liechtenstein, US Embassy (2012) Embassy of the Principality of Liechtenstein in Washington, DC. "100 Years of Liechtenstein Postage Stamps." Available at http://www.liechtensteinusa.org/index.php?mact=CGBlog,cntnt01,detail,0&cntnt01articleid=28&cntnt01returnid=123. Accessed March 30, 2014.

Liechtenstein v. Guatemala (1955) International Court of Justice, judgment of April 6.

Liechtensteiner Vaterland (2003) Article on the prince's response to the Council of Europe's criticism. February 15.

Liechtensteiner Vaterland (2015) "Employees Shall Pay the Price for the Strong Swiss Franc." January 25, page 1.

Lindsell, Jonathan (2015) "The Norwegian Way: A Case Study for Britain's Future Relationship with the EU." *Civitas: Institute for the Study of Civil Society*, February.

Lipson, Charles (2003) *Reliable Partners: How Democracies Have Made a Separate Peace*. Princeton: Princeton University Press.

Lisimachio, Georges (1983) *La Principauté de Monaco: un État souverain*. Thèse de droit public soutenue à Nice le 21 février.

Llobet, Salvador (1947) *El Medio y la Vida en Andorra: Estudio geográfico*. Barcelona: Industrial Gráfica.

Lomas, Ulrika (2012) "Liechtenstein FMA Seeks Stronger Ties with Switzerland." *Tax News Brussels*. Available at http://www.tax-news.com/news/Liechtenstein_FMA_Seeks_Stronger_Ties_With_Switzerland___58832.html. Accessed November 5, 2013.

Lorenz, Pierre-Louis (2013) "Luxembourg." In *Strategic Cultures in Europe: Security and Defence Policies Across the Continent*, edited by Heiko Biehl, Bastian Giegerich, and Alexandra Jonas, 229–42. New York: Springer.

Lubell, Mark (2007) "Familiarity Breeds Trust: Collective Action in a Policy Domain." *Journal of Politics* 69, no. 1 (February): 237–50.

Lucas, Edward (2009) *The New Cold War: Putin's Russia and the Threat to the West*. New York: Palgrave Macmillan.

Macy, Michael (2007) "Cooperation Without Trust? Review." *Social Forces* 86, no. 2 (December): 851–53.

Magone, José M. (2017) *The Statecraft of Consensus Democracies in a Turbulent World: A Comparative Study of Austria, Belgium, Luxembourg, the Netherlands and Switzerland*. New York: Routledge.

Majerus, Jean-Marie (2011) "Pierre Wener & Gaston Thorn: La Perception de la Politique Européene du Luxembourg dans the Annees 1970." In *Quelles Architectures Pour Quelle Europe? Des Projets d'une Europe Unie à l'Union Européenne (1945–1992). Actes des duexième journées d'études de la Maison de Robert Schuman, Metz, 9–11 Mai, 2010*, edited by Sylvain Schirmann, 45–64. New York: P.I.E. Peter Lang.

Malin, George (2007) "200 Jahren Liechtenstein Fürstentum Souveranität." *Liechtenstein Politische Schriften Band* 42: 225–50.

Marshall, Andrew (1993) "The Single Market, Political Geography and Anomalies." *IBRU Boundary and Security Bulletin* (October): 657–61.

Martin, Lawrence (1993) *Pledge of Allegiance: The Americanization of Canada in the Mulroney Years*. Toronto: McClelland & Stewart.

Martin, Lisa (2000) *Democratic Commitments: Legislatures and International Cooperation*. Princeton: Princeton University Press.

Maten, Maria (2013) Vice chair of the International Relations Committee, Andorran General Council. Former minister of foreign affairs. Interview with the author, May 16, Andorra-la-Vella.

Matlock, Jack F. Jr. (2004) *Reagan and Gorbachev: How the Cold War Ended*. New York: Random House.

McDonald, Marci (1993) *Taking Orders: How the U.S. Shaped Canada's Foreign Policy*. Toronto: Atkinson Charitable Foundation.

McGregor, Janyce (2015) "TPP Deal Protects Canadian Jobs, Stephen Harper Says." CBC News, October 5, 2015. Available at http://www.cbc.ca/news/politics/canada-election-2015-tpp-agreement-atlanta-1.3254569. Accessed October 5, 2015.

McKenzie, Baker (2016) "New Double Tax Treaty between Spain and the Principality of Andorra." *Lexology*, March 8. Available at http://www.lexology.com/library/detail.aspx?g=1974af2c-719c-443a-b2c9–7a81a2ce084f. Accessed January 28, 2017.

McNamara, Robert S., James Blight, Robert Brigham, Thomas Bietsteker, and Col. Herbert Schandler (1999) *Argument Without End: In Search of Answers to the Vietnam Tragedy*. New York: Public Affairs.

Meade, James E. (1957) "Negotiations for Benelux: An Annotated Chronicle 1943–1956." *Princeton Studies in International Finance* no. 6.

Mearsheimer, John (1994/95) "The False Promise of International Institutions." *International Security* 19, no. 3 (Winter): 5–49.

Meehan, Elizabeth (1993) "Citizenship and the European Community." *Political Quarterly* 62, no. 2 (April-June): 172–86.

Micó, Joan (2013) Director of sociology, Andorran Studies Institute. Interview with the author. May 17, Santa Julià de Lòria, Andorra

Middlemas, Keith (1995) *Orchestrating Europe: The Informal Politics of the European Union 1973–1995*. New York: Fontana Press.

Miller, Edward (2013) *Misalliance: Ngo Dinh Diem, the United States, and the Far of South Vietnam*. Cambridge, MA: Harvard University Press.

Mills, Kelly-Ann (2016) "North Korea Begs World for Aid After Devastating Floods Despite Spending Millions on Nuclear Weapons." *Mirror*, September 16. Available at http://www.mirror.co.uk/news/world-news/north-korea-begs-world-aid-8847251. Accessed September 19, 2016.

Ministère des affaires étrangères, France (2013) *Projet de loi autorisant l'approbation de la convention entre le Gouvernement de la République française et le Gouvernement de la Principauté d'Andorre en vue d'éviter les doubles impositions et de prévenir l'évasion et la fraude fiscale en matière d'impôts sur le revenu*. NOR: MAEJ1401144L/Bleue-1. Paris.

Monaco, Principality of (1918) "Letter from Envoy Extraordinary and Minister Plenipotentiary of the Principality of Monaco Count Balny d'Avricourt to Mr. Stephen Pinchon, Senator, Minister for Foreign Affairs of the French Republic." July 17, Paris.

Monaco, Principality of (1953) "Ordonnance n. 758 du 01/06/1953 rendant exécutoire la convention signée à Paris le 1er avril 1950 tendant à éviter les doubles impositions et à codifier les règles d'assistance en matière successorale." Monaco.

Monaco, Principality of (1963a) "Ordonnance n. 3.037 du 19/08/1963 rendant exécutoire à Monaco la Convention fiscale signée à Paris le 18 mai 1963." Monaco.

Monaco, Principality of (1963b) "Ordonnance n. 3.038 du 19/08/1963 rendant exécutoire à Monaco la Convention douanière signée à Paris le 18 mai 1963." Monaco.

Monaco, Principality of (1963c) "Ordonnance n. 3.039 du 19/08/1963 rendant exécutoire à Monaco la Convention de voisinage signée à Paris le 18 mai 1963." Monaco.

Monaco, Principality of (1972) "Ordonnance n. 4.919 du 18/05/1972 rendant exécutoire l'échange de lettres franco-monégasques du 6 août 1971 modifiant les règles de partage des recouvrements de taxes sur le chiffre d'affaires, fixées par l'échange de lettres annexé à la convention fiscale du 18 mai 1963." Monaco.

Monaco, Principality of (1999) "Ordonnance n. 13.916 du 01/03/1999 rendant exécutoires les dispositions de léchange de lettres franco-monégasques concernant l'introduction de l'Euro à Monaco." Monaco.

Monaco, Principality of (2000a) "Ordonnance n. 14.513 du 20/06/2000 rendant exécutoire l'échange de lettres relatif à l'application de l'article 7 modifié de la convention de voisinage signée à Paris le 18 mai 1963." Monaco.

Monaco, Principality of (2000b) "Ordonnance n. 14.513 du 20/06/2000 rendant exécutoire l'échange de lettres relatif à l'application de l'article 10 modifié de la convention de voisinage signée à Paris le 18 mai 1963." Monaco.

Monaco, Principality of (2001) "Ordonnance n. 14.892 du 28/05/2001 rendant exécutoire l'accord sous forme d'échange de lettres concernant la surveillance harmonisée des établissements de crédit de la Principauté de Monaco, sous forme de filiale ou de succursale." Monaco.

Monaco, Principality of (2006a) "Ordonnance n. 407 du 15/02/2006 rendant exécutoire le Traité déstiné à adapter et à confirmer les rapports d'amitié et de cooperation entre la Principauté de Monaco et la République française, signée à Paris le 24 octobre 2002." Monaco.

Monaco, Principality of (2006b) "Avenant à la Convention fiscale entre le gouvernement de Son Altesse Sérénissime le Prince de Monaco et le governement de la République française, signé à Paris le 18 mai 1963 et modifiée par l'avenant du 25 juin 1969, signé à Monaco le 26 mai 2003." Annexé au Journal de Monaco #7.741, 3 février.

Monaco, Principality—Office of Communication (2016) "Etat des négociations entre Monaco et l'Union européenne." Circa June 1.

Monaco Life (2016) "Minister of State discusses Monaco's EU negotiations with Euronet." Available at http://www.monacolife.net/?p=5603. Accessed May 31, 2017.

Montinola, Garbriella R. (2004) "Corruption, Distrust and the Deterioration of the Rule of Law." In *Distrust*, edited by Russell Hardin, 298–323. New York: Russell Sage Foundation.

Moore, Gregory J. (2014) "Beijing's Problem with an Operationally Nuclear North Korea." In *North Korean Nuclear Operationality: Regional Security & Nonprolifera-*

tion, edited by Gregory J. Moore and Graham T. Allison, 77–103. Baltimore: Johns Hopkins University Press.

Moore, Jack (2016) "North Korea Threatens 'Physical Action' Over U.S. Anti-Missile System." *Newsweek*, July 11. Available at: http://www.newsweek.com/north-korea-threatens-physical-action-us-anti-missile-system-479267. Accessed July 11, 2016.

Moravcsik, Andrew (1998) *The Choice for Europe: Social Purpose and State Power from Messina to Maastricht*. Ithaca: Cornell University Press.

Moravcsik, Andrew (2000) "The Origins of Human Rights Regimes: Democratic Delegation in Postwar Europe." *International Organization* 54, no. 2 (Spring): 217–52.

Moravcsik, Andrew (2004) "Is There a 'Democratic Deficit' in World Politics? A Framework for Analysis." *Government and Opposition* 39, no. 2: 336–63.

Morello, Carol (2016) "Iran Nuclear Deal Could Collapse under Trump." *Washington Post*, November 9. Available at https://www.washingtonpost.com/world/national-security/iran-nuclear-deal-could-collapse-under-trump/2016/11/09/f2d2bd02-a68c-11e6-ba59-a7d93165c6d4_story.html?utm_term=.936ed984b969. Accessed December 30, 2016.

Moshes, Arkady (2003) "Lukashenka's Role in Russian Politics." In *Independent Belarus: Domestic Determinants, Regional Dynamics, and Implications for the West*, edited by Margarita M. Balmaceda, James I. Clem, and Lisbeth L. Tarlow, 197–221. Cambridge, MA: Harvard University Press/Ukrainian Research Institute and Davis Center for Russian Studies.

Muirhead, Bruce (2004) "From Special Relationship to Third Option: Canada, the U.S., and the Nixon shock." *American Review of Canadian Studies* (Autumn): 439–62.

Mullins, Christopher W. (2011) "War Crimes in the 2008 Georgia-Russia Conflict." *British Journal of Criminology* 51: 918–36.

Museo San Marin (2014) Exhibit on San Marino history. San Marino.

Musi, Aurelio (2003) "L'Italia dal Sacro Romano Impero allo Stato nazionale." In *Il Piccolo Stato: Politica, Storia, Diplomazia*, edited by Laura Barletta, Franco Cardini, and Guiseppe Galasso, 171–96. Sarravalle, San Marino: AIEP Editore.

Nanto, Dick K., and Mark E. Manyin (2011) "China-North Korea Relations." *North Korea Review* 7, no. 2 (Fall): 94–101.

Narveson, Jan (1971) "Promising, Expecting, and Utility." *Canadian Journal of Philosophy* 1, no. 2 (December): 207–330.

Nasmyth, Peter (1992) *Georgia: A Rebel in the Caucasus*. London: Cassell.

National Archives (2015) Statistical Information about Fatal Casualties of the Vietnam War. Available at http://www.archives.gov/research/military/vietnam-war/casualty-statistics.html. Accessed July 6, 2015.

National Defense—Government of Canada (2016) "Canadian Armed Forces Expands Contribution to Global Coalition to Defeat ISIL." May 19. Available at: http://news.gc.ca/web/article-en.do?mthd=index&crtr.page=9&nid=1068259. Accessed January 17, 2017.

National Post (2001) "PM Links Attacks to 'Arrogant' West," September 13. Available at http://www.nationalpost.com/home/story.html?id=758F9920-A876-4A04-85AF-5B93736230F1. Accessed September 18, 2015.

NATO (1989) *The North Atlantic Treaty Organization: Facts and Figures*. Brussels: NATO.

Nesvetailova, Anastasia (2003) "Russia and Belarus: The Quest for the Union; or Who Will Pay for Belarus's Path to Recovery." In *Contemporary Belarus: Between Democracy and Dictatorship*, edited by Elena A. Korosteleva, Colin W. Lawson, and Rosalind J. Marsh, 152–64. London: Routledge Carzon.

New York Times (1910) "Is Monaco Doomed? Other Nations Want It." December 11.

New York Times (1971) *The Pentagon Papers as Published by the New York Times Based on Reporting by Neil Sheehan*. New York: Bantam Books.

Newcomer, John (1984) *The Grand Duchy of Luxembourg: The Evolution of Nationhood, 963–1983*. Lanham, MD: University Press of America.

Newman, Michael (1996) *Democracy, Sovereignty and the European Union*. New York: St. Martin's Press.

Nichol, Jim (2008) *Russia-Georgia Conflict in South Ossetia: Context and Implications for U.S. Interests*. Congressional Research Service RL34618, October 24. Washington, DC: Government Printing Office.

Nichol, Jim (2009) *Georgia [Republic] and NATO Enlargement: Issues and Implications*. Congressional Research Service 7–5700, RS22829, March 6. Washington, DC: Government Printing Office.

Nikonov, Vyacheslav (1999) "The Place of Belarus on Russia's Foreign Policy Agenda." In *Belarus at the Crossroads*, edited by Sherman W. Garnett and Robert Legvold, 105–29. Washington: Carnegie Endowment for International Peace.

Nodia, Ghia, and Álvaro Pinto Scholtbach (2006) *The Political Landscape of Georgia: Political Parties: Achievements, Challenges and Prospects*. Delft: Eburon.

Noesselt, Nele (2014) "China's Contradictory Role(s) in World Politics: Decrypting China's North Korea Strategy." *Third World Quarterly* 35, no. 7: 1307–25.

Non-Proliferation of Nuclear Weapons (1995) Letter dated April 17, 1995 from the representatives of France, the Russian Federation, the United Kingdom of Great Britain and Northern Ireland, and the United States of America addressed to the Secretary-General of the 1995 Review and Extension Conference of the parties to the Treaty on the Non-Proliferation of Nuclear Weapons. NPT/CONF.1995/20 April 19, 1995.

Nooteboom, Bart (2002) *Trust: Forms, Foundations, Functions, Failures and Figures*. Cheltenham: Edward Elgar.

NORAD (2005) Continental Air Command Historical Summary, July 1956–June 1957. Available at http://www.northcom.mil/Portals/28/Documents/Supporting%20documents/(U)%201956-1957%20NORAD%20CONAD%20History.pdf. Accessed February 16, 2017.

NORAD (2012) *A Brief History of NORAD*. Office of History. Colorado Springs, CO.

Nugent, Nigel (1989) *The Government and Politics of the European Community*. Durham, NC: Duke University Press.

Oddone, David (2014) Interview with the author. *La Tribuna Sammarinese*. June 25, San Marino.

OECD (2009a) *Agreement between the Government of the United States of America and the Government of the Principality of Monaco for the Exchange of Information Relat-*

ing to Tax Matters. September 8. Available at: http://www.oecd.org/countries/monaco/43662746.pdf. Accessed May 6, 2015.

OECD (2009b) "Andorra, Liechtenstein and Monaco removed from OECD List of Unco-operative Tax Havens," April 3. Available at http://www.oecd.org/countries/monaco/andorraliechtensteinandmonacoremovedfromoecdlistofunco-operativetaxhavens.htm. Accessed May 26, 2015.

OECD (2009c) "The Liechtenstein Declaration." Available at http://www.oecd.org/general/42340216.pdf. Accessed March 25, 2013.

OECD (2011) *Supplementary Peer Review Report, Phase 1, Legal and Regulatory Framework: Monaco*. Paris: OECD.

OECD (2013) "Andorra Deepens Commitment to Fight Offshore Tax Avoidance and Evasion," May 11. Available at http://www.oecd.org/countries/andorra/andorra-deepens-commitment-to-fight-offshore-tax-avoidance-and-evasion.htm. Accessed May 26, 2015.

OECD (2014a) "Andorra Commits to Automatic Exchange of Information in Tax Matters." Available at http://www.oecd.org/countries/andorra/andorra-commits-to-automatic-exchange-of-information-in-tax-matters.htm. Accessed May 26, 2015.

OECD (2014b) "Monaco Deepens Commitment to Fight Offshore Tax Avoidance and Evasion." October 10. Available at http://www.oecd.org/newsroom/monaco-deepens-commitment-to-fight-offshore-tax-avoidance-and-evasion.htm. Accessed May 6, 2015.

Olson, James S., and Randy Roberts (2008) *Where the Domino Fell: America and Vietnam, 1945–1995*. 5th ed. Malden, MA: Blackwell.

Olson, Mancur, and Richard Zeckhauser (1966) "An Economic Theory of Alliances." *Review of Economics and Statistics* 48 (August): 266–79.

Oneal, John (1990) "The Theory of Collective Action and Burden Sharing in NATO." *International Organization* 44, no. 3 (Summer): 379–402.

Orbell, John M., Alphonse J. van der Krugt, and Robyn M. Dawes (1991) "Covenants Without the Sword: The Role of Promises in Social Dilemma Circumstances." In *Social Norms and Economic Institutions*, edited by Kenneth J. Koford and Jeffrey B. Miller, 117–33. Ann Arbor: University of Michigan Press.

Osborne, Lucy (2012) "How 2,000 Britons Living in Monaco Are Costing UK £1bn a Year in Lost Taxes." *Daily Mail*, September 19. Available at http://www.dailymail.co.uk/news/article-2205884/How-2–000-Britons-living-Monaco-costing-UK-1bn-year-lost-taxes.html. Accessed May 6, 2015.

Osgood, Charles (1962) "Reciprocal Initiative." in *The Liberal Papers*, edited by James Roosevelt. Garden City, NY: Anchor Books.

Otarashvili, Maia (2015) "Russia's Quiet Annexation of South Ossetia." *Foreign Policy Research Institute E-Notes*. February. Philadelphia: Foreign Policy Research Institute.

Out-Law (2004) "Princess Caroline of Monaco Wins Privacy Ruling." June 28. Available at http://www.out-law.com/page-4663. Accessed May 6, 2015.

Owen, John M. (1997) *Liberal Peace, Liberal War: American Politics and International Security*. Ithaca: Cornell University Press.

Pace, Julie (2016) "Trump Signals Shift from Obama's Focus on Multilateralism." Associated Press, December 28th. Available at: http://www.realclearpolitics.

com/articles/2016/12/28/trump_signals_shift_from_obamas_focus_on_multilateralism_132658.html. Accessed December 29, 2016.

Panke, Diana (2010) *Small States in the European Union: Coping with Structural Disadvantages*. Farnham, UK: Ashgate.

Pauly, Louis B. (2003) "Canada in a New North America." In *The Rebordering of North America: Integration and Exclusion in a New Security Context*, edited by Peter Andreas and Thomas J. Biersteker, 90–109. New York: Routledge.

Pearson, James (2014) "Front Companies, Embassies Mask North Korean Weapons Trade," Reuters: World. March 11. Available at http://www.reuters.com/article/2014/03/11/us-korea-korea-un-idUSBREA2A08020140311. Accessed August 11, 2015.

Pearson, L. B. (1989/1951) "Canada, the United States, and Korea, 1951." In *Partners Nevertheless: Canadian-American Relations in the Twentieth Century*, edited by Norman Hillmer, 108–15. Toronto: Copp Clark Pitman Ltd.

Pelkmans, Jacques, and Philipp Böhler (2013) *The EEA Review and Liechtenstein's Integration Strategy*. Brussels: Center for European Policy Studies.

Péporté, Pit, Sonja Kmec, Benoît Majerus, and Michel Margue (2010) *Inventing Luxembourg: Representations of the Past, Space and Language from the Nineteenth to the Twenty-First Century*. Leiden: Brill.

Peppers, Don, and Martha Rogers (2012) *Extreme Trust: Honesty as a Comparative Advantage*. New York: Penguin.

Perepelitsa, Hrihoriy (1999) "Belarusian-Russian Integration and Its Impact on the Security of Ukraine." In *Belarus at the Crossroads*, edited by Sherman W. Garnett and Robert Legvold, 81–103. Washington: Carnegie Endowment for International Peace.

Perras, Galen Roger (1998) *Franklin Roosevelt and the Origins of the Canadian-American Security Alliance, 1933–1945: Necessary, But Not Necessary Enough*. Westport, CT: Praeger.

Perrett, David (2010) "Why Women Fall for Men Who Look Like Their Father . . . and Other Astonishing Secrets of the Science of Attraction." *Daily Mail*, September 23. Available at: http://www.dailymail.co.uk/femail/article-1314344/Why-women-fall-men-look-like-father.html. Accessed October 12, 2015.

Perron, Celeste (2009) "Why You're Likely to Marry Your Parent." CNN, February 11. Available at: http://www.cnn.com/2009/LIVING/personal/02/11/lw.programmed.,to.marry.parents/. Accessed October 12, 2015.

Pervez, Muhammed S. (2013) *Security Community in South Asia: India-Pakistan*. London: Routledge.

Phinnemore, David (2013) *The Treaty of Lisbon: Origins and Negotiation*. Basingstoke: Palgrave Macmillan.

Pirchner, Herman, Jr. (2005) *Reviving Greater Russia? The Future of Russia's Borders with Belarus, Georgia, Kazakhstan, Moldova and Ukraine*. Lanham, MD: University Press of America.

Plant, Thomas, and Ben Rhode (2013) "China, North Korea and the Spread of Nuclear Weapons." *Survival* 55, no. 2 (April–May): 61–80.

Politico (2016) "Full Transcript: Third Presidential Debate—October 20, 2016." Available at http://www.politico.com/story/2016/10/full-transcript-third-2016-presidential-debate-230063. Accessed December 30, 2016.

Pollin, Edra J. (2012) "When Does Cohabitation Become a Common Law Marriage?" *Huffington Post*, January 5. Available at http://www.huffingtonpost.com/edra-j-pollin/when-does-cohabitation-be_b_1184994.html. Accessed June 21, 2016.

Popescu, Nicu (2006) "'Outsourcing' De Facto Statehood: Russia and the Secessionist Entities in Georgia and Moldova." Center for European Policy Studies: Policy Brief. July.

Portes, Alejandro (1998) "Social Capital: Its Origins and Applications in Modern Sociology." *Annual Review of Sociology* 24: 1–24.

Potolidis-Beck, Panagiotis (2013) Diplomatic officer, Office for Foreign Affairs, Principality of Liechtenstein. Interview with the author, May 9, Vaduz.

Potolidis-Beck, Panagiotis (2015) Diplomatic officer, Office for Foreign Affairs, Principality of Liechtenstein, correspondence with the author, March 11.

Potter, Nancy Nyquist (2002) *How Can I Be Trusted? A Virtue Theory of Trustworthiness*. Lanham, MD: Rowman & Littlefield.

Pouliot, Vincent (2016) *International Pecking Orders: The Politics and Practice of Multilateral Diplomacy*. New York: Cambridge University Press.

Pratt, Michael G. (2007) "Promises, Contracts and Voluntary Obligations." *Law & Philosophy* 26, no. 6 (November): 531–74.

Preston, Richard A. (1977) *The Defence of the Undefended Border: Planning for War in North America 1867–1939*. Montreal: McGill-Queen's University Press.

Pritchard, Charles L. (2007) *Failed Diplomacy: The Tragic Story of How North Korea Got the Bomb*. Washington, DC: Brookings Institution.

Pryce, Roy (1973) *The Politics of the European Community*. London: Butterworths.

Putnam, Robert (2000) *Bowling Alone: The Collapse and Revival of American Community*. New York: Simon & Schuster.

Quaderer, Rupert (2000) "Jahre der Retardation: Liechtensteins innenpolitische Entwicklung 1815–1848." In *Liechtenstein und die Revolution 1848*, edited by Arthur Brunhart, 61–76. Chronos: Zurich.

Radio Free Asia (2015a) "North Korea Discharges Soldiers Amid Wider Military Downsize." July 20. Available at http://www.rfa.org/english/news/korea/discharges-07172015142820.html. Accessed August 11, 2015.

Radio Free Asia (2015b) "Kim Jong Un Orders North Korean Markets to Get Rid of Foreign Products." July 17. Available at http://www.rfa.org/english/korea/kim-jong-un-orders-north-korean-markets-to-get-rid-of-foreign-products-07172015144036.html. Accessed August 11, 2015.

Radio Free Europe (2015) "Obama Says Iran Nuclear Deal Relies On Verification, Not Trust." August 28. Available at http://www.rferl.org/a/obama-iran-deal-relies-on-verification/27214668.html. Accessed December 30, 2016.

Radoman, Milena (2013) "La BNP Paribas Monaco dans le Collimateur." *Monaco Hebdo*, May 15, 22–23.

Raeder, Vadin (2004) "Coping with Distrust in Emerging Russian Markets." in *Distrust*, edited by Russell Hardin, 233–48. New York: Russell Sage Foundation.

Rathbun, Brian C. (2009) "It Takes All Types: Social Psychology, Trust and the International Relations Paradigm in Our Minds." *International Theory* 1, no. 3 (Summer): 345–80.

Rathbun, Brian C. (2011) "The 'Magnificent Fraud': Trust, International Cooperation, and the Hidden Domestic Politics of American Multilateralism after World War II." *International Studies Quarterly* 55, no. 1 (March): 1–21.

Rathbun, Brian C. (2012) *Trust in International Cooperation: International Security Institutions, Domestic Politics and American Multilateralism*. New York: Cambridge University Press.

Raton, Pierre (1970) *Liechtenstein: History and Institutions of the Principality*. Vaduz: Liechtenstein-Verlag.

Rawls, John (1955) "Two Concepts of Rules." *The Philosophical Review* 74, no. 1 (January): 3–32.

Ray, Hemen (1983) *China's Vietnam War*. New Delhi: Radiant Publishers.

Raz, Joseph (1982) "Promises in Morality and Law: Review." *Harvard Law Review* 95, no. 4 (February): 916–38.

Reixach, Jaume (2015) "The Co-Princes of Andorra Kidnap the Future." March 16. Available at http://www.eltriangle.eu/cat/notices/2015/03/els-coprinceps-segresten-el-futur-d-andorra-40501.php. Accessed May 26, 2015.

Reuters (2015) "China Denies Rushing Forces to Border During Korean Tensions." August 27. Available at http://www.reuters.com/article/2015/08/27/us-china-northkorea-idUSKCN0QW12Y20150827?feedType=RSS&feedName=topNews. Accessed August 31, 2015.

Risse, Thomas, Stephen C. Ropp, and Kathryn Sikkink (1999) *The Power of Human Rights: International Norms and Domestic Change*. New York: Cambridge University Press.

Roberts, John (1989) "Acid Rain: The Poison in Canadian-American Relations." In *Friends So Different: Essays on Canada and the United States in the 1980s*, edited by Lansing Lamont and J. Duncan Edmonds, 75–82. Ottawa: University of Ottawa Press.

Rontoyanni, Clelia (2005) "Belarus and the East." In *Postcommunist Belarus*, edited by Stephen White, Elena Korosteleva, and John Löwenhardt, 123–42. Lanham, MD: Rowman & Littlefield.

Ropp, Theodore (1963) "Politics, Strategy, and the Commitments of a Middle Power." In *Canada-United States Treaty Relations*, edited by David R. Deener, 81–101. Durham, NC: Duke University Press.

Ross, Robert S. (1988) *The Indochina Triangle: China's Vietnam Policy, 1975–1979*. New York: Columbia University Press.

Rothstein, Bo (2011) *The Quality of Government: Corruption, Social Trust, and Inequality in International Perspective*. Chicago: University of Chicago Press.

Roussel, Stéphane (2004) *The North American Democratic Peace: Absence of War and Security Institution-Building in Canada-US Relations, 1867–1958*. Montreal: McGill-Queen's University Press.

Rowen, Meredith, and Gerard A. Finin (2010) "Trust in Government in the Pacific Islands." In *Building Trust in Government: Innovations in Governance Reform in Asia*, edited by G. Shabbir Cheema and Vesselin Popovski, 134–65. New York: United Nations University Press.

Rozanov, Anatoly (1999) "Belarus: Foreign Policy Priorities." In *Belarus at the Crossroads*, edited by Sherman W. Garnett and Robert Legvold, 19–35. Washington, DC: Carnegie Endowment for International Peace.

RTT News (2014) "Talks On EU Association Agreement With Andorra, Monaco and San Marino Authorized," December 16. Available at http://www.rttnews.com/2431758/talks-on-eu-association-agreement-with-andorra-monaco-and-san-marino-authorized.,aspx. Accessed May 22, 2015.

Rudling, Per Anders (2008) "Belarus in the Lukashenka Era: National Identity and Relations with Russia." In *Belarus, Moldova, and Ukraine between Russia and the European Union*, edited by Oliver Schmidtke and Serhy Yekelchyk, 55–77. New York: Palgrave Macmillan.

Russell, Mary (1991) *Please Don't Call it Soviet Georgia: A Journey Through a Troubled Paradise*. London: Serpent's Tail.

Russett, Bruce, and John Oneal (2000) *Triangulating Peace: Democracy, Interdependence, and International Organizations*. New York: W. W. Norton.

Ruzicka, Jan, and Nicholas J. Wheeler (2010) "The Puzzle of Trusting Relationships in the Nuclear Non-Proliferation Treaty." *International Affairs* 86, no. 1 (January): 69–85.

Ryzhkov, Vladimir (2014) "The New Putin Doctrine." *Moscow Times*, April 3. Available at http://www.themoscowtimes.com/opinion/article/the-new-putin-doctrine/497316.html. Accessed July 16, 2015.

Saakashvili, Mikheil (2005) "Interview with Mikheil Saakashvili." in *"Enough!": The Rose Revolution and the Republic of Georgia 2003*, edited by Zurab Karumidze and James V. Wertsch, 23–28. New York: Nova Science.

Sadowski, Rafal (2009) "Belarus Between the European Union and Russia: The Polish Perspective." in *Belarus: External Pressure, Internal Change*, edited by Hans-Georg Heinrich and Ludmilla Lobova, 177–91. Frankfurt: Peter Lang.

San Marino Site (2015) San Marino History: Eighteenth Century and Garibaldi. Available at: http://www.sanmarinosite.com/en/history/eighteenth-century/. Accessed May 18, 2015.

San Marino, Republic of (2015) Ministry of Foreign Affairs—Bilateral Conventions between San Marino and Italy. Available at http://www.esteri.sm/on-line/en/home/foreign-affairs/international-treaties/bilateral-conventions/bilateral-conventions---bilateral-agreements-with-italy.html. Accessed May 11, 2015.

Sandholtz, Wayne, and Kendall Stiles (2009) *International Norms and Cycles of Change*. New York: Oxford University Press.

Sandler, Todd (2004) *Global Collective Action*. New York: Cambridge University Press.

Sandler, Todd, and Keith Hartley (1999) *The Political Economy of NATO: Past, Present, and Into the 21st Century*. New York: Cambridge University Press.

Sandler, Todd, and Hirofumi Shimizu (2014) "NATO Burden Sharing 1999–2010: An Altered Alliance." *Foreign Policy Analysis* 10: 43–60.

Sands, Christopher (2012) "Has Obama Really 'Lost Canada'?" *Huffington Post Canada*. Available at http://www.huffingtonpost.ca/christopher-sands/how-obama-lost-canada_b_1627876.html. Accessed July 23, 2015.

Sang-hun, Choe (2015) "North Korea Moves Forces amid Talks with South," *New York Times*, August 23. Available at http://www.nytimes.com/2015/08/24/world/asia/with-force-deployments-north-korea-raises-stakes-of-talks-with-south.html. Accessed August 31, 2015.

Sang-sook, Lee (2011) "North Korea-China Treaty of Friendship: New Implications and Current Bilateral Relation." *Korea Focus*, November 11. Available at http://www.koreafocus.or.kr/design2/layout/content_print.asp?group_id=103907. Accessed August 4, 2015.

Sannikov, Andrei (2003) "Russia's Varied Roles in Belarus." in *Independent Belarus: Domestic Determinants, Regional Dynamics, and Implications for the West*, edited by Margarita M. Balmaceda, James I. Clem, and Lisbeth L. Tarlow, 221–31. Cambridge, MA: Harvard University Press/Ukrainian Research Institute and Davis Center for Russian Studies.

Savchenko, Andrew (2009) *Belarus: A Perpetual Borderland*. Leiden: Brill.

Scalbert, Augustin (2010) "Le co-prince Nicolas Sarkozy fraîchement attendu en Andorre." *L'Obs*. Available at http://tempsreel.nouvelobs.com/rue89/rue89-politique/20100728.RUE7759/le-co-prince-nicolas-sarkozy-fraichement-attendu-en-andorre.html. Accessed May 31, 2017.

Scanlon, Thomas (1990) "Promises and Practices," *Philosophy and Public Affairs* 19, no. 3 (Summer): 199–226.

Schoon, Ingrid, and Helen Cheng (2011) "Determinants of Political Trust: A Lifetime Learning Model." *Developmental Psychology* 47, no. 3: 619–31.

Scobell, Andrew (2004) *China and North Korea: From Comrades-in-Arms to Allies at Arm's Length*. Carlisle, PA: Strategic Studies Institute.

Seger, Otto (1978) "History." In *The Principality of Liechtenstein: A Documentary Handbook*, 4th edition, edited by Walter Kranz. Translated by C. D. C. Martin, 7–24. Schann: Buch U. Offsetbruckerei.

Seger, Paul (2013) Permanent representative to the United Nations, former ambassador to Liechtenstein, Swizz Federation. Interview with the author, March 5, Provo, Utah.

Seigel, Robert (2016) "The View from Luxembourg, where a 'Brexit' is Unthinkable." *National Public Radio*, June 20. Available at http://www.npr.org/sections/parallels/2016/06/20/482772593/the-view-from-luzembourg-where-a-brexit-is-unthinkable?ft=nprml&f-1001. Accessed January 17, 2017.

Selva, Alvaro (2012) *Storia delle Instituzioni Della Repubblica di San Marino*. Sarravalle, San Marino: AIEP Editore.

Selva, Alvaro (2014) Professor of legal studies, University of San Marino and former senior government official. Interview with the author, June 25, San Marino.

Senate, United States (2008) *Russia's Aggression against Georgia: Consequences and responses: Hearing before the Committee on Foreign Relations*. September 17. Available at http://www.gpo.gov/fdsys/pkg/CHRG-110shrg46828/html/CHRG-110shrg46828.htm. Accessed August 10, 2015.

Senate, United States (2012) *China's Impact on Korean Peninsula Unification and Questions for the Senate: A Minority Staff Report prepared for the use of the Committee on Foreign Relations, December 11*. 77–566 PDF. Washington: Government Printing Office.

Sengupta, Somini and Choe Sang-hun (2016) "U.N. Toughens Sanctions on North Korea in Response to Its Nuclear Program." *New York Times*, March 2. Available at http://www.nytimes.com/2016/03/30/world/asia/north-korea-un-sanctions.html?_r=0. Accessed March 7, 2016.

Sengupta, Somini, and Jane Perez (2016) "U.N. Stiffens Sanctions on North Korea." *New York Times*, December 1, A4.

Serra, Eva (2008) "The Treaty of the Pyrenees, 350 Year Later." *Catalan Historical Review* 1: 81–99.

Servei de Politicá Lingüística (2011) *Coneixements i Usos Lingüístics de la Població d'Andorra: Situació actual i evolució (1995–2009)*. Andorra: Govern d'Andorra.

Severini, Patrizia Sabbatucci (1995) "Nel cuore dell'Italia. Economia e politica nelle relazioni Italia e San Marino, 1860–1960." In *Sindacato politica economia a San Marino in età contemporanea*, edited by Francesco Casadei, Marco Pelliconi, Laura Rossi and Patrizia Sabbatucci Severini, 123–231. Quaderni del Centro di Studi Storici (n. 12), Ostra Vetere.

Severini, Patrizia Sabbatucci (2003) "Un microstato e il suo tutore: San Marino e l'Italia. 1861–1960." In *Il Piccolo Stato: Politica, storia, diplomazia*, edited by Laura Barletta, Franco Cardini and Guiseppe Galasso, 251–82. Sarravalle, San Marino: AIEP Editore.

Shen, Zhihua, and Yafeng Xia (2012) "China and the Post-War Reconstruction of North Korea, 1953–1961." North Korea International Documentation Project Working Paper #4. May. Princeton: Woodrow Wilson International Center for Scholars.

Shlapentokh, Dmitry (2012) "The Role of Small States in the Post-Cold War Era: The Case of Belarus." In *Belarus: Development, Relations and U.S. Interests*, edited by Alexander T. Gardner and Marcus Payne, 43–95. New York: Nova Science.

Shore, Sean M. (1998) "No Fences Make Good Neighbors: The Development of the Canadian-US Security Community, 1871–1940." In *Security Communities*, edited by Emanuel Adler and Michael Barnett, 333–67. New York: Cambridge University Press.

Silva, Cristina (2016) "North Korea's Kim Jong Un Tells Troops 'Wipe Out South Korea': Will Seoul and Pyongyang Go to War?" *International Business Times*, December 2. Available at: http://www.ibtimes.com/north-koreas-kim-jong-un-tells-troops-wipe-out-south-korea-will-seoul-pyongyang-go-2454096. Accessed December 10, 2016.

Silva, Susana Costa e, Frank Bradley, and Carlos M. P. Sousa (2012) "Empirical Test of the Trust-Performance Link in an International Alliances Context." *International Business Review* 21: 293–306.

Slobodchikoff, Michael O. (2014) *Building Hegemonic Order Russia's Way: Order, Stability and Predictability in the Post-Soviet Space*. London: Lexington Books.

Smith, David J. (2009) "The Saakashvili Administration's Reaction to Russian Policies Before the 2008 War." In *The Guns of August 2008: Russia's War in Georgia*, edited by Svante E. Cornell and S. Frederick Starr, 122–42. London: M. E. Sharpe.

Snyder, Scott (2009) *China's Rise and the Two Koreas: Politics, Economics, Security*. Boulder, CO: Lynne Rienner.

Soldatkin, Vladimir, and Timothy Heritage (2015) "Russian Treaty with Rebel Georgian Region Alarms West." Reuters, March 18. Available at http://www.reuters.com/article/2015/03/18/us-russia-georgia-southossetia-idUSKBN0ME1G620150318. Accessed September 8, 2015.

Stacey, Charles P. (1963) "Twenty-One Years of Canadian-American Military Co-operation." In *Canada-United States Treaty Relations*, edited by David R. Deener, 102–22. Durham, NC: Duke University Press.

Stevenson, Michael D. (2013) "'A Very Careful Balance:' The 1961 Triangular Agreement and the Conduct of Canadian-American Relations." *Diplomacy & Statecraft* 24: 291–311.

Stiles, Kendall (2015) *State Responses to International Law*. New York: Routledge.

Stokes, Bruce (2016) "Republicans, Especially Trump supporters, See Free Trade Deals as Bad for U.S." Pew Research, March 31. Available at http://business insider.com/kim-jong-uns-overseas-billions-2013-3. Accessed November 10, 2017.

Tansill, Charles Callan (1943) *Canadian-American Relations, 1875–1911*. New Haven: Yale University Press.

Taylor, Adam (2013) "Kim Jong-un Estimated to Have Up to $5 Billion in Secret Overseas Accounts." *Business Insider*, March 13. Available at http://business insider.com/kim-jong-uns-overseas-billions-2013-3. Accessed November 10, 2017.

Taylor, Bayard (2002/1876) *La república dels Pirineus/The Republic of the Pyrenees: Andorra 1867*. Andorra: Ministry of Foreign Affairs.

Taylor, James H. (1989) "Bilateral Relations in the Global Context." In *Friends So Different: Essays on Canada and the United States in the 1980s*, edited by Lansing Lamont and J. Duncan Edmonds, 240–50. Ottawa: University of Ottawa Press.

Teacy, W. T. Luke, Michael Luck, Alex Rogers, and Nicholas R. Jennings (2012) "An Efficient and Versatile Approach to Trust and Reputation using Hierarchical Bayesian Modelling." *Artificial Intelligence* 193 (December): 149–85.

Telegraph (2009) "San Marino Turns on Bogus Residents over Tax Avoidance." August 31. Available at http://www.telegraph.co.uk/news/worldnews/europe/sanmarino/6118304/San-Marino-turns-on-bogus-residents-over-tax-avoid ance.html. Accessed May 15, 2015.

Telegraph (2012) "Italians Smuggle Cash into San Marino to Beat Tax Crackdown." By Nick Squires, January 31. Available at http://www.telegraph.co.uk/finance/financialcrisis/9052082/Italians-smuggle-cash-into-San-Marino-to-beat-tax-crackdown.html. Accessed May 15, 2015.

Tessman, Brock, and Wolfe Wojtek (2010) "Great Powers and Strategic Hedging: The Case of Chinese Energy Security Strategy." *International Studies Review* 13, no. 2: 214–40.

Thompson, John H., and Stephen J. Randall (2008) *Canada and the United States: Ambivalent Allies*, 4th ed. Athens: University of Georgia Press.

Thompson, Kenneth (1994) "Understanding Political Realism." In *Community, Diversity, And a New World Order: Essays in Honor of Inis L. Claude, Jr.*, edited by Kenneth Thompson, 249–65. Lanham, MD: University Press of America.

Thomson, Robert (2011) *Resolving Controversy in the European Union: Legislative Decision-Making Before and After Enlargement*. New York: Cambridge University Press.

Thorhallsson, Baldur (2000) *The Role of Small States in the European Union*. Aldershot: Ashgate.

Tiefenthaler, Rupert (2000) "Alarmierende Gerüchte: Liechtenstein und die Revolution 1848 aus der Sicht Vorarlbergs." In *Liechtenstein und die Revolution 1848*, edited by Arthur Brunhart, 51–60. Zurich: Chronos.

Timothy, Dallen J., Jaume Guia, and Nicolas Berthet (2012) "Tourism as a Catalyst for Changing Boundaries and Territorial Sovereignty at an International Border." *Current Issues in Tourism* 1, no. 1: 1–7.

Torry, Jack (2015) "Don't Blame Nixon for Scuttled Peace Overture." *Real Clear Politics*, August 9. Available at http://www.realclearpolitics.com/articles/2015/08/09/dont_blame_nixon_for_scuttled_peace_overture_127667.html. Accessed January 20, 2017.

Traunmüller, Richard (2011) "Moral Communities? Religion as a Source of Social Trust in a Multilevel Analysis of '97 German Religions." *European Sociological Review* 27, no. 3: 346–63.

Trausch, Gilbert (1982) *Ministry of Foreign Affairs in the Grand Duchy. The Times Survey of Foreign Ministries of the World*. London: Times Books.

Trausch, Gilbert (2003) *Histoire du Luxembourg: Le Destin Européen d'un Petit Pays*. Toulouse: Privat.

Treaty of London (1867) *Treaty of May 11, William III Proclamation*.

Tsygankov, Andrei P., and Matthew Tarver-Wahlquist (2009) "Dueling Honors: Power, Identity and the Russia-Georgia Divide." *Foreign Policy Analysis* 5: 307–26.

United Nations (2006) "Final Script: To Serve with Pride." Issued at the High Level Conference on Eliminating Sexual Exploitation and Abuse. December, New York.

United Nations Department of Peacekeeping Operations (2009) *Georgia—UNOMIG—Background*. New York: United Nations.

Uslaner, Eric (2000) "Producing and Consuming Trust." *Political Science Quarterly* 115 (December): 569–90.

Van Aaken, Anne (2014) "Smart Flexibility Clauses in International Investment Treaties and Sustainable Development: A Functional View." *Journal of World Investment and Trade* 15: 827–61.

Van Milders, Lucas (2012) "Does Cooperation at the International Level Require Trust?" E-IR Info, April 29. Available at http://www.e-ir.info/2012/04/29/does-cooperation-at-the-international-level-require-trust/. Accessed November 25, 2012.

Van Roon, Ger (1989) *Small States in Years of Depression: The Oslo Alliance, 1930–1940*. Assen/Maastricht: Van Gorcum.

Veenendaal, Wouter (2014) *Politics and Democracy in Microstates*. London: Routledge.

Venturini, Karen (2014) Professor of history, University of San Marino. Interview with the author, June 24, San Marino.

Veterans Affairs Canada (2017) "The 1942 Dieppe Raid." Available at http://www.veterans.gc.ca/eng/remembrance/history/second-world-war/1942-dieppe-raid. Accessed February 16, 2017.

Villaró, Albert (2013) "Els Invasors." *Diari Andorra* blog post, March 9. Available at http://www.diariandorra.ad/blocs/avillaro/2013/04/09/els-invasors/. Accessed April 11, 2013.

Visani, Claude (2012) *Gli Intrighi di una Repubblica: San Marino e Romagna. Ottant'anni di storia raccontata dai protagonisti*. Bologna: Pendragon.

Vitek, William (1993) *Promising*. Philadelphia: Temple University Press.

Volkan, Vamık D. (2004) *Blind Trust: Large Groups and Their Leaders in Times of Crises and Terror*. Charlottesville, VA: Pitchstone Publishing. (*Blindes Vertrauen: Grossgruppen und Ihre Führer in Kriesezeiten*. Giessen: Psychosozial-Verlag, 2005.)

Wagner, John, and Karoun Demirjian (2016) "After Obama Sanctions Russia, Trump Says It's Time 'to move on to bigger and better things." *Washington Post*, December 29. Available at https://www.washingtonpost.com/news/post-politics/wp/2016/12/29/after-obama-sanctions-russia-trump-says-its-time-to-move-on-to-bigger-and-better-things/?utm_term=.f3e55c891569. Accessed December 30, 2016.

Walder, Adam (2013) Reporter at *Wort.lu*. Interview with the author, May 2, Luxembourg.

Walsh, John (2013) "All That Glitters in Monte Carlo." *The Independent*, June 1. Available at http://www.independent.co.uk/travel/europe/all-that-glitters-in-monte-carlo-8639110.html. Accessed May 1, 2015.

Weber, Linda R., and Allison I. Carter (2003) *The Social Construction of Trust*. New York: Kluwer Academic.

Weber, Patrick (2007) *Monaco: La Saga Grimaldi*. Paris: Timée-Editions.

Weitsman, Patricia (2004) *Dangerous Alliances: Proponents of Peace, Weapons of War*. Stanford, CA: Stanford University Press.

Weller, Matthias (2015) "Mutual Trust: In Search of the Future of European Union Private International Law." *Journal of Private International Law* 11, no. 1: 64–102.

Wheeler, Nicholas J. (2013) "Investigating Diplomatic Transformations." *International Affairs* 89, no. 2 (March): 477–96.

Willbanks, James H. (2004) *Abandoning Vietnam: How America Left and South Vietnam Lost Its War*. Lawrence: University Press of Kansas.

Williams, William Appleman, Thomas McCormick, Lloyd Gardner, and Walter LaFeber, eds. (1985) *America in Vietnam: A Documentary History*. New York: W. W. Norton.

Willie v. Liechtenstein (1999) European Court of Human Rights (application no. 28396/95). Judgment, Strasbourg, October 28.

Wilson, Robert R. (1963) "Canada-United States Treaty Relations and International Law." In *Canada-United States Treaty Relations*, edited by David R. Deener, 3–27. Durham, NC: Duke University Press.

Wimmer, Andreas (2008) "The Making and Unmaking of Ethnic Boundaries: A Multi-level Process Theory." *American Journal of Sociology* 113, no. 4: 970–1022.

Wivel, Anders (2016) "From Small State to Smart State: Devising a Strategy for Influence in the European Union." In *Small States in Europe: Challenges and Opportunities*, edited by Robert Steinmetz and Anders Wivel, 15–29. London: Routledge.

Wong, Edward (2011) "China Exerts Influence Nurtured over Decades." *New York Times*, December 21. Available at http://www.nytimes.com/2011/12/21/world/asia/china-exerts-influence-nurtured-over-decades.html?_r=0. Accessed July 30, 2015.

Wood, Stepan, Anne-Marie Slaughter, and Andrew Tulumello (1998) "International Law and International Relations Theory: A New Generation of Interdisciplinary Scholarship." *American Journal of International Law* 92, no. 3 (July): 367–97.

World Bank (2015) San Marino data. Available at: http://data.worldbank.org/country/san-marino. Accessed May 18, 2015.

World Trade Organization–Liechtenstein (2000) *Trade Policy Review—Switzerland and Liechtenstein, December. Report by the Government of Liechtenstein—Part III.* Press release/TPRB/150, 6 December. Available at http://www.wto.org/english/tratop_e/trp_e/tp150_e.htm#fntext1. Accessed November 5, 2013.

Wort.lu (2014) "Expats in Luxembourg want 'More Europe.'" *Luxembourger Wort* on-line, April 25. Available at https://www.wort.lu/en/luxembourg/expats-in-luxembourg-want-more-europe-535a86c0e4b00047c4ef2e90. Accessed May 7, 2014.

Xu, Beina, and Jayshree Bajoria (2014) "The China-North Korea Relationship." CFR Backgrounders, August 22. Available at http://www.cfr.org/china/china-north=korea=relationship/p11097. Accessed August 4, 2015.

Yekelchyk, Serhy (2008) "Out of Russia's Long Shadow: The Making of Modern Ukraine, Belarus, and Moldova." In *Belarus, Moldova, and Ukraine between Russia and the European Union*, edited by Oliver Schmidtke and Serhy Yekelchyk, 9–29. New York: Palgrave Macmillan.

Yovel, Jonathan (1999/2000) "What Is Contract Law 'About'? Speech Act Theory and a Critique of 'Skeletal Promises.'" *Northwestern University Law Review* 94, no. 3: 931–62.

Zak, Paul (2008) "How to Run a Con: Why Our Brains Make Us Vulnerable to Con Men." November 13. Available at https://www.psychologytoday.com/blog/the-moral-molecule/200811/how-run-con. Accessed October 8, 2015.

Zetzche, Dirk (2013) Propter Homines Chair for Banking and Securities Law at the University of Liechtenstein. Interview with the author, May 10, Vaduz.

Zheng, Jun, Elizabeth Veinott, Nathan Bos, Judith S. Olson, and Gary M. Olson (2002) "Trust without Touch: Jumpstarting Long-Range Trust with Initial Social Activities." *Collaboratory for Research on Electronic Work* (April): 1–25.

Index